Renault 5 Owners Workshop Manual

by J H Haynes
Member of the Guild of Motoring Writers
and Tim Parker

Models covered:

UK: Renault 5 L, TL, TS & GTL, 845, 956 & 1289 cc
USA: Renault 5 TL & GTL. 79 cu in (1289 cc)

ISBN 0 85696 141 8

Printed in England   *(141 - 10C1)*

HAYNES PUBLISHING GROUP
SPARKFORD YEOVIL SOMERSET ENGLAND
distributed in the USA by
HAYNES PUBLICATIONS INC
861 LAWRENCE DRIVE
NEWBURY PARK
CALIFORNIA 91320
USA

Acknowledgements

No book is the work of one person. This Owners Workshop Manual is the work of many and due credit should go to each and everyone of them.

Thanks are due to Regie Renault - in particular Renault Limited (UK), for their assistance with technical information and the provision of certain illustrations. Castrol Limited supplied lubrication data, and the Champion Sparking Plug Company supplied the illustrations showing the various spark plug conditions. The bodywork repair photographs used in this manual were provided by Lloyds Industries Limited who supply 'Turtle Wax', 'Dupli-Color Holts', and other Holts range products.

Lastly, special thanks to all of those people at Sparkford who helped in the production of this manual. Particularly, Brian Horsfall and Les Brazier who carried out the mechanical work and took the photographs, respectively; Stanley Randolph who planned the layout of each page and Rod Grainger the editor.

Introduction to this manual

Its aim

This manual is written for the interested owner or driver of a Renault 5. It will not only give him or her a description of the car, its specifications and very workings, but will also give an 'in depth' experienced guide as to how to maintain and repair/ overhaul the Renault 5.

We actually buy a version of the car concerned and strip and rebuild its major components in our own workshop. Throughout this operation the author is present, as are a skilled mechanic and a photographer. By working in this way the author is able to experience, first hand, the same problems as the average owner is likely to encounter and also to note the methods by which these problems are overcome. Our workshop is not extensively equipped, instead we make do with a pit, an engine hoist and a fairly basic set of tools - in this way authenticity is ensured. However, it should be appreciated that it will sometimes be necessary to use a special tool to accomplish some tasks. Where this is the case the Renault number for the special tool is given in the text, together with a description of the tool's usage.

Using the manual

The manual is divided into twelve Chapters, each one a logical division of the car. The two models of the Renault 5 are dealt with together, differences being pointed out constantly. Where there is significant design differences, the Sections are divided into two parts.

Constant cross-reference is made by using the Chapter, Section and paragraph numbers. Each Section has a number as does each paragraph. For example: Chapter 1, Section 3 paragraph 4 would appear as Chapter 1, 3.4. Where only 3.4 is given it refers to Section 3, paragraph 4 in the same Chapter. Thus a photograph captioned 3.4 refers to that Section and paragraph in the same Chapter as the photograph.

Two types of illustration are used. Line illustrations are annotated as a figure, ie; Fig. 1.3 is the third figure in Chapter 1. Photographs, usually in an overhaul sequence simply have the Section and paragraph number with their caption. There is a contents page and an index.

The left side of the car (nearside) and right side (offside) must be taken as pertinent to someone sitting in the front seat and facing forwards. Certain line illustrations will be left-hand drive cars. They are used only if no confusion is possible unless a special caption is given.

Whilst every care has been taken to ensure the accuracy of this manual, no liability can be accepted by the authors or publishers for any loss, damage or injury caused by any errors in, or omissions from, the information given.

Contents

NB. General descriptions and specifications are given in each Chapter, where applicable, after the 'list of contents', and 'fault diagnosis' is given at the end of the Chapter.

Introduction to the Renault 5

Think of the Renault 5 as a first. It's a first in many ways. The first £1000, 1000 cc car; the first 'comfortable' mini production car; the first fully equipped small car and it is first, in front of the competition.

The Renault 5 is not like the other small front wheel drive Renaults. Unlike the 4 and 6 it does not have a separate chassis but is of monocoque construction like the bigger 16, and it only has three doors rather than five (the tailgate makes the doors uneven in number). It is much more a small Renault 16 rather than a better Renault 6. It has plastic 5 mph impact proof front and rear bumpers which have been designed into the car rather than simply stuck on the ends. Unlike most other Renaults it can be described universally as attractive. It is a superb car.

Introduced into the UK in late 1972 demand has always far exceeded supply, particularly for the 5TL (956 cc). The other model, the 5L (845 cc) sells well but cannot be such good value even though it performs more economically. Demand is high because of the need for a practical small car which is not as well fulfilled by the competition. The European car is with us, less specific national character but more universal acceptance. The Renault 5 could only be French but it would surprise many who would normally never sit in anything which is not British!

Recently Renault UK sent a survey out to all owners who are on their records. One question asked was demanding a subjective answer to what they could improve on their car. This Renault 5 owner could only demand the fitting of mudflaps - the car is that good!

Modifications to the Renault 5 range

Such is the complexity of modern car production in all its aspects, it is not possible to list all the modifications that may have been made to one range of cars. Details of a given component may change overnight without any announcement, and any significance to the repair of the car. Regie Renault have a purchasing policy so that the production line does not stop if there is a shortage of a given manufacturer's parts. They simply switch to another supplier. Consequently it is possible to have three or four 'different' parts fitted in one week's production of cars. All major design modifications obviously have been mentioned. Nevertheless, it does mean that when purchasing parts and when reading this manual that you should be sure precisely as to what you are buying and what you are doing. Significant charges have taken place in late 1973 to cover all 1974 models - mention is made here.

1974 version of the Renault 5TL. (R1222). This is the actual car used in our workshops and subsequently run by the Company for well over 40,000 miles. The 5L looks very similar but is without wheel trims and side strips. The wheels are much plainer

The Renault 5 is fitted with rubber floor covering as standard. The degree of comfort is very high

Quick reference general data

Capacities and settings

Engine sump (excluding filter)	5.25 Imp pints/3 litres (R1222)	4.5 Imp pints/2.5 litres (R1221)
Extra capacity for oil filter change	0.4 Imp pints/0.25 litres	0.4 Imp pints/0.25 litres
Gearbox	3.25 Imp pints/1.85 litres	
Cooling system	11 Imp pints/6.25 litres (R1222)	10.25 Imp pints/5.82 litres (R1221)
Spark plug gap	0.6 to 0.7 mm (0.024 to 0.028 in)	
Points gap	0.4 mm (0.016 in)	

Rocker clearance:

	Hot	Cold
Inlet	0.18 mm (0.0075 in)	0.15 mm (0.006 in)
Exhaust	0.25 mm (0.010 in)	0.20 mm (0.008 in)

Petrol tank ... ... 8.5 Imp gallons (38.6 litres)

Tyre pressures

	Front	Rear
Normal	24 psi	27 psi
For heavy loading or continuous high speed running	26 psi	28 psi

Voltage ... ... 12 volts

Dimensions and weights

Overall length	11 ft 5 3/16 in. (3.50 metres)
Overall width	4 ft 11 7/8 in. (1.52 metres)
Overall height (unladen)	4 ft 7 1/8 in. (1.40 metres)
Ground clearance (laden)	6 ft 11/16 in. (144.5 mm)

Wheelbase:

Right	7 ft 10 1/2 in. (2.40 metres)
Left	8 ft (2.43 metres)

Track (front):

R1222	4 ft 2 13/16 in. (1.29 metres)
R1221	4 ft 2 3/8 in. (1.28 metres)

Track (rear): ... ... 4 ft 13/16 in. (1.24 metres)

Turning circle (between walls) ... ... 33 ft 3 5/8 in. (10.15 metres)

Kerb weight:

R1222	1731 lb (785 kg)
R1221	1610 lb (730 kg)

Maximum permissible all-up weight:

R1222	2459 lb (1115 kg)
R1221	2337 lb (1060 kg)

Buying spare parts and vehicle identification numbers

Buying spare parts

Spare parts are available from many sources, for example: Renault garages, other garages and accessory shops, and motor factors. Our advice regarding spare parts is as follows:

Officially appointed Renault garages - This is the best source of parts which are peculiar to your car and otherwise not generally available (eg; complete cylinder heads, internal gearbox components, badges, interior trim etc). It is also the only place at which you should buy parts if your car is still under warranty; non-Renault components may invalidate the warranty. To be sure of obtaining the correct parts it will always be necessary to give the storeman your car's engine and chassis number, and if possible, to take the old part along for positive identification. Remember that many parts are available on a factory exchange scheme - any parts returned should always be clean! It obviously makes good sense to go straight to the specialists on your car for this type of part for they are best equipped to supply you.

Other garages and accessory shops - These are often very good places to buy material and components needed for the maintenance of your car (eg; oil filters, spark plugs, bulbs, fan belts, oils and grease, touch-up paint, filler paste etc). They also sell general accessories, usually have convenient opening hours, charge lower prices and can often be found not far from home.

Motor factors - Good factors will stock all of the more important components which wear out relatively quickly (eg; clutch components, pistons, valves, exhaust systems, brake cylinders/pipes/hoses/seals/shoes and pads etc). Motor factors will often provide new or reconditioned components on a part exchange basis - this can save a considerable amount of money.

Vehicle identification numbers

Modifications are a continuing and unpublished process in vehicle manufacture quite apart from major model changes. Spare parts manuals and lists are compiled upon a numerical basis, the individual vehicle numbers being essential to correct identification of the component required.

Both of the models in this manual are known as the Renault 5 - however, there are considerable specification differences between the two. Always use the correct Renault model number when describing your car to a Renault storeman:

Renault 5L (845 cc) = R1221
Renault 5TL (956 cc) = R1222

The storeman will also need to know the *oval plate number* under all circumstances. For engine and transmission parts he will need to know the *engine number* and the *gearbox number* respectively in addition. For certain chassis and body parts he may need to know the *diamond plate number*. The *paint code* may be required if the shade of the car is not easily described. All these numbers are located in readily visible places. (See the diagrams).

Very few parts from other Renault models will fit this range except for some mechanical parts from the Renault 4 and 6 (850 cc) on the 5L and the 6 (1100 cc) for the 5TL. Be wary of secondhand used parts!

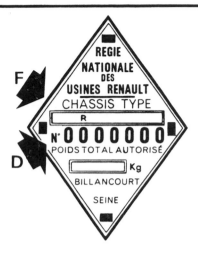

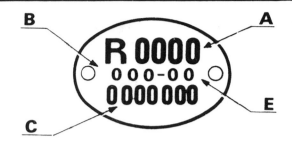

Lozenge (diamond) plate (on the bulkhead)

F — The vehicle type
D — The chassis number

Oval plate (on the bulkhead)

A — The first three figures give vehicle group type, the fourth gives the engine type
B — Gives the basic equipment type (ie; poor road etc)
C — The fabrication number
E — The version number

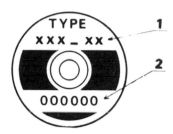

Gearbox plate (fixed to the top cover)

1   The gearbox type
2   The fabrication number

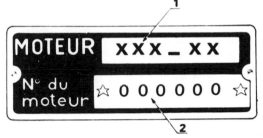

Engine plate (riveted to the engine block)

1   The engine type
2   The fabrication number

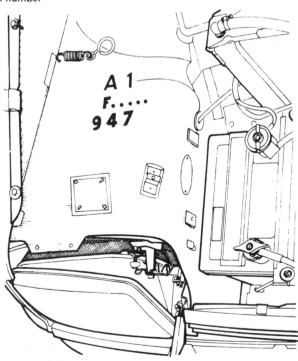

Paint code
A white stencilled code on the right side inner wing

Routine maintenance

Maintenance is essential for ensuring safety and desirable for the purpose of getting the best in terms of performance and economy from the car. Over the years the need for periodic lubrication - oiling and greasing - has been drastically reduced if not totally eliminated. This has unfortunately tended to lead some owners to think that because no such action is required the components either no longer exist or will last for ever. This is a serious delusion. If anything, there are now more places, particularly in the steering and suspension, where joints and pivots are fitted. Although you do not grease them any more you still have to look at them - and look at them just as often as you may previously have had to, to grease them. It follows therefore that the largest initial element of maintenance is visual examination. This may lead to repairs or renewals.

At the beginning of each Chapter in the manual the routine maintenance details covering that Chapter are given.

In the summary given here the 'essential for safety' items are shown in **bold type**. These **must** be attended to at the regular frequencies shown in order to avoid the possibility of accidents and loss of life. Other neglect results in unreliability, increased running costs, more rapid wear and more rapid depreciation of the vehicle in general.

Every 250 miles/400 kms (or weekly, whichever comes first)

Steering and suspension
> **Check tyres pressures - the ride and handling of this car can be severely altered by incorrect tyre pressures.**
> **Examine tyres for wear or damage.**
> **Is the steering smooth and accurate?**
> Take note of any unusual noises when travelling and visually check the suspension and shock absorbers.

Brakes
> **Is there a fall-off of braking efficiency?**
> **Try an emergency stop. Is adjustment necessary?**

Lights, wipers and horns
> **Do all the bulbs work at the front, rear, interior: and work well?**
> **Are the headlight beams aligned properly?**
> **Do both wipers and horn work fully?**

Battery
> Check the electrolyte level and top-up if necessary.

Engine
> Check the sump oil level and top up if required. The oil required to top-up from 'MIN' to 'MAX' level on the dipstick is 2½ Imperial pints (1.42 litres).
> Check for visible coolant leaks (check coolant level in expansion bottle).
> Check for any fluid leak puddles left under the car overnight.

Every 1000 miles/1600 kms (or monthly, whichever comes first)

Check all 250 mile points and anything which you feel is not quite right.

Steering
> **Is there any free-play between the steering wheel and the roadwheels?**

Brakes
> **Check the fluid level in the master cylinder reservoir. Top-up if necessary. If significantly or regularly lower examine the system immediately for leaks.**

Bodywork
> Clean away with water any mud and road dirt from the petrol tank feed pipe inside the right-hand rear wing.
> Lubricate headlight adjusting screws and beam level levers.

General
> Check the condition and the tension of the fan belts.
> Apply glycerine (not oil) to the windscreen wiper arm spindles.

Every 3000 miles/5000 kms (or four monthly, whichever comes first)

Undertake all the items listed previously, plus the following:

Steering
> **Examine all steering linkage, joints and bushes for signs of wear or damage.**
> **Check the front and rear wheel hub bearings.**
> **Check tightness of steering rack/radiator mounting bolts.**
> **Check driveshafts for wear at the outer universal joint and the rubber bellows for leaks.**

Brakes
> **Adjust the brakes and lubricate the adjusters to stop them rusting solid.**
> **Inspect the front brake disc pads on the R1222 and replace when worn (in full sets).**

Suspension
> **Examine all bolts and bushes securing the suspension and shock absorbers. Tighten as necessary.**

Engine
> Drain the sump, you will need a container of at least 5 Imp. pints (2.84 litres), and either a 23 mm socket or a hexagonal key (10 mm) to undo the sump plug, depending on type fitted. Allow to drain when hot for five minutes. Refit sump plug and refill with 5.25 Imp. pints/3 litres (R1222) or 4½ Imp. pints/2.5 litres (R1221) of engine oil.

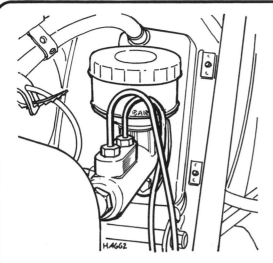

Master cylinder fluid reservoir. A level check is stamped on the container

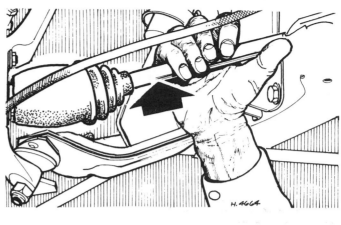

Grip the driveshaft and try to twist. The handbrake must be on

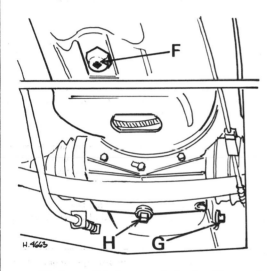

Oil change. F is the sump drain plug, H is the gearbox drain plug and G is the gearbox filler plug

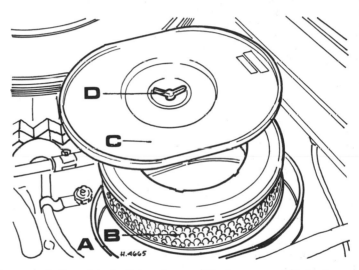

Carburettor air filter. D is the fixing wing nut, C is the top cover, B the element and A the base

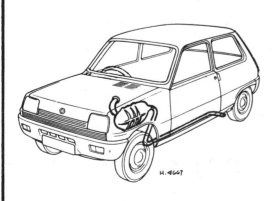

The exhaust system in skeleton form looks like this. Check the joints and surfaces

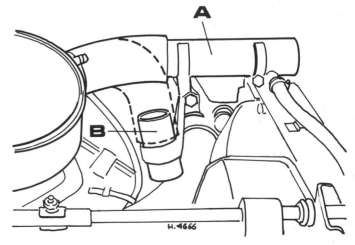

The air filter intake moves. For the summer use position A, for winter months use position B

Check the tension of the fan belts.
Check the spark plugs.

Transmission

Check level of oil by undoing the side filler plug with a 10 mm open ended spanner. If no oil starts to flow out top-up with gear oil using a flexible spout. The check should be made with the oil hot. Place in reverse gear to assist filling.

Bodywork

Lubricate all hinges including the bonnet, catches and locks with engine oil. Do not forget the car's jack and 'courtesy' door plungers.

Electrics

Check proper functioning of electric cooling fan of the R1222 as well as the heated rear window.

Every 9000 miles/15000 kms (or annually, whichever comes first)

Undertake all the checks and tasks already mentioned plus the following:

Brakes

Examine brake drum shoes front and rear and replace if necessary.
Check the condition of the wheel cylinder rubbers for leaks.
Check, properly, the condition of the hydraulic rigid and flexible hoses, particularly the fronts for chafing, dents and any other form of deterioration and rectify if necessary.
Lubricate the handbrake linkage, and adjust if necessary.

Suspension

Have the front wheel track checked and adjusted at your Renault garage.

Engine

Change the oil filter cartridge (if fitted).
Lubricate the dynamo end 'greaser' with three drops of engine oil. (Not R1221).
Oil the felt pad under the rotor arm of the distributor very carefully with three drops of engine oil and grease the cam.
Fit new contact points, and adjust the gap, then the static timing.
Check static ignition timing.
Check the condition of the distributor cap and plug leads.
Fit new spark plugs set to the correct gap.
Fit new carburettor air cleaner element, and clean carburettor float chamber.
Clean the fuel pump and filter gauze of sediment.
Check the tightness of the inlet/exhaust manifold.

Transmission

Drain the gearbox oil, when hot, into a container of at least 3.25 Imp. pints (1.8 litres). You should undo both the drain plug(s) and the filler plug and place the car in reverse gear to obtain easier flow both on draining and refilling. Replace the sump plug(s). Refill with gear oil until it just overflows from the filler plug. (On some cars fitted with special transmission undershields you may have to remove them to do this task). Capacity 3.25 Imp. pints (1.8 litres).

Clutch

Adjust clearance if necessary.

Bodywork

Check and adjust if necessary the underbody height.
Check the tightness of all body parts particularly the bumpers and their mounting and all mechanical assemblies such as the gearbox mounting, and door and tailgate catches. (Check sun-roof fittings if current).
Check seat belt mountings and their fittings.
Check fixing of all rubber grommets particularly handbrake moulding.

Every 18 months/2 years

Renew brake fluid.
Flush out the sealed cooling system and replenish.
Check underbody and wheel arches after cleaning and re-underseal if necessary.

In addition, time should be spent on the following:

Cleaning

The best way to examine a car and know what sort of a state it is in, is to thoroughly clean it, inside and out. One of the principal results of this, which is not covered by other maintenance operations, is the finding of any traces of rust in the body panels. If rust is allowed to go unchecked it could affect some panels which may make the car unsafe and keep it off the road.

Exhaust system

An exhaust system must be leakproof and keep engine noise below a level of 86 decibels. Leaks may cause dangerous fumes to enter the interior and affect the driver and passengers - thus having an adverse effect on the driver's capabilities. Excessive noise constitutes a public nuisance. Both these faults can result in the vehicle being declared unfit for use.

Special safety note: Do not rely on the car jack supplied. It is not able to do any more than just support the car for changing a wheel. For more ambitious work (even during routine maintenance) purchase a better, stronger type.

Never fill the fuel tank to the brim - you will lose fuel at the first corner.

Never tow the car with the tow rope fixed to the driveshaft, bumper or tie-rod. Never tow with the bumper. In each case tow fixed around a major component or on the tow ring.

Most of the tasks just listed can be carried out with a small set of metric tools and feeler gauges together with a normal selection of screwdrivers and a hammer. Always prepare your ground first and make sure you have the time, the correct replacement parts and are fully in command of the tasks which you wish to start.

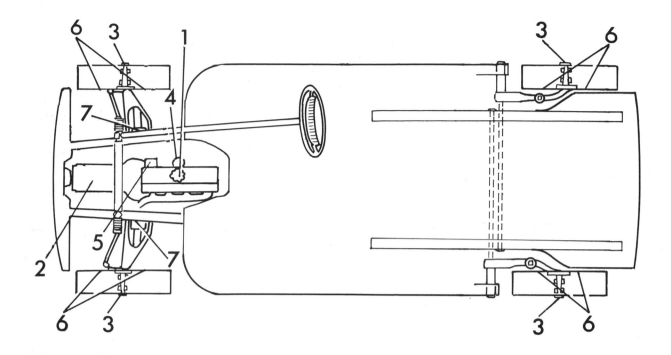

Recommended lubricants and fluids

Component	Castrol Product
Engine (1)	Castrol GTX
Transmission (2)	Castrol Hypoy Light (80 EP)
Wheel bearings (3)	Castrol LM Grease
Distributor (4)	Castrol GTX/Castrol Everyman
Dynamo bushes - R1221 (5)	Castrol GTX/Castrol Everyman
Brake mechanisms - adjuster cams and shoes to backplates (6) ...	Castrol PH Grease
Driveshafts - inner joints (7)	Specific Renault lubricant
Chassis - general	Castrol LM Grease
Hinges, locks, pivots etc.	Castrol GTX/Castrol Everyman
Hydraulic system	Castrol Girling Universal Brake and Clutch Fluid
Coolant	Water (soft) and Castrol Antifreeze
Distributor cam and battery terminals	Petroleum jelly (vaseline)
Battery	Distilled water
Hydraulic system pistons	Rubber grease

With regard to lubrication the above are general recommendations. Lubrication requirements vary from territory-to-territory and also with vehicle usage - consult the operators handbook supplied with your car.

Chapter 1 Engine

Contents

Specifications

Engine - general (R1222)

Type	4 cylinder, in line, ohv, pushrod operated. Cast iron block with removable cylinder liners. Aluminium cylinder head
Renault type number	689 - 01 (Sierra engine)
Cubic capacity	956 cc (58.3 cu. in)
Bore	65 mm (2.559 in)
Stroke	72 mm (2.835 in)
Compression ratio	9.25 to 1
Firing order	1 - 3 - 4 - 2
BHP (maximum) SAE	47 bhp at 6,000 rpm
Torque (maximum) SAE	47 lb/ft at 3,500 rpm
Engine weight (dry)	200 lbs (approx)
Normal operating temperature	78°C

Camshaft (R1222)

Number of bearings	4, running direct in block (one sleeved)
Endfloat	0.06 to 0.11 mm (0.002 to 0.005 in)

Connecting rods and big-end bearings (R1222)

Bearing type ... ... Shell
Bearing material ... ... Aluminium tin
Nominal diameter ... ... 43.98 mm (1.731 in)

Crankshaft and main bearings (R1222)

Number of main bearings 5
Bearing material ... ... Aluminium tin
Nominal diameter ... ... 46 mm (1.811 in)
Regrind sizes available for all crankshaft bearings ... ... 0.25 mm (0.010 in), 0.50 mm (0.020 in), 1 mm (0.040 in)
Grinding tolerances ... ... 0.020 mm (0.001 in)

Pistons and cylinders (R1222)

Cylinder block and liners ... ... Cast iron, removable liners
Water jackets ... ... Full length
Liner bottom locating diameter ... ... 75.5 mm (2.972 in)
Liner protrusion ... ... 0.05 to 0.12 mm (0.002 to 0.005 in) (paper)
Piston type ... ... Aluminium alloy, 3 ring
Overbore sizes available ... ... 0.25 mm (0.010 in), 0.50 mm (0.020 in), 1 mm (0.040 in)
Gudgeon pin fitting ... ... Press fit in connecting rod
Direction of assembly ... ... Arrow on piston towards flywheel
Gudgeon pin length ... ... 57 mm (2.25 in)
Gudgeon pin diameter ... ... 18 mm (0.709 in)
Oil pressure at 4,000 rpm ... ... 55 psi

Pushrods (R1222)

Length ... ... 172 mm (6.75 in)
Diameter ... ... 5 mm (0.197 in)

Valves (R1222)

Inlet:
    Diameter of head ... ... 33.5 mm (1.319 in)
    Stem diameter ... ... 7 mm (0.276 in)
Exhaust:
    Diameter of head ... ... 30.3 mm (1.193 in)
    Stem diameter ... ... 7 mm (0.276 in)
Valve guides match respective valves:
    Internally ... ... 7 mm + 0.018 mm (0.276 in)
    Externally ... ... 11 mm + 0.4 mm, available in two oversizes: 0.10 mm and 0.25 mm
Valve seats ... ... 90°
Seat widths:
    Inlet ... ... 1.1 to 1.4 mm (0.043 to 0.055 in)
    Exhaust ... ... 1.4 to 1.7 mm (0.055 to 0.067 in)
Valve spring free-length ... ... 42 mm (1.21/32 in)
Wire diameter ... ... 3.4 mm (0.134 in)
Internal diameter of coil ... ... 21.6 mm (0.850 in)
Valve rocker arm clearances:
    Hot engine:
        Inlet ... ... 0.18 mm (0.007 in)
        Exhaust ... ... 0.25 mm (0.010 in)
    Cold engine:
        Inlet ... ... 0.15 mm (0.006 in)
        Exhaust ... ... 0.20 mm (0.008 in)
Cylinder head depth ... ... 71.70 mm (2.823 in)
Maximum safe regrind on cylinder head ... ... +0.30 mm (0.012 in)
Combustion chamber volume ... ... 33.3 cc (2.032 cu. in)
Spark plug electrode gap ... ... 0.6 mm (0.024 in)
Engine oil sump capacity:
    Excluding filter ... ... 5.25 Imp. pints (3 litres)
    Including filter ... ... 5.7 Imp. pints (3.25 litres)

Torque wrench settings (R1222)

	lb f ft	kg f m
Cylinder head bolts	50	6.91
Manifold nuts	45	6.22
Crankshaft main bearing bolts	50	6.91
Flywheel bolts	40	5.42
Big-end bolts	25	3.45

Engine - general (R1221)

Type	4 cylinder, in line, ohv, pushrod operated. Cast iron block with removable cylinder liners. Aluminium cylinder head
Renault type number	800 - 01 (Ventoux engine)
Cubic capacity	845 cc (51.56 cu. in)
Bore	58 mm (2.284 in)
Stroke	80 mm (3.150 in)
Compression ratio	8 to 1
Firing order	1 - 3 - 4 - 2
BHP (maximum) SAE	38 bhp at 5,000 rpm
Torque (maximum) SAE	40.5 lb/ft at 3,000 rpm
Engine weight (dry)	178 lb (81 kg)
Normal operating temperature	84°C (183°F)

Camshaft (R1221)

Number of bearings	3, running direct in block
Endfloat	0.06 mm to 0.14 mm (0.002 to 0.0055 in)

Connecting rods and big-end bearings (R1221)

Bearing type	Shell
Bearing material	White metal/lead indium
Nominal diameter	38 mm (1.496 in)

Crankshaft and main bearings (R1221)

Number of main bearings	3
Bearing material	White metal/lead indium
Nominal journal diameter	40 mm (1.575 in)
Regrind sizes available for all crankshaft bearings	0.25 mm (0.010 in), 0.50 mm (0.020 in), 1 mm (0.040 in)
Grinding tolerances	0.025 mm (0.001 in)

Pistons and cylinders (R1221)

Cylinder block and liners	Cast iron, removable liners
Water jackets	Full length
Height of block	215 mm (8 7/16 in)
Liner bottom locating diameter	62.5 mm (2. 15/32 in)
Liner protrusion	0.04 to 0.012 mm (0.002 to 0.005 in) impregnated paper 0.08 to 0.015 mm (0.003 to 0.006 in) copper
Piston type	Aluminium alloy, 3 ring
Piston length	64 mm
Overbore sizes available	0.25 mm (0.010 in), 0.50 mm (0.020 in), 1 mm (0.040 in)
Gudgeon pin fitting	Press fit in connecting rod
Direction of assembly	Arrow on piston towards the flywheel
Gudgeon pin length	49 mm (1. 15/16 in)
Gudgeon pin diameter	16 mm (0.630 in)
Oil pressure at 4,000 rpm	34 psi

Pushrods (R1221)

Length	131 mm (5.5/32 in)
Diameter	5 mm (0.197 in)

Valves (R1221)

Inlet:

Diameter of head	28.2 mm (1.110 in)
Stem diameter	7 mm (0.276 in)

Exhaust:

Diameter of head	25 mm (0.984 in)
Stem diameter	7 mm (0.276 in)

Valve guides match respective valves:

Internally	+0.018 mm (0.276 in)
Externally	+ 4 mm, available in two oversizes: 0.10 mm, 0.25 mm
Valve seats - (7 mm diameter valve stem)	90°

Seat widths:

Inlet	1.5 mm (0.059 in)
Exhaust	1.8 mm (0.071 in)
Valve springs - Free-length	39 mm (1.17/32 in)
Wire diameter	2.7 mm (0.106 in)
Internal diameter of coil	16.8 mm (0.661 in)
Tappets - diameter	Nominal 19 mm (0.748 in) Oversizes available +0.20 mm (0.008 in), 0.50 mm (0.020 in)

Valve lift:

Inlet	5.75 mm (0.226 in)
Exhaust	6.00 mm (0.238 in)

Valve rocker arm clearances:

Hot engine:

| | lb f ft | kg f m |

Inlet ... ...   0.18 mm (0.007 in)
Exhaust ... ...   0.25 mm (0.010 in)

Cold engine:

Inlet ... ...   0.15 mm (0.006 in)
Exhaust ... ...   0.20 mm (0.008 in)

Cylinder head depth ... ...   94.7 mm (3.728 in)
Maximum safe regrind on cylinder head ... ...   +0.40 mm (0.015 in)
Combustion chamber volume ... ...   27.3 cc
Spark plug electrode gap ... ...   0.6 mm (0.024 in)

Engine oil sump capacity:

Excluding filter ... ...   4.5 Imp. pints (2.5 litres)
Including filter ... ...   4.8 Imp. pints (2.75 litres)

Torque wrench settings (R1221)

	lb f ft	kg f m
Cylinder head bolts	45	6.22
Manifold nuts	45	6.22
Crankshaft main bearing bolts	45	6.22
Flywheel bolts	35	4.84
Big-end bolts	25	3.45

1 General description

The Renault 5TL (from now on described by the number R1222) and the Renault 5L (the R1221) have different engines. The R1222 has the 'Sierra' engine of 956 cc; this is the five bearing crank engine taken from the Renault 8, 10, 6-1100 and 12. The R1221 has the old 'Ventoux' engine of 845 cc; this is a three bearing crank engine designed over twenty years ago and used also in the Dauphine, the 4 and 6-850. There is another capacity of engine used in the R1220, of 782 cc. This model is not imported into the UK although it is virtually identical to the R1221. Whilst the two engines covered in this manual are quite different in terms of the parts used, they are very similar in design. Consequently it must be assumed that the methods given in this book apply to both engines, and both cars unless special mention is made.

Both engines have a longer stroke than bore, the smaller having very long stroke characteristics. Both engines are fitted with aluminium cylinder heads. Engines are four cylinder, fitted with two valves per cylinder, which are operated by overhead rockers and pushrods from a single camshaft mounted in the right-hand side of the engine block.

The crankshaft runs in five/three main bearings and the end-float is controlled by a pair of semi-circular thrust washers located in the upper half of the centre main bearing. The camshaft is driven by a single chain from a sprocket on the rear end of the crankshaft. The chain is controlled by a tensioner. The camshaft in turn drives the oil pump through a skew gear and the oil pump drive shaft also drives the distributor.

The pistons are a semi-floating fit to the connecting rods and the gudgeon pins are retained in the piston with circlips. The connecting rod small end bush is renewable to be reamed to fit the gudgeon pin. The lubricating system is of the forced-feed type to the crankshaft main bearings, connecting rod, big-end bearings, camshaft and valve rocker gear. The oil pump is fully submerged and is of the twin gear type.

The engine is flexibly mounted in the car at three points on the chassis: one either side of the block onto the monocoque and the third at the end of the gearbox on the front cross-member. It will be appreciated that neither the engine nor the gearbox is fully supported when any one mounting is removed. All versions of the engines covered here are fitted with single downdraught fixed jet carburettor.

2 Major operations which may be carried out with the engine in place

The following work may be conveniently carried out with the engine in place:

1 *Removal and replacement of the cylinder head assembly.*
2 *Removal and replacement of the clutch assembly (removal of gearbox necessary).*
3 *Removal and replacement of the engine mountings.*
4 *Removal and replacement of the sump.*
5 *Removal and replacement of the oil pump.*
6 *Removal and replacement of the connecting rod big-end bearings.*
7 *Removal and replacement of pistons and connecting rods (after the removal of the cylinder head and sump).*
8 *Removal and replacement of the flywheel (after removing the gearbox and clutch).*

3 Major operations which entail the engine removal

1 Removal and replacement of the timing cover and timing chain.
2 Removal and replacement of the camshaft.
3 Removal and replacement of the crankshaft main bearings.
4 Removal and replacement of the crankshaft.

4 Method of engine removal

There is only one method of engine removal for this car and that is a straight up and out lift, together with the gearbox. It is **not** possible to take the engine out without the gearbox.

5 Engine removal - R1222

1 The engine is removed together with the gearbox. There is no other method. Together the two components are not very heavy although it helps to have two people doing the job. The removal should take 1½ hours.
2 Position the car's nose under the centre of a roof beam or tripod to be used as the lifting support. Have adequate access to

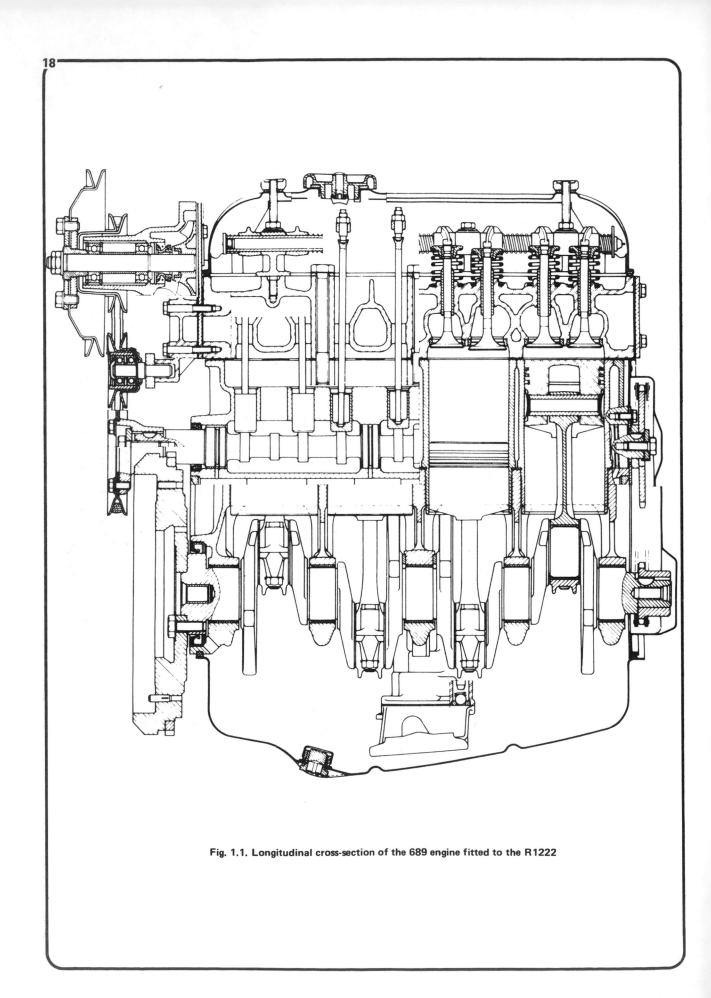

Fig. 1.1. Longitudinal cross-section of the 689 engine fitted to the R1222

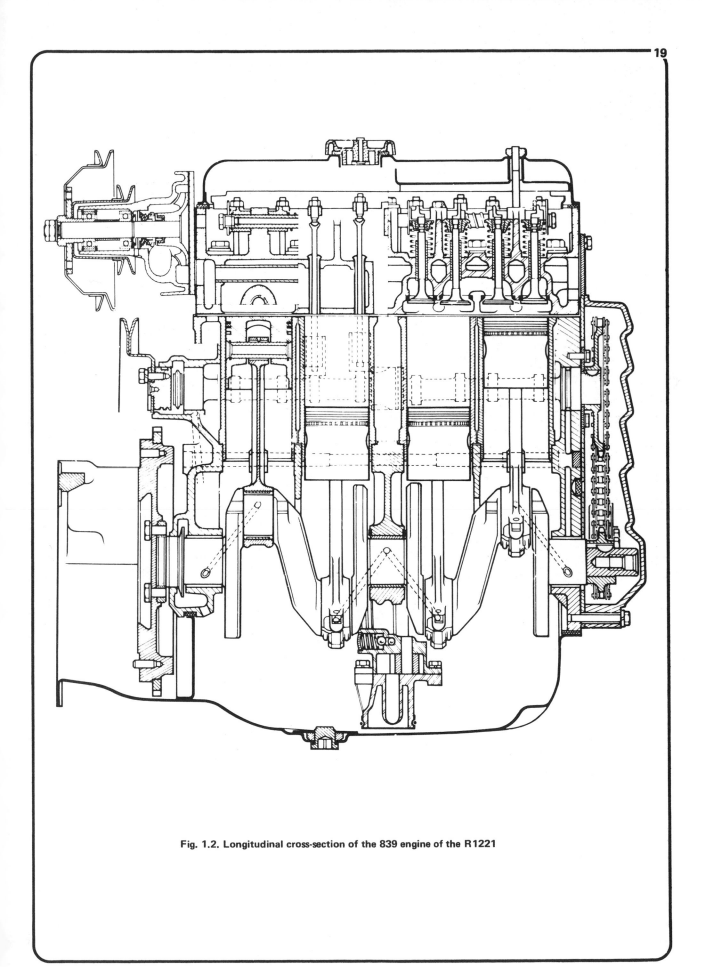

Fig. 1.2. Longitudinal cross-section of the 839 engine of the R1221

the side and to the front of the car. Chock the rear wheels, back and front, release the handbrake.

3 Get under the front of the car and remove the front gearbox protective undertray. You can see how the tray is fixed - around its edge with captive setscrews. Remove all these in turn. Now drain the oil from both the engine and the gearbox. Both drain plugs require specific spanners; remove the filler plug for the gearbox as well, this aids draining. Use a funnel to avoid the engine oil splashing on the front anti-roll bar. (photos)

4 To remove the bonnet it is necessary to remove both headlamps. These are located by a simple clip and a hook, on a pivot. Unhook the spring clip from its slot, tilt the light forward and withdraw the light towards the centre of the car. Carefully pull off the electrical connection. Store both light units in a safe place - they are expensive! (photos)

5 With the bonnet still open, mark round the hinge positioning on the front crossmember and then undo the four fixing bolts, two for each hinge and remove the bonnet lid. Remove its check strap from behind the headlamp inner plate. It helps to have another person to help. Store the bonnet carefully, preferably resting on some cloth. (photos)

6 Remove the spare wheel and the jack from the engine compartment.

7 Unscrew the positive (red) battery connection and place aside out of the way.

8 Remove the top of the air cleaner. Take out the element and then unscrew the three exposed nuts which fix the air cleaner base to the carburettor. Pull up the base with its washers, once you have pulled off the 'trumpet' hose from the inner wing fixing. (photos)

9 Loosen the alternator top fixing/belt adjusting brace, loosen the pivot bolt from behind the alternator and slacken the belt and remove it. (photos)

10 There are three electrical connections on the back of the alternator, two are 'screw' fixings, the third a pull-off tag. Remove all three and tie back the wiring. (photos)

11 Remove the alternator pivot bolt and withdraw the alternator from the car. Again store this carefully.

12 Now remove the second drive belt from the front of the engine. On the opposite side to the alternator is a simple belt tensioner. Loosen the locking nut and tensioner bolt and then loosen the clamping bolt, take up the tension and slip off the second belt. (photo)

13 The more you can take off the engine at this stage the better it will be. However, some of the operations next described are not strictly necessary for engine removal but have been described now for this is how the job was tackled in our workshop. Drain the cooling system. Remove the hexagonal cap from the top of

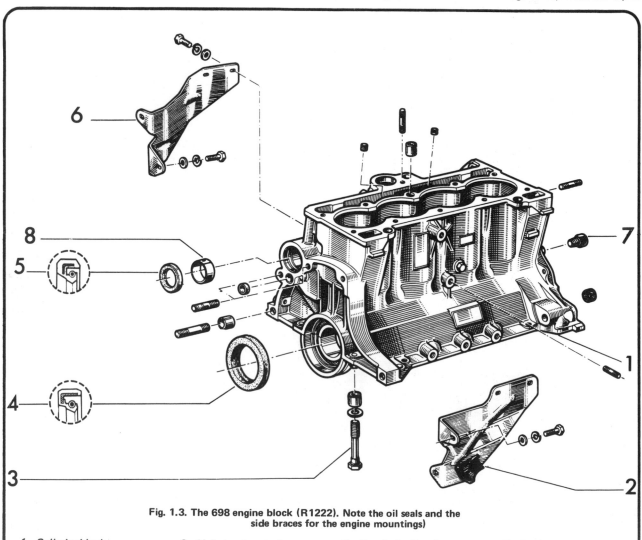

Fig. 1.3. The 698 engine block (R1222). Note the oil seals and the side braces for the engine mountings)

1 Cylinder block	3 Main bearing stud	5 Camshaft oil seal	7 Engine block coolant
2 Engine mounting plate	4 Countershaft oil seal	6 Engine mounting plate	drain plug
			8 Camshaft end bush

5.3a The gearbox undershield is easily removed from below

5.3b The engine oil will inevitably drain onto the anti-roll bar

5.3c The gearbox oil drains less messily

5.4a This clip finally locates the headlamp shell on its pivots

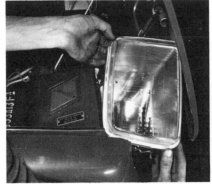

5.4b The headlamp shell is in cramped conditions; it has to come out from above

5.4c Carefully pull off the connector once the shell is loose

5.5a This is the best method of removing the bonnet, not the hinge pin itself

5.5b Don't forget the check strap; it's surprisingly heavy

5.8a The top of the air cleaner has a sealing ring made of rubber

5.8b The air cleaner base is also rubber mounted

5.8c Pull off the flexible feed hose, don't undo the hose clip

5.9a This area looks crowded but the alternator is readily accessible

5.9b The generator drivebelt will need careful but firm easing to remove

5.10a This is the first electrical connection on the alternator; use a spanner

5.10b The second electrical connection

5.12 Once the adjustment is loosened the inner drivebelt will ease off

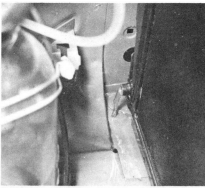

5.13a The coolant will always drain and splash over the inner bodywork

5.13b Note the 'once only' hose clip on this heater hose

5.13c The thermostat is held in the hose with a hose clip

5.13d The second heater hose is removed

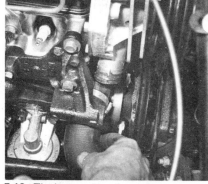

5.13e The bottom hose is much more accessible once the alternator is removed

5.15a The water pump pulley is only held by three setscrews

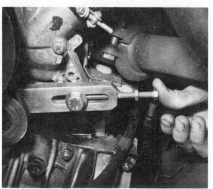

5.15b The inner drivebelt adjuster is very simple to use

5.15c The inner drivebelt adjuster is actually bolted to the water pump

the radiator and then remove the drain plug from its lower near-side position inside the car. Most of the coolant will be lost as it is not possible to collect it directly beneath the outlet. Pull off the four top hoses from the water pump. The original hose clips are 'once only' affairs. Throw them away and obtain some proper worm-drive hose clips for replacement. The largest hose will contain the thermostat safe and intact within it. (photos)

14 Remove the fifth hose to the water pump below. This too has the throw-away hose clips.

15 To remove the water pump at this stage (not strictly necessary), undo the three bolts which locate the top pulley to the water pump. Now remove the second/inner drive belt tensioner fixing bolt and remove the tensioner. (photos)

16 Six setscrews secure the water pump to the cylinder head. Use a small ring or socket spanner. Pull off cleanly with its

gasket and backing plate. (photos)

17 To remove the carburettor (not strictly necessary although its connections are), first disconnect the throttle tension spring. Then pop-off the linkage which operates the butterfly on the body of the carburettor, pivoting on the rocker cover. (photo)

18 Pull off the fuel pipe and lead it back to the fuel pump. (photo)

19 Disconnect the choke cable. Both the inner and the outer of the cable are located and need to be loosened from their clamps. (photos).

20 Undo the two nuts on the carburettor fixing studs and gently pull off the carburettor body with its gaskets. (photos)

21 Undo the exhaust clamp between the manifold and the connecting exhaust pipe. Remove the clamp. (photos)

22 Using a socket and an extension (it helps to have a 3/8 inch

5.16a This shows the water pump fixing screws, six in all

5.16b The water pump is removed, do not remove the front from the backing plate until the whole unit is removed

5.16c Once the water pump is removed there is much more room to work

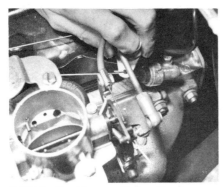
5.17 The throttle operating rod has a 'pop-on' fixing. Note the spring attached

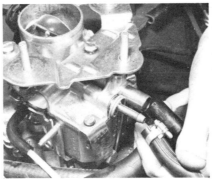
5.18 The fuel pipe is fixed by a clip to the carburettor. Always replace it

5.19 The choke cable uses a fragile, stiff wire to operate it

5.20a The carburettor fixing nuts are difficult to locate and undo

5.20b Always handle the carburettor with care, it is both fragile and costly

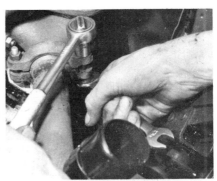
5.21a With use the exhaust clamp bolts 'heat' together. They may be stiff

5.21b Retain this clip, it works well and is difficult to substitute

5.22a This is the type of wrench needed to remove the exhaust manifold

5.22b Use two hands to remove the manifold, pull off square

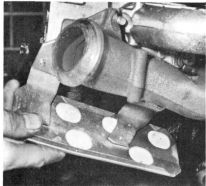

5.22c R1222, retain the necessary heat shield when the manifold comes away

5.23a The major starter motor electrical connection

5.23b A short spanner is necessary for the other starter motor electrical connection

5.23c Another tricky removal task; use this type of spanner for starter motor removal

5.23d The starter motor is heavy; it may need juggling to remove

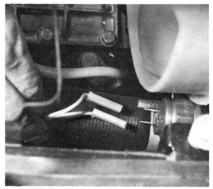

5.25a Coolant temperature sender unit for the radiator fan

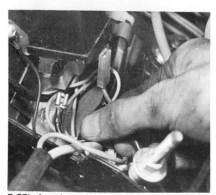

5.25b Another connection for the cooling fan, this time at the relay

5.26 The radiator cross brace preforms an essential task and should never be left out

5.27a The windscreen washer pump is best removed to save it from possible damage

as opposed to ½ inch drive), loosen and remove the exhaust manifold nuts from their studs - the manifold should then be free to remove, the water hoses will come with it. A heat shield for the starter motor will come away too. Disconnect the vacuum ignition pipe. (photos)

23 Disconnect the two cables to the end of the starter motor which will now be obvious. Loosen the three mounting bolts of the starter motor. This is quite tricky as there is hardly sufficient room to work. A socket extension is nearly essential. Remove the starter motor. (photos)

24 Remove the windscreen washer reservoir from its bracket next to the battery.

25 Pull off the electrical connection to the thermostatic switch in the radiator core. This is below the electric fan. Remove also the electrical connection on the relay which is in the circuit to activate the fan. (photos)

26 Remove the cross-brace between the radiator and the transverse tubular brace. (photo)

27 Loosen and remove the electric windscreen washer pump from the inner wing and tie it, as well as the hose, up and back. Then loosen the top hose from the radiator and lift away. (It should already be loose at the other end). (photos)

28 Unscrew the top of the expansion bottle taking great care with the sealing washer: do not force with grips. Then pull off the overflow pipe from the radiator.

29 Loosen the battery top clamp and then pull off the top frame. This will need the negative (green) connection undoing. Then pull the battery out of the car. (photos)

30 Pull the bottom hose from the bottom of the radiator. This will give access to the last two fixing bolts of the radiator, to enable the radiator, plug the fan housing, to be removed. (photos)

31 Loosen the clutch cable adjuster locknut. Slacken off and then disconnect the clutch cable at the lever arm. Pull it round to the offside of the car and tie back. (photo)

32 Split the gearshift rod. This is easily done by removing the two centre clamps and sliding one end out of the other. Leave the end still through the eye of the bush on the transverse top member. For floor change vehicles remove the 'below' changer from the slection arm on the top of the casting. (photos)

33 Now remove the transverse top member. This is located on each side of the car by setscrews. On the nearside bracket the air cleaner 'trumpet' is held behind. Lift out the member with the end gear rod, once the roll pin on the gearshift is removed. (photos)

34 Disconnect the engine/gearbox earth from the body frame and then loosen and remove the speedometer drive cable from the top end of the gearbox. This is located close to the earth cable. (photo)

35 Pull off the HT lead to the centre of the distributor (king lead) and then using the appropriate spanner disconnect the LT lead on the side. Tie these leads back towards the coil.

36 Pull off the fuel line from the tank to the fuel pump on the side of the engine block. Push this back out of the way. (photo)

37 Now the steering rack has to be removed. First from inside the engine compartment remove the through bolt connecting each steering arm with the ends of the steering rack. (photo)

38 Disconnect the rack from the steering column at the flexible coupling. This is an easy and obvious task, only two bolts need to be removed. (photo)

39 The rack is secured to the bodyframe by two through bolts on its under side. Remove these but be sure to retain, and record their exact position, the shims used on each side. Lift out the rack. (photos)

40 Jack-up the car at the front as high as is safe having removed the hub caps, place on supports and loosen the wheel nuts. Obtain some flexible wire or string and a ball joint 'remover'. Split the top ball joint on the two sides of the front suspension once both wheels have been removed. Do not allow the upright to hang on the brake hose but tie it up so that it is out of the way but not under any strain - use the wire or string. (photos)

5.27b The top hose may well need a certain amount of force to push it off

5.29a The battery is held down with a sturdy sprung frame

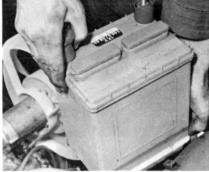
5.29b When lifting the battery watch for electrolyte spillage

5.30a The bottom hose's clip broke whilst being removed. It may in fact be easier to remove these clips by cutting them

5.30b The radiator sits on rubber feet

5.31 Slacken the clutch adjustment before removing the cable connection

5.32a The gear selector rod splits by removing one of the joints

5.32b The gear selector rod is in two parts, one inside the other

5.33a This tube is used for the air cleaner summer setting, the other, lower left, is for the winter

5.33b The cross brace should come away with part of the gear selector

5.34 The speedometer drive is only fixed by a locknut

5.36 At the fuel pump end, the fuel feed pipe is a push-on fit only

5.37 It may be necessary to wriggle the steering arm pin out

5.38 It is only necessary to undo two opposing bolts on the flexible coupling

5.39a The steering rack itself only has two fixings

5.39b It is best to use a ratchet drive to loosen the steering rack fixing bolts

5.39c Always record the position of the steering rack shims

5.39d Move the rack through the housing to facilitate removal

5.40a Loosen the ball joint nut before using a ball joint remover

5.40b Always be careful with the ball joint bellows once removed

5.43a Undo the front gearbox mounting pad on the gearbox first

5.43b This is the other side of the same pad

5.43c The pad simply clips onto the cross member

5.44 The driveshafts are not held in the gearbox by anything other than their splines

41 Go further under the car and loosen the two side engine mounting stud nuts. This must be done from below and with an open-ended spanner. Remove the nuts.

42 Place a sling around the engine and the gearbox. The best mounting places are just in front of the drive shaft take-off and under the rear end of the engine. Connect the sling to the hoist and just take the weight.

43 Remove the front gearbox mounting pad from the car (and gearbox). Its fixing bolts and nuts are obvious. The sling should now be taking the weight at the front. (photos)

44 Carefully pull out the driveshafts from each side of the differential housing. Watch the seals on the housing. They should easily pull out now that the suspension is disconnected. Tie them back and up out of the direct line of the power unit removal, but not under any strain. (photo)

45 Make sure that there are no wire or pipes connected between the engine and the body shell. There should be two - the water temperature sender unit on the cylinder head and the oil pressure warning light sender - pull these two off and tie back! Unhook the gearshift spring.

46 Lift the engine and gearbox up and out, carefully. It does not require any great angle of tilt. The car must remain stationary and the hoist pulled forward to clear the bodywork. Lower the power unit gently onto a suitable working surface - preferably, not the floor. (photo)

6 Engine removal - R1221

1 For the purposes of engine removal there is little difference in this model, the R1221, from the R1222 just described. The fundamental change is the positioning of the radiator and the use of a conventional fan. Therefore, the procedure given in the previous Section should be followed up to paragraph 25. For 'alternator', however, read 'dynamo' and ignore the adjusting

5.46 Be careful when hoisting the engine out; watch for any components which could catch

brace - a jockey wheel is fitted instead.

2 Remove the brace from the top of the radiator down to the front body crossmember. At the same time loosen the gearshift through bush on the top of the radiator.

3 Now go back to paragraphs 27, 28, 29, 30 and 31 and do those operations.

4 Go on to paragraphs 34, 35, 36 and 37. When you remove the steering rack using this method, you will also disconnect the radiator. It is easiest to remove the radiator with the rack rather than to remove it from the top of the rack. The radiator sits on a bracket which is located through the same setscrews as the rack.

5 Paragraphs 38 onwards to the end of Section 5 still apply.

Dismantling

7 Engine - dismantling (general)

1 Owners who have previously dismantled engines will know the need for a strong work bench and many tools and pieces of equipment, which make life much easier when going through the process of dismantling an engine. For those who are doing a dismantling job for the first time, there are a few 'musts' in the way of preparation which, if not acquired, will only cause frustration and long delays in the job in the long run. It is essential to have sufficient space in which to work. Dismantling and reassembly is not going to be completed all in one go and it is therefore absolutely essential that you have sufficient area to leave things as they are when necessary. A strong work bench is also necessary together with a good engineer's vice. If you have no alternative other than to work at ground level, make sure that the floor is at least level and covered with a suitable wooden or wood composition material on which to work. If dirt and grit are allowed to get into any of the component parts all work which you carry out may be completely wasted. Before actually placing the engine wherever it is that you may be carrying out the dismantling, make sure that the exterior is now completely and thoroughly cleaned.

2 Once dismantling begins it is advisable to clean the parts as they are removed. A small bath of paraffin is about the best thing to use for this, but do not let parts which have oilways in them become immersed in paraffin otherwise there may be a residue which could cause harmful effects later on. If paraffin does get into oilways every effort should be made to blow it out. For this it may be necessary to carry the particular part to a garage fitted with a high pressure air hose. Short oilways such as there are in the crankshaft can be cleared easily with pipe cleaners.

3 Always obtain a complete set of gaskets when the engine is being dismantled - no gaskets on an engine are re-usable and any attempt to do so is quite unjustified in view of the relatively small cost involved. Before throwing any gaskets away, however, make sure that you have the replacement to hand. If, for example, a particular gasket cannot be obtained it may be necessary to make one, and the pattern of the old one is useful in such cases.

4 Generally speaking, it is best to start dismantling the engine from the top downwards. In any case, make sure it is firmly supported at all times so that it does not topple over whilst you are undoing the very tight nuts and bolts which will be encountered. Always replace nuts and bolts into their locations once the particular part has been removed, if possible. Otherwise keep them in convenient tins or pots in their groups, so that when the time comes to reassemble there is the minimum of confusion.

8 Engine dismantling - ancillaries

1 A word of warning at this stage is that you should always be sure that it is more economic to dismantle and overhaul a worn engine rather than simply to exchange it on the Renault Factory scheme. It is not always.

2 If you are intending to obtain an exchange engine complete, it will be necessary first of all to remove all those parts of the engine which are not included in the exchange. If you are stripping the engine completely yourself in the likelihood of some outside work to be done by specialists, all these items will be taken off anyway.

3 Short engines are not available from Renault Limited. It is as well to check with whoever may be supplying the replacement

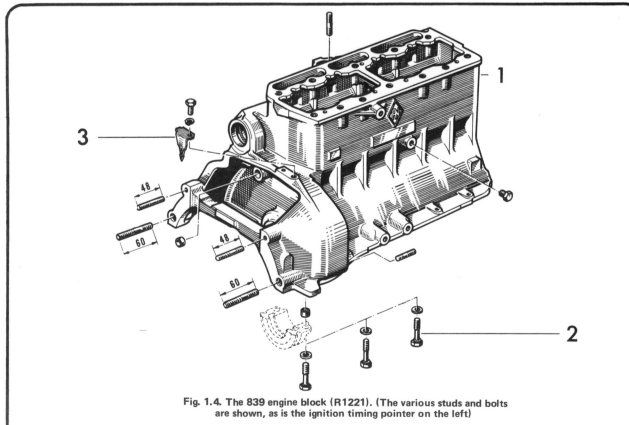

Fig. 1.4. The 839 engine block (R1221). (The various studs and bolts are shown, as is the ignition timing pointer on the left)

1   Cylinder block   2   Main bearing bolts   3   Ignition static timing marker

exchange unit what it is necessary to remove, but as a general guide the following items will have to be taken off. Reference is given to the appropriate Chapter for details of removal of each of these items:

Generator - Chapter 9
Distributor - Chapter 4
Thermostat - Chapter 2
Carburettor - Chapter 3
Inlet/exhaust manifold - Chapter 1
Fuel pump - Chapter 3
Engine mounting brackets - Chapter 1
Distributor/oil pump drive - Chapter 4
Gearbox - Chapter 6
Ignition coil - Chapter 4
Static timing pointer - Chapter 1
Belt tensioner - Chapter 2
Dipstick
Water pump - Chapter 2
Starter motor - Chapter 11

Always clean the engine before exchanging.

9 Inlet/exhaust manifold - removal

1 If the engine is being completely dismantled or if the cylinder head is being removed, it is not necessary to detach either the inlet/exhaust manifold, prior to carrying out this work.

2 The only occasions when one would expect to have to remove the manifold would be to renew a suspected leaking gasket or, of course, a cracked or damaged manifold.

3 Both manifolds have to be removed together as they are one unit and are mounted to the engine on a common gasket.

4 First of all disconnect all the carburettor controls and fuel pipe connection to the carburettor and remove the carburettor together with its air cleaner from the inlet manifold flange. Details are given in Chapter 3. Next disconnect the exhaust pipe from the flange on the manifold by undoing the clamp removing it completely. The exhaust pipe to the silencer will then hang limp with the silencer. It supports itself quite safely. Pull off the water hoses from the water heated manifold block. Undo and remove with a tubular spanner the four nuts which hold the whole manifold to the head. On the R1222 there is a special heat shield which will come away too. (On some models there is a bracing piece between the inlet manifold carburettor studs and two cylinder head bolts. It is essential to remove these two cylinder head studs to remove the bracing piece and then the manifold. A 14 mm socket or ring spanner will undo these. Even if the cylinder head is not going to be removed these bolts must be undone. It should not disturb the cylinder head gasket if done carefully, and the bolts replaced correctly).

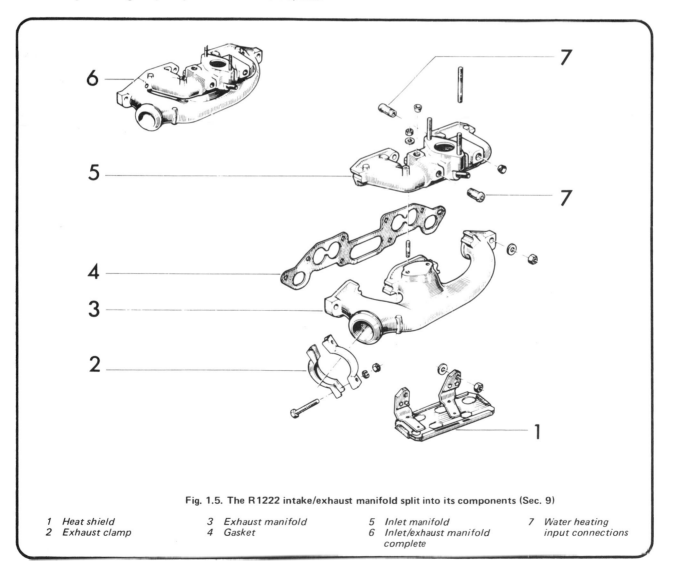

Fig. 1.5. The R1222 intake/exhaust manifold split into its components (Sec. 9)

1 Heat shield	3 Exhaust manifold	5 Inlet manifold	7 Water heating
2 Exhaust clamp	4 Gasket	6 Inlet/exhaust manifold complete	input connections

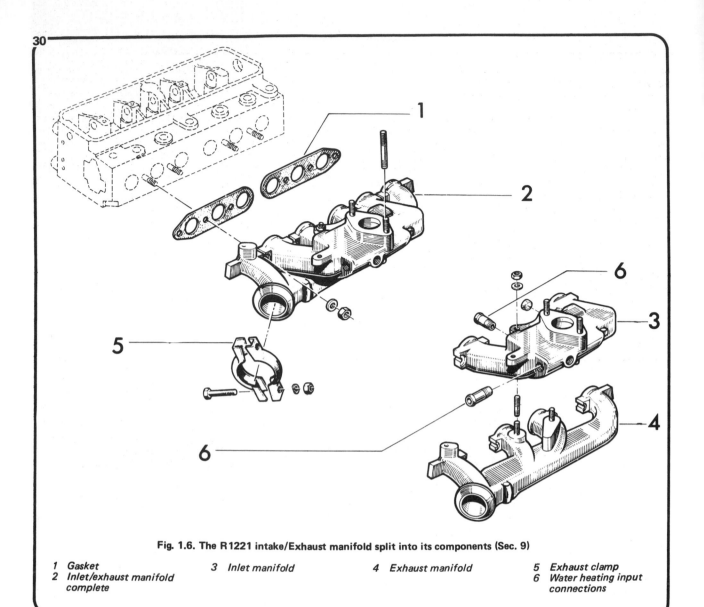

Fig. 1.6. The R1221 intake/Exhaust manifold split into its components (Sec. 9)

1 Gasket
2 Inlet/exhaust manifold
   complete

3 Inlet manifold

4 Exhaust manifold

5 Exhaust clamp
6 Water heating input
   connections

10.2 The rocker cover itself holds the gasket

10.3 The R1222 (shown here) and the R1221 differ in their
rocker gear

10 Valve rocker gear - removal

1 It is not necessary to remove the valve rocker gear from the cylinder head in order to remove the cylinder head from the engine, either in or out of the car. In fact the valve rocker gear can only be removed under the following conditions:

  a) *The cylinder head is removed from the engine with the engine still in the car.*
  b) *The engine is removed from the car with the cylinder head still attached to the engine.*
  c) *The water pump must be removed from the cylinder head under ALL CONDITIONS.*

2 Remove the rocker cover by undoing the two retaining nuts and lift off. Lift off the rocker cover gasket. (photo)

3 Breather pipes etc will differ from model to model and should be extracted with care. All lift out easily. For the R1222 removal is now simple. Undo progressively the four pedestal stud nuts and then lift the rocker arms and shaft upwards directly. (photo) For the R1221 read on.

4 We assume that the water pump is off the cylinder head. Remove the cylinder head end plate.

5 Extract the little rubber grommet from the end of the cylinder head away from the water pump. Prise it outwards with a screwdriver.

6 Undo the two locking nuts located on the centre pedestals, having prised the locking flat with a screwdriver. These nuts, 8 mm, locate the split rocker shaft in the pedestals. Remove together with the locking washers.

7 Unscrew the shaft end plugs and remove the four clips, two end springs and the two shaft end plug setscrews.

8 If the cylinder head is still on the engine but it is out of the car, slacken off all the valve rocker arms using a ring spanner. Unscrew the eight adjusting pins about two turns.

9 A shaft extractor can be made by using a bolt of 11 mm diameter about two inches long, threaded for about an inch. Unscrew the end bolts and screw in this bolt through the end of the cylinder head into the rocker shaft until it is fairly tight. Then lever the bolt out of the hole again as straight as you can, having removed the locking springs. With luck the shaft will follow it and the rocker arms will fall off the shaft together with their floating springs. Retrieve the rocker arms noting their position, with the springs. Repeat for the other end. Be careful, it is not too easy without the real tool - the head is made of aluminium and does not take kindly to bashing around. (It is this form of shaft extraction which does not allow the removal in the car).

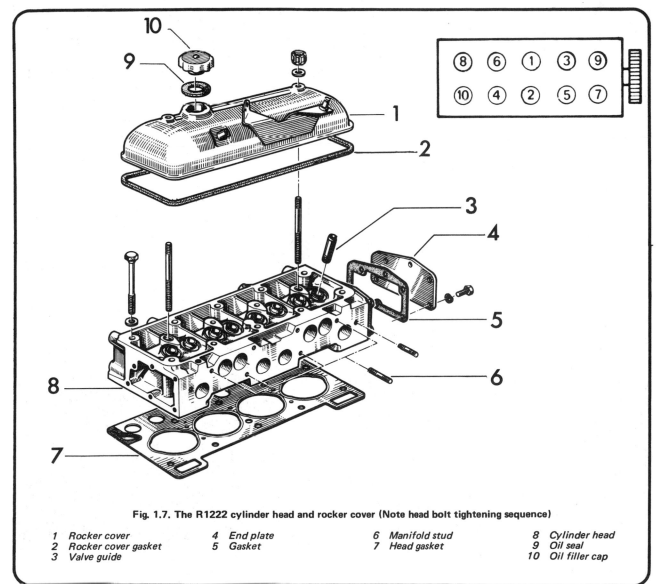

Fig. 1.7. The R1222 cylinder head and rocker cover (Note head bolt tightening sequence)

1	Rocker cover	4	End plate	6	Manifold stud	8	Cylinder head
2	Rocker cover gasket	5	Gasket	7	Head gasket	9	Oil seal
3	Valve guide					10	Oil filler cap

11 Cylinder head - removal

1 The cylinder head may be removed with the engine either in or out of the car.

2 If the engine is to remain in the car, the following must be done first:

    a) Drain the cooling system.

    b) Remove the air cleaner from the carburettor and pre-ferably remove the carburettor also as a safety precaution.

    c) Remove both top and bottom radiator hoses completely.

    d) Disconnect all the leads from the spark plugs.

    e) Disconnect the heater water pipes from the water pump housing at the front of the cylinder head.

    f) Disconnect and remove the fuel feed pipe from the fuel pump which goes to the carburettor.

    g) Undo the exhaust manifold to exhaust pipe clamp and allow pipe to hang.

    h) Pull away the throttle cable (R.H.D. cars only) and tie to right-hand side inner wing.

    i) Undo and push forward the gear shift rod and the radiator tie rod on the R1221.

    j) Remove electrical lead to water temperature sender unit in water pump casting.

    k) Remove the outer fan belt which runs round the fan pulley and the generator, then the other fan belt (see Chapter 2) and the generator.

Note: The water pump should remain on the head for ease of movement but this is not essential. It is however easier to remove the water pump with the head out of the car.

3 With the foregoing completed removal of the cylinder head is now the same whether the engine is in or out of the car. Remove

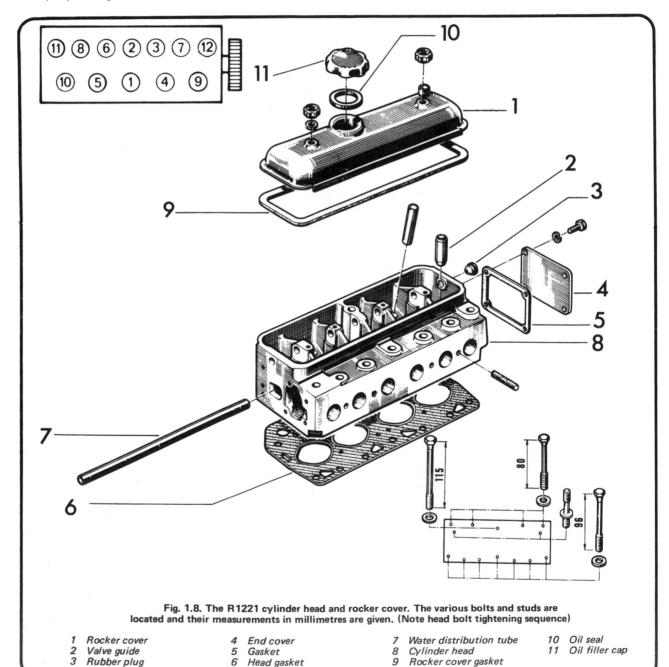

Fig. 1.8. The R1221 cylinder head and rocker cover. The various bolts and studs are located and their measurements in millimetres are given. (Note head bolt tightening sequence)

1 Rocker cover	*4 End cover*	*7 Water distribution tube*	*10 Oil seal*
2 Valve guide	*5 Gasket*	*8 Cylinder head*	*11 Oil filler cap*
3 Rubber plug	*6 Head gasket*	*9 Rocker cover gasket*	

the nuts which locate the rocker cover; remove the rocker cover with the gasket.

4 If the engine is still in the car make absolutely sure at this stage that it is **out of gear** and the handbrake is on. Leaving the valve rocker gear in place undo the 12 cylinder head bolts.

5 If you are working on the R1221 engine it is essential that you have the correct socket with which to undo the cylinder head bolts. This is Renault Part Number 'Mot 23-12 384', it is a special 14 mm socket with a 3/8 inch drive which has been machined very finely on its outside. You will need a 3/8 inch-converter-to-½ inch-drive, if you have the normal type of socket set drive in current use. Purchase this socket and special extension at the outset - there is no other way - you will break something, if only yourself, if you attempt this task without these tools.

6 Once all the bolts are out, the head should lift straight off. (Keep the bolts in the correct order for refitting). It is an aluminium head - do not hit it if it is reluctant to lift off. Tap the spark plug side very, very gently in a horizontal plane and it will move. Place the head on a flat, safe surface. (photo)

7 Do not turn the engine over to remove the head because you will disturb the removable cylinder liners. Once these are disturbed the pistons have to be removed etc and if it was only your intention to replace the cylinder head gasket you have created a lot of unnecessary work. When the head is removed the pushrods will be left floating in the tappet chest. Remove these and place them through a piece of cardboard in their correct order for replacement. Be careful that the cam followers do not become dislodged at this stage. (photo)

8 Remove the old cylinder head gasket and retain for inspection.

9 Once the head is removed and you do not wish to dismantle the pistons, liners and their seals, place retaining clamps on the liners. These can be made from large washers about 1½ inches in diameter, and some metal tubing - galvanised pipe used on building sites is ideal - about 2 inches long. You will need four of each. Replace the four head bolts which go between cylinders one and two and three and four with the washers flat on the block and the tube over them. Once the bolts are fairly tight the liners will not shift.

Special Note: Apart from the removal of the valve rocker gear, the valves and the valve springs, all dealt with in this Chapter, there is one further task to be carried out on the cylinder head: checking and replacing the internal water distribution tube, its cover plate and gasket. This will be dealt with in Chapter 2 on the Cooling System.

12 Valves - removal

1 With the valve rocker gear removed and the water pump taken off, see Chapter 2, the valves are relatively easy to remove

with the cylinder head on the bench, even though there is no proprietary spring compressor on sale in the United Kingdom which will help on this head. Do not buy one, it will not work!

2 Start at one end of the head by placing some highly compressed rag in the combustion chamber and then placing it face down onto the bench. This effectively holds the valves in place on that cylinder, when you remove the valve spring and collets.

3 With the aid of a second person to extract the two collet halves from the top of the valve stem, press down on the top of the valve spring washer/cap with two equally sized screwdrivers both with blades of about 3/8 inch across. The spring will compress with its cap and because the valve is held up by the compressed rag the collets will fall outwards to be collected. This is not dangerous - the valve springs are not very strong and provided the motions are undertaken precisely and are unrushed, all will be well. Retain the collets in order - they differ from inlet to exhaust valve. (photo)

4 Release the pressure on the valve cap once the collets are extracted, remove the cap (sometimes known as spring seat), the spring (single springs only are used on all valves, but be sure to record those from the inlet valves and those from the exhaust separately - they differ in strength) and the lower washers.

5 Do one combustion chamber at a time before extracting the valves themselves. Repeat the process for each chamber and record the order in which the valves are removed. Place them through a piece of cardboard in order, as you would the pushrods, for further inspection. (photo)

13 Tappets - removal

1 With the cylinder head and the pushrods removed the tappets can be extracted.

2 Each one can be removed by pushing one's index finger right into the tappet, pushing out the oil and then pulling it upwards. A technique will soon be developed to raise them up in this way. (photo)

3 Place the tappets in their correct order for inspection and correct replacement.

14 Timing cover, gears and chain - removal

1 The timing cover is located at the rear end of the engine, nearest to the bulkhead, and can only be removed with the engine out of the car because of its close proximity with the bulkhead. (It has been removed with the engine in the car albeit with great difficulty but it was found to be pointless because nothing else could be done to the timing gear without the engine out). It is located by eleven setscrews, some direct into the block, some tightened with nuts.

2 Remove the timing cover and its gasket by undoing the

11.6 The cylinder head should never be prised off the block

11.7 Note the location of the pushrods

12.3 Instead of two screwdrivers, an alternative, a bent piece of steel

12.5 The valves are small but relatively hardy

13.2 Fingers are best for removing cam followers

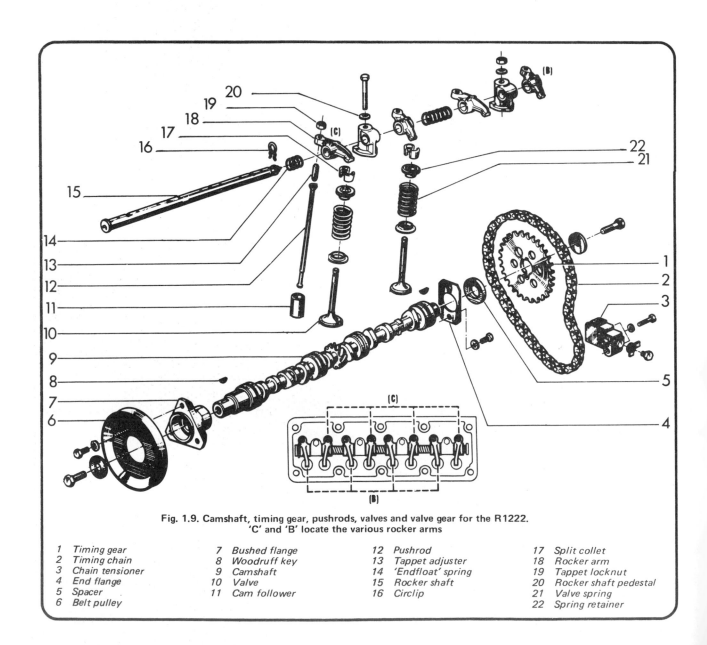

Fig. 1.9. Camshaft, timing gear, pushrods, valves and valve gear for the R1222.
'C' and 'B' locate the various rocker arms

1 Timing gear	7 Bushed flange	12 Pushrod	17 Split collet
2 Timing chain	8 Woodruff key	13 Tappet adjuster	18 Rocker arm
3 Chain tensioner	9 Camshaft	14 'Endfloat' spring	19 Tappet locknut
4 End flange	10 Valve	15 Rocker shaft	20 Rocker shaft pedestal
5 Spacer	11 Cam follower	16 Circlip	21 Valve spring
6 Belt pulley			22 Spring retainer

14.2a The timing cover is very heavy and has sharp edges

14.2b Record the position of the pulley on the camshaft

14.2c Always remove the pulley before attempting dismantling at the other end of the camshaft

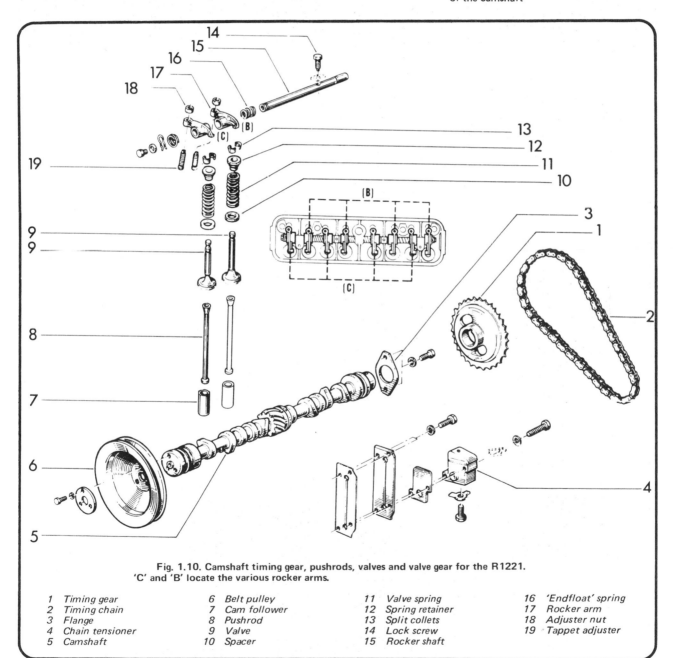

Fig. 1.10. Camshaft timing gear, pushrods, valves and valve gear for the R1221.
'C' and 'B' locate the various rocker arms.

1	Timing gear	6	Belt pulley	11	Valve spring
2	Timing chain	7	Cam follower	12	Spring retainer
3	Flange	8	Pushrod	13	Split collets
4	Chain tensioner	9	Valve	14	Lock screw
5	Camshaft	10	Spacer	15	Rocker shaft

16	'Endfloat' spring
17	Rocker arm
18	Adjuster nut
19	Tappet adjuster

screws. The cover is quite heavy and has some sharp machined edges. Remove the camshaft belt pulley from the other end. (R1221). (photos)

3 Remove the chain tensioner by unlocking and unscrewing the retaining cylinder bolt. Insert a 3 mm Allen key into the retaining cylinder, turn the key in a clockwise direction until the pad carrier assembly is no longer under tension and the tensioner and its thrust plate should be free. (photos)

4 *R1221:* To remove the timing chain and sprockets a two legged puller is necessary. Do not attempt to take off either of the sprockets without drawing them both away together with the camshaft.

5 Remove the two camshaft flange fixing bolts through the camshaft sprocket. Then draw off the crankshaft sprocket. Make sure the tappets and the distributor drive is away; also the fuel pump.

6 Once the crankshaft sprocket is clear the chain can be lifted away. The camshaft is now ready to pull out. (photo)

7 *R1222:* The principle for this engine is the same except that the camshaft sprocket is located to the camshaft with a setscrew through its centre, a location tab and a locking tab. Once this sprocket is loosened it should pull off enabling the chain to be removed. The crankshaft sprocket does not need pulling off.

8 The backplate can now be removed.

15 Camshaft - removal

1 The camshaft runs directly in the block without shell bearings. Unlike more conventionally designed cars, the camshaft drives pulleys or sprockets at both ends which means that it can only be removed once the engine is out of the car. The cylinder head must also be removed as must the tappets or cam followers, so must the distributor, its drive pinion and drive gear (see Chapter 4) and so must the fuel pump (see Chapter 3). (photo)

2 Remove the pulley at the end of the camshaft nearest the flywheel. It is held by three setscrews and spring washers. It should fall off as it is only a face to face fit.

3 The R1221 camshaft removal was described in the previous Section as its removal is necessary to facilitate timing gear and chain removal. (photo)

4 The R1222 camshaft is removed in the same way as that of the R1221 was, once the sprocket has been removed. (photo)

5 Do not damage the camshaft lobes.

16 Sump - removal

1 The sump may be removed with the engine and gearbox in the car and, of course, with it out, provided the engine has been separated from the gearbox and is lying on its side. With the engine still in the car it is really arm aching work if you are lying on the ground under the car, it is not much better with the car on a ramp or over a pit. (photo)

2 Drain the sump of its oil. A 5 Imp. pint (3.1 litres) container is necessary. Replace the sump plug after five minutes.

3 Remove the anti-roll bar (Chapter 10).

4 Undo the four bolts which hold the tubular crossmember between the chassis rails and the suspension mounting brackets. Then remove the crossmember altogether.

5 Undo the four bolts which locate its front edge to the gearbox if still fitted in the car. These are clearly visible.

6 With a long screwdriver undo the two setscrews which have cuts in their heads first. These are located at the rear of the sump and must be got at by passing the screwdriver through the two holes in the floor of the car close to the edge. This will not apply with the engine out of the car.

7 Undo and remove all the sump setscrews which remain. (Two at the front end will be nuts on locating studs). Catch the square star washers. Lower the sump and remove the gasket which should come away in four parts.

17 Oil pump - removal

1 The oil pump may be removed from the engine whilst the engine is still in the car. It is necessary first of all to remove the sump. As the oil pump drive spindle also drives the distributor, care must be taken to ensure that the ignition timing is not lost when the oil pump is removed and eventually replaced. It is, therefore, necessary also to remove the distributor cap and turn the engine until the rotor is in line with the number one plug high tension lead contact. The timing marker on the crankshaft pulley wheel must then also be against the top dead centre position. For full details of engine timing refer to Chapter 4.

2 Once the crankshaft has been set to the correct position the distributor should be removed. By looking down into the distributor mount opening it will be possible to see the top of the oil pump spindle and the position of the offset slot. Take a careful note of this position.

3 The pump may be removed by undoing the three 10 mm setscrews. The inner of the three is difficult to get at with a spanner and much patience should be exercised with this screw. The pump should pull out. (photo)

18 Big-end bearings, pistons, connecting rods and liners - removal

1 With the engine in the car it is possible to change the big-end bearings only on the R1222; on the R1221 it is possible to change the pistons, liners and connecting rods as well. With the engine removed from the car, the task is much easier and generally cleaner but, of course, it is understood that if a quick emergency repair job is to be done and speed is of the essence, then it would be in order to do any work with the engine still in the car. The pistons and their connecting rods must be removed from the top of the engine once their connecting rod end caps have been removed. It will not be possible to do this with the improvised cylinder liner retainers in position. It must therefore be assumed that if a piston or pistons is removed that the liners will be disturbed and have to be replaced. It is possible to buy from Renault Limited some special liner retainers quite cheaply which will retain the liners and allow pistons to be removed. It is a good idea if you are going to the extent of replacing the pistons to relocate and reseal the liners anyway at the same time cleaning the sludge away from their outside. But if speed is the essence - buy the proper liner retainers.

2 With the sump removed and the crankshaft exposed, each of the big-end bearing caps can be detached after removing the two bolts which hold each cap to the connecting rod stud. Rotate the engine to bring each connecting rod cap into position for unscrewing the nuts. (photo)

3 With the nuts removed, each big-end bearing cap can be pulled off. It must be noted that the connecting rods and big-end caps are marked with a small punch mark on the end of the connecting rod and cap, which matches up on each one. If the same connecting rods and caps are to be re-used, they must be replaced exactly as they came out. The same applies to the big-end bearing shells which will be released as soon as the connecting rods are detached from the crankshaft. It is inadvisable to re-use these shells anyway, but if they are not renewed they must be put back in exactly the same location from which they came.

4 If any difficulty is experienced in removing the big-end bearing caps from the studs of the connecting rods, it will help if the crankshaft is revolved in order to dislodge them. If this is done, however, care must be taken to ensure that nothing gets jammed when the connecting rod comes away from the crankshaft at the top of its stroke. Once released, connecting rods and pistons can be pushed up through the cylinder bores and out of the top of the block. Make sure that the pistons are kept in such a way that they can be easily identified and replaced in the same bore, if necessary.

5 If you have had to leave the liner retainers off you should

14.3a Note the location of various parts before further dismantling

14.3b This is how the chain tensioner works

14.6 The timing chain must always come away with the timing chain in this way

15.1 Always remove the fuel pump before the camshaft

15.3 The final component needing to be removed before the camshaft itself

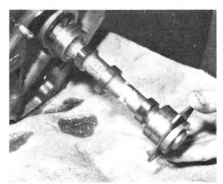

15.4 When you remove the camshaft, do so very carefully

16.1 The sump needs just as much care as the other engine components

17.3 The fixing setscrews on the oil pump are difficult to get at

18.2 Bearing shells should be retained for further inspection

now remove the liners. If they are still fitted and you wish to remove the liners for reboring or replacement, now remove the retainers.

6   Tap the bottom of the liners from beneath with a hard piece of wood which will not tend to split. If you hit them with steel of any kind they will crack without fail and will be 'instant scrap'.

7   Tap all four loose before you remove one. Lift them upwards and note where they were fitted and which way round. Provided you have drained the cooling system well, little liquid sediment will be left although there will almost certainly be a lot of rust particles there. If the crankshaft is to remain in the block, cover it as well as you can from below with non-fluffy rag to stop the likelihood of liquid or sediment falling on the journal surfaces - it will not actually do them any harm but it is difficult to remove when you are ready to reassemble. Only now remove the gaskets which seal the liners to the block.

19 Gudgeon pins - removal

The gudgeon pins float in the piston and are an interference fit in the connecting rods. This 'interference fit' between gudgeon pin and connecting rod, means that heat is required (230–260°C/450–500°F) before a pin can be satisfactorily replaced in the connecting rod. If it is necessary to replace either the piston or connecting rod, we strongly recommend that the assembly of the two be entrusted to someone with experience. Misapplied heat can ruin one, or all, of the components very easily.

20 Flywheel - removal

1   The flywheel may be removed with the engine in the car

provided that the gearbox and clutch assemblies and the sump are removed first. The flywheel would normally be removed in these circumstances for purposes of renewing the starter ring, which may have damaged teeth, or because of a badly scored face due to a badly worn clutch friction disc.

2   With the gearbox and clutch removed as described in Chapter 6 and 5 respectively, the bolt heads which secure the flywheel to the crankshaft flange will come into view. These bolts are locked into position by tab washers. Knock back the tabs and then undo and remove the securing bolts. It may be necessary to lock the flywheel to obtain leverage on the securing bolts. Use a

screwdriver on the starter ring and lock it onto the block. It is obvious where to do this. As there are two positions to locate the dowel pin (R1221) in the crankshaft flange and no dowels for the R1222, it is necessary to mark the exact locating position of the flywheel. Note the position of the dowel pin relative to the machined timing cut on the edge of the flywheel. It will be necessary to use a little leverage in order to draw the flywheel off and great care should be taken that it does not come off with a sudden jerk and fall down. One way of preventing this is by putting a stud, another, longer bolt with the head sawn off, into one of the bolt holes so that when the flywheel comes free, the

20.2 The flywheel must be marked for exact replacement

21.4 If possible, have everything clean before dismantling

21.5 Even if the crankshaft is worn, treat it with care

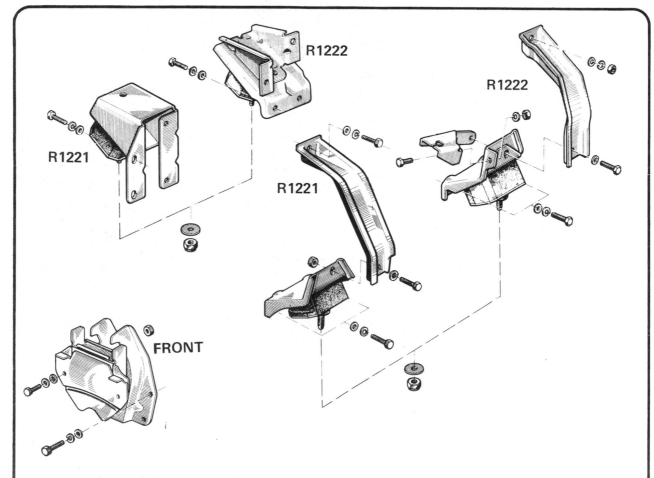

Fig. 1.11. The R1222 and R1221 use different engine mountings. The left and right-hand sides are illustrated for each engine. The front gearbox mounting, lower left, is universal (Sec. 23)

end of the stud will support it. Should the locating dowel (R1221) come out, replace it in the crankshaft immediately - in the correction position! (photo)

21 Crankshaft and main bearing - removal

1 It is only possible to inspect and replace two/four of the three/five main bearing shells (R1221/R1222) with the engine still in the car, at least for all practical purposes. For this reason if you want to be really sure of an adequate inspection and replacement of these bearings, they must only be looked at as a total operation: ie; all the main bearings together, and this can only be done with the engine out of the car and the timing cover removed. Main bearings seldom need replacing by themselves, it is more than likely that further overhaul is necessary and therefore the engine is likely to be out of the car.

2 With the engine removed from the car it is necessary for the sump, oil pump, timing cover and gear (but not crankshaft sprocket) to be removed, together with the flywheel. It is also desirable that the cylinder head should have been removed so that the engine may be stood inverted. If the liners are to be retained the engine should be placed on its side.

3 The connecting rod bearing caps should all have been removed and, of course, this will have been done if the pistons are being removed from the engine as well.

4 Using a good quality socket spanner remove the two bolts from each of the main bearing caps. Then lift off each of the caps. (photo)

5 With the main bearing caps removed the crankshaft may be carefully lifted out of the block and it should then be placed somewhere safe where it cannot fall or be damaged. The upper half main bearing shells may then be removed from the crankcase, together with the semi-circular thrust washers fitted at the centre main bearing. (photo)

22 Lubrication system - description

The engine has a very basic but effective oil flow system. Oil from the sump is pumped by the submerged oil pump up to the centre main bearing and then up to the main oil gallery under pressure. From there it is distributed through drillings to the other main bearings, the big-end bearing, the camshaft bearing surfaces, the rocker shafts and arms, the timing gear and the cylinder bores. A film of oil should be maintained on all these surfaces by this method. There are normally adequate gaskets to keep the oil inside the block at the sump, rocker cover and timing cover and aluminium plugs at each end of the oil gallery. Two types of oil seal thrower stop the oil leaking at the ends of the crankshaft. Oil drips back into the sump to be recirculated. There is a removable cartridge oil filter; a gauze filter is however fitted to the oil pump inlet to keep the worst sludge at bay.

23 Engine mountings - removal

1 The engine mountings (those fixed to the engine block) are basically rubber blocks which connect and hold the engine onto the chassis rails. They are mounted either side, half way along the block and are not interchangeable. They can be replaced individually with the engine in the car provided the engine is supported suitably.

2 The right-hand side mounting is a simple metal fabrication which is stuck to the hard rubber block. This has to be replaced as a unit and is held to the engine block by four setscrews. Undo the nut which locates the rubber block to the chassis rail then, with the engine suitably supported (if still in the car), unscrew the setscrews, one will have to be located from underneath the car. The mounting block will then come away as will the coil mounting bracket, but separately. The chassis rail mount can be removed by undoing four bolts which pass through the chassis and be lifted away.

3 The left-hand side mounting is constructed with two metal fabrications, one acting as a brace to the other on which is stuck the hard rubber block. However three setscrews can be undone after the one nut locating the block to the chassis rail has been undone, and the two fabrications will come away together (one is bolted at right angles to the other). Only the one fabrication attached to the rubber block need be replaced. The chassis rail mount can be removed in the same way as the one on the right-hand side.

Inspection and overhaul

24 Engine - examination

1 Examination of an engine runs in two phases. The first is a visual and aural examination when it is running and in the car, and the second is when it is out of the car, having decided that something is wrong and needs repairing. It is a matter to decide when to take the car off the road, and do something about putting right whatever faults may be. In general, if the oil and fuel consumption are perfectly reasonable, the performance is satisfactory, and it is not suffering from overheating, over cooling, or any other fault which causes aggravation and irritation on the road to a large degree, it is best left alone. Provided the regular maintenance requirements are carried out there is no need to take it to pieces.

2 The first indications of an engine becoming worn (if one has not been able to get the exact mileage that the engine has travelled) are an increase in oil consumption and possibly a corresponding increase in fuel consumption. This may also be accompanied by a falling off in performance. On any car it is not always easy to detect a falling off in performance and it is quite a good idea to drive another car of the same type which is known to be in very good condition, to make a comparison. If the signs are that the engine is performing poorly, using too much petrol and beginning to burn oil, then one of the first things to do is to test the compression in each cylinder with a proper compression testing gauge. This will indicate whether the pistons are leaking in the cylinders or the valves are leaking in the head. Depending on the results, the cylinder head may be removed and further examination carried out to the bores and head as described in subsequent Sections. Early action at this stage could well restore the engine to a satisfactory condition. Furthermore, such action would not call for a great deal of either money or time. If the condition is left, however, it will get progressively worse until such a time as the simple repairs which would have been needed earlier have reached the stage where more major operations are necessary. This will be proportionately much more expensive and time consuming.

25 Crankshaft and main bearings - examination and renovation

1 With the crankshaft removed examine all the crankpins and main bearing journals for signs of scoring or scratches. If all the surfaces of the bearing journals are obviously undamaged, check next that all the journals are round. This can be done with a micrometer or caliper gauge, taking readings across the diameter of each journal at six or seven points. If you do not own a micrometer or know how to use one, you should have little difficulty at any garage that has good mechanics to get someone to measure it for you.

2 If the crankshaft has ridges or severe score marks in it, it must be reground. The manufacturers of the Renault go further and say that a crankshaft in this condition should be renewed but as this can be a very expensive procedure, it is felt that regrinding should suffice in all but the most extraordinary situation. If there are no signs of ridging or severe scoring of the journals, it may be that the measurements indicate that the journals are not round. If the amount of ovality exceeds 0.002 inch (0.050 mm) it is probable that regrinding is necessary but it is best to get the advice of someone who is experienced and

familiar with crankshafts and regrinding them to give an opinion.
3 The main bearing shells themselves are normally a matt grey in colour all over and should have no signs of pitting or ridging or discolouration as this usually indicates that the surface bearing metal has worn away and the backing material is showing through. It is worthwhile renewing the main bearing shells anyway if you have gone to the trouble of removing the crankshaft, but they must, of course, be renewed if there is any sign of damage to them or if the crankshaft has been reground. When the crankshaft is reground the diameter is reduced and consequently one must obtain the proper undersized bearing shells to fit. These will normally be supplied by the firm which has reground the crankshaft. Regrinding is normally done in multiples of 0.010 inch (0.25 mm) as necessary and bearing shells are obtainable to suit these standard regrinding sizes. If the crankshaft is not being reground, yet bearing shells are being renewed, make sure that you check whether or not the crankshaft has been reground once before. This will be indicated by looking at the back of the bearing shell and this will indicate whether or not it is minus 0.010 inch (0.25 mm) or more. The same type of shell bearing must be used when they are renewed.

26 Big-end bearings - examination and renovation

The big-end bearings are subject to wear at a greater rate than those for crankshaft. Signs that one or more big-end bearings are getting badly worn is a pronounced knocking noise from the engine, accompanied by a significant drop in oil pressure due to the increased clearance between the bearing and the journal permitting oil to flow more freely through the resultantly larger space. If this should happen quite suddenly and action is taken immediately, and by immediately is meant within a few miles, then it is possible that the bearing shell may be replaced without any further work needing to be done. If this happens in an engine which has been neglected and oil changes and oil filter changes (on those models so fitted) have not been carried out as they should have been, it is most likely that the rest of the engine is in a pretty terrible state anyway. If it occurs in an engine which has been recently overhauled, then it is almost certainly due to a piece of grit or swarf which has got into the oil circulation system and finally come to rest in the bearing shell and scored it. It is in these instances where a replacement of the

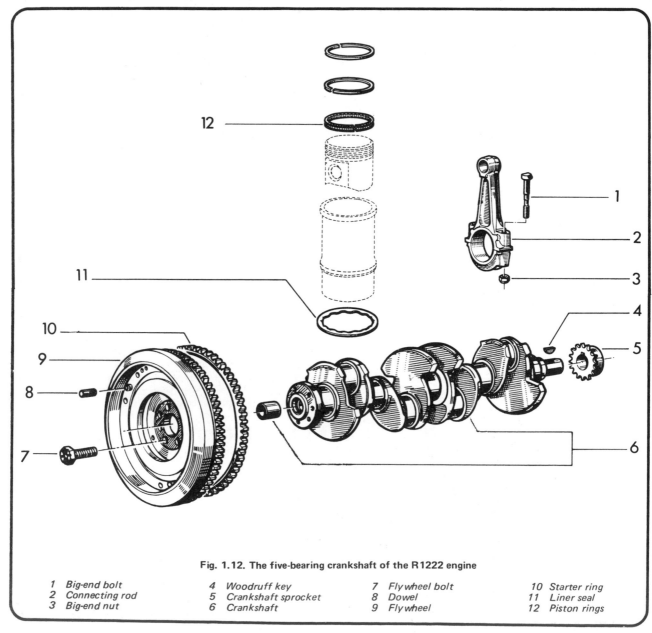

Fig. 1.12. The five-bearing crankshaft of the R1222 engine

1	Big-end bolt	4	Woodruff key	7	Flywheel bolt	10	Starter ring
2	Connecting rod	5	Crankshaft sprocket	8	Dowel	11	Liner seal
3	Big-end nut	6	Crankshaft	9	Flywheel	12	Piston rings

shell alone accompanied by a thorough flush out of the lubrication system may be all that is required.

27 Cylinder liner bores - examination and renovation

1   The liner bores may be examined for wear either in or out of the engine block; the cylinder head must, of course, be removed in each case. If the liners are still in the block and it is hoped that they will not need renovation the liner retainers must be left in place so that relocation does not have to take place. However, if you have got to the stage where the pistons are out it is better to remove the liners for inspection even if they do not require renovation. Relocation itself does not take much time, skill or money. Each bore may be examined in turn with the piston at the bottom of its stroke. A perfect cylinder is, as its name implies, perfectly cylindrical in shape. That is, the sides are parallel and a cross section is perfectly circular.

2   First of all examine the top of the cylinder about a quarter of an inch below the top of the liner and with the finger feel if there is any ridge running round the circumference of the bore. In a worn cylinder bore a ridge will develop at the point where the top ring on the piston comes to the uppermost limit of its stroke. An excessive ridge indicates that the bore below the ridge is worn. If there is no ridge, it is reasonable to assume that the cylinder is not badly worn. Measurement of the diameter of the cylinder bore both in line with the piston gudgeon pin and at right angles to it, at the top and bottom of the cylinder, is also another check to be made. A cylinder is expected to wear at the sides where the thrust of the piston presses against. it. In time this causes the cylinder to assume an oval shape. Furthermore, the top of the cylinder is likely to wear more than the bottom of the cylinder. It will be necessary to use a proper bore measuring instrument in order to measure the differences in bore diameter across the cylinder and variations between the top and bottom ends of the cylinder. As a general guide it may be assumed that any variations more than 0.010 inch (0.25 mm) indicates that the liners need reboring. Provided all variations are less than 0.010 inch (0.25 mm) it is probable that the fitting of new piston rings will cure the problems of piston to cylinder bore

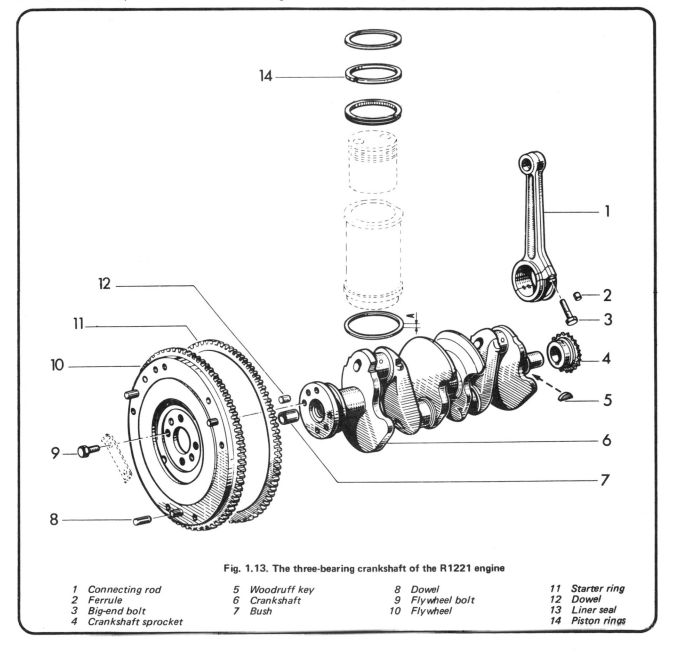

Fig. 1.13. The three-bearing crankshaft of the R1221 engine

1 Connecting rod	5 Woodruff key	8 Dowel	11 Starter ring
2 Ferrule	6 Crankshaft	9 Flywheel bolt	12 Dowel
3 Big-end bolt	7 Bush	10 Flywheel	13 Liner seal
4 Crankshaft sprocket			14 Piston rings

clearances. Once again it is difficult to give a firm ruling on this
as so much depends on the amount of time and effort which the
individual owner is prepared or wishes to spend on the task.
Certainly, if the cylinder bores are obviously deeply grooved or
scored, they must be rebored regardless of any measurement
differences in the cylinder diameter. If the engine has been
removed from the car for overhaul anyway, any cylinder bore
wear in excess of 0.005 inch (0.127 mm) certainly qualifies it for
a rebore, to do otherwise would be a waste of time and effort.
However, one must bear in mind again the fact that a rebore will
require the fitment of new pistons and the expense of this once
again could affect the owner's decision.
Special note: Contrary to a widely held belief these liners can be
safely rebored and pistons are available in various sizes of
oversize. (The liners have to be removed from the block though).
Do have the liners checked for cracks by a qualified engineering
shop.

---

28 Connecting rods, pistons and piston rings - examination and renovation

1   Pistons and rings are normally examined in relation to the
cylinder bores. With the cylinder head removed it is possible to
check the amount of movement between the piston and the wall,
both visually and with the aid of a feeler gauge. Liner retainers
must be fitted. If the condition of the bores seems to be
satisfactory, any excessive clearances between piston and bore
(0.010 inch/0.25 mm and upwards) could be due to wear of the
piston itself. Piston ring wear is almost certain to have taken
place also if this is the case, and will necessitate removal of the
pistons for further examination. First of all, look for signs of
damage to the piston ring grooves, and to the sides of the piston
where scoring may be apparent. Any deep scoring or any obvious
breakage between the piston ring grooves and the top of the
piston will, of course, call for a new piston. If the pistons do not
appear worn or damaged, next check the clearance between the
piston rings and the piston ring grooves. This can be done with a
feeler gauge and if it is in excess of the specified clearances the
pistons should be renewed. Excessive clearance between the rings
and the grooves allows the rings to chatter and they will break
very easily. Unfortunately, the wear usually occurs on the piston
rather than on the piston rings, although new rings should be
used as a check before condemning the pistons.
2   To check the condition of the rings it will be necessary to
remove them from the piston. Only the top ring on each piston
need be checked and, in fact, if one of the four piston rings is
bad it is reasonable to assume that the others will be similar and
the whole lot should be replaced. Remove the top piston ring by
spreading the ends apart sufficiently to enable it to be pulled out
of the groove and over the top of the piston. Care must be taken
not to twist the ring or draw it off unevenly, otherwise it could
easily break. The ring should then be placed inside the cylinder
bore from which it came pressed down approximately two
inches. It should lie perfectly horizontal across the bore and this
can be achieved by using a piston from which all the rings have
been removed to press it down square. Then the gap between the
ends of the piston rings should be measured with a feeler gauge;
if the piston ring gap exceeds that specified then the piston ring
is worn out and should be replaced. If the top ring is worn it is
reasonable to assume that the other two are worn on the same
pistons as well. Rings are normally only obtainable in sets
anyway so any thoughts of economy by renewing one or two
rings on a set of four pistons are really not worthwhile.
3   Provided the engine has not seized up or had some other
calamitous damage caused to it, it is most unlikely that the
connecting rods are in need of renewal at any time. In cases of
seizure one or more could have become bent and to check this
they will need setting up on a special jig. This is normally only
within the competence of a specialist engineering organisation.

29 Valve rocker gear - examination and renovation

Each rocker should move freely on the rocker shaft without
any signs of looseness or slackness. If any slackness is apparent it
will be necessary to dismantle the assembly. If either the rocker
bushes in the rocker arms and/or pedestals or the rocker shaft
are obviously scored and worn at those points where the rockers
are pivoting then they should be renewed. The rockers
themselves should also be examined on the faces where they bear
onto the top of the valve stems and if signs of wear are excessive
they should also be renewed.

30 Cylinder head, valves, valve springs and guides - examination and renovation

1   Once the cylinder head has been removed, it should be placed
upon a work bench so that a thorough examination can be
carried out.
2   First of all, all the valves should be removed.
3   The valves should be examined for signs of pitting or burning,
particularly around their edges and where they seat into the
cylinder head. If the valves are very much contaminated with
carbon, this should first of all be removed with a wire brush.
Very hard spots of carbon may need chipping off with the edge
of a very hard blade or tool. Be very careful; it is an aluminium
head! Exhaust valves are the ones most likely to suffer from
burning and if this is apparently quite severe, then the valves
should be discarded. Next replace each valve into its own guide,
after thoroughly cleaning the guide and valve stem, and check to
see that there is no sideways movement of the valve in the guide.
A very small amount of play is permissible but if it is very
considerable, then it means that oil and exhaust gases can all
make their way past the stem of the valve and this is not
conductive of good performance. If the guides are obviously
badly worn, then it will be necessary to have new ones fitted,
together with new valves. The fitting of valve guides on this
engine is a specialist task as they have to be reamed out to give a
very close tolerance after fitting. If it is thought that the wear is
on the valve stem rather than in the guide, the best way to check
is to obtain a new valve and try it in position.
4   If the valves are apparently in good general condition the
next thing to do is to examine the valve seats themselves in the
cylinder head. Here again, there should be no signs of pitting or
burning. The valve seats should also be checked to make sure
there are no cracks. If there are signs of damage to the seat in
any way, then the head itself may need fitting with a new valve
seat insert. Possibly, the existing valve seats may be recut. Give
this job to a specialist. Provided the valves and seats are in good
condition, then it is possible to reseat them by grinding in
position using a carborundum paste. This grinding-in process
should also be carried out when a new valve is being fitted.
5   The carborundum paste used for this job is normally supplied
in a double ended tin with coarse paste at one end and fine paste
at the other. In addition, a suction tool for holding the valve
head so that it may be rotated is also required. To grind in a
valve, first smear a trace of the coarse paste onto the seat face
and fit the suction grinder to the valve head. Then with a semi-
rotary motion grind the valve head into its seat, lifting the valve
occasionally to redistribute the grinding paste. When a dull matt
continuous line is produced on both the valve seat and the valve
then the paste can be wiped off. Apply a little fine paste and
finish off the grinding process. If a light spring is placed over the
valve stem behind the head this can often be of assistance in
raising the valve from time to time against the pressure of the
grinding tool so as to redistribute the paste evenly round the job.
The width of the line which is produced after grinding should
not be more than 1.8 mm. If, after a moderate amount of
grinding, it is apparent that the seating line is much wider than
this then it means that the seat has already probably been cut
back once or more times previously, or else the valve has been
ground several times. Here again, specialist advice is best sought

on occasions such as this.

6 After each valve has been ground in, the traces of carborundum paste which will remain in the area of the seat and inlet port must be thoroughly flushed away with paraffin. If possible, a high pressure air line should be used to blow away the final traces. Obviously, particles of carborundum grit are not wanted anywhere inside the engine.

7 Before the valves are finally replaced, all traces of carbon should be cleaned from them and also from the cylinder head itself. A wire cup brush and an electric drill are very useful in doing this work in the head. The face of the cylinder head should also be scraped perfectly clean and free from accumulations of carbon which may be upon it. Do not use any abrasive paper for cleaning but rather a flat bladed scraper. Make sure that no odd particles of gasket or carbon fall into the orifices in the casting. If they should, get them blown out.

8 Examine all the valve springs to make sure that they are of the correct length according to the specifications. It will have been noticed when they were being removed whether any were broken, and if they are then they should be replaced. It is a good idea to replace all the valve springs anyway. If you have reached this stage it is false economy not to do so. They are relatively cheap.

9 It is a good idea to replace the valve spring seating washers which sit directly on the cylinder head. These wear reasonably quickly.

10 Before reassembling the valves and springs to the cylinder head make a final check that everything is thoroughly clean and free from grit and then lightly smear all the valve stems with engine oil prior to reassembly.

31 Timing chain and sprockets - examination and renovation

Examine the teeth of both sprockets for wear. Each tooth on the sprocket is in the shape of an inverted 'V' and if the side of the tooth is concave in shape it is an indication that the tooth is worn badly and the sprocket should therefore be replaced. If the sprockets are worn and have to be renewed then the chain should also be renewed. If the sprockets are satisfactory, examine the chain to make sure there is no play between the links and if the chain is held out it should not bend when held horizontal. In view of the relative cheapness of these items it is worthwhile putting on a new chain anyway. Examine the tensioner pivot for signs of excessive wear which could cause rattling and also the tensioner itself. If the chain has gouged a deep groove into the tensioner renew it.

32 Camshaft and tappets - examination and renovation

1 The camshaft lobes should be examined for signs of flats or scoring or any other form of wear and damage. At the same time the tappets should also be examined, particularly on the faces where they bear against the camshaft, for signs of wear. If the case hardened surfaces of the cam lobes or tappets faces have been penetrated it will be quite obvious as there will be a darker, rougher pitted appearance to the surface in question. In such cases, the tappet of the camshaft will need renewal. Where the camshaft or tappet surface is still bright and clean and showing slight signs of wear it is best left alone. Any attempt to reface either will only result in the case hardened surface being reduced in thickness with the possibility of extreme and rapid wear later on.

2 The skew gear in the camshaft which drives the oil pump shaft and indirectly the distributor also should be examined for signs of extreme wear on the teeth. Here again if the skew gear teeth are badly worn and ridged, it will mean renewal of the complete camshaft. This is quite probable on 'tired' engines. Examine also in conjunction with this the teeth on the driven gear.

3 The camshaft bearing journals should be perfectly smooth and show no signs of pitting or scoring as they are relatively free

from stress. If the bearing surfaces are scored or discoloured it would suggest that the camshaft is not 'running true'. This will certainly mean camshaft renewal - if very bad have your local engineering works or Renault agent check the alignment of the block and the camshaft as the camshaft runs directly in the block. Proprietary camshafts replacement bearings are not available. Fortunately, it is rare for the camshaft journals and bearings to wear out at anything like the same rate as the rest of the engine. Having ascertained that the faces of the tappets are satisfactory, check also that the tappets are not a loose fit in their respective bores. It is not likely that they are loosely fitting, but if so they should be renewed.

33 Flywheel - examination and renovation

1 There are two areas in which the flywheel may have been worn or damaged. Firstly, is on the driving face where the clutch friction plate bears against it. Should the clutch plate have been permitted to wear down beyond the level of the rivets, it is possible that the flywheel has been scored. If this scoring is severe it may be necessary to have it refaced or even renewed.

2 The other part to examine is the teeth of the starter ring gear around the periphery of the flywheel. If several of the teeth are broken or missing, or the front edges of all teeth are obviously very badly chewed up, then it would be advisable to fit a new ring gear.

3 The old ring gear can be removed by cutting a slot with a hacksaw down between two of the teeth as far as possible, without cutting into the flywheel itself. Once the cut is made a chisel will split the ring gear which can then be drawn off. To fit a new ring gear requires it to be heated first to a temperature of 220°C (435°F), no more. This is best done in a bath of oil or an oven, but not, preferably, with a naked flame. It is much more difficult to spread and heat evenly and control it to the required temperature with a naked flame. Once the ring gear has attained the correct temperature it can be placed onto the flywheel making sure that it beds down properly onto the register. It should then be allowed to cool down naturally. If by mischance, the ring gear is overheated, it should not be used. The temper will have been lost, therefore softening it, and it will wear out in a very short space of time.

4 Although it is not actually fitted into the flywheel itself, there is a bush in the centre of the crankshaft flange onto which the flywheel fits. Although this bush is more correctly associated with the gearbox or clutch it is mentioned here as well as it would be a pity to ignore it whilst carrying out work on the flywheel. If it shows signs of wear it should be renewed. If suitable extractors are not available to get it out another method is to fill the recess with grease and then drive in a piece of close fitting steel bar. This should force the bush out. A new bush may be pressed in.

34 Oil pump - examination and renovation

1 Only work on the oil pump with it removed from the block.

2 Unscrew the four setscrews which hold the cover face and filter to the main body.

3 Take care with the ball seating boss, the ball bearing and the pressure relief spring which will come away when the cover face is removed.

4 Take out the driven gear and then the drive gear and the shaft.

5 Clean all the parts with petrol or paraffin and check the condition of the splines on the driveshaft. They should be unchewed and straight.

6 Check the condition of the ball bearing and its seating. There should be no irregularity nor ridges in either. The ball should be replaced anyway if you have reached this stage.

7 Check the spring. If possible replace it anyway at this stage. Obtain the correct replacement without fail.

8 Check the clearance between the pump gears and their body.

If over 0.008 in. (0.20 mm) replace the gears. Also check the cover joint face for marks and irregularities. Replace if scored.

9   It may be found that if two or more parts need replacing that it is more economic and quicker to replace the whole pump. There is no exchange scheme.

35 Inlet/exhaust manifold - inspection

Exhaust and inlet manifolds should be examined for signs of cracks or other breakages, particularly on the mounting lugs. The mating faces of both manifolds where they join the cylinder head should be examined to make sure that they are completely flat and free from pitting or burrs of any sort. Use a straight-edge to check the faces of the manifold for distortion. If there is any distortion or signs of severe pitting or burning the manifold should be renewed. Provided the manifolds are sound, accumulations of carbon within the ports may be removed with a wire brush or scraper.

36 Decarbonisation

1   Modern engines, together with modern fuels and lubricants have virtually nullified the need for the engine to have a 'decoke' which was common enough only a few years ago. Carbon deposits are formed mostly on the modern engine only when it has to do a great deal of slow speed, stop/start running, for example, in busy traffic conditions. If carbon deposit symptoms are apparent, such as pinking or pre-ignition and running on after the engine has been switched off, then a good high speed run on a motorway or straight stretch of road is usually sufficient to clear these deposits out. It is beneficial to any motor car to give it a good high speed run from time to time.

2   There will always be some carbon deposits, of course, so if the occasion demands the removal of the cylinder head for some reason or another, it is a good idea to remove the carbon deposits when the opportunity presents itself. Carbon deposits in the combustion chambers of the cylinder head can be dealt with

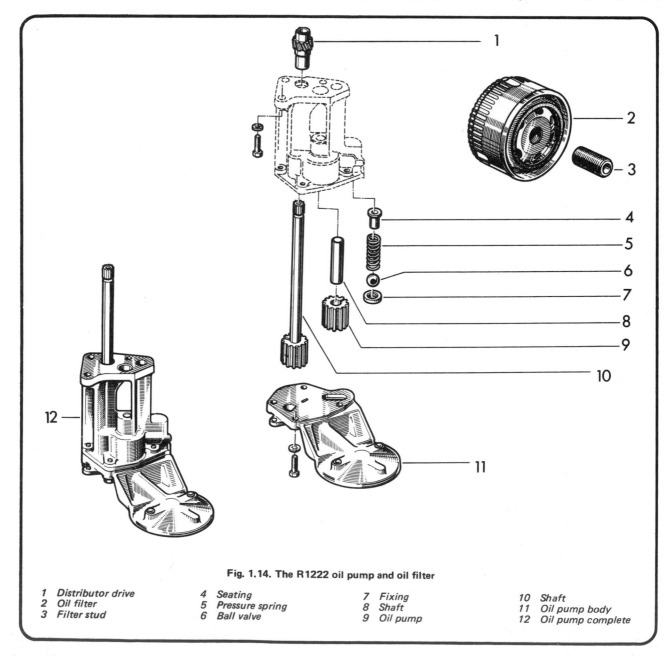

Fig. 1.14. The R1222 oil pump and oil filter

1 Distributor drive	4 Seating	7 Fixing	10 Shaft
2 Oil filter	5 Pressure spring	8 Shaft	11 Oil pump body
3 Filter stud	6 Ball valve	9 Oil pump	12 Oil pump complete

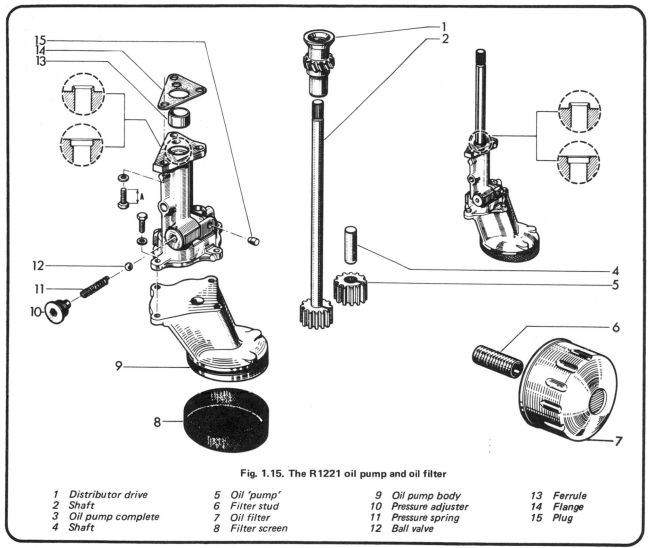

Fig. 1.15. The R1221 oil pump and oil filter

1	Distributor drive	5	Oil 'pump'
2	Shaft	6	Filter stud
3	Oil pump complete	7	Oil filter
4	Shaft	8	Filter screen

9	Oil pump body	13	Ferrule
10	Pressure adjuster	14	Flange
11	Pressure spring	15	Plug
12	Ball valve		

as described. The other carbon deposits which have to be dealt with are those on the crowns of the pistons. This work can easily be carried out with the engine in the car, but great care must be taken to ensure that no particles of dislodged carbon fall either into the cylinder bores and down past the piston rings or into the water jacket orifices in the cylinder block. Liner retainers must be fitted.

3 Bring the first piston to be cleaned to the top of its stroke and then using a sheet of strong paper and some self adhesive tape, mask off the other three cylinders and surrounding block to prevent any particles falling into the open orifice in the block. To prevent small particles of dislodged carbon from finding their way down the side of the piston which is actually being decarbonised press grease into the gap between the piston and the cylinder wall. Carbon deposits should then be scraped away carefully with a flat blade from the top of the crown of the piston and the surrounding top edge of the cylinder. Great care must be taken to ensure that the scraper does not gouge away into the soft aluminium surface of the piston crown.

4 A wire brush, either operated by hand or a power drill, should not be used if decarbonising is being done with the engine still in the car. It is virtually impossible to prevent carbon particles being distributed over a large area and the time saved by this method is very little.

5 After each piston has been attended to clean out the grease and carbon particles from the gap where it has been pressed in. As the engine is revolved to bring the next piston to the top of

its stroke for attention, check the bore of the cylinder which has just been decarbonised and make sure that no traces of carbon or grease are adhering to the inside of the bore.

Reassembly

37 Engine reassembly - general

It is during the process of engine reassembly that the job is either made a success or a failure. From the very word go there are three basic rules which it is folly to ignore namely:

1 Absolute cleanliness. The working area, the components of the engine and the hands of those working on the engine must be completely free of grime and grit. One small piece of carborundum dust or swarf can ruin a big-end in no time, and nullify all the time and effort you have spent. No matter what the pundits say this engine and its other components can be reconditioned and rebuilt very successfully and continue working efficiently. It is necessary to rebuild this engine in operating theatre conditions - warmth, light and space.

2 **Always,** no matter what the circumstances may be, use new gaskets, locking tabs, seals, nyloc nuts and any other parts mentioned in the Sections in this Chapter. It is pointless to dismantle an engine, spend considerable money and time on it and then to waste all this for the sake of something as small as a failed oil seal. Delay the rebuilding if necessary.

3   Don't rush it. The most skilled and experienced mechanic can easily make a mistake if he is rushed.

4   Check that all nuts and bolts are clean and in good condition and ideally renew all spring washers, !ockwasher and tab washers as a matter of course. A supply of clean engine oil and clean cloths (to wipe excessive oil off your hands only!) and a torque spanner are the only things which should be required in addition to all the tools used in dismantling the engine.

38 Engine block - preparation for reassembly

1   Assuming that the engine has been completely stripped for reconditioning and that the block is now bare, before any reassembly takes place it must be thoroughly cleaned both inside and out.

2   The ideal situation is to dip the block in a garage's cleaning tank usually fitted with a mixture of paraffin and cleaning fluid, and then to leave it submerged for an hour or so. Then get to work on it with a wire brush and screwdriver. Clean out all the crevices, do not scratch any machined surfaces, and scrub both the inside and out. The tappet chest is prone to hide sludge. A great deal of sediment often collects around the liner seatings. Chip this away if necessary.

3   Hose down the block with a garden hose and if possible dry it off with an air jet. Dry and thoroughly clean out the block with non-fluffy rag until it is spotless. The water will not make it go rusty provided you dry it off well.

4   Clean out all the oilways with a test tube/bottle brush and finally dry these. You should now not need to worry if you had to eat your lunch from the side of the block!

5   Check the two oil gallery aluminium plugs at each end of the block and the two screw-in camshaft bearing plugs on the top of the block. These should be solidly intact and show no signs of being weepy. If they do, drill a hole in their centre and cork-screw them out. Tap and peen in new ones very gently. These are supplied with the gasket sets necessary for the rest of the overhaul. (If you are reluctant to do this job ask your engineering works to do it for you - it is, however, quite easy).

39 Crankshaft and main bearing - reassembly

1   Stand the cylinder block inverted on the bench and gather together the bearing caps, new bearing shells and have the crankshaft without the flywheel fitted alongside line up in the way in which it will eventually be placed into the cylinder block. Make sure that the oilways in the crankshaft are all quite clear.

2   Make sure that the bearing housings in the cylinder block are perfectly clean and smooth in preparation for the fitting of the

top halves of the main bearing shells. Each bearing shell has an oil hole in it, some have two, and this must line up with the corresponding hole in the cylinder block. Each shell is notched, and this notch also must line up with the corresponding notch in the cylinder block. Carefully fit each shell into its proper position, taking care not to bend, distort or scratch it in any way. When they are in position lubricate the shells with a liberal quantity of clean engine oil. (photos)

3   Making sure that the crankshaft is the right way round, next pick up and very carefully lower it square and straight into position on the shell bearings in the crankcase.

4   Again, make sure that the bearing caps are perfectly clean and fit the shells so that the notches in their ends line up and fit snugly into the grooves in the bearing caps. There are no oilways in the bearing caps so that the holes in the end bearing shells will not line up with anything. (photo)

5   The crankshaft endfloat is controlled by two semi-circular thrust washers which fit at the sides of the centre main bearing journal. Place these in position and slide them round into the gap between the bearing housing and the flange of the crankshaft, making sure that the white metal/grooved face abut onto the crankshaft. Once these are in position the endfloat can be checked by pushing the crankshaft as far as it will go in one direction and measuring the gap between the face of the thrust washer and the machined surface of the flange with a feeler blade. Endfloat should be between 0.002 and 0.005 in. (0.05 and 0.125 mm). (Adjusting flanges of differing size are available - the correct ones should have been supplied with the new bearing by your machinists). (photo)

6   Next arrange all the bearing caps complete with their shells so that you know precisely where each one should go. They are easily identifiable by their particular shape. As there is the possibility of a seepage of oil through the end main bearing cap mating faces it is permissible to put a very thin smear of non-setting jointing compound onto the outside edge of the vertical face where the bearing cap locates into the crankcase. Lubricate the main journals of the crankshaft liberally with clean engine oil and place all the bearing caps in position and fit the bolts. The front main bearing cap has a machined front face and this must line up with the rear suface of the cylinder block. Make sure that this is done with a straight edge before finally tightening down the bolts. (photo)

7   When all the caps are settled correctly in position, tighten the bolts down evenly, starting at No. 1, at the flywheel end and working to No. 3 (R1221) or No. 5 (R1222), using a torque spanner, to the correct torque as given under the specifications. When this has been done revolve the crankshaft to make sure that there are no intermittent tight spots. Any signs that something is binding whilst the crankshaft is being revolved indicates that something is wrong and there may be a high spot on the bearings or on the crankshaft itself. This must be investigated or a damaged bearing could result. (photo)

8   Now fit the front main bearing oil seal. This is a circular oil seal, which has a very fragile inner lip. Always fit a new one. Oil it well with engine oil, and press it by hand into the correct position. Tap it gently fully home with a piece of wooden dowel

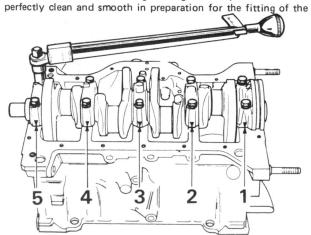

Fig. 1.16. The numbering sequence of the R1222 main bearings (Sec. 39)

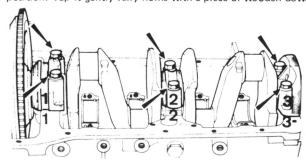

Fig. 1.17. The R1221 main bearings (Sec. 39)

39.2a Always use new bearing shells if the engine is dismantled

39.2b Liberal oiling is better than being too mean

39.2c Note the clinical conditions; it pays in the end with engine longevity

39.3 Place the crankshaft onto the main bearings with extreme care

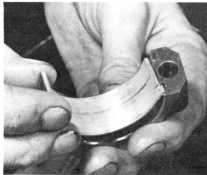

39.4 Each bearing and bearing cap has only one locating notch

39.5 For clarity we have shown the position of the thrust washers

39.6 Main bearing cap location should be accurate and unrushed

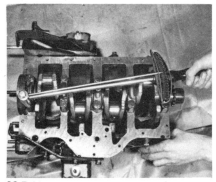

39.7 Always use a good torque wrench

39.8 Treat the crankshaft oil seal with extreme care; always use a new one

until it is fully in. There should be a slight recess between it and the outer edge of the block/bearing cap. (photo)

40 Pistons, gudgeon pins and connecting rods - reassembly

As mentioned in Section 18 the connecting rods and gudgeon pins are an interference fit requiring heat to enable them to be correctly assembled. This work should be entrusted to someone with the necessary experience and equipment. It is important that the piston and connecting rod are assembled the proper way round to ensure that the offset of the piston is on the thrust side of the cylinder.

With the connecting rod lying on the bench have the number stamped on the 'big-end' facing you, the arrow on the piston top **must** face upwards.

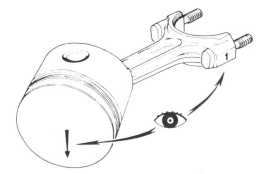

Fig. 1.18. Piston location on the connecting rod. Note the arrow direction and the stamped number. (R1222 and R1221) (Sec. 40)

41 Piston rings - replacement

1 Before fitting new piston rings to the old pistons, make sure the ring grooves in the piston are completely clean and free of carbon deposits. A piece of old, broken piston ring is a useful tool for doing this, but make sure that the sharp edge is not permitted to gouge out any pieces of metal. Check also that the specified gap between the edge of the new piston ring and the groove is correct.

2 All rings must be fitted from the top of the piston. To get the new rings into position involves spreading them sufficiently to clear the diameter of the piston itself and then moving them down over the existing grooves into their appropriate positions. Care must be taken to avoid straining them to a point where they could break. A piece of thin shim steel or an old feeler gauge blade is a very useful means of guiding the ends of the rings over the grooves to prevent them inadvertently dropping in, rather than passing over each groove.

3 Before fitting the rings to the piston it is important to check that the end gap matches the cylinder bore into which they will eventually be fitted. Push the rings down the bores using the piston until they are about 2½ inches (64 mm) below the top surface of the top of the liner. Then measure the gap. If the gap is too large you have either got the wrong piston rings or the cylinder bores are worn more than you had anticipated. If the gap is too small then it will be necessary to remove a piece of material from the end of the ring. The gap may be increased to the correct specification by clamping the end of the ring in a vice so that a very small portion of the end projects above the top of the vice. Then use a fine file to take off the material in very small quantities at a time. Do not clamp the ring so that the end being filed projects too far above the vice jaws or it may easily be snapped off while the filing is being done.

4 When every ring has been checked and the gaps made correct the rings should be assembled to the piston to prevent them being mixed up with other rings which will be fitted to other bores. Fit the bottom scraper ring first placing it over the top of the piston and spreading the ends. Move it down the piston a little at a time, taking care to prevent it from snagging in the grooves over which it will pass. The next ring to be fitted is the lower compression ring and this only goes on one way up. The top edge of the ring will be marked 'top' and this, of course, means that the ring is the top one on the piston. The top compression ring, which is the last one to go on then can be fitted either way up on the piston. When all the rings are in position in their grooves, try and arrange the gaps to be equally spaced around the piston. Place the gap of the oil control ring over an undrilled portion of the groove. Obviously, if the gaps of all the rings are in a straight line there will be a much greater tendency for compression loss at that point.

42 Liner fitment check

1 If the liners have been removed to be checked, rebored and relocated or just to be reseated they should be located after the crankshaft has been fitted - to ease the fitting of the crankshaft, but it in fact matters little. In the majority of cases the crankshaft is in the block and the procedure for fitting is the same whether the engine is in or out of the car.

2 If new liners are purchased with new pistons as a set you must keep the piston with its liner. This means that if you have already fitted the pistons to the rods that you must be careful as to the order in which the liners go into the block, ie, that No. 1 rod with its piston still goes into its respective liner in the No. 1 position.

3 When fitting liners into the block you must first do so without the pistons fitted in the liners, but this is only a trial run. It is in fact a good idea to make this trial run without committing yourself to placing any piston and its liner to any position, place your liner before you fit the piston to any particular connecting rod. Once the liners are placed in their

easiest position you can then match the position of the liner to the piston to the connecting rod. All liners are interchangeable in the block.

4 Check that the liners are in good, clean condition without any cracks, even hairline ones, on the outside. Make sure you have a selection of 'O' ring seals of different thicknesses. These seals are available in 0.007 mm marked with a blue spot, 0.10 mm marked with a red spot and 0.14 mm marked with a green spot. Buy the latest type. They are now usually paper.

5 Lightly oil the holes in the block into which the liners must fit and hold the block upright on the bench by supporting the sump face on the blocks of wood. (It is easier to do this with the block held in position in the car!)

6 Hold a liner on the bench and slide the thinnest of the seals over the end. With the seal fully home place the liner carefully into the block until it sits firmly in. Do not place the seal in the block and then slide in the liner; it does not work!

7 Repeat this with the other three liners using the same thickness of seal. Tap all four liners very gently with a rubber faced hammer to make sure they are fully home. (photo)

8 Using a metric feeler gauge measure the projection of the top of each liner in turn above the surface of the block. This is done by placing the blade or blades on the block face and running your finger across (you should have clean hands anyway) from the feeler gauge to the liner top. The projection should be between 0.04 and 0.011 mm. The nearer 0.011 mm the better. If you are some way out remove the liners and then replace them using a different thickness of seal. Go through the permutations until you have it right. Provided you have all four liners with the same projection it matters little that one liner has used one thickness of seal and the other another.

9 Now that you have found out which seals to use, you cannot know without doing this, you should remove the liners, recording their order and the seals used, to fit them with their

42.7 Hold the gasket to the liner with grease and treat with care

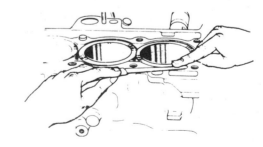

Fig. 1.19. Piston liner clearance fit (R1222 and R1221) (Sec. 42)

pistons and connecting rods outside the engine. If the liners have been removed, never fit the liners to the block and then fit the pistons.

43 Pistons, connecting rods and big-end bearings - reassembly into liners

1 Do not fit the pistons to the liners with the liners in the block, whether the engine is in or out of the car. Remove the liners and fit them on a bench.

2 If new piston rings, on either new pistons or the old pistons, are going into the original cylinder bores it is important that the piston ring gaps should be checked before fitting the piston assemblies. This will mean removing the rings from a new piston in order to check them. In order to assist the bedding in of the new piston rings to the original cylinder bore, it is a good idea to remove the oil glaze which builds up on a bore as an engine becomes more used. This can be done with very fine emery cloth, wrapped round a wooden plug of suitable diameter. Careful and thorough cleaning out afterwards will also be necessary, so unless you are perfectly sure that you can do this job safely, it is best not to do it at all.

3 Place the liners in their order of fitment, positioned with the 'front' face of the liner facing the left, as if it were the flywheel end.

4 Oil the piston. Tap the piston and connecting rod assembly into the top of the liner making sure the arrow on the crown of the piston faces **left** and that the number stamped on the big-end faces away from the camshaft (once all is assembled in the block). Fit a suitable clamp around all the piston rings to compress them into the grooves of the piston. It is possible to improvise a ring compressor out of a suitably sized hose clip, but great care should be exercised if this is done as it is not possible to get it to lie dead flat due to the adjusting screw housing projecting beyond the edge of the clip. This can permit the edge of a piston ring to escape its control and then be trapped against the cylinder block face and consequently break. If a strip of sheet metal is cut from an old tin and used in conjunction with a hose clip this is less likely to happen. With the rings suitably clamped, the piston may then be gently tapped into the bore. (photos)

5 Fit a new shell bearing into the connecting rod half of the big-end, making sure that the notch in the end of the shell lines up with the notch in the connecting rod. (photo)

6 Repeat for each piston and then place the liners and piston assemblies into the block, as has been described in the previous Section.

7 Lubricate the big-end journal on the crankshaft with clean engine oil and pull the connecting rod down onto the journal. Fit a new shell bearing into the cap, lining up the notch accordingly. Oil the shell and replace it onto the big-end studs. With the big-end bearing caps marked there should be no difficulty in making sure that the same cap goes onto the same connecting rod the right way round. Refit the nuts and tighten them down to the correct torque. It is a good idea to purchase a set of new big-end nuts each time this job is done. These nuts do sometimes stretch and weaken. Loctite is a good additional safety measure. (photo)

8 With the pistons and liners assembled in the block, recheck the liner projection with a feeler gauge as previously described. If now outside the tolerance you must dismantle and start again.

9 Do not now turn the engine over until the liner retainers are installed or the cylinder head is replaced.

44 Flywheel - replacement

1 Before replacing the flywheel to the crankshaft flange, the mating faces must be examined carefully for any signs of dents

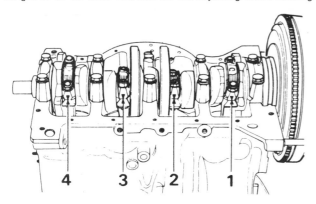

Fig. 1.20. The big-end bearings numbered from the flywheel (R1222) (Sec. 43)

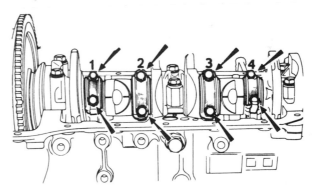

Fig. 1.21. The R1221 big-end bearings (Sec. 43)

43.4a Liberally oil the piston rings

43.4b Note the direction the piston is facing

43.4c Proprietry piston ring clamps are the best to use

43.4d Push the piston into the liner slowly but positively

43.4e Only at this stage fit the liner seating gasket

43.5 Big-end bearing shells are fitted in a similar manner to mains' shells

43.7 Again, as always, use a torque wrench

44.2 Correct location and proper torque-tightening are essential

45.2 The oil pump does not have a gasket

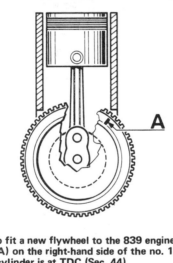
Fig. 1.22. To fit a new flywheel to the 839 engine, line up the TDC mark (A) on the right-hand side of the no. 1 crankpin, when no. 1 cylinder is at TDC (Sec. 44)

or burrs and be cleaned up as necessary. All traces of oil and grit must also be removed, and the locating dowel peg (R1221) should be in position on the crankshaft flange. Offer up the flywheel to the flange squarely and locate it carefully into position without damaging the edges of the mating faces.

2   Once the flywheel is securely mounted the set bolts should be fitted and progressively tightened up to the specified torque. If possible, it is a good idea to check the flywheel run-out at the outer edge of the clutch facing. If this exceeds a total of 0.08 mm (0.0031 in.) then it means that the flywheel is not fitted square with the crankshaft and serious vibration problems could result when the engine is running. A micrometer clock gauge will be needed to check this run-out. (photo)

45 Oil pump - replacement

1   Wipe clean the mating surfaces of the oil pump and the cylinder block.
2   With a new paper gasket (R1221 only) offer up the pump and screw up the three holding setscrews. Do not forget their spring washers. Tighten hard, it is not possible to use a torque wrench. You do not have to worry about engine timing at this stage. (photo)

46 Sump - replacement

1   Replacing the sump gasket is quite one of the most difficult jobs to do on Renault engines with the engine out of the car - with the engine in the car it is worse! With the engine on the bench it is only the flywheel which gets in the way; with the engine in the car and you are underneath everything gets in the way!
2   With the engine on the bench make sure that it is cylinder head down resting on wooden blocks. The flywheel must be fitted and torqued down. Before replacing the sump make quite sure that all big-end bearing cap nuts are tight, all main bearing cap bolts are tight, and that the oil pump has been replaced and securely tightened down. Clean the block and sump mating surfaces until they are quite clean and dry. Allow the two front and rear cork sections (R1221) of the gasket to soak in warm water for about ten minutes. The R1222 has 'rubber' end gaskets, like an oil seal, and these should be fitted in a similar manner. For clarity see the photos.
3   Fit four studs one at each end of the cylinder block, two on each side, into the sump bolt holes. Smear the rear main bearing cap sealing face with vaseline and mould over its appropriate section of cork gasket.

Fig. 1.23. The R1222 sump and timing cover and their gasket location

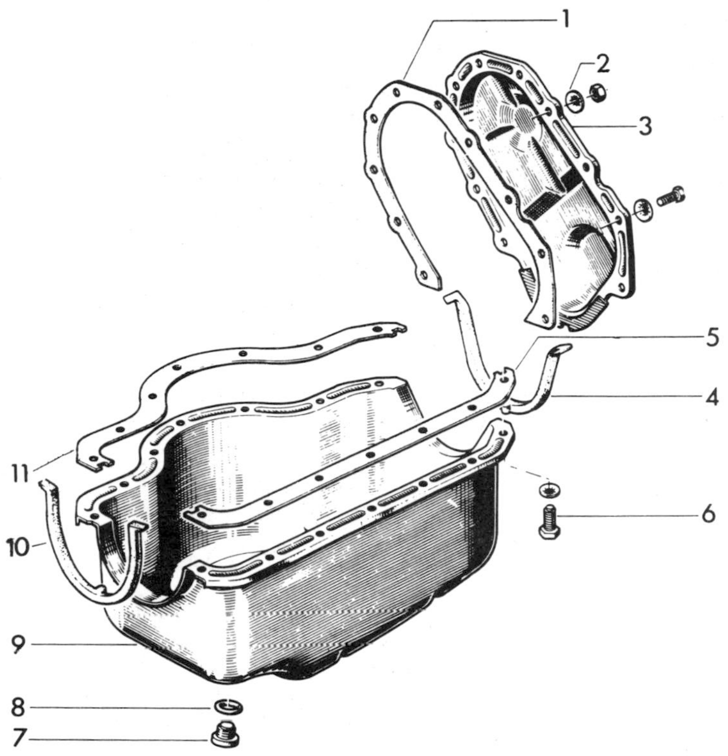

1 Timing cover gasket
2 Timing cover nuts
3 Timing cover
4 Sump end gasket
5 Sump side gasket
6 Sump bolt
7 Sump plug
8 Copper washer
9 Sump
10 Sump end gasket
11 Sump side gasket

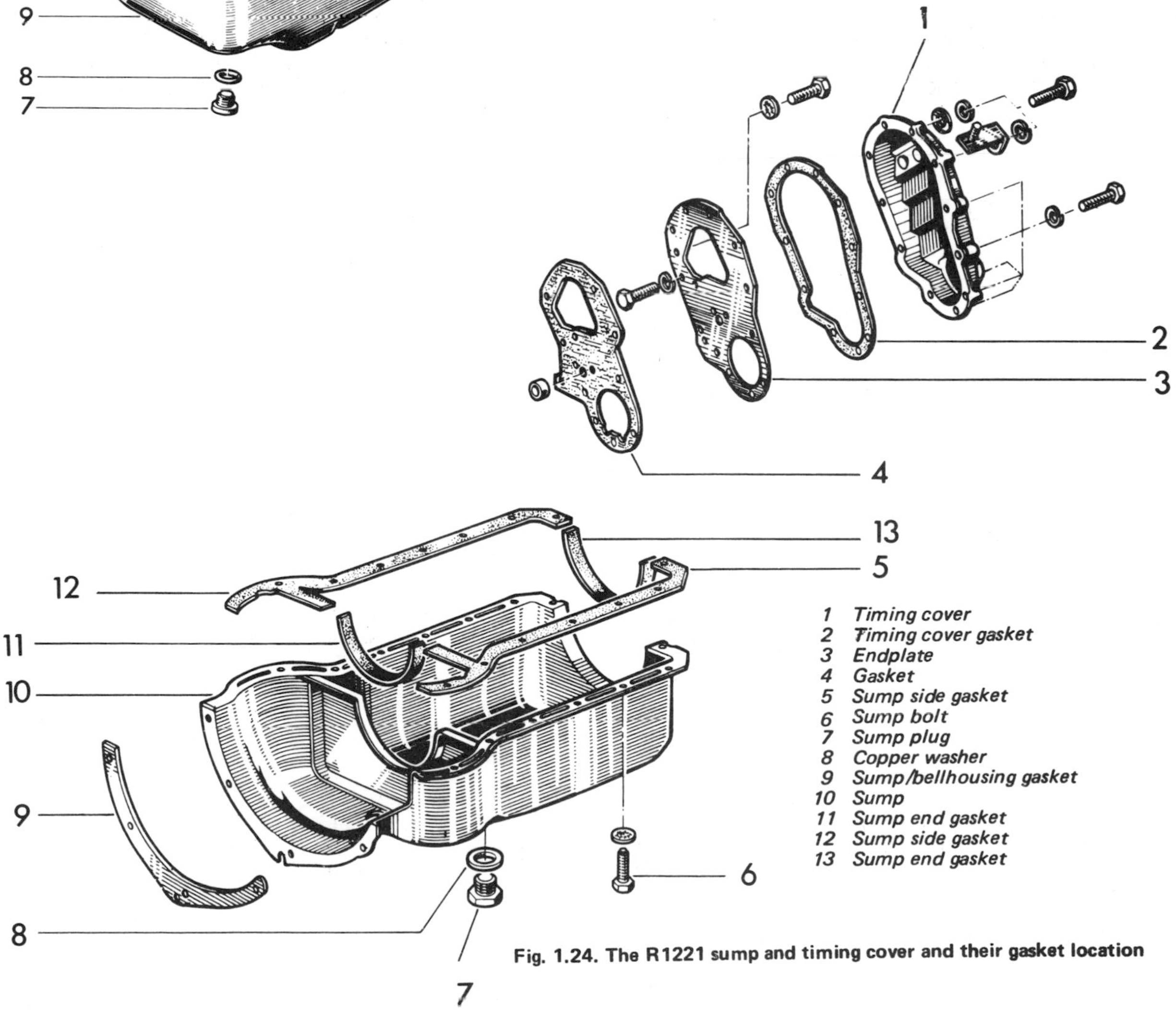

1 Timing cover
2 Timing cover gasket
3 Endplate
4 Gasket
5 Sump side gasket
6 Sump bolt
7 Sump plug
8 Copper washer
9 Sump/bellhousing gasket
10 Sump
11 Sump end gasket
12 Sump side gasket
13 Sump end gasket

Fig. 1.24. The R1221 sump and timing cover and their gasket location

4 Fit the two long side pieces of cork gasket over the four locating studs. The tips of these two sections will just overlap the ends of the rear main bearing cap section. Place some vaseline on these joints. With luck the three sections now fitted will stay in place. (photo)

5 This is the difficult piece to fit. Smear some vaseline in the front main bearing cap sealing groove and place into it the last piece of cork gasket. Its ends should overlap the two long sections this time. Wait a few moments to make sure that it does not move.

6 Carefully place over the sump on the four locating studs. Once in position do not move it. Quickly but carefully screw in the sump bolts until they are all in, half done up. Quickly check that the rear and side cork sections have not disappeared inside the sump. You cannot see the front main bearing cap section. (photo)

7 Tighten the securing bolts in a rotational manner, taking care not to move the sump pan. Place nuts on the four studs and tighten. You should now have a good seal.

8 The procedure for refitting the sump pan when the engine is in the car is the same as just described up until paragraph 3, except that you must only fit locating studs to the front of the block, not to the rear. This time smear all the mating edges of the block with vaseline. Press up the rear main bearing cap cork section, then the two long side members - the vaseline and the locating studs should keep them in place for a short time.

9 Press into place the front main bearing cap cork section - this too should hold itself in place because of the vaseline, the grip of the groove and because it has lost most of its springiness by being soaked in warm water.

10 Again quickly but carefully offer up the sump to the block. Offer up the rear end first tilting it so that the end of the sump hits the rear main bearing cap first, and rests on the lip of the floor section. Holding the sump pan very steady with one hand, fit two securing bolts at the rear end and tighten just a fraction. Offer up the other end now onto the front main bearing cap and the two locating studs. Hold steady with one hand and secure those two studs with nuts, tightening just a fraction.

11 Before tightening any more replace all the other sump bolts and then tighten them all, including the four nuts in a rotational manner. Again with luck and a steady hand you should have a good seal. (Remember to use the two screw top bolts at the very rear end. You will have to balance them on the top of a screwdriver and push it through the two holes in the floor).

12 If the engine is in the car you should now replace the bolts which mate the front end of the sump to the gearbox. This is a straight reversal of the disassembly. Some sumps are fitted with a bracing piece. Also you should replace the anti-roll bar and relocate the crossmember.

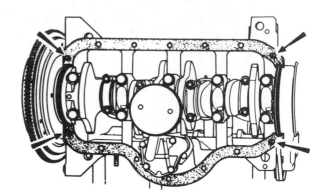

Fig. 1.25. The critical location of the R1222 sump gasket (Sec. 46)

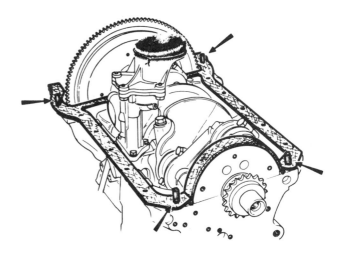

Fig. 1.26. Always locate the side gasket pieces over the ends of the end gaskets (R1221) (Sec. 46)

47 Camshaft and tappets - replacement

1 The engine must be out of the car for the camshaft to have been removed. With the camshaft removed the tappets must first have been removed. Also the cylinder head should have been removed. Refitting the camshaft and tappets is virtually the reversal of their removal no matter what type of timing gear is fitted. Never refit the tappets before the camshaft; it does not matter however whether the oil pump is fitted. The distributor, and the skew gear drive must be removed.

2 Clean all old gasket cement from the timing cover end of the block. Fit the timing gear-to-block end plate (time timing gear only) and its gasket, smearing it with gasket cement. Fit its two

46.2a This is one of the special end sump gaskets in position

46.2b This is the other end with its locating lip

46.4 Cork is generally used for the long side gaskets; they fit over the end gasket lips

46.6 Sumps are difficult to fit well

47.5a Oil the camshaft well before insertion and be careful with the lobes

47.5b This is the fixing plate for the camshaft housing

47.5c This part of the camshaft housing must be spotlessly clean

47.5d Simply an interference fit stops oil leaks

47.7 The distributor drive must locate readily but not loosely

holding setscrews.

3   Have the engine resting on its sump on some soft material. Lubricate the lobes and bearing surfaces of the camshaft well.

4   *R1221:* Always refit the camshaft with its sprocket attached. Have a Renault agency align it for you if a new sprocket is to be fitted. Now reverse the removal procedure but tap on the crankshaft sprocket over its woodruff key with a hide headed hammer. Insert the camshaft in straight and gently.

5   *R1222:* Replace the camshaft as a direct reversal of the removal. (photos)

6   In each case read Section 49 before going further.

7   Refit the oil pump drive skew gear. Then fit the distributor drive offset slotted key. See Chapter 4. (photos)

8   Replace the tappets into their respective chambers once well oiled, if you are in the least bit doubtful as to their condition. Once fitted do not turn the block on its side without the cylinder head in place otherwise they may fall out.

48 Engine mountings - replacement

1   Engine mounting replacement is the exact reversal of their removal (see Section 22).

2   If the engine is out of the car and you have assembled it in the ordered sequence here, it is now a good time to replace the mountings for they will allow much greater manoeuvrability. You can just about lift the whole engine by them and they will afford good propping sections.

3   Engine mountings on this car should be replaced with reasonable frequency, for they weaken quite soon. If you are rebuilding your engine, then replace them. Weak engine mountings allow too much movement back and forth of the engine on acceleration, and the exhaust pipe will hit the inner wing through which it passes.

49 Timing gear and cover - replacement and engine timing

1   *R1221:* Because the camshaft has to be replaced with its sprocket the timing chain must be replaced with the camshaft/sprocket and the crankshaft sprocket.

2   Heat the crankshaft sprocket in hot water. Put the timing chain on it and the camshaft sprocket as shown in Fig. 1.27.

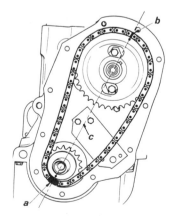

Fig. 1.27. R1221 timing chain alignment (Sec. 49)

a   *Yellow link of chain to meet dot on crankshaft sprocket, outer*
b   *Scribed mark on chain to meet dot on camshaft sprocket, outer*
c   *Points 'a' and 'b' to align with dot 'c', 'a' and 'b' to be on outer edges of sprockets*

Push in the camshaft and top on the crankshaft sprocket. Once fully home check the timing with the figure.

3   Tighten the camshaft flange through the camshaft sprocket. Replace the chain tensioner (see paragraph 6).

4   Check once again all is well, with the chain tensioner adjusted and replace the cover using a new gasket.

5   *R1222:* The *R1222* timing gear is replaced in a very similar way except that Fig. 1.28 should be looked at. Also the camshaft and the crankshaft sprocket do not need to be removed. (photo)

6   The chain tensioner is easily replaced and adjusted.

7   Refit the chain tensioner together with its thrust plate. (photos)

8   Insert the 3 mm Allen key into the retaining cylinder and turn in a clockwise direction until the pad carrier presses against the chain, with tension. Do not overtighten, you will wear out the pad.

9   Tighten the retaining cylinder block and lock it. Then tighten the timing gear-to-block plate and the oil feed plate. Replace the timing cover. (photo)

10   Timing the engine is now important although it is not necessary to fit the distributor yet. Study the two Figures 1.29 and 1.30 for the two engines and then fit the distributor drive/oil pump skew key. It must be accurate.

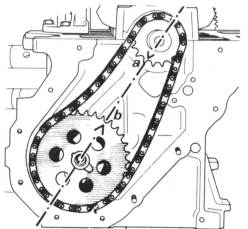

Fig. 1.28. The timing chain position for the R1222 (Sec. 49)

a   Crankshaft sprocket mark to oppose 'b'
b   Camshaft sprocket mark to oppose 'a' upon shortest line

49.5 Note the markings tie up with the diagram to obtain correct camshaft timing

49.7a Oil and assemble the chain tensioner

49.7b Make sure it sits readily on the timing chain before tightening

49.9 Always use a new gasket on the timing cover; once the engine is installed the cover cannot be reached

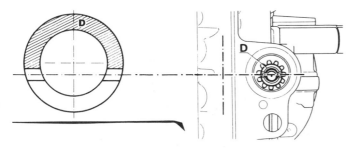

Fig. 1.29. R1222 distributor shaft drive alignment with no. 1 cylinder in firing position (Sec. 49)

Note: Driveshaft slot set at 90° to longitudinal line of engine. Also, largest offset 'D' of drive towards no. 1 cylinder

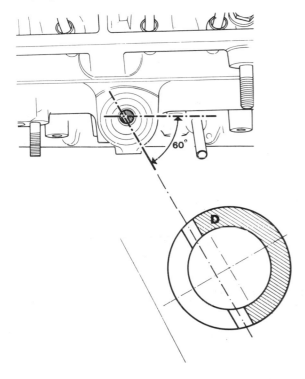

Fig. 1.30. R1221 distributor shaft drive alignment with no. 1 cylinder in firing position (Sec. 49)

Note: Driveshaft slot set at 60° to longitudinal line of engine. Also, largest offset of drive towards no. 1 cylinder

50 Valves and springs - reassembly to cylinder head

1   With the head perfectly clean and having carried out all the necessary renewals and renovations as required, lightly lubricate the valve stem for the first valve to be replaced and fit it in its guide. If the same valves are being used again they should have been kept in order so that they may go back in the same place. (photos)

2   Use the same process with the compressed rag and two equal screwdrivers as used on the disassembly: 11.3. Have a second person pop in the collets when the spring is compressed, release the pressure and go onto the next valve in that combustion chamber. Remember that not only are the inlet valves and their springs different from the exhaust but so are the collets. The inlet collets have two round ridges, one at the bottom, and the exhaust has one 'square' ridge in its centre.

51 Valve rocker gear - reassembly

1   If the engine is in the car you must refit the rocker gear to the cylinder head before you replace the cylinder head. If the engine is out of the car it does not matter whether you replace it before you replace the head or not. Basically it cannot be replaced once the cylinder head is fitted to the engine in the car. However, the water pump and its end plate must not be fitted.

2   Replacing the valve rocker gear is a direct reversal of its removal without exception. You should however always oil all the parts upon refitting. R1221 - always replace the rubber end plug with new every time the rocker gear is dismantled. A further point to remember - do not overtighten the rocker shaft pedestal locking bolts, they may strip their threads! Relock the tab washers. (photo)

52 Inlet/exhaust manifold - replacement

1   In all situations it is preferable to refit the manifold to the cylinder head before fitting the head to the block. This will then not make it necessary to undo any head studs to mount the manifold bracing piece, after the head has been refitted, and it is considerably easier to tighten the securing nuts.

2   Always use new manifold gaskets, slip these over the studs. It does not matter which way they face. Place on the manifold over the studs and using new nuts and spring washers, bolt up the manifold. Tighten hard but do not overtighten, making sure that the studs do not strip out of the head. Should they do so you will have to dismantle and refit new studs having had helicoils fitted by your Renault agent. (If you have removed the cylinder head studs make absolutely sure you remount them the right way round, they have different length threads at each end and it matters!) (photos)

50.1a The valve springs sit on a steel collar

50.1b Valve springs are cheap; always replace them on a major engine overhaul

51.2 The rocker gear, fitting is simple but should be tightened progressively

52.2a Never skimp on the exhaust manifold gasket; use a new one every time

52.2b If the studs have been removed make sure they are correctly located before replacing the manifold

53.1 Once again a new gasket is essential for the water pump

54.4 The cylinder head gasket needs no cement

54.5a Be most careful when refitting the cylinder head that the gasket is the right way up

54.5b The pushrods should be returned to their original locations

53 Water pump - refitting

1   Under any circumstances it makes little difference whether you refit the water pump before refitting the cylinder head to the block. Fitting is a reversal of the removal, exactly. (photo)

54 Cylinder head and pushrods - refitting

1   Again the procedure for refitting the head is similar whether the engine is in or out of the car.
2   Make sure that the new cylinder head gasket is the correct one. Clean the top of the block of all dust and make sure that it and the head surfaces are perfectly flat.
3   Remove the cylinder liner retaining clamps.
4   Fit the gasket in position on the block, crimped edges towards the block. Do not use any gasket cement or grease. (photo)
5   Position the cylinder head on the gasket and fit the bolts and their washers. Make sure that the right length bolts go in the right place - this does matter. (Do not forget to fit the manifold bracing piece before fitting the centre left-hand bolt). The pushrods will have to be guided in. Refit the pushrods into the respective tappets, cup end up. You should, of course, make sure that the rocker clearances are very wide. It is a good idea to use new washers. (photos)
6   Tighten the bolts in the correct sequence progressively (Figs. 1.7 and 1.8). First to 10 lb ft and then finally to 50 lb ft (R1222) or 45 lb ft (R1221). You must, of course, use the correct socket and drive together with a torque spanner. (photo)
7   After the first 300 miles of running with a new cylinder head gasket wait until the engine is cold then undo all the cylinder head bolts ¼ of a turn and retorque them in the correct sequence to the correct setting.

55 Valve rocker clearances - checking and adjustment

1   The valve rocker clearances are important as they control the amount a valve opens and when it opens and thus can affect the efficiency of the engine.
2   The clearances should be measured and set by using a feeler blade between the rocker arm and the end of each valve stem. This is done when the valve is closed and the tappet is resting on the lowest point of the cam. (photo). The clearances are given in Fig. 1.31.
3   To enable each valve to be in the correct position for checking with the minimum amount of engine turning the procedure and order of checking should follow the sequence given in the following tables. In the table the valves are numbered 1 to 8, starting from the front of the cylinder head. A valve is fully open when the rocker arm has pushed the valve down to its lowest point. (Note: the clearances are the same for both engines).

Open Valve	Adjust clearance (cold)
No 8 (ex)	No 1 (ex)
No 6 (in)	No 3 (in)
No 4 (ex)	No 5 (ex)
No 7 (in)	No 2 (in)
No 1 (ex)	No 8 (ex)
No 3 (in)	No 6 (in)
No 5 (ex)	No 4 (ex)
No 2 (in)	No 7 (in)

4   Using two spanners, first slacken the locknut on the adjusting stud and then put the feeler blade, of appropriate thickness, between the rocker arm and valve stem of the valve being adjusted. Slacken the stud adjuster if the gap is too small to accept the blade. (photo)
5   Turn the adjusting screw until the feeler blade can be felt to

54.6 The aluminium cylinder head needs careful torquing down

55.2 For most accurate setting, always use metric feeler blades

55.4 Two proper spanners are essential

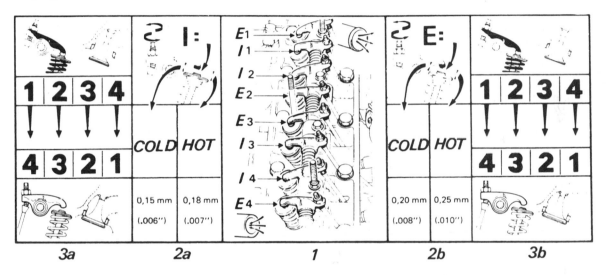

Fig. 1.31. Valve clearance adjustment (both models) (Sec. 55)

1   Shows inlet (1) and exhaust (e) valve numbering
2a Shows clearances for inlet valves in hot or cold state
2b Shows clearances for exhaust valves in hot or cold state

3a Shows which inlet valve is closed when a given inlet valve is open
3b Shows which exhaust valve is closed when a given exhaust valve is open

drag lightly when it is drawn out of the gap.

6   Hold the adjuster with a screwdriver and tighten the locknut. Check the gap once more to make sure it has not altered as a result of locking the stud.

7   After the first 300 miles of running following any operation which necessitated removal of the cylinder head (see paragraph 7 of the previous Section) recheck the valve rocker clearances.

56 Engine reassembly - final stages

1   Before replacing an engine into the car, all those ancillary parts which are removed before the engine was stripped should be replaced. These items were listed in Section 7. One possible exception is the carburettor which projects in a somewhat vulnerable way and could be damaged expensively if any mishap occurred on replacing the engine.

2   Refit the rocker gear cover, even though it has to be taken off again, as this will protect the rocker gear from damage and dust. Leave the new gasket to be fitted latter. (photo)

57 Engine - replacement

Generally speaking, the replacement of the engine is a reversal of the removal procedure but the following points should be borne in mind.

56.2 A new rocker cover gasket each time will save leaks

1   The engine and gearbox have been removed together, they should be reassembled and replaced together. This takes care of the possible difficulties one may encounter fitting the gearbox input shaft into the clutch.

2   When lowering the engine into the car make sure first that it is suspended at the correct attitude. It is difficult and possibly dangerous to have to alter the angle of tilt whilst it is suspended.

3   Always lower the engine very slowly and watch it all round all the way. It is easy to wrench out wire and pipes due to being in too much of a hurry and not noticing these things when they flip back in the way - as they always seem to do.

4   If the engine will not go where it should, look and find out why. Do not try and force anything.

5   Always fit a new oil filter, air cleaner element, spark plugs and contact points, and fill with fresh oil and coolant.

6   Replace all the suspension and steering parts as well as the driveshafts before attempting to start the engine. Always lower the car to the ground and use the following check list, as well as reading the relevant parts in the rest of this book concerning those components which you have had to touch to remove the engine but which are not actually engine components, before attempting to start the car.

7   Once the engine has started and all is well you must have the car retracked at the front wheels before undertaking any regular use.

8   The following check list should ensure that the engine starts safely and with little or no delay and that the car is ready to move:

a) Fuel pipes to fuel pump and carburettor connected and tight.
b) Coolant hoses to radiator and heater connected and tight.
c) Radiator and block coolant drain plugs shut and tight.
d) Cooling system filled and bled.
e) Sump drain plug screwed and tight.
f) Oil filter cartridge tight.
g) Oil in sump and dipstick replaced.
h) Oil in transmission unit and plugs tight.
i) LT wires connected to the distributor.
j) Spark plugs clean and tight.
k) Valve rocker clearance set.
l) HT leads all connected and secure.
m) Distributor rotor arm fitted.
n) Choke and accelerator cable fitted and working through their total range.
o) Earthing cable from engine block to battery and battery to earth secure.
p) Starter motor cable to battery connected and secure.
q) Generator leads connected.
r) Oil pressure warning, coolant temperature sender unit and electric fan (R1222) cables connected.
s) Battery charged and secure in position.
t) All loose tools removed from the engine compartment.
u) Clutch cable refitted and adjusted.
v) Gear change linkage replaced.
w) Steering rack replaced and all ball joints secure and tight.
x) Steering column reconnected.
y) Driveshafts refitted to transmission unit and greased, and speedometer cable replaced. See Chapter 7.
z) Handbrake cables, linkage and engine mountings secure.

Leave the bonnet off and the lights unconnected for the initial start but replace before venturing on to the road!

9   As soon as the engine starts, run it steadily at a fast tick-over for several minutes and look all round for signs of leaks and loose or unclipped pipes and wires. Watch the instrument and warning lights and stop the engine at the first indications of anything nasty!

58 Fault diagnosis - engine

Symptom	Reason/s	Remedy
Engine will not turn over when starter switch is operated	Flat battery Bad battery connections Bad connections at solenoid switch and/or starter motor	Check that the battery is fully charged and that all connections are clean and tight
	Starter motor jammed	With a pre-engaged starter fitted, rock the car back and forth with a gear engaged. If this does not free pinion remove starter
	Defective solenoid	Bridge the main terminals of the solenoid switch with a piece of heavy duty cable in order to operate the starter
	Starter motor defective	Remove and overhaul starter motor
Engine turns over normally but fails to fire and run	No spark at plugs	Check ignition system according to procedures given in Chapter 4
	No fuel reaching engine	Check fuel system according to procedures given in Chapter 3
	Too much fuel reaching the engine (flooding)	Check the fuel system as above
Engine starts but runs unevenly and misfires	Ignition and/or fuel system faults	Check the ignition and fuel systems as though the engine had failed to start
	Incorrect valve clearances	Check and reset clearances
	Burnt out valves Blown cylinder head gasket, dropped liners	Remove cylinder head and examine and overhaul as necessary
	Worn out piston rings Worn cylinder bores	Remove cylinder head and examine pistons and cylinder bores. Overhaul as necessary
Lack of power	Ignition and/or fuel system faults	Check the ignition and fuel systems for correct ignition timing and carburettor settings
	Incorrect valve clearance	Check and reset the clearances
	Burnt out valves Blown cylinder head gasket	Remove cylinder head and examine and overhaul as necessary
	Worn out piston rings Worn cylinder bores	Remove cylinder head and examine pistons and cylinder bores. Overhaul as necessary
Excessive oil consumption	Oil leaks from crankshaft front oil seal timing cover gasket and oil seal, rocker cover gasket, sump gasket, sump plug washer	Identify source of leak and renew seal as appropriate
	Worn piston rings or cylinder bores resulting in oil being burnt by engine (smoky exhaust is an indication)	Fit new rings or rebore cylinders and fit new pistons, depending on degree of wear
	Worn valve guides and/or defective valve stem	Remove cylinder head and recondition valve stem bores and valve and seals as necessary
Excessive mechanical noise from engine	Wrong valve to rocker clearance	Adjust valve clearances
	Worn crankshaft bearings Worn cylinders (piston slap)	Inspect and overhaul where necessary
	Slack or worn timing chain and sprockets, or disintegrating fibre cog	Adjust chain and/or inspect all timing mechanism
Unusual vibration	Fan blade broken off (R1221)	Break off another fan blade to balance fan until renewal is possible
	Broken engine/gearbox mounting	Renew mounting
	Misfiring on one or more cylinders	Check ignition system

Note: When investigating starting and uneven running faults do not be tempted into a snap diagnosis. Start from the beginning of the check procedure and follow it through. It will take less time in the long run. Poor performance from an engine in terms of power and economy is not normally diagnosed quickly. In any event the igniton and fuel systems must be checked first before assuming any further investigation needs to be made

Chapter 2 Cooling system

Contents

Specifications

Type of system	Pressurised with centrifugal circulation pump, fan and thermostat. Sealed system
Coolant capacity	R1222: 11 pints R1221: 10.25 pints Both to include heater and expansion chamber
Coolant	Mixture of equal proportions of antifreeze (glycol) and distilled water
Expansion chamber	Glass bottle adjacent to radiator
Radiator	Row, grilled tube type cooled by fan
Fan	R1222: Electric, thermostatically controlled fan mounted remote from the engine R1221: Conventional belt driven 6 bladed fan
Water pump	Centrifugal-driven by belt from camshaft pulley
Fan belt tension	¼ in. at longest run
Thermostat opening temperature	84°C (183°F) normal
Electric fan cut-in temperature (R1222)	92°C (198°F)
Cut-out temperature	82°C (180°F)

For the heater fan and R1222 cooling fan - See Chapter 9.

1 General description

The engine cooling liquid is circulated round the system on the thermosyphon principle, assisted by a belt driven impeller type pump.

The system is pressurised and sealed so that boiling will only occur at abnormally high temperatures and that there is no loss of coolant. As the coolant heats up it expands and flows into the expansion chamber, which is fitted with a blow-off valve should the pressure and therefore the temperature get too great. No coolant should be lost as air pressure and not water pressure is ever lost because the expansion chamber is never more than about 1/3 filled with coolant. As the coolant becomes cool it will flow back into the radiator under the vacuum principle.

The circuit also incorporates a thermostatically controlled valve which restricts the amount of water passing through the radiator until the correct engine operating temperature is reached. This assists rapid warming up and keeps the engine at a constant running temperature regardless of ambient conditions.

The principle of operation is as follows. The water heated by the engine rises out of the cylinder head towards the thermostat which, if cold, is closed. It then diverts via the heater (or heater by-pass pipe if the heater valve is shut) straight to the pump and thence back to the engine.

When the engine warms up a proportion of the warm water will pass via the thermostat valve to the top of the radiator down through which it will pass and cool. The pump will then draw the cold water from the bottom of the radiator and pass it back to the engine (the pump has two inlets). If the engine temperature should rise excessively the thermostat valve will close off the by-pass outlet thus directing all water through the radiator.

It is important that the system is always sealed properly and

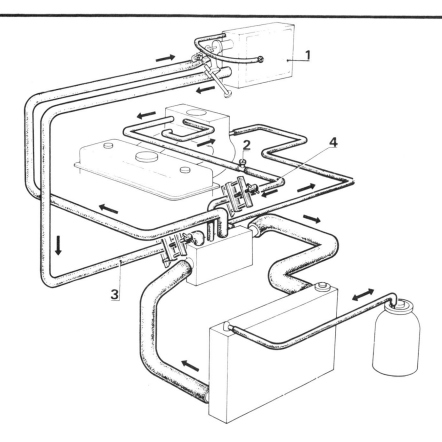

Fig. 2.1. The R1222 cooling/heating system. 1 shows the heater radiator bleed valve, 2 the central bleed valve and 3 & 4 the two clamp positions. The arrows indicate flow direction

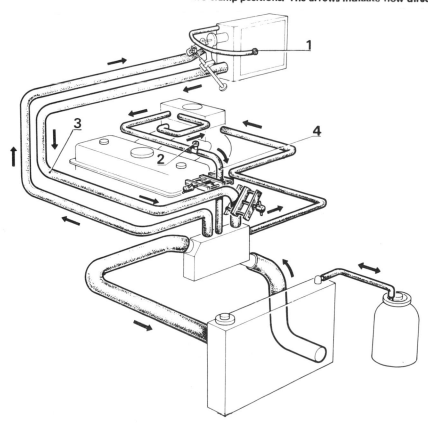

Fig. 2.2. The R1221 cooling/heating system. 1 shows the heater radiator bleed valve, 2 the control bleed valve and 3 & 4 the two clamp positions. The arrows indicate flow direction

that it is filled with the correct coolant which ideally is 50% antifreeze (glycol) and 50% distilled water. To maintain correct antifreeze properties and to safeguard against internal damage to the aluminium cylinder head this mixture should be adhered to at all times. Because of the sealed system this mixture is safe during the whole year in any climate.

The R1221 utilises a belt driven cooling fan whilst the R1222 has a thermostatically controlled electric fan. The R1221 has a centrally mounted radiator over the transmission unit whilst the R1222 radiator is bolted to the front body cross panel.

2 Fan belts - removal, replacement and adjustment

1 Two 'fan' belts are fitted to both models. One, the inner drives the water pump from the camshaft pulley whilst the other drives the generator from a second 'outer' pulley from the water pump.

2 It is fairly simple to replace both belts but obviously the outer belt must come off first before the inner one can come off. On the R1221 only is a belt driven cooling fan fitted; the belts must be spread over it.

3 To remove the outer, generator belt, loosen the generator pivot bolt and push the generator towards the engine. The generator is the tensioner for this belt. For the R1221 it is slightly more difficult because of the proximity of the distributor to the generator. Slacken the generator pivot only enough to allow slight movement. The belt will fall off the R1222 but will have to be threaded over the R1221 fan.

4 To move the inner, or water pump belt, it is necessary to loosen the belt tensioner. For the R1222 this means loosening the tensioner plate bolt and then slackening the tightening setscrew which is at right-angles to it. Loosen enough for the jockey wheel just to slip back from beneath the belt. For the R1221 the same principle will apply except that the tensioner only has the tensioner plate fitting and not the tightening screw.

5 Replacement of both belts is quite straightforward and simply a reversed removal sequence. For the R1222 the inner belt tension should be measured between the camshaft and water pump pulleys whilst that of the R1221 should be between the tensioner jockey wheel and the water pump. In each case the deflection should be ¼ inch (6.35 mm). The R1221 tensioner is levered up with a screwdriver resting on the water pump body.

For the outer generator drivebelt the tension is taken with the pivoting of the generator. Again the tension should be measured along the length; that on the top run is easiest. A deflection of ¼ inch (6.35 mm) is correct for both models.

6 After a new belt has run for a few hundred miles, check the tension again as the initial stretch may need re-adjustment. There are no definite rules as regards frequency of checking but it only takes a second every time the oil level is checked.

7 The jockey wheel or tensioner of each model runs on a single ball bearing held onto its spindle by two circlips on each side. If and when this bearing fails its replacement is straightforward. It may however be necessary to purchase a pulley/bearing complete if failure takes place. These bearings should be greased on fitting.

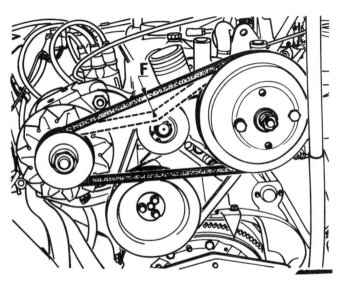

Fig. 2.3. Generator (alternator R1222, dynamo R1221) drive belt adjustment. 'F' indicates measurement point (Sec. 2)

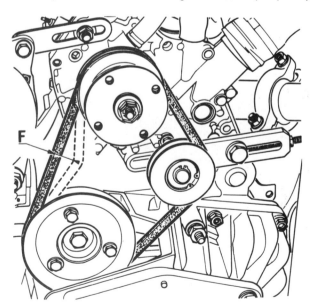

Fig. 2.4. R1222 'fan' belt (water pump drive) adjustment. 'F' indicates measurement point (Sec. 2)

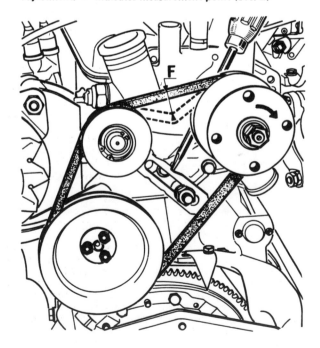

Fig. 2.5. R1221 'fan' belt water pump drive adjustment. 'F' indicates the measurement point (Sec. 2)

3 Cooling system - draining, flushing, refilling and bleeding

1 Stand the car on level ground and if hot allow to cool for at least 15 minutes. Remove the expansion chamber safety valve cap. The safety valve is undone by unscrewing the large knurled plastic cap. If very stiff use a rag over the top and undo carefully with a pair of adjustable grips.

2 Undo the radiator drain plug located at the bottom left-hand side of the radiator. Use the correct spanner - it is a brass plate and does not like pliers. To save the coolant is pointless - most of it will drain under the car at various points and you would need a recepticle the size of a bath to claim it all. However, it is a good idea to lay newspaper underneath the car to soak up the worst of it. The coolant will trickle out at first. Wait until it begins to gush before unsealing the radiator cap. This indicates that the expansion chamber is empty; you cannot see, the bottles are usually pretty dirty.

3 Make sure at this stage that the heater is in the 'on' position and then open the bleed plug for the heating system which is located on the bulkhead. There is a second one on the R1222 close to the water pump. Open this too. Undo it fully but do not remove.

4 Now drain the cylinder block but removing the plug located at the rear of the engine block on the right-hand side, about halfway down. This is quite fiddly.

5 Allow the car to stand for another five minutes before tackling anything else so that the last drip can fall.

6 It is possible to drain these parts mentioned separately so that you need not drain the block for example, simply because you wish to change a radiator top hose. It is a simple enough system to understand and functions in a conventional manner.

7 If sediment blocks the drain holes poke them gently with some wire to free.

8 Every so often it is a good practice to flush out the system to remove any loose sediment, and scale which may have accumulated. The time to do this is when the coolant is being drained. With the sealed system, however, the need for topping up should be very infrequent so that the deposits of lime and so on, from regular additions of new water, are negligible. The need for flushing, therefore, is usually only caused by some other factor - such as a leak which allows air to enter the system and cause oxidisation or the use of an antifreeze of a type which may cause corrosion.

9 To check the need for flushing open the radiator drain tap and if the liquid coming out is obviously very dirty, although it can be a deep colour, and full of solid particles let it run out. If it clears as more runs out and the outflow is in no way restricted then there is no great problem. If, however, constant poking with a piece of wire is needed and the liquid continues very dirty then obviously a flush is needed.

10 To flush out, simply leave the radiator and block drain taps open and after removing the radiator cap, run a hose through the system for about 15 minutes (ordinary water is quite safe). If the taps show signs of blockage keep poking them out. If the blocking is persistent remove the tap completely so that a larger orifice may permit the obstruction to clear itself. In some bad cases a reverse flush may help and this is easily done by removing the radiator and running the hose into the bottom tank so that it flows out of the filler neck.

11 If the radiator flow is restricted by something other than loose sediment then when no amount of flushing will shift it and it is then that a proprietary chemical, suitable for aluminium heads, is needed. Use this according to the directions and make sure that the residue is fully out afterwards. If leaks develop after using a chemical cleaner, a proprietary radiator sealer may cure them but the signs are that the radiator has suffered considerable chemical corrosion and that the metal is obviously getting very thin in places.

12 Always flush out before refilling if the old coolant was particularly dirty. (Clean out the glass expansion chamber too).

13 Screw up both block and radiator drain plugs. Make sure that a copper washer is fitted to the radiator plug. Make sure all the hose clips are tight and that the hoses are in good condition.

14 Mix 50% distilled water and 50% antifreeze in a clean gallon can. Mix a further pint of the coolant. It is essential to use a glycol based antifreeze, so that it cannot damage the cylinder head. Ideally distilled water should be used to ensure long life of the system as it is by definition very pure. However, it is possible to use clean soft water, if distilled water is not available.

15 Pour 1¼ pints (0.7 litre) of the liquid through a funnel (a flexitop bottle is ideal) into the glass bottle, to 1.3/16 in. (30 mm) above maximum mark, and replace the safety valve. (Check the bottle sealing rings).

16 Fill the rest of the cooling system through the radiator top, leaving the heater in the on position and bleed screws still undone.

17 Once the radiator is full, use two clamps as near to the water pump as possible on the two hoses feeding the two bleed screws.

18 Start the engine and run at a fast tickover (1500 rpm) keep filling the radiator with more coolant.

19 When continuous coolant flows out of the bleed screws without a trace of air, close them. Do not now touch them.

20 Remove the clamps. Top up the radiator and replace the cap.

21 Stop the engine, allow to cool and then recheck the level and check for leaks.

4 Radiator (R1222) - removal and replacement

1 The fixing of the R1222 radiator is nearer the front of the car, on the cross panel. It is held by two horizontal studs and nuts and rests on two rubber channels on the front cross panel.

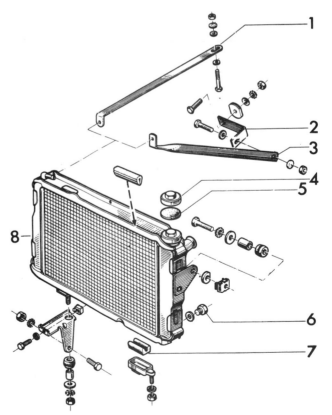

Fig. 2.6. R1222 radiator components and fixings - the electric cooling fan is not shown (Sec. 4)

1 Radiator stay	5 Rubber seal
2 Bracket	6 Drain plug
3 Second radiator stay	7 Rubber seat
4 Radiator cap	8 Radiator

An electric fan is attached to it.

2 Removal and replacement of this radiator is much simpler than that of R1221. Disconnect the electrical connections to the fan and to its thermostat. Disconnect the top and bottom hoses and the top expansion chamber feed. Remove the two stud nuts and washers and top braces and lift the radiator away. (See Chapter 1).

3 Remove the electric fan mechanism by undoing the three outer fan cowling nuts and studs.

4 Thoroughly clean the exterior of the radiator. It has presumably been removed in order to repair a leak or for further examination of a suspected blockage (except of course, as part of a procedure to get access to something else).

5 Some radiators are made of steel and brass, some of all brass. If the steel has rusted through, little short of replacement can take place but all brass parts can be repaired with solder where exterior leaks are accessible. The technique of soldering is not discussed here, but suffice it to say that the surfaces to be joined must be thoroughly cleaned, then tinned and the solder able to 'run' in the repair. It is fruitless merely depositing blobs of solder about the place. It would be better to use a resin filler paste which in fact can be used for such repairs in limited applications. Care must also be taken when soldering to localise any heat used. Otherwise the radiator may start to disintegrate where you least want it to. A leak in the internal parts of the honeycomb, if not severe, can be cured with one of the specialist sealers added to the cooling liquid. If severe, professional attention will be needed. Another way for emergencies only, is to block the whole of the honeycomb in the suspect area with resin filler paste. Old fashioned remedies such as mustard, egg whites and porridge oats added to water, are not recommended as they have been known to have sinister effects on water pumps and thermostats. There is much less liquid in modern systems and these foodstuffs cannot be digested so readily!

6 Replacement of the radiator is a direct reversal of removal. Make sure the bottom mounting top rubber bushes are in good condition between the bracket and the radiator.

5 Radiator (R1221) - removal and replacement

1 Drain the cooling system as described earlier in Section 3.

2 Slacken the clip and remove the top radiator hose where it connects to the radiator. Slacken also the clip securing the

Fig. 2.7. Disconnection points for the R1221 radiator (Sec. 5)

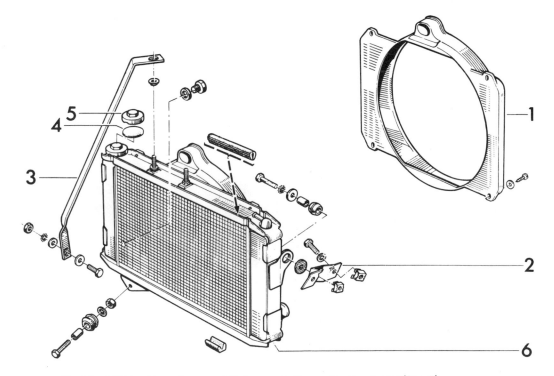

Fig. 2.8. R1221 radiator, brace and fixings - note the cooling fan shroud (Sec. 5)

1 Fan cowl	3 Radiator stay	5 Radiator cap
2 Lower bracket	4 Rubber seal	6 Radiator

bottom hose to the radiator and pull off the hose.

3 The radiator is held onto a special bracket which is itself held by two studs to the steering rack. There is also a tie rod from the front crossmember to the top of the radiator which is held there by one more stud which, with another, also locates the gear shift rod front bush.

4 Remove the tie rod and then the radiator itself as described in Chapter 1.

5 Read the previous Section for radiator cleaning. Replacement is a reverse procedure. Also be sure that the two through bolts which locate this bracket and the steering rack are really tight. Have the steering/wheel alignment checked after removing the radiator - always.

6 Expansion bottle - general

1 Removal of the glass expansion bottle is very easy. Unscrew the two screws which locate its wire strap to the inner wing and lift out.

2 Replacement is again a reversal of its removal. It can be cleaned with hot water and soap and should be well rinsed.

7 Thermostat - general

1 If the engine gets too hot or stays too cool, then the thermostat is probably to blame.

2 Drain out sufficient coolant to lower the level about 4 inches (100 mm) (say a quart) so that no more will be lost when the top radiator hose is next detached from the thermostat housing. Remove the air cleaner on the R1222.

3 Remove the top radiator hose at the water pump. In the largest diameter end should be the thermostat. It does sometimes fall into its housing if the bottom hose clip is fully undone. Pull the thermostat out.

4 To test the thermostat, suspend it on a piece of cotton in a pan of water and see how it behaves at the necessary opening temperatures. The valve should start to open within 3°C (5°F) of the normal operating temperature. Then, after another 2 or 3 minutes, it should open 6.5 mm (¼ inch) to the 'bypass port closed' position. After being once more placed in cooler water it should close within 15 to 20 seconds.

5 If a thermostat does not operate correctly it should be renewed. If one is not immediately available leave the old one out to avoid damage by possible overheating of the engine.

6 Refit the thermostat by placing it in its housing, checking that one of its bridges is not obstructing a blocked water circulation hole and push the radiator hose over it (it is obvious which end of the hose fits), making sure that it is not necessary, when fitting the other end of the hose to the radiator, to twist it. Secure the jubilee clips, refill the radiator with coolant and check for leaks. Refit the air cleaner on the R1222.

8 Water pump - general

1 If the water pump leaks or the bearing is obviously worn it will need to be removed for renewal. It can be done with the engine in the car and without removing the radiator or cylinder head. However, it is a nasty job on either car, the R1221 has to have its radiator loosened and the R1222 the centre cross brace pulled forward.

2 Drain the cooling system and then undo the hoses which are connected to the pump.

3 Slacken the generator mounting bolts and belt tension adjuster bolt so that the 'fan' belts may be removed. The generator should then be allowed to rest down.

4 Disconnect the battery.

5 Loosen the radiator as described in Chapter 1, (R1221) but do not actually remove the radiator. Undo the centre cross brace on the R1222 and pull towards the radiator having unclipped the

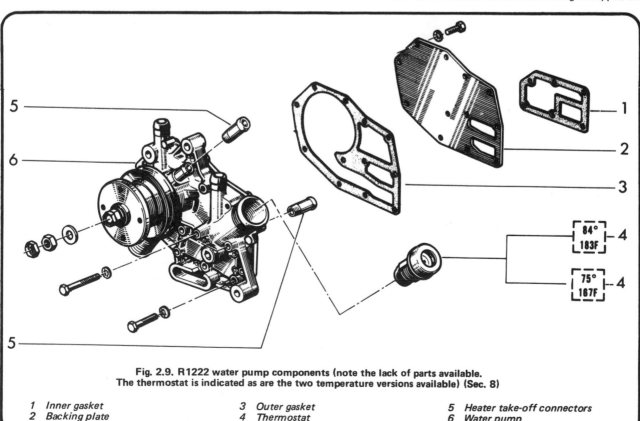

Fig. 2.9. R1222 water pump components (note the lack of parts available. The thermostat is indicated as are the two temperature versions available) (Sec. 8)

| 1 Inner gasket | 3 Outer gasket | 5 Heater take-off connectors |
| 2 Backing plate | 4 Thermostat | 6 Water pump |

two radiator hoses on it.

6   Pull the radiator away from the pump so that the fan blades will clear it (R1221).

7   Remove the water pump securing nuts and bolts. (It is easier to get at all these if the radiator is removed but it is by no means essential). Some bolts do not actually locate the pump to the cylinder head but only the pump backplate to its body.

8   Tap the water pump with a soft faced hammer and draw it out and up, taking care not to hit the radiator.

9   To remove the fan (R1221) and its pulley hold the pulley and the pump in a soft faced vice and remove the Pal locking washer on the centre shaft of the pump at the fan. Remove the securing nut and washer.

10 Take the pump out of the vice and replace in the vice, this time without bearing on the pulley. Lever the pulley/fan off the pump spindle equally all the way round and very carefully. It is located on a Woodruff key onto the impeller spindle.

11 To replace a broken fan or pulley undo the two locking tab washers and undo the four setscrews and part one from the other. Replacement of both fan and pulley is a reversal of the removal procedure.

12 Water pumps cannot be repaired. Exchange pumps only are available.

13 Reassembly is a reversal of its dismantling procedure. Make sure the drive pulley nut is torqued to 15 lb f ft (2.07 kg fm).

14 Before replacing the pump to the cylinder head the mating faces of both the impeller housing and the head must be perfectly clean and free of traces of old gaskets. Fit a new gasket, using jointing compound, on both sides and tighten the bolts evenly to ensure a watertight joint.

15 Refit the fan and pulley, replace the 'fan' belts and adjust the tension and connect the water hoses. Refix the radiator or centre cross brace. Refill the system with coolant. Examine for leaks when cold and at normal running temperature. Make sure that pulleys all run true to each other.

9 Coolant hoses - general

1   All Renaults are fitted with 'once only' hose clips when new. If any work is undertaken on the cooling system, buy replacement hose clips to start with. Buy only Jubilee type hose clips and throw the original fitments away! (photo)

2   All coolant hoses are easily and obviously removed and replaced. Never skimp and always use proprietary replacements. The R1221 is fitted with some very 'shaped' hoses whilst the R1222 has some long trunkated ones, also it has a water heated manifold which requires more hoses.

3   A coolant leak is always obvious because of the searching nature of the 'green' antifreeze used for all seasons in the Renault engine.

10 Water temperature sender unit - general

1   The water temperature sender unit is located into the bottom of the thermostat housing (R1221). The R1222 fitment is on the rear end of the cylinder head.

2   Whilst operating in the same way in the majority of its applications its actual warning can differ from car to car. Most cars are fitted with an orange warning light on the facia panel which is lit by the sender unit when the coolant is overheating. The temperatures at which it operates vary from application to application.

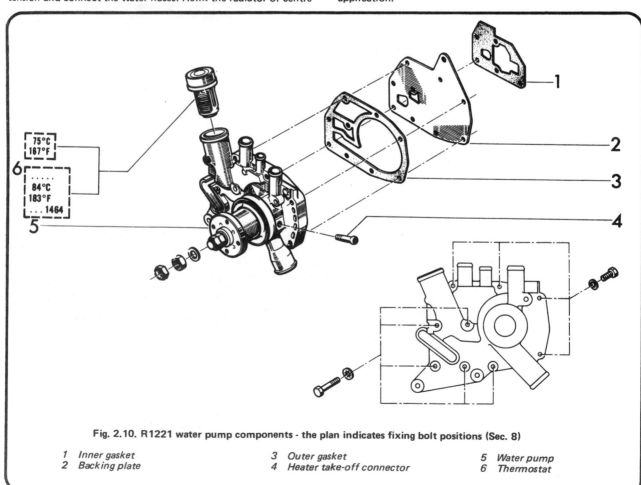

Fig. 2.10. R1221 water pump components - the plan indicates fixing bolt positions (Sec. 8)

| 1 | Inner gasket | 3 | Outer gasket | 5 | Water pump |
| 2 | Backing plate | 4 | Heater take-off connector | 6 | Thermostat |

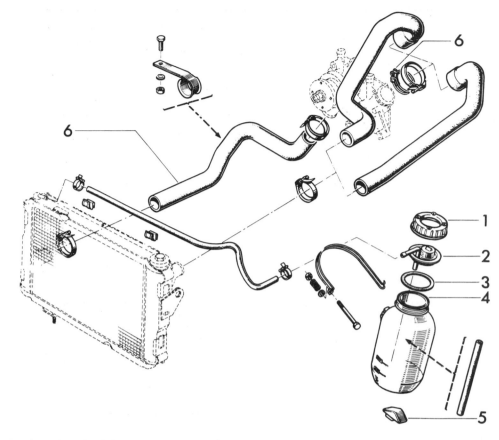

Fig. 2.11. R1222 hoses and ancillary cooling system components (Sec. 9)

1	Expansion chamber seal cap	3	Seal	5	Seat
2	Valve	4	Expansion bottle	6	Coolant hoses

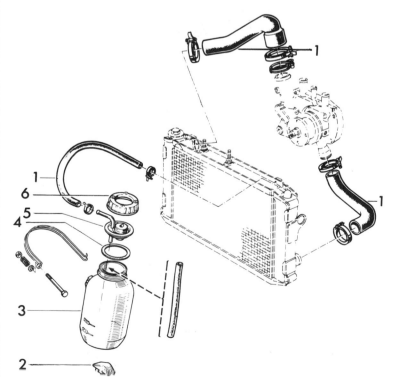

Fig. 2.12. R1221 hoses and ancillary cooling system components (Sec. 9)

1 Coolant hoses
2 Seat
3 Expansion bottle
4 Seal
5 Valve
6 Expansion chamber seal cap

9.1 Constantly check hose conditions, it is easy to overlook small failures

3 If it ceases to work it is easily replaced in a similar method to the thermostat. Drain the coolant sufficiently and unscrew, having removed its connecting wire. Replace with a new unit but make sure that you have also replaced its copper sealing ring.

11 Water distribution tube (R1221) - general

1 At the opposite end to the water pump on the cylinder head is a small rectangular cover plate located by four setscrews. The cover plate hides the end of the water distribution tube in the cylinder head. Although the cover plate and a possible leaking gasket can be replaced with the engine and cylinder head in the car, the distribution tube cannot, nor even be inspected.

2 To replace a leaking cover plate gasket drain the coolant from the system and undo the four securing screws. Clean the mating surfaces and using gasket cement replace with the proper gasket and tighten sufficiently.

3 To inspect the water distribution tube, a task only worth doing when the cylinder head or engine are being overhauled, requires the cylinder head to be removed from the block. Remove the cover plate as described and check to see if the cylindrical steel tube, its end visible through the cover plate end in the circular hole is corroded badly, disintegrated, or otherwise damaged. If it is damaged it will have to be drifted very

delicately from the cover plate end through to the water pump end. This means removing the water pump. Check that replacement parts are available and have a skilled engineer to do the job for you. He should also replace the tube for you in the reverse motion.

4 The holes drilled in the tube should face towards the exhaust valve seats at an angle of 30% to the vertical and the end which has the two holes close together should be positioned at the cover plate end. Peen the ends after insertion to prevent any twisting movement. Replace the water pump and cover plate.

12 Heating system - general

1 The heating system for the interior of the car which also incorporates the windscreen demisting system, is coupled to the engine cooling system. A system of 'heater' hoses connect the cooling system to a special heater matrix or radiator under the dashboard. Flow of 'hot' coolant is controlled by a hot water valve situated at the heater matrix. A special electric fan is fitted to force air through the 'hot' matrix and into the car, when the car is stationary or moving slowly. Normally the force of the air as the car runs is sufficient to heat the car.

2 The heating system is invisible under the bonnet. It is made up of three major components, all of which can be removed

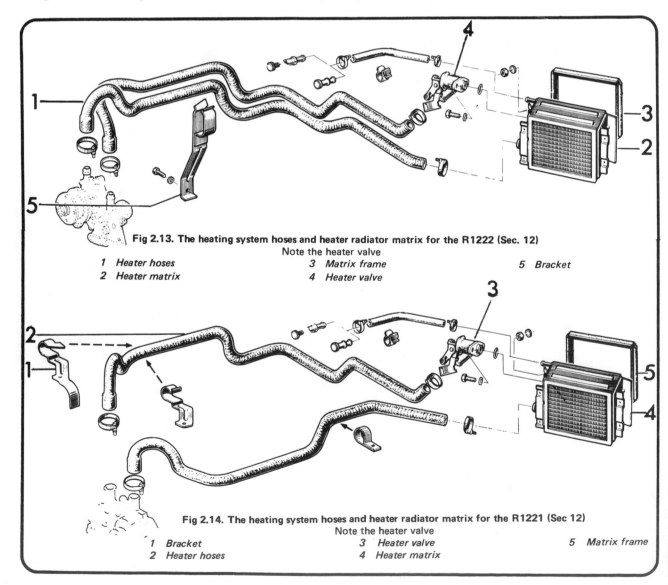

Fig 2.13. The heating system hoses and heater radiator matrix for the R1222 (Sec. 12)
Note the heater valve

1 Heater hoses	*3 Matrix frame*	*5 Bracket*
2 Heater matrix	*4 Heater valve*	

Fig 2.14. The heating system hoses and heater radiator matrix for the R1221 (Sec 12)
Note the heater valve

1 Bracket	*3 Heater valve*	*5 Matrix frame*
2 Heater hoses	*4 Heater matrix*	

from the car from under the bonnet. These are the heating/ventilating unit, the heater fan and the heater matrix. Additionally, there are hoses and cables. If there is any failure in any part of the system it is easier to remove the component to tackle repair than to work on it, on the car.

3   To remove the heating/ventilating unit, disconnect the battery and remove the air filter unit. Uncouple the flap lever control cable and unclip its outer sleeve from the unit. Disconnect the heater fan electrical conection and then unclip the heating system bleed screw hose from the front of the unit. Remove the air inlet trunking by loosening the hose clip. The heating/ventilating unit is now loose.

4   To remove the fan, it is necessary to remove it together with the matrix. Uncouple the hot water valve control cable and unclip its outer sleeve. Unscrew the two nuts securing the matrix to the bulkhead and the assembly as a whole should be loose but not free from the car.

5   To remove the fan from the matrix, now unscrew the four nuts securing the motor/fan unit. The motor/fan unit can be split by releasing the three anti-vibration rubber mounted nuts on the fan.

6   The matrix can be fully removed from the car by releasing the two heater hoses from it. The hot water valve is secured to the matrix by two screws and a suitable washer.

7   The whole system is replaced in a reverse sequence to its removal. Always make sure that motor/fan anti-vibration washers are seated properly and that all the flaps and valves work properly.

8   It is not possible to undertake any repair on the heater motor except that of changing the brushes. This is a simple operation which may require either crimping or soldering. If in doubt have this done by an auto-electrician once the motor is removed.

9   It is possible to change the hot water valve without removing anything more than the heating/ventilating unit. Do this, then clamp the two hoses next to the matrix, remove them from the valve and remove the valve as just described. Refitting is a reverse sequence.

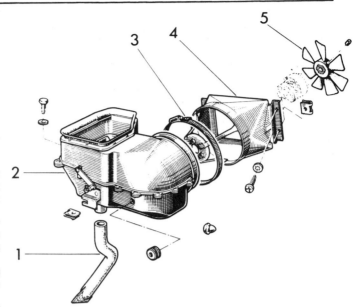

Fig. 2.15. The heater blower components (Sec. 12)

1 Drain tube	4 Shroud
2 Vent body	5 Fan blades
3 Hose clip	

10   Always bleed the cooling/heating system if the heater matrix or hot water valve have been removed and replaced. See Section 3.

13 Fault diagnosis - cooling system

Symptom	Reason/s	Remedy
Loss of coolant but no overheating provided	Expansion bottle empty Small leaks in system	Half fill expansion bottle. Examine all hoses and connections for signs of cracks and leaks when engine is both cold and hot, stationary and running. If no signs, use proprietary sealer in coolant to stop any invisible leaks.
Overheating and loss of coolant only when overheated	Faulty thermostat Fan belt slipping/electric fan faulty Engine out of tune due to ignition and/or fuel system settings being incorrect Blockage or restriction in circulation of cooling water Radiator cooling fins clogged up Blown cylinder head gasket or cracked cylinder head Sheared water pump impeller shaft Cracked cylinder body New engine still tight.	Check and renew if faulty. Check and adjust. Check ignition and fuel systems and adjust as required. Check that no hoses have collapsed. Drain, flush out and refill cooling system. Use chemical flushing compound if necessary Remove radiator and clean exterior as needed Remove cylinder head for examination. Remove pump and check. Remove engine and examine and repair (if possible). Adjust engine speeds to suit until run in.
Engine runs too cool and heater inefficient	Thermostat missing or stuck open	Remove housing cover and inspect.

Chapter 3 Carburation; fuel & exhaust systems

Contents

Specifications

Fuel pump

Type	SEV or Guiot mechanical
Delivery pressure	Between 2.5 and 4 psi

	R1221	R1222
	Solex 32 SEIA (543)	**Solex 32 SE1A (507)**
Carburettor		
Settings:		
Choke tube	23	23
Main jet	122.5	120
Air compensator jet	150	140
Slow running jet	42.5	40
Needle valve	1.5 mm	1.5 mm
Accelerator pump	45	40
Stangler/choke	Manual by cable	

Idling speed (engine)	675 to 725 rev/min
Fuel tank capacity	9 Imp galls (41 litres)
Air cleaner	Paper element with summer/winter setting
Exhaust	Single silencer under 'nearside' inner front wing. In four pieces from manifold

1 General description

The fuel tank is mounted underneath the car at the rear and from this fuel is drawn by a mechanical pump and delivered to the carburettor.

The pump, of either SEV or Guiot manufacture, is operated by an arm actuated by a lobe on the camshaft and is located halfway down the cylinder block on the left-hand side, the opposite side of the carburettor. The pump incorporates a filter screen. Fuel is delivered to a single fixed choke carburettor. Two types of carburettor have been fitted, manufactured by Solex depending on model. The output of the pump exceeds all normal requirements of the carburettor and the level of the fuel in the carburettor float chamber is regulated by a float operated needle valve. When the valve is closed, shutting off the flow, the pump freewheels. The diaphragm is held up by the pressure in the line until such time as the carburettor needle valve opens allowing the spring action of the pump to resume oscillating the diaphragm and deliver more fuel.

The air taken in through the carburettor to mix with the fuel vapour is filtered by a renewable paper element.

2 Air filter element - removal and renewal

1 Unscrew the bolt which holds the whole air cleaner assembly to the carburettor. Then disconnect the inlet hose from the air cleaner. (Throw the original hose clip away and refit with a worm drive clip). Once clear the whole unit may be lifted off and separated to give access to the filter element. Clean out the interior of the filter housing. If the same element is to be refitted tap it on a flat surface to remove any loose accumulations of dust. On some models the rocker cover breather pipe feeds into the air cleaner body. **Do not** try and wash it, brush it - or blow it with compressed air.

2 When reassembling the unit make sure that the sealing ring is intact and in place. When fitting the element, it should seat snugly over the locating ridges in the housing.

3 The air intake pipe may be positioned for 'Summer' or 'Winter' conditions by choosing the appropriate 'inlet' pipe fixing on the inner wing so that for 'Summer' conditions the pipe points towards the inner wing at right angles to the exhaust pipe, and for 'Winter' conditions the pipe intakes directly above the exhaust pipe to enable it to draw in warm air. Tighten the

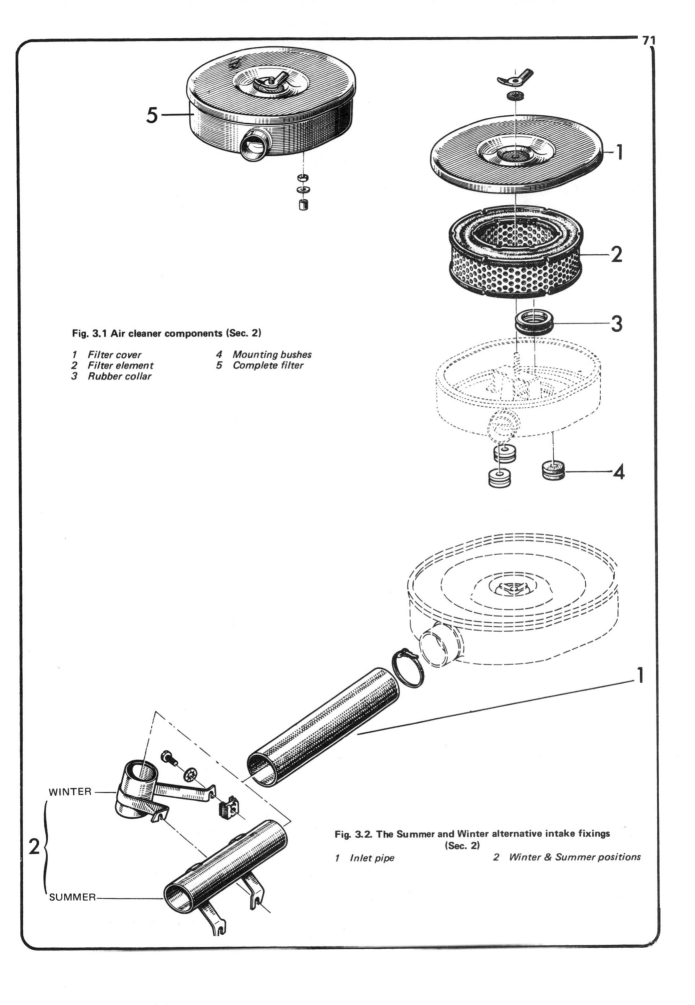

Fig. 3.1 Air cleaner components (Sec. 2)

1   *Filter cover*   4   *Mounting bushes*
2   *Filter element*   5   *Complete filter*
3   *Rubber collar*

WINTER

SUMMER

Fig. 3.2. The Summer and Winter alternative intake fixings
(Sec. 2)

1   *Inlet pipe*   2   *Winter & Summer positions*

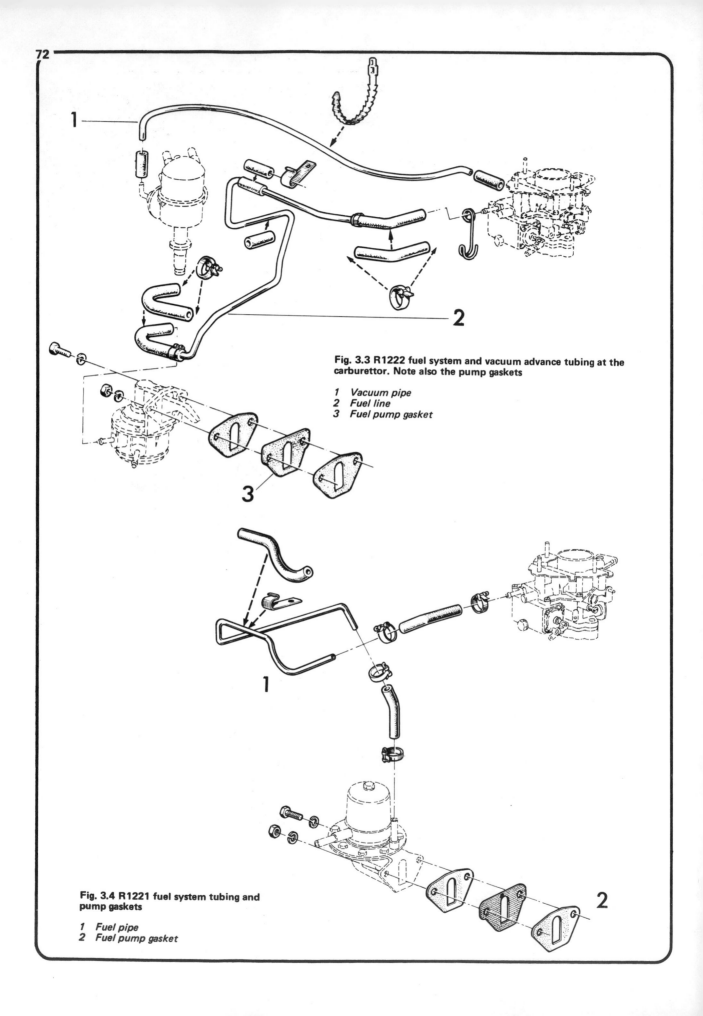

Fig. 3.3 R1222 fuel system and vacuum advance tubing at the carburettor. Note also the pump gaskets

1 Vacuum pipe
2 Fuel line
3 Fuel pump gasket

Fig. 3.4 R1221 fuel system tubing and pump gaskets

1 Fuel pipe
2 Fuel pump gasket

centre bolt. **Note**: The stud onto which the whole assembly fits should remain in the carburettor body when the filter is changed.

3 Carburettor - descriptions and principle

1 Although each model has a different carburettor Solex 32 SEIA (543) and Solex 32 SEIA (507), they are similar in principle and operation. Both use water heated manifolds (photo).
2 Petrol is pumped into the float chamber and is regulated by the needle valve. This fuel is sucked into either the main or pilot jet at a rate depending upon the depression in the venturi, or choke of the carburettor, which in turn is controlled by the speed of the engine. It is fed into the venturi as a fine spray to be mixed with air, the flow of which is controlled by the butterfly, and then when mixed, into the combustion chambers of the engine to be combusted. The running of the engine with regard to carburation is controlled by the throttle or butterfly stop screw and its relative position when compared with the air volume control screw. The flow of petrol once passed the float chamber is fixed by the jet size and therefore the tuning of the carburettor is totally controlled by the rate of the air flow

3.1 Each carburettor should be marked externally with its specification

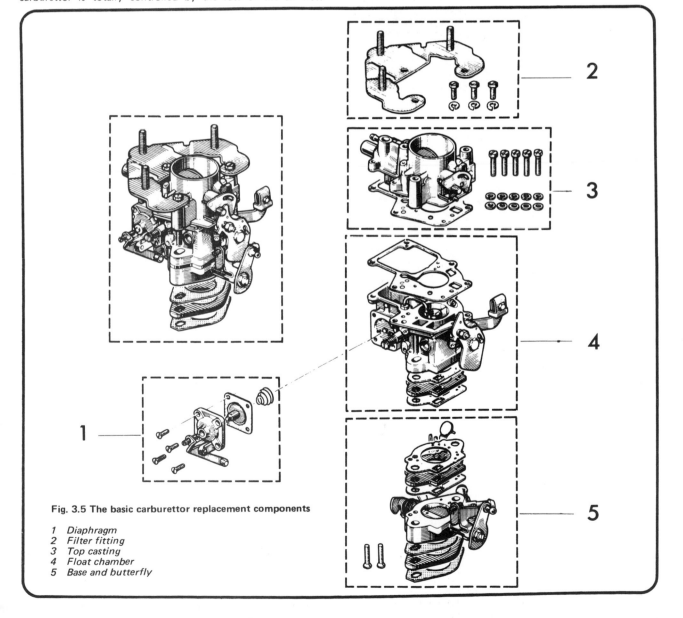

Fig. 3.5 The basic carburettor replacement components

1 Diaphragm
2 Filter fitting
3 Top casting
4 Float chamber
5 Base and butterfly

through the carburettor.

3 At low engine speeds the fuel flows through the pilot jet (idling jet), but as the speed increases there is a point of change over when sufficient depression is available to draw the fuel from the float chamber and bypass the pilot jet through the main jet. The operation of the choke when starting an engine from cold in effect feeds excess petrol, and to a certain extent air, into the venturi through a separate drilling in the carburettor because there is insufficient depression in the engine to draw enough fuel through the idling or main jets. The manual choke is controlled by the driver who can judge when the engine is warm enough not to need this excess of fuel.

4 Carburettor - removal and replacement

R1221

1 The carburettor may be removed easily with the engine in the car, for inspection and cleaning. Under some circumstances it may be wise to remove it from the manifold before removing an engine from the car.

2 Remove the air cleaner top and then the three fixing nuts inside the filter base. Pull off the air cleaner body.

3 Undo the holding bolt on the choke lever arm at the end of the choke cable and the outer cable casing grip on the carburettor. Pull out the cable away from the carburettor and tie back.

4 Unhook the throttle spring and allow to hang on its catch.

5 Pull off the fuel pipe from the carburettor and plug the end with a pencil or suitable instrument to stop fuel dripping out.

6 Release the throttle cable and then the rod from its lever, and tie back. This will be a push-on ball fit, and a setscrew with a hole drilled through it. Do not be surprised if the throttle pedal rests on the floor of the car. The throttle pedal is described in Chapter 8.

7 With an open ended spanner undo the two fixing nuts from their studs and remove together with their washers.

8 Clamp the hoses at the base of the carburettor seating block and then disconnect these water heating hoses. Remove also the rocker cover oil rebreathing pipe.

9 Lift off the carburettor and retrieve the gaskets and fixing bracket. Plug the manifold inlet with some clean rag.

10 Replacement of the carburettor is an exact reversal of removal but you must be sure that the correct number of gaskets have been replaced and that all the operating controls be they cable or rod are fitted in their correct positions and that they are not fully tightened up until total adjustment has taken place. It is silly to run with the choke out all the time because you overtightened the cable!

R1222

11 Removal and replacement of the R1222 carburettor is exactly similar to that of the R1221 except for the vacuum advance pipe which should be pulled off carefully.

5 Carburettor - setting and adjustment

1 Before making any adjustments to the carburettor settings make sure that your reasons for the adjustment are sound and that you only do one setting at a time. Check the result of each adjustment after it it made. The carburettor is a finely balanced and a relatively delicate instrument and can easily be put off tune.

2 Control settings are important. Make sure that the operation of the choke cable moves the lever easily throughout its full range of movement and returns to its closed position when the control knob is pushed home. Adjustment can be made by repositioning the inner cable relative to the operating arm at the clamping screw. The outer cable can be repositioned as necessary where it clips to the bracket on the carburettor.

3 The throttle cable and rod should also be checked for movement throughout its range. Make particularly sure that when the throttle flap is in the fully open position the position of the accelerator pedal is as far down as it could possibly be, even with the cable disconnected. Otherwise pressure on the pedal will impact severe strain on the cable, and more important on the throttle spindle and bearings. Adjustment should be made at the point where the end of the cable outer is located into the bracket near the carburettor. Slacken the locknuts and move the outer cable so that when the accelerator pedal is fully depressed the throttle is just fully open. Twist the head on the end of the rod to achieve the same result. Relock it (Fig. 3.13).

4 Slow running adjusment is controlled by an airflow screw. This regulates the air mixture with that of the fuel. The single jet screw controls fuel mixture throughout the full operational range. If satisfactory slowrunning cannot be achieved with the airflow screw adjustment, then it will be necessary to proceed to the following check which affects the carburettor performance at all speeds.

Special Note: Under no circumstances must the settings of the carburettor throttle bleed screw and cold start setting be altered. These are set at manufacture. If you do you will defeat the fine workings of your carburettor.

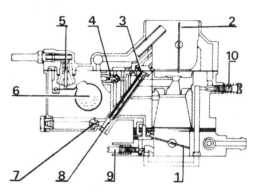

3.6 Cross-section of the Solex 32 SEIA carburettor

1	Throttle butterfly	6	Float
2	Choke flap	7	Main jet
3	Air compensator jet	8	Emulsion tube
4	Idling speed jet	9	Fuel screw
5	Needle valve	10	Air screw

Fig. 3.7 Description and settings (Sec. 5)

K	Choke tube	l	Accelerator pump
Gg	Main ket	a	Air correction jet
g	Slow running jet		

5 Make sure that the car has reached its fully operational temperature which should take at least ten minutes from cold.

6 Turn the air screw to obtain a normal tickover speed (by ear, in fact 675 rpm).

7 Then turn the fuel screw until the engine reaches its maximum speed.

8 Repeat both operations until the maximum engine speed lies between 675 and 700 rpm when turning the fuel screw. Then screw in the fuel screw 'a fraction' to just lower the engine speed but keeping its smoothness.

9 If the tickover setting is not obtainable or is racing the engine then you should recheck your carburettor controls for correctness of fitting and start again. If you are not able to obtain a reasonable tickover such are the variables which can affect the smooth running of the engine that you should look once more at the carburettor and then go on and check the

ignition system and other more serious mechanical parts.

10 Apart from setting the idling speed as just described, there are three other adjustments: throttle butterfly angle, initial throttle opening and position of the defuming valve. Strictly

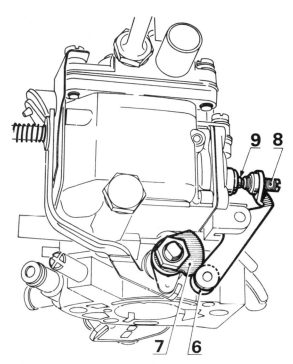

Fig. 3.9 '6' roller, '7' cam, '8' adjusting screw, '9' plunger - accelerator pump travel (Sec. 5)

Fig. 3.8 'A' air screw, 'B' fuel screw (Sec. 5)

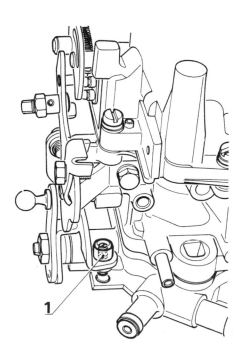

Fig. 3.10 Throttle butterfly adjustment screw. Remove the cap over '1' (Sec. 5)

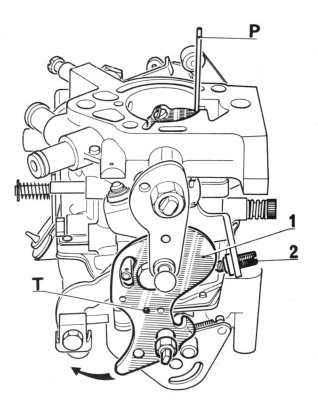

Fig. 3.11 Initial throttle opening: 'P' gauge rod, 'T' hole, '1' lever, '2' turn screw (Sec. 5)

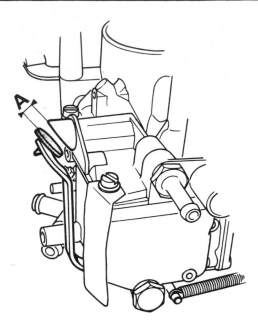

Fig. 3.12 Defuming valve, 'A' = 3 to 4 mm (1/8 to 5/32 inch) (Sec. 5)

speaking these adjustments should never need making unless the carburettor has been dismantled. If you have dismantled your carburettor (see next Section) you should have the three adjustments checked by a Renault garage. It is impractical to check them at home.

6 Carburettor - dismantling, inspection and reassembly

1 Do not dismantle the carburettor unless it is absolutely necessary. This should be only for cleaning at intervals of 9000 miles or when systematic diagnosis indicates that there is a fault with it. The internal mechanism is delicate and finely balanced and unnecessary tinkering will probably do more harm than good.

2 Although certain parts may be removed with the carburettor still attached to the engine, nevertheless, it is considered safer to remove it and work over a bench.

3 With the carburettor off the car disassembly is as follows (this covers all carburettors fitted, with slight variations which, because of their simple and obvious nature, are not specifically mentioned each time). Remove the air filter base fitting. This is

fixed by three screws. Remove the top of the carburettor by undoing its fixing screws with the correct size screwdriver. These screws are made of comparatively soft metal and will damage very easily. With the top should come the choke mechanism (both types), fuel inlet pipe and filter (if fitted), and needle valve. The gasket and float itself should remain in the body of the carburettor.

4 Remove the gasket and the float placing bracket or spindle and then the float itself.

5 Remove any jets and their washers which have screwdriver cuts in their heads and are removable from the top and inside of the carburettor.

6 Unscrew all the external adjusting screws but note Section 5, paragraph 4 now. Retain all washers and springs and code for their relevant positions.

7 Turn the top of the carburettor upside down and remove the needle valve and its washer.

8 On Solex carburettors you will be able to remove the choke tube itself from the body of the carburettor.

9 There is no point under any circumstances in removing any more parts from the carburettor. If any of these parts are in need of attention then a complete new carburettor is needed. It is safer and more efficient, if you have reached this stage of need of repair to replace the complete unit.

10 All the parts which have been separated should be thoroughly cleaned in methylated spirits or clean petrol by hand and without the help of anything more than a soft non-fluffy rag. Do not use any scrapers, emery paper, wire wool or hard projections such as a pin on these parts. All have been machined to extremely fine tolerances. Blow all parts dry.

11 Inspect for blockages and scoring, the float for a puncture and the needle valve for easy operation. On floats make sure the metal tag is not bent or distorted. Replace if it is. There is no room for float level adjustment. Replace any parts which are obviously worn or damaged but also do so to any which you even suspect. (Make sure that parts are still available though before throwing away - you may need a temporary repair).

12 Replace all parts in the reverse of their removal using new copper washers and gaskets all the way through. Do not over-tighten anything, and do not use any gasket cement. If the top of the carburettor does not fit flat it needs replacing. **Special note:** No mention has been made of throttle, choke and butterfly spindles. As these spindles run directly in the body or top of the carburettor they are likely over a period of usage to wear. It is impractical to replace parts of these and any wear or failure in these parts must mean complete replacement.

7 Choke cable - general

The choke cable should not need touching unless it snaps or receives a permanent kink in it. It is of stiff steel wire. Its

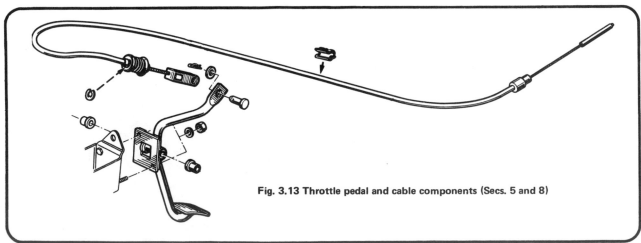

Fig. 3.13 Throttle pedal and cable components (Secs. 5 and 8)

removal and replacement is conventional and straightforward. Its pull knob must be removed by unscrewing the nut behind the dashboard. Both inner and outer cable must be removed and replaced from inside the car.

8 Throttle cable - general

The flexible throttle cable is easily replaced if broken. Make sure all the fixings at the carburettor are re-installed. Also make sure it does not 'go through' any tight curves. It helps to lubricate a new cable with light oil. There is a compressing spring at the carburettor's end. It should be nearly compressed when the throttle is fully open.

9 Fuel pump - removal and replacement

1 The mechanical fuel pump will need removing if it is to be dismantled for overhaul, but the filter can be cleaned in-situ. Disconnect the fuel lines on the inlet and outlet sides by pulling off the connector pipes on both sides.
2 Undo the two nuts, one is a nut on a stud the other is a setscrew, holding the pump flange to the crankcase, and take the pump off. Keep the spacer and gaskets together and do not discard them. If necessary blank off the fuel line from the tank to prevent loss of fuel. (photo)
3 Replacement is a reversal of the removal procedure. Make sure that the total thickness of gaskets and spacer is the same as came off. Check that the fuel line connections are not leaking after starting the engine.
4 Two types of mechanical pump are fitted. The R1221 is strictly conventional, whilst the R1222 is essentially similar but is fitted 'upsidedown' ie., the operating lever is above the diaphragm and the fuel inlet and outlet below.

9.2 Note that the fuel pump has one stud and one setscrew fixing

10 Fuel pump - inspection, dismantling and reassembly

1 First clean the pump exterior thoroughly and mark the edges of the two halves of the body.
2 Undo the cover retaining screw(s) and lift off the cover. The gasket and gauze filter may then be removed.
3 Remove the screws and washers holding the two halves of the pump together and the top (R1221)/bottom (R1222) half may

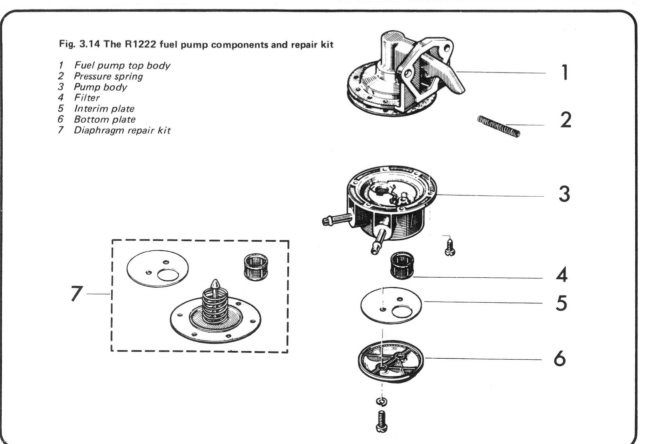

Fig. 3.14 The R1222 fuel pump components and repair kit

1 Fuel pump top body
2 Pressure spring
3 Pump body
4 Filter
5 Interim plate
6 Bottom plate
7 Diaphragm repair kit

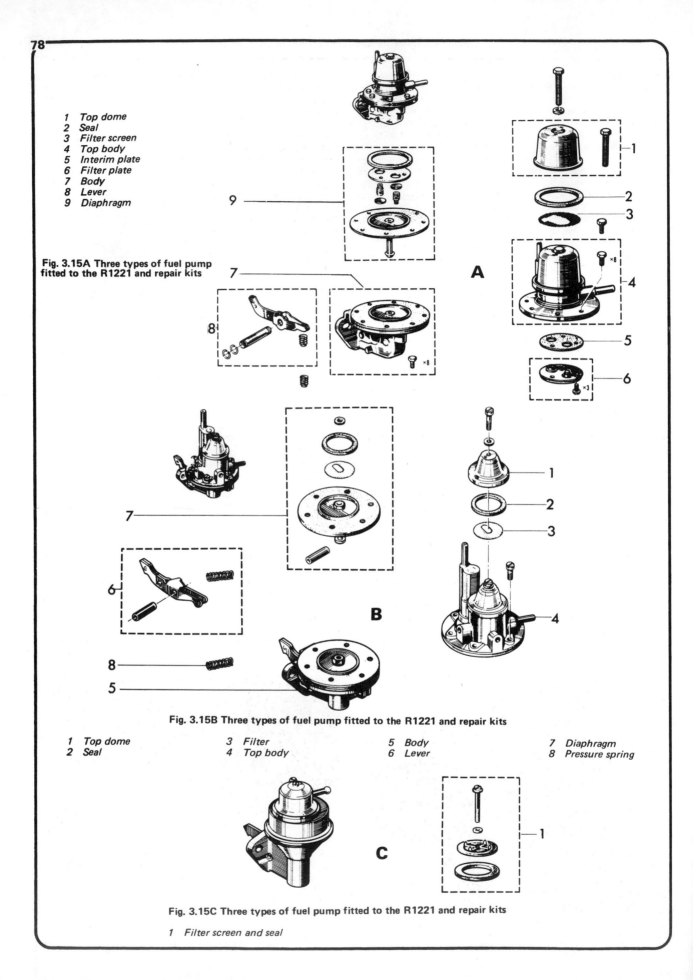

1 Top dome
2 Seal
3 Filter screen
4 Top body
5 Interim plate
6 Filter plate
7 Body
8 Lever
9 Diaphragm

Fig. 3.15A Three types of fuel pump fitted to the R1221 and repair kits

A

Fig. 3.15B Three types of fuel pump fitted to the R1221 and repair kits

B

1	Top dome	3	Filter	5	Body	7	Diaphragm
2	Seal	4	Top body	6	Lever	8	Pressure spring

Fig. 3.15C Three types of fuel pump fitted to the R1221 and repair kits

C

1 Filter screen and seal

then be lifted off.

4 The diaphragm and pushrod should be removed next but you will have to remove the pump lever and its spindle to release it. This is done by releasing one of the spindles circlips. This can prove to be very fiddly but with patience and a strong blunt penknife blade the circlip can be 'peeled' off. The R1221 differs slightly here but it will be obvious. Push the spindle through and pull out the lever. Retrieve the lever spring. Lift out the diaphragm and its rod carefully. This spindle is usually known as the rocker arm pivot pin.

5 If there are signs of wear in the rocker arm pivot pin, and rocker arm and link bushes then they should be renewed.

6 The valve assemblies should only be removed from the upper body if renewal is necessary. They are staked into the body and are destroyed when levered out.

7 Examine the diaphragm for signs of cracking or perforation and renew if necessary.

8 Overhaul kits are usually available for all pumps and are supplied with a new diaphragm, valves and sealing rings. Check the manufacture of the pump first as well as the supply.

9 When fitting new valve assemblies to the body, first fit the seating washers and then place the valves, making sure that they are the correct way up according to inlet and outlet. The body will have to be restaked at six (different) places around the edge so that the assemblies are firmly held in their positions. If this is not done properly and leakage occurs between the valve assembly and the seating ring the pump will not operate efficiently.

10 To replace the diaphragm and lever arm it will be necessary to place the diaphragm spring in the body of the pump. Then the diaphragm and its rod. Press the diaphragm spring down and fit the spring, push in the lever (the right way up) and connect over the top of the machined stop on the rod. Push in the rocker arm pivot pin and push through the lever. Replace the circlip on the pivot pin. Always use a new circlip.

11 Fit the upper half of the pump body and line up the mating marks. In order to assemble the two halves and the diaphragm properly push the rocker arm upwards so that the diaphragm is drawn level. Then place the eight screws in position lightly. It is best if the base of the pump is held in a vice whilst the rocker arm is pushed right up to bring the diaphragm to the bottom of its stroke. A short piece of tube over the rocker arm will provide easy leverage. In this position the eight screws should be tightened evenly and alternately.

12 Fit a new filter bowl gasket carefully in the groove of the upper body, making sure that it does not twist or buckle in the process. Replace the cover and screw it tight.

13 When the pump is reassembled the suction and delivery pressure can be felt at the inlet and outlet ports when the rocker arm is operated. Be careful not to block the inlet port completely when testing suction. If the rocker arm were to be operated strongly and the inlet side was blocked the diaphragm could be damaged.

11 Fuel gauge - tank sender unit

1 The fuel gauge sender unit is mounted on the top of the tank where the fuel outlet pipe connection is also made, sucking up the petrol through a filter on the end of a tube. If the fuel gauge appears faulty first check the wiring connections at the base of the instrument panel. See Chapter 9. Then go on to the sender unit which is a variable resistance giving different readings with both a full and empty tank by the operation of a varnished cork float. If the fault lies here and you are sure that the sender unit was properly connected, you will have to replace the whole unit. It is not possible to replace parts of it.

2 To remove the sender unit, you will have to remove the fuel tank. See Section 13.

Having presumably pulled off the fuel and electrical contents to remove the tank from the car, unclip the locking ring - it has three lips which must be bent back carefully - and lift out carefully turning the body of the unit to release the float and filter tube. When replacing always use a new gasket and do not over-tighten. Make sure that the two connections are clean and tight.

3 These are reliable instruments and are usually non-functioning because of some mechanical defect rather than electrical, ie; the float arm is bent, or the float has been perforated.

12 Exhaust system

1 The exhaust system, although peculiar in its arrangement is conventional in its working and extremely simple to repair as it has one silencer. It is wise only to use original type exhaust clamps and proprietary made systems. (photos)

2 When any one section of the exhaust system needs renewal it often follows that the whole lot is best replaced.

3 It is most important when fitting exhaust systems that the twists and contours are carefully followed and that each connecting joint overlaps the correct distance. Any stresses or strain imparted, in order to force the system to fit the hanger rubbers, will result in early fractures and failures.

4 When fitting a new part of a complete system it is well worth removing ALL the system from the car and cleaning up all the joints so that they fit together easily. The time spent struggling with obstinate joints whilst flat on your back under the car is

12.1a This clip is one of three major exhaust support systems; make sure it fits well and is always tight

12.1b The exhaust system on the Renault 5 is hardy and long lived; this is the tailpipe rubber support

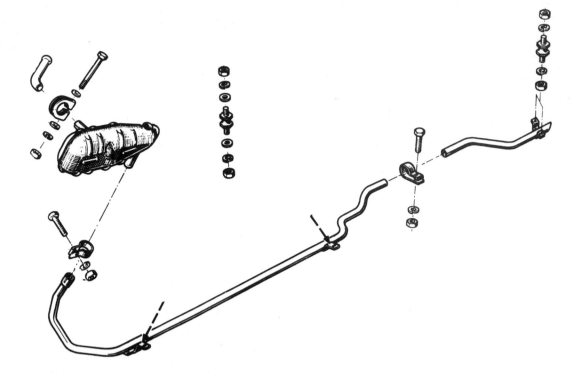

Fig. 3.16 The exhaust system. Whilst many of the components appear not to be the same for the two models, they are in fact (Sec. 12)

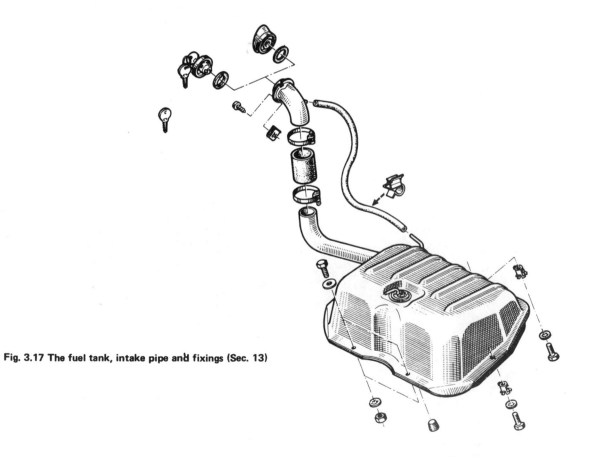

Fig. 3.17 The fuel tank, intake pipe and fixings (Sec. 13)

eliminated and the likelihood of distorting or even breaking a section is greatly reduced. Do not waste a lot of time trying to undo rusted and corroded clamps and bolts. Cut them off. New ones will be required anyway if they are that bad.

5 The critical fitting point is the exit hole of the first pipe through the inner wing direct to the silencer. Only adjust this point when the whole system is in place but not fully tightened. The pipe should run through the centre of the hole. Tighten the two exhaust clamps from under the bonnet first, get this right and rigid before finally fixing the rear of the system.

13 Fuel tank - general

1 The fuel tank is located at the rear of the car directly below the boot floor. Its removal is simple if a little messy. On previous small front wheel drive Renaults the tanks have been prone to internal rusting. It appears that this has been overcome on the Renault 5, although the exterior of the tank and the filler neck are still liable to hold road dirt which will eventually rust through, outside to in.

2 To remove the tank, jack-up the rear of the car, as high off the ground as possible. Place supports under both sides at the rear and remove the rear roadwheels. Clean out the inner wing on the filler cap side.

3 Undo the two hose clips visible on the filler neck, remove and squeeze off the rubber centre hose. Remove the filler cap and take out the two screws which hold its captive head to the bodyshell. These are visible once the cap is removed. Remove then the overflow pipe from inside the rear wing to the captive head, ie; ½ curved entry pipe and then remove that.

4 The tank is held by four spire screws and two nuts and bolts, around its lipped edge. Remove all these from below. Slide the tank one inch forwards and then down and left, towards the nearside rear suspension arm. This should clear the filler neck.

5 Unclip the electrical lead to the sender unit in the top of the tank and the fuel feed pipe nearby. The tank should then come away.

6 Replacement is a reverse process.

14 Fault diagnosis - Fuel system and carburation

Unsatisfactory engine performance and excessive fuel consumption are not necessarily the fault of the fuel system or carburettor. In fact they more commonly occur as a result of ignition and timing faults. Before acting on the following it is necessary to check the ignition system first. Even though a fault may lie in the fuel system it will be difficult to trace unless the ignition is correct. The faults below, therefore, assume that this has been attended to first (where appropriate).

Symptom	Reason/s	Remedy
Smell of petrol when engine is stopped	Leaking fuel lines or unions Leaking fuel tank	Repair or renew as necessary Fill fuel tank to capacity and examine carefully at seams, unions and filler pipe connections. Repair as necessary
Smell of petrol when engine is idling	Leaking fuel line unions between pump and carburettor Overflow of fuel from float chamber due to wrong level setting, ineffective needle valve or punctured float	Check line and unions and tighten or repair Check fuel level setting and condition of float and needle valve, and renew if necessary
Excessive fuel consumption for reasons not covered by leaks or float chamber faults	Worn jets Over-rich jet setting Sticking mechanism	Renew jets or carburettor body if not removable Adjust jet Check correct movement of mechanism
Difficult starting, uneven running, lack of power, cutting out	One or more jets blocked or restricted Float chamber fuel level too low or needle valve sticking Fuel pump not delivering sufficient fuel	Dismantle and clean out float chamber and jets Dismantle and check fuel level and needle valve Check pump delivery and clean or repair as required

Chapter 4 Ignition system

Contents

Specifications

Spark plugs

Type	(R1222) AC42FS, Champion L87Y, Eyquem Renault 705 S
	(R1221) AC43FS, Champion L87Y, Eyquem Renault 705 S
Electrode gap	0.6 to 0.7 mm (0.024 to 0.028 in)

Coil

Coil	SEV or Ducellier 12 volts

Distributor

Type	R1222 Ducellier 4360 or 4440
	R1221 Ducellier 4444 or SEV 400 02702
Rotation	Clockwise
Firing order	1 - 3 - 4 - 2 (No. 1 nearest radiator)
Contact points gap	0.4 mm (0.016 in)
Ignition timing	R1222 4/6° BTDC (10 mm/3/8 in. at flywheel)
	R1221 5/7° BTDC (12 mm/15/32 in. at flywheel)
Dwell percentage	63 +/− 3
Cam angle	57° +/− 3°

---

1 General description

In order that the internal combustion engine with spark ignition can operate properly, it is essential that the spark be delivered at the spark plug electrodes at the precise moment it is required. This moment varies - in relation to the position of the pistons and crankshaft - depending on the speed and loading of the engine. This control of the spark timing is automatic. When it is realised that at 50 mph approximately 100 sparks per second are being produced then the importance of the need for precise setting is realised. The majority of minor faults and cases of poor performance and economy can be traced to the ignition system.

The principles are as follows: Battery voltage (12 volts) is fed through a circuit which passes through a coil developing high voltage.

Without going into electrical principles it is sufficient to say that when the 12 volt circuit is 'made', current is fed into a capacitor (condenser). When the circuit is broken the condenser discharges its current into the low voltage line and a high voltage current is boosted from the core of the coil and along the HT lead. This current is delivered to the centre contact of the distributor cap and from there, via the rotor arm, to each of the other four contacts in turn. Each of these is linked by a 'high tension' lead to each spark plug.

Obviously the timing of the break in the circuit decides the moment at which the spark is made. The contact points (or breaker points!) are in effect a switch. Not only do they open and close four times for every 2 revolutions of the crankshaft -

delivering a spark to the four plugs in turn - they also open earlier or later in relation to the position of the crankshaft/pistons. Ignition advance and retard are the terms used to express this condition and it is measured in degrees - being degrees of angle of any crank on the shaft. Zero degrees is top dead centre, being the highest point of the arc made by a crank. Timing setting is therefore expressed as so many degrees BTDC (before top dead centre).

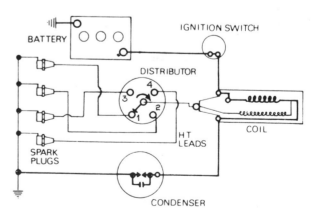

Fig. 4.1 The basic ignition system

In order to vary the ignition timing the contact opening cam is able to revolve a certain amount around the centre spindle. This is controlled by spring-loaded weights which move out under centrifugal force. When they move out, the spindle to cam position is altered.

Vacuum advance is fitted to the R1222 but not to the R1221.

Timing varies with different engines but normally ranges from the static (at rest) advance of approximately 0° BTDC to 28° BTDC for the R1222 and 13° BTDC for the R1221. When accelerating and under open throttle conditions the centrifugal control is in operation. The static timing is important of course as the automatic timing advance device starts from this point and consequently if it is incorrect the whole range is affected.

The manual clamp adjustment on the body clamp adjusts the static ignition setting entirely.

Whilst little is in fact identical in the way of components between the R1221 and R1222 the principles, dismantling and reassembly, services and checks are all similar and can be discussed together. Any specific differences are pointed out.

Any work on the ignition system necessitates removal of the spare wheel. It is therefore not mentioned here on each occasion.

2 Routine maintenance

a) Spark plugs

Remove the plugs and thoroughly clean away all traces of carbon. Examine the porcelain insulation round the central electrodes inside the plug and if damaged discard the plug. Reset the gap between the electrodes. Do not use a set of plugs for more than 9000 miles. It is false economy.

At the same time check the plug caps. Always use the straight tubular ones normally fitted. Good replacements can come from a Renault agency.

b) Distributor

Every 9000 miles remove the cap and rotor arm and put one or two drops of engine oil into the centre of the cam recess. Smear the surfaces of the cam itself with petroleum jelly. Do not overlubricate as any excess could get onto the contact points surfaces and cause ignition difficulties.

Every 9000 miles examine the contact point surfaces. If there is a build up of deposits on one face and a pit in the other it will be impossible to set the gap correctly and they should be refaced or renewed. Set the gap when the contact surfaces are in order.

Check the proper functioning of the R1222 vacuum advance mechanism.

c) General

Examine all leads and terminals for signs of broken or cracked insulation. Also check all terminal connections for slackness or signs of fracturing of some strands of wire. Partly broken wire should be renewed.

The HT leads are particularly important as any insulation faults will cause the high voltage to 'jump' to the nearest earth and this will prevent a spark at the plug. Check that no HT leads are loose or in a position where the insulation could wear due to rubbing against part of the engine.

3 Contact breaker points - adjustment

1 Remove the distributor cap by unclipping the two leaf springs, one each side of the distributor.
2 Pull off the rotor arm from the cam spindle and remove the plastic dust shield (if fitted). (photo)
3 First examine the points by carefully levering them apart with a small screwdriver or something similar. If the faces of the circular contacts are pitted or rough then they cannot be properly set and should be removed for renewal or cleaning up.
4 If the faces are clean then turn the engine so that the moving arm of the breaker rests with the following on one of the four high points on the cam. The engine can be turned by engaging a gear and moving the car.
5 Select a feeler blade (0.4 mm/0.016 in) applicable for both models and place it between the points. If the gap is too great, slacken the fixed point locking screw and move the plate to alter the gap. If the gap is too small the feeler blade may still fit between the points as the spring loaded arm can simply move back. When setting them, therefore, the feeler gauge blade should only be a very light touch on each contact face. (photos)
6 Lock the fixed plate screw and recheck the gap. Replace the rotor arm making sure that the lug in the rotor recess is fully engaged in the slot on the cam spindle.
7 Check the inside of the distributor cap before replacing it and

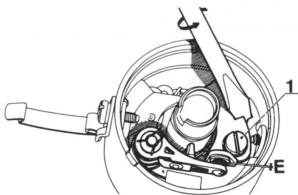

Fig. 4.2 Contact breaker gap adjustment. '1' is the screw to loosen the fixed point and 'E' is the gap (Sec. 3)

3.2 Always pull off the rotor arm before attempting points adjustment

3.5a Try to use metric feeler blades; fit the blade at right angles and exert no pressure

3.5b Always use a screwdriver which fits properly; the screw head will burr easily

verify that the four contacts are clean and the centre carbon brush is intact and moves freely.

4 Contact breaker points - removal and replacement

1 The contact points will need removal if the surfaces are bad enough to require renewal or refacing. Generally it is best to renew the contacts completely as refacing never produces a surface as good as the original and they will deteriorate again much more rapidly.

2 Remove the distributor cap, rotor arm and dust shield as described .in the previous Section and remove the fixed plate locking screw.

3 Remove the small circlip on the terminal post which also secures the end of the spring and lift off the washer. Undo until loose the small nut which secures the lead to the condenser and the spring of the contact breaker arm. Lift upwards the spring contact from the pivot post. Now remove the fixed contact locking screw and lift out this contact. It is wise even for changing contact points to have a set of metric distributor spanners to avoid the use of pliers. (photos)

4 Replacement is the *exact* reversal of the removal sequence. Do not get anything muddled and take your time.

5 Condenser - testing, removal and replacement

1 A faulty condenser causes interruptions in the ignition circuit or total failure. Elaborate testing methods are pointless as the item is cheap to renew.

2 If the contact points become pitted after a relatively small mileage (under 1000) and if starting is difficult then it is a good idea to replace the condenser when replacing the points. Another way to check is to remove the distributor cap, rotor arm and dust shield and turn the engine so that the points are closed. Then switch on the ignition and open the points using an insulated screwdriver. There should be a small blue spark visible but if the condenser is faulty there will be a fat blue spark.

3 The condenser is external to the working of the types of distributor fitted to these engines although it may be in either a vertical or horizontal position. Using the correct spanner undo the lead from the condenser to the fixing post on the side of the distributor. (Some models may be fitted with a metal tag instead). Remove the body of the condenser from the other fixing post which also holds one of the distributor cap clips. Fit a new one in reverse order. Make sure you fit the correct condenser.

4.3a Loosen the external LT fixing nut then pull off the lead

4.3b Carefully release the spring clip with a screwdriver

4.3c Delicately ease up the moving points from the pivot post

4.3d The fixed points are still in the distributor

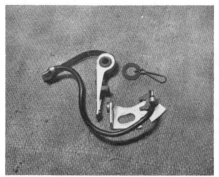

4.3e The components for removal when changing the points. The washer and spring clip do not come in a points set

6.3 There is little room around the distributor; work carefully recording where things go

6.6 The distributor is located and held by one stud and nut only

6 Distributor - removal and replacement

1 The distributor will need removal if there are indications that the drive spindle is a sloppy fit in the bushes (causing contact gap setting difficulties) or if it is to be dismantled and thoroughly cleaned and checked. It should also be removed before the oil pump is taken out.

2 Before removing the distributor it is helpful to prevent future confusion if the engine is positioned with No 1 piston at TDC on the firing stroke. This can be done by noting the position of the No 1 plug lead in the cap and then turning the engine to TDC so that the rotor is adjacent to the No 1 plug position in the cap. (The cap of course, will be removed to do this). For details see Section 8 - 'Ignition timing'.

3 Detach the plug leads from the spark plugs and the coil HT lead from the distributor cap or coil. Remove the cap by unclipping the leaf spring clip at each side. (photo)

4 Undo the LT lead at the coil - this should be a screw on connector, and pull off the vacuum advance pipe from the R1222 distributor.

5 Undo the one setscrew which locates the baseplate to the cylinder block on the side of the distributor drive casing. Do not at this stage undo the clamp bolt which fixes the baseplate to the distributor body (R1221). If this is removed you will have to retime the engine. Of course it may be necessary if a new distributor is fitted, but wait until the distributor is away from the engine.

6 Lift the distributor up and out, the locating flange and sealing ring should come with it. Before proceeding any further, note the position of the eccentric slot in the end of the drive shaft inside the distributor mounting recess in the block. This will give a firm timing reference if the oil pump is to be removed. (photo)

7 Replacement is a reversal of the removal procedure. Check that the rubber sealing ring between the flange and block is in good condition. Line up the eccentric tongue on the distributor shaft with the slot in the drive shaft and when the sleeve of the body is being pushed down be prepared to rotate the shaft either way a little so as to engage the drive.

8 Upon camshaft removal and replacement this slotted drive gear will have been removed. Refit into the oil pump drive skew gear in exactly the same position from which it was removed.

7 Distributor - dismantling, inspection and reassembly

1 If the distributor is causing trouble (ie; not holding its adjustment, giving ragged performance etc), it will require replacement. Apart from contact points, rotors, condensers, base plates, automatic advance and retard springs and for the R1222, vacuum advance units, virtually no parts are available. There is, therefore, little point in disassembly with a view to rebuilding, only one with a view to confirmation of diagnosis, although

unless you do rebuild it will not be possible to exchange the unit. If in any doubt, exchange the unit.

2 Quick diagnosis and dismantling, inspection and reassembly is now given. Without proper test equipment it is difficult to diagnose whether or not the centrifugal advance mechanism is performing as it should (It is possible to check on the vacuum advance of the R1222). However, play in the shaft bushes can be detected by removing the rotor arm and gripping the end and trying to move it sideways. If there is any movement then it means that the cam cannot accurately control the contact points gap. This must receive attention.

3 With the distributor removed take off the rotor, condenser and contact points as described in Section 4.

4 If, at this stage, you consider that the distributor is in need of replacement and that you will have to retime the engine then you should remove the base clamp now R1221 only (the R1222 has one forked clamp which is always loosened!) otherwise it can be left on throughout the dismantling stages. Release the clamp bolt and pull off the plate.

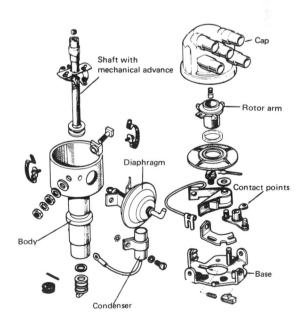

Fig. 4.3 The R1222 distributor components

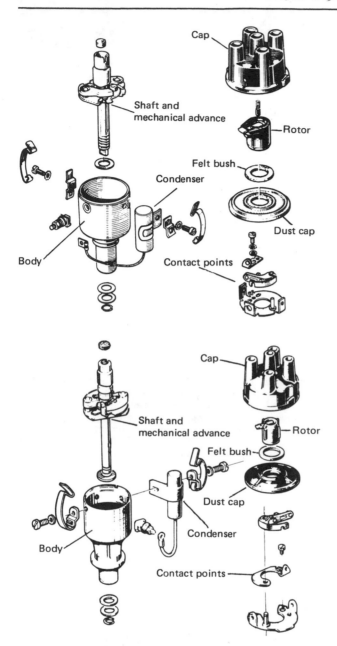

**Fig. 4.4 The R1221 distributors. (Above) SEV Marchal,
(below) Ducellier**

5   Remove the felt oil-soak washer from the top of the cam.

6   On R1222 distributors disconnect the vacuum advance piston from the base plate by removing the small circlip from the fixing stud and lifting off. Unscrew the two fixing screws from outside the casing and pull the mechanism out through and away.

7   Remove the contact point baseplate by removing totally the two distributor cap clip fixing setscrews through the side of the distributor body and the condenser/contact spring fixing point. Pull upwards the contact point baseplate and remove.

8   Remove the shaft circlip and washers at the bottom end of the distributor by 'peeling' it off with a penknife.

9   Pull up through the body of the distributor the shaft with the automatic advance mechanism still intact.

10 Remove the advance mechanism springs gently. Do not twist or distort them.

11 Reassembly of the distributor is a reversal of the dismantling process. Do not stretch the centrifugal springs. Smear the

contact breaker baseplate with a thin film of oil or grease between it and the moving plate.

8   Ignition timing

1   It is necessary to time the ignition when it has been upset due to overhauling or dismantling which may have altered the relationship between the position of the pistons and the moment at which the distributor delivers the spark. Also, if maladjustments have affected the engine performance it is very desirable, although not always essential, to reset the timing starting from scratch. In the following procedures it is assumed that the intention is to obtain standard performance from the standard engine which is in reasonable condition. It is also assumed that the recommended fuel octane rating is used. It is possible today to have an engine checked on special equipment designed to indicate where different faults may be. These instruments are excellent for indicating what may be wrong with your engine in a variety of areas. They do not, however, compute the full combination of settings needed to get the best possible performance from your particular engine as it is. The final check for ignition timing depends solely on the performance of the car on the road in all the variety of conditions that it meets.

2   The static or datum timing is getting the spark to arrive at a particular position of the crankshaft. (See Section 1). Most manufacturers stick to the convention of using No 1 cylinder for this adjustment and the Renault is no exception. The flywheel visible between and below the water pump and the radiator (R1221) and water pump and gearchange (R1222) has a notch marked on its outer circumference. A pointer is fitted on the cylinder block, just beneath the heater pipe, pointing down on to this outer edge of the flywheel. If the engine is turned, TDC on No 1 piston will be achieved when the pointer is the correct distance from the mark on the flywheel. See specifications for the correct distance according to engine type. Do this and then look at the distributor cap and see at which position the HT lead from No 1 spark plug connects. Then remove the cap and see whether the top of the rotor arm is facing the No 1 plug contact. If it is, good! If not then the engine must be turned another complete revolution to the TDC mark again. The rotor arm should then be in the correct positon. Should the rotor arm still be way out, check whether the distributor body can be rotated enough to compensate by slackening the clamp and trying it. It may be possible, with alterations to plug lead lengths.

3   Now the engine should be set at the correct static advance position.

4   As discussed in the opening section the spark is produced when the contact points in the LT circuit open. It is now necessary to slacken the distributor clamping screw so that the body of the distributor may be turned (whilst the rotor spindle stays still). The distributor should now be turned slightly, one way or the other, so that the contact points are fully open on the cam. The contact gap **must** be set correctly. As it is difficult to see exactly when the points are just closed a means of doing this electrically is necessary. Use a continuity tester or 12 volt bulb and a jumper lead. If the latter is used, put one lead to the terminal where the coil LT lead joins the distributor and the other to a good earth on the engine block. With the ignition switched on the bulb will now light. Turn the body of the distributor anticlockwise until the light just goes out. Then, lightly holding the rotor arm with clockwise pressure, turn the body clockwise again until the light just comes on again. Then tighten the clamping screw. If desired the correctness of the setting can be checked with a stroboscopic timing light but such a device is not essential for accurate setting of the static timing.

5   The performance of the engine should now be checked by road testing. Make any adjustments by loosening the clamp screw and moving the distributor body very slightly to the right (anticlockwise) to advance it. Lock it again and retest. If the performance is worse repeat the procedure but turn to the left (clockwise) to retard. After a little time going one way or the

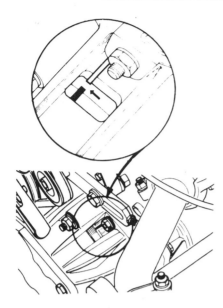

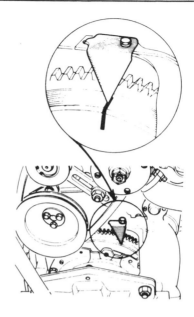

Fig. 4.5 The R1222 static ignition timing marks. The inset enlarges the pointer marks (Sec. 5)

Fig. 4.6 The R1221 static ignition timing marks. The inset enlarges the pointer marks (Sec. 8)

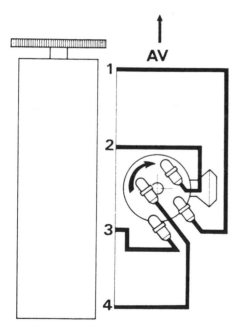

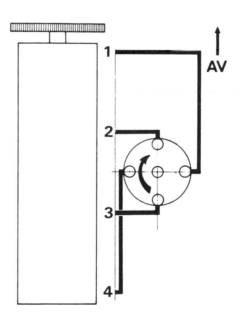

Fig. 4.7. The R1222 firing order and distributor rotor rotation. 'AV' indicates the front of the engine (flywheel end)

Fig. 4.8. The R1221 firing order and distributor rotor rotation. 'AV' indicates the front of the engine (flywheel end)

other, in very small progression, the 'optimum' timing will result.

6   Should the owner wish, he may check the centrifugal advance characteristics of the distributor. For this he will need to employ an accurate tachometer and a stroboscopic timing light. If the distributor was seriously wrong then the performance of the car would be noticeably affected. Should the distributor be suspected of malfunction in this respect it would be best to get it tested on the specialised equipment available at some garages, or simply fit a new one. Often the cost of thorough checking (which involves removing the distributor if it is to be done very precisely) is not far short of the cost of a new unit.

9   Spark plugs and HT leads - general

1   With the development of modern technology and materials, spark plugs are generally very reliable and require minimal attention. When they are due for checking and cleaning it is good practice to have them thoroughly sand blasted, gapped and checked under pressure on the machine that most garages have installed. They can also be used as good indications of engine condition, particularly as regards the fuel mixture being used and the state of the pistons and cylinder bores. Check each plug as it

is possible that one cylinder condition is different from the rest. Plugs come in different types to suit the particular type of engine. A 'hot' plug is for engines which run at lower temperatures than normal and a 'cold' plug is for the hotter running engines. If plugs of the wrong rating are fitted they can either damage the engine or fail to operate properly. Under normal running conditions a correctly rated plug in a properly tuned engine will have a light deposit of brownish colour on the electrodes. A dry black sooty deposit indicates an over-rich fuel mixture. An oily blackish deposit indicates worn bores or valve guides. A dry hard whitish deposit indicates too weak a fuel mixture. If plugs of the wrong heat ranges are fitted they will have similar symptoms to a weak mixture together with burnt electrodes (plug too hot) or to an over-rich mixture caked somewhat thicker (plug too cold). Do not try and economise by using plugs beyond 9000 miles. Unless the engine remains in exceptionally good tune, reductions in performance and fuel economy will outweight the cost of a new set.

2 The HT leads and their connections at both ends should always be clean and dry and, as far as possible, neatly arranged away from each other and nearby metallic parts which could cause premature shorting in weak insulation. The metal connections at the ends should be a firm and secure fit and free from any signs of corrosive deposits. If any lead shows signs of cracking or chafing of the insulation it should be renewed. Remember that radio interference suppression is required when renewing any leads. **Note:** It is advisable when removing spark plugs from this engine to use a fully cranked 'short' spark plug remover. Be especially careful when refitting plugs to do so without force and screw them up as far as possible by hand first. Do not overtighten. The aluminium head does not take kindly to thread crossing and extra force. The proprietary non-cranked plug caps should always be used to ease fitting and to ensure against HT lead shorting. (photo)

10 Coil - general

1 The coil needs an equal amount of attention to the rest of the ignition system. Testing the coil is dealt with in Section 12.
2 The coil is easily removed by loosening the right-hand mounting stud nut, then the left-hand one. It can then be swung in a clockwise direction on the right-hand stud and lifted upwards. Its actual mounting plate can remain on the cylinder block for R1221. The coil for the R1222 is mounted on the offside inner ring and is more easily accessible. Make sure you have a replacement coil of the correct connector type.

11 Ignition/starter switch - general

1 All vehicles are fitted with a switch which is incorporated in the steering column lock. In both cases the switch is in a similar position and can be replaced without removing the locking device.
2 Disconnect the battery, before attempting anything. Before removing to replace check that it is not functioning properly and that there is not a fault either in the starter motor or in the ignition light.
3 Remove the bottom protective panel under the steering column. See Chapter 11.
4 Disconnect the electrical junction box below the switch and unscrew its securing screws.
5 Press on the retaining ring with a screwdriver and push up from behind the switch.
6 Once the total unit is released the switch key is easily removed from the body. Two screws connect it and it slides towards the rear once these are released.
7 Reassembly is a straight reverse sequence. Do not play with these switches for they are very expensive.

9.2 Cross threads are easily started in an aluminium cylinder head; go carefully and use a proper plug spanner. Do not overtighten

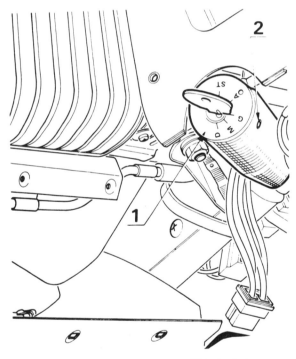

Fig. 4.11 The ignition/starter switch. '2' is the fixing screw, '1' is the retaining catch (Sec. 11)

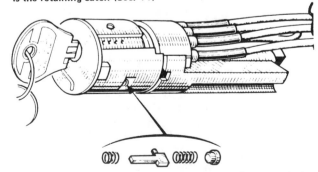

Fig. 4.12 The locking tumbler from the ignition/starter switch (Sec. 11)

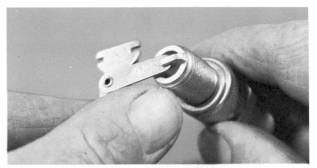

Measuring plug gap. A feeler gauge of the correct size (see ignition system specifications) should have a slight 'drag' when slid between the electrodes. Adjust gap if necessary

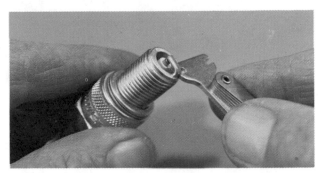

Adjusting plug gap. The plug gap is adjusted by bending the earth electrode inwards, or outwards, as necessary until the correct clearance is obtained. Note the use of the correct tool

Normal. Grey-brown deposits lightly coated core nose. Gap increasing by around 0.001 in (0.025 mm) per 1000 miles (1600 km). Plugs ideally suited to engine and engine in good condition

Carbon fouling. Dry, black, sooty deposits. Will cause weak spark and eventually misfire. Fault: over-rich fuel mixture. Check: carburettor mixture settings, float level and jet sizes; choke operation and cleanliness of air filter. Plugs can be re-used after cleaning

Oil fouling. Wet, oily deposits. Will cause weak spark and eventually misfire. Fault: worn bores/piston rings or valve guides; sometimes occurs (temporarily) during running-in period. Plugs can be re-used after thorough cleaning

Overheating. Electrodes have glazed appearance, core nose very white - few deposits. Fault: plug overheating. Check: plug value, ignition timing, fuel octane rating (too low) and fuel mixture (too weak). Discard plugs and cure fault immediately

Electrode damage. Electrodes burned away; core nose has burned, glazed appearance. Fault: initial pre-ignition. Check: as for 'Overheating' but may be more severe. Discard plugs and remedy fault before piston or valve damage occurs

Split core nose (may appear initially as a crack). Damage is self-evident, but cracks will only show after cleaning. Fault: pre-ignition or wrong gap-setting technique. Check: ignition timing, cooling system, fuel octane rating (too low) and fuel mixture (too weak). Discard plugs, rectify fault immediately

12 Ignition faults - symptoms, reason and remedies

Engine troubles normally associated with, and usually caused by, faults in the ignition system are:

a) *Failure to start when the engine is turned.*
b) *Uneven running due to misfiring or mistiming.*
c) *Smooth running at low engine revolutions but misfiring when under load or accelerating or at high contact revolutions.*
d) *Smooth running at high revolutions and misfiring or cutting-out at low speeds.*

a) First check that all wires are properly connected and dry. If the engine fails to catch when the starter is operated do not continue for more than 5 or 6 short burst attempts or the battery will start to get tired and the pistons made worse. Remove the spark plug lead from a plug and turn the engine again holding the lead (by the insulation) about ¼ inch from the side of the engine block. A spark should jump the gap audibly and visibly, if it does then the plugs are at fault or the static timing is very seriously adrift. If both are good, however, then there must be a fuel supply fault, so go on to that.

If no spark is obtained at the end of a plug lead detach the coil HT lead from the centre of the distributor cap and hold that near the block to try and find a spark. If you now get one, then there is something wrong between the centre terminal of the distributor cap and the end of the plug lead. Check the cap itself for damage or damp, the 4 terminal lugs for signs of corrosion, the centre carbon brush in the top (is it jammed?) and the rotor arm.

If no spark comes from the coil HT lead check next that the contact breaker points are clean and that the gap is correct. A quick check can be made by turning the engine so that the points are closed. Then switch on the igniton and open the visible spark and, once again, if the coil HT lead is held near the block at the same time proper HT spark should occur. If there is

a big fat spark at the points but none at the HT lead then the condenser is done for and should be renewed.

If neither of these things happen then the next step in this tale of woe is to see if there is any current (12 volts) reaching the coil (+ terminal). (One could check this at the distributor, but by going back to the input side of the coil a longer length of possible fault line is bracketed and could save time).

With a 12 v bulb and piece of wire suitably connected (or of course a voltmeter if you have one handy) connect between the + or SW terminal of the coil and earth and switch on the ignition. No light means no volts so the fault is between the battery and the coil via the ignition switch. This is moving out of the realms of just ignition problems - the electrical system is becoming involved in general. So to get home to bed get a piece of wire and connect the + terminal of the coil to the + terminal on the battery and see if sparks occur at the HT leads once more.

If there is current reaching the coil then the coil itself or the wire from its - terminal to the distributor is at fault. Check the - or CB terminal with a bulb with the ignition switched on. If it fails to light then the coil is faulty in its LT windings and needs renewal.

b) Uneven running and misfiring should first be checked by seeing that all leads, particularly HT, are dry and connected properly. See that they are not shorting to earth through broken or cracked insulation. If they are, you should be able to see and hear it. If not, then check the plugs, contact points and condenser just as you would in a case of total failure to start.

c) If misfiring occurs at high speed check the points gap, which may be too small, and the plugs in that order. Check also that the spring tension on the points is not too light this causing them to bounce. This requires a special pull balance so if in doubt it will be cheaper to buy a new set of contacts rather than go to a garage and get them to check it. If the trouble is still not cured then the fault lies in the carburation or engine itself.

d) If misfiring or stalling occurs only at low speeds the points gap is possibly too big. If not, then the slow running adjustment on the carburettor needs attention.

Chapter 5 Clutch

Contents

Specifications

Clutch		R1222	R1221
Type and designation		Diaphragm spring, single plate	
		160 DBR 260	160 DBIR 215
Operation		Cable	
Plate diameter		160.02 mm (6.3 in)	
Disc thickness		7 4 mm (0.291 in)	
Thrust bearing		Ball bearing sealed unit	
Adjustment		End of release fork	
		3 to 4 mm (1/8 to 5/32 in)	

Torque wrench settings		lb f ft	kg f m
Cover to flywheel (R1222)		40	5.53
Cover to flywheel (R1221)		30	4.14

1 General description

The clutch is a cable operated single dry plate diaphragm type.

The clutch pedal pivots on the same shaft as the brake pedal (see Chapter 9) and operates a cable to the clutch release arm. The release arm activates a thrust bearing (clutch release bearing) which bears on the diaphragm spring of the pressure plate. The diaphragm then released or engages the clutch driven plate which is splined onto the gearbox primary shaft. The clutch driven plate (disc) spins in between the clutch cover and the flywheel face when it is released, and is held there when engaged, to connect the drive from the engine to the transmission unit.

As wear takes place on the driven plate the clearance between the clutch release bearing and the diaphragm increases. This wear is compensated for, up to the point where the driven plate is worn out, by altering the length of the clutch cable. This adjustment takes place next to the release arm with an adjuster nut on the cable.

There is only one fundamental difference in operation between the R1222 and R1221, although few parts are interchangeable. The clutch release arm of the R1221 pivots on the face plate of the transmission unit whilst the R1222 pivots on a rod pressed through the bellhousing of the transmission unit. Otherwise all operations are similar.

2 Clutch cable - removal and replacement

1 The clutch cable travels directly from the end of the clutch pedal to the clutch operating lever. It is very easy to replace. There have been several types of clutch cable fitted from various manufacturers and various types of lever at the release mechanism. It also matters whether the car is left or right-hand drive. No cables are interchangeable, it is therefore important that you are certain of the type when ordering a replacement. Generally, cables only need replacing when they have broken. They require no maintenance themselves.

2 To replace a cable first slacken off the clutch release lever completely. See the next Section.

3 Depress the clutch pedal inside the car by hand and release that end of the cable. It may be attached to the top of a quadrant or bolted by a U piece to the pedal.

4 From under the bonnet, release the other end of the cable from the rod mechanism. The R1221 threads through the lever arm; the R1222 passes through a ferrule which is slotted into a double drilling.

5 Pull out the outer cable from its fixing in the bulkhead, the other side of the end of the clutch pedal. It is a push-in fit using a special alloy split splined collar to locate the outer cable.

6 Check also at this stage, with the cable removed, the swivel mechanism through which the cable moves. It should not be sloppy.

7 Replacement is an exact reversal of its removal. Adjust the release bearing clearance as described in Section 3.

3 Clutch - adjustment

1 Clutch adjustment to compensate for its free play is taken up at the rod connecting the clutch cable to the release bearing arm. Undo the locknut on its end and tighten the inner nut until the correct clearance is made. Retighten the locknut and tighten the two together. There is no compensatory adjustment of the clutch cable outer. The R1221 and R1222 use similar adjusting

12

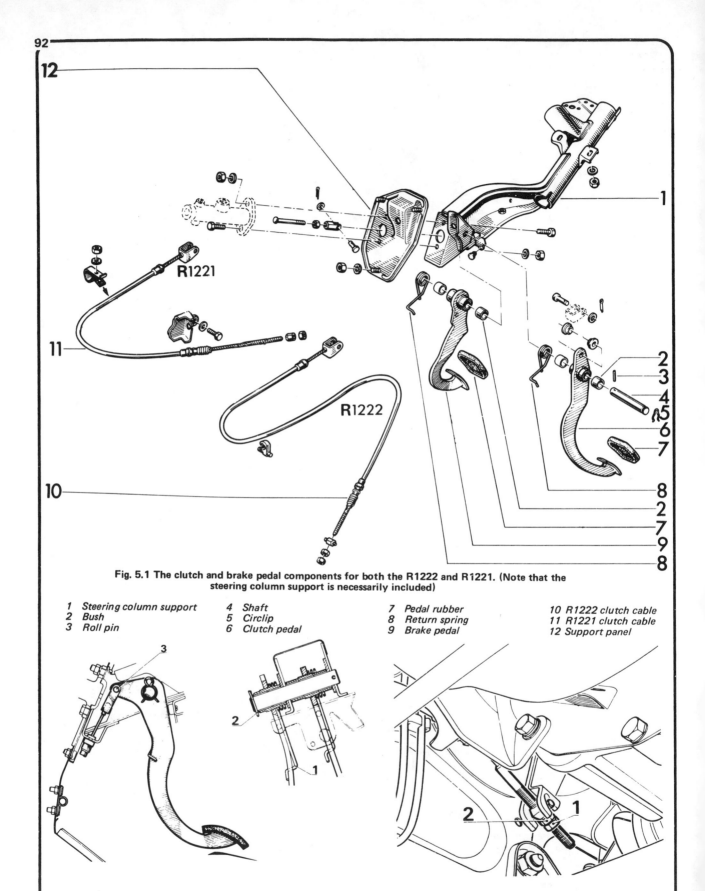

R1221

R1222

11

10

1

2
3
4
5
6
7

8
2
7
9
8

Fig. 5.1 The clutch and brake pedal components for both the R1222 and R1221. (Note that the steering column support is necessarily included)

1 Steering column support	4 Shaft	7 Pedal rubber	10 R1222 clutch cable
2 Bush	5 Circlip	8 Return spring	11 R1221 clutch cable
3 Roll pin	6 Clutch pedal	9 Brake pedal	12 Support panel

3

2

1

2   1

Fig. 5.2 The clutch cable fixing and pedal fixing at the pedal. '1' is the return spring, '2' is the pivot shaft locating clip and '3' is the ferrule locating the cable to the pedal (Sec. 2)

Fig. 5.3 The cable fixing at the clutch release end. '1' is the locknut, whilst '2' is the adjuster (Secs. 2 and 3)

methods.

2   The correct adjustment is measured at the end of the release lever and must be 3 to 4 mm (1/8 to 5/32 in). It is felt when pressing the release arm in a releasing motion onto the clutch. It must be between the point of full release and just touching the clutch plate.

4   Clutch - removal

1   If it is necessary to renew the friction plate or examine the clutch in any way it will first of all be necessary to remove the gearbox (see Chapter 6) in order to get at it. If the engine has been removed then the clutch is, of course, accessible. Once the gearbox is removed or the engine taken out the succeeding operations are the same although work is easier with the engine out when no pit or ramp is available. If the engine and gearbox have been removed from the car together they will have to be separated or course.

2   Before removing the clutch cover bolts mark the position of the cover in relation to the flywheel so that it may be put back the same way.

3   Slacken off the cover retaining bolts ½ a turn at a time in a diagonal fashion evenly so as to relieve the diaphragm spring pressure without distorting it.

4   When the bolts are removed the friction plate inside will be released. The cover will then come away easily. The friction plate will fall down from the flywheel face.

5   Clutch - inspection and renovation

1   The clutch driven plate should be inspected for wear and for contamination by oil. Wear is gauged by the depth of the rivet heads below the surface of the friction material. If this is less than 0.025 inch (0.6 mm) the linings are worn enough to justify renewal.

Examine the friction faces of the flywheel and clutch pressure plate. These should be bright and smooth. If the linings have worn too much it is possible that the metal surfaces may have been scored by the rivet heads. Dust and grit can have the same effect. If the scoring is very severe it could mean that even with a new clutch driven plate, slip and juddering and other malfunctions will recur. Deep scoring on the flywheel face is serious because the flywheel will have to be removed and machined by a specialist, or renewed. This can be costly. The same applies to the pressure plate in the cover although this is a less costly affair. If the friction linings seem unworn yet are blackened and shiny then the cause is almost certainly due to oil. Such a condition also requires renewal of the plate. The source of oil must be traced also. It will be due to a leaking seal on the transmission input shaft (Chapter 6 gives details of renewal) or on the front of the engine crankshaft (see Chapter 1 for details of renewal).

2   If the reason for removal of the clutch has been because of slip and the slip has been allowed to go on for any length of time it is possible that the head generated will have adversely affected the pressure springs in the cover. Some or all may have been affected with the result that the pressure is now uneven and/or insufficient to prevent slip, even with a new friction plate. It is recommended that under such circumstances a new assembly is fitted.

3   Although it is possible to dismantled the clutch cover assembly and, in theory, renew the various springs and levers the economics do not justify it. Clutch cover assemblies are available on an exchange basis. It will probably be necessary to order an assembly in advance as most agencies other than the large distributors carry stocks only sufficient to meet their own requirements. However, it is possible to get assemblies from reputable manufacturers other than Renault; Borg and Beck for

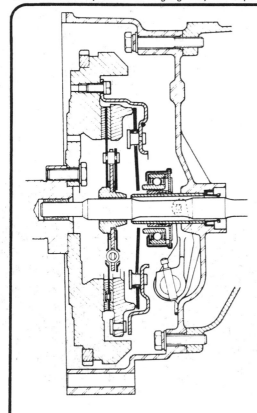

Fig. 5.4 Cross-section of the R1222 clutch and release bearing

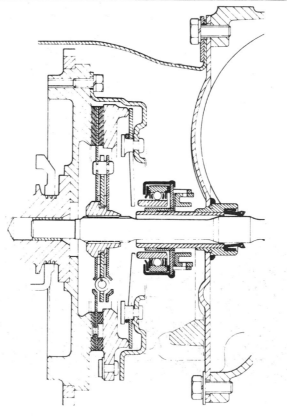

Fig. 5.5 Cross-section of the R1221 clutch and release bearing

instance. Be absolutely sure as to what you are ordering for many types of clutch have been fitted.

6 Clutch - replacement

1 If the original cover is being re-used line up the marks made before removal, and support the friction plate on one finger between cover and flywheel so that the offset side of the driven plate, on the side of the boss with the largest diameter, faces the flywheel. (photo)

2 Locate the cover on the flywheel and then place all the cover bolts in position and screw them up lightly by hand.

3 It is necessary to line up the centre of the friction disc with the exact centre of the flywheel. This is easily done if a piece of shouldered bar can be placed in the counter bore at the flywheel centre with the larger diameter supporting the friction disc. If you do not have such a thing, the disc may be lined up by eye if the engine is out of the car. If this is not done, great difficulty (and possible damage to the gearbox input shaft) may be experienced when the time comes to refit the gearbox to the engine. (photo)

4 With the friction plate centralised the cover bolts should be tightened diagonally, evenly and progressively. Be careful with the diaphragm type so as not to distort it or strip threads in the flywheel. It is a good idea to replace the fixing bolts with new each time a new clutch is fitted. Remove the centralising tool. Before refitting the gearbox to the engine do not forget to check the clutch release bearing and operating mechanism.

7 Clutch operation rod/fork and release bearing (R1222) - dismantling, inspection and reassembly

1 Full examination is only possible when the gearbox is removed and is normally undertaken when the clutch is in need of repair. The mechanism is carried in and attached to the transmission casing/bellhousing. Check the bearing itself. The guided ball type should be shiny, and smooth running without any looseness in its revolutions. The retaining spring clips at each side must be a tight fit so that the bearing does not rattle about on its mounting.

2 To inspect the lever fork it is necessary to remove the release bearing by unclipping the holding spring clips and sliding the bearing off the input shaft. Little should go wrong with the lever fork. Renault require a special tool (Emb. 384) to withdraw the fork retaining pins, however it should be possible to use a tubular extractor to pull them out.

3 Do not clean any parts with any cleaning fluid for it will spoil

the release bearing. If in doubt replace the bearing; it is safer and less trouble in the long run.

4 Replacement is a straight reversal of its removal of all components here. To lubricate the lever bearing surfaces and the release bearing faces use a little molybdenum paste - never grease or oil. Replacing the fork retaining pins is critical. Always use a new rubber seal and then tap the new pins into place. See Fig. 5.8 and leave the shanks protruding 1 mm.

5 Re-adjust the pedal free play once the gearbox is re-installed.

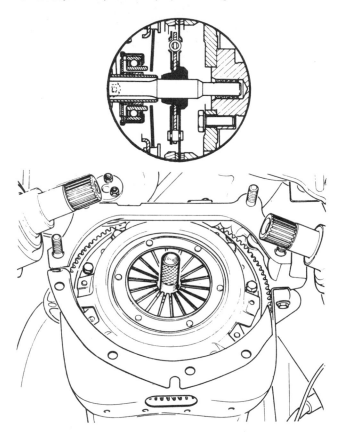

Fig. 5.6 Centring the clutch plate. Here the proper tool is shown; any suitable 'dowel' can be used (Sec. 6)

6.1 The clutch is one of the most simple components but one which is often not understood

6.3 Here the gearbox shaft is being used to centre the driven plate

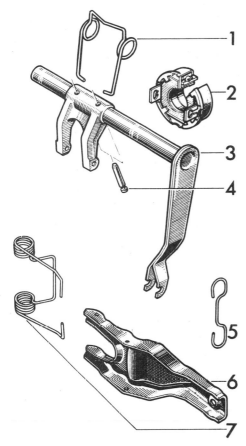

8 Clutch operation lever and release bearing (R1221) dismantling, inspection and reassembly

1 When the clutch pedal is depressed the cable actuates the lever which pivots on the gearbox face and forces a ball release bearing against the steel boss at the centre of the releasing mechanism of the clutch cover. The ball bearing release bearing is unlikely to wear but it may become dry and fail. It is often very noisy, and should be replaced if it runs out of true.

2 To renew the release bearing the clutch bellhousing/gearbox must be separated from the engine. The bearing is held to the actuating arm by two spring steel clips which, when released, allow it to be drawn off over the gearbox input shaft. Replacement is a reversal of the removal procedure. Should the release arm require removal the pivot pin clip holding it in position may be released by unhooking the wire holding spring. With the release arm removed check its own bearing surface and replace if very worn. Check also the face of the gearbox at this position and replace under extreme circumstances. Once again check that you are using the correct replacement part. This cannot be overstressed.

Fig. 5.7. The clutch release arms. Whilst the R1222 (top) and R1221 (bottom) release arms differ, the release bearing is the same for both

1 Return spring
2 Release bearing
3 R1222 clutch shift
4 Pin
5 Retention clip
6 R1221 clutch shift
7 Return spring

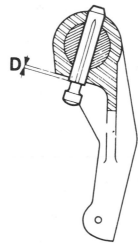

Fig. 5.8 Clutch fork pin position (R1222). 'D' = 1 mm (1/32 in.) (Sec. 7)

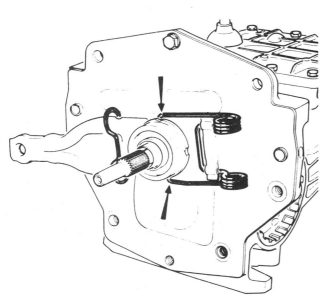

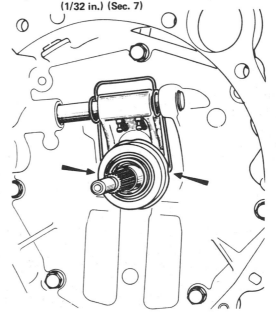

Fig. 5.9 The release bearing return spring fixings; R1221 (left); R1222 (right) (Secs 7 and 8)

9 Fault diagnosis - clutch

Symptom	Reason/s	Remedy
Judder when taking up drive	Loose engine/gearbox mountings or over-flexible mountings	Check and tighten all mounting bolts and replace any 'soft' or broken mountings
	Badly worn friction surfaces or friction plate contamination with oil carbon deposit	Remove engine and replace clutch parts as required. Rectify any oil leakage points which may have caused contamination
	Worn splines in the friction plate hub or on the gearbox input shaft	Renew friction plate and/or input shaft
Clutch spin (or failure to disengage) so that gears cannot be meshed	Clutch actuating cable clearance too great	Adjust clearance
	Clutch friction disc sticking because of rust on splines (usually apparent after standing idle for some length of time)	As temporary remedy engage top gear, apply handbrake, depress clutch and start engine (If very badly stuck engine will not turn) When running rev up engine and slip clutch until disengagement is normally possible Renew friction plate at earliest opportunity
	Damaged or misaligned pressure plate assembly	Replace pressure plate assembly
	Incorrect release bearing fitted	Replace with correct part
Clutch slip - (increase in engine speed does not result in increase in car speed-especially on hills)	Clutch actuating cable clearance from fork too small resulting in partially disengaged clutch at all times	Adjust clearance
	Clutch friction surfaces worn out (beyond further adjustment of operating cable) or clutch surfaces oil soaked	Replace friction plate and remedy source of oil leakage

Chapter 6 Gearbox

Contents

Specifications

Gearbox - general

	R1222	R1221
Renault type number	354—15 (dash change) 354—21 (floor change)	354—14
Number of gears	4 forward, 1 reverse	
Synchromesh	All forward gears	
Forward gears	Helical cut gears	
Reverse gear	Straight cut	
Oil capacity	3 Imp pints (1.8 litres)	
Oil grade	EP80W	
Ratios:		
1st	3.67	
2nd	2.24	
3rd	1.46	
4th	1.03	
Reverse	3.23	

Differential - general

Type ... ... Integral with gearbox, consisting of 2 sun wheels and 2 planet wheels. (As the R1222 and R1221 engines revolve in different directions the differential crownwheels are mounted on opposite sides in each gearbox fitment)

Ratio ... ... 33 x 18 (4.125 to 1)
Road speed at 1000 rev/min in top gear ... ... 14.6 mph
Casing ... ... One piece

1 General description

Upon the introduction of the Renault 5 the transmission unit fitted was that used in the late model Renault 6. It is a four speed gearbox and has a conventional shifts pattern (all forward speed in an 'H') and a one piece casing.

Because the R1222 and R1221 engines revolve in different directions, the transmission units have their crownwheel and pinions on opposing sides in the casing, the final drive, of course, being within the same casting.

The primary shaft transmits motion via four forward gears to the secondary or pinion shaft on which is the main gear cluster and synchromesh. The reverse gear is on a third shaft fixed to the gear casing. Motion is then transmitted when a gear is engaged, by the pinion gear on the end of the pinion shaft to the crownwheel and then to the driveshafts. Gear selector forks are mounted in the top of the casing and are operated by a to-and-fro and sideways motion of the gear lever bolted to the top. These forks select gears on the primary shaft which then mesh with the appropriate gear on the pinion shaft.

Various gear ratios have been used. The speedometer is gearbox driven. Although relatively simple transmission units there are nevertheless a few words of warning which must be seated before any potential dismantlers start work, to let them know what they are letting themselves in for.

First of all decide whether the fault you wish to repair is worth all the time and effort involved. Secondly, if the transmission unit is in a very bad state then the cost of the necessary component parts may well exceed the cost of an exchange factory unit. Thirdly, be absolutely sure that you understand how the transmission unit works.

Returning to the second point just mentioned, it is possible to dismantle the unit with tools from a normal tool kit but only so far. Fortunately this is the point, if further dismantling is decided to be necessary, to check whether an exchange unit would be a cheaper method of repair. Renault cannot supply individual component parts, rather parts assembled into units, past this point.

Check very carefully the availability and cost of transmission unit parts before dismantling.

2 Transmission unit (R1222) - removal and replacement

1   The transmission unit can be removed either with the engine, see Chapter 1, or by itself leaving the engine in the vehicle. If only wishing to work on the gearbox or clutch rather than the engine as well, it is a simple task to remove the transmission alone. This unit alone is reasonably light and compact.

2   Place the car on level ground and apply the handbrake.

3   Now follow the sequence in Chapter 1 from Section 5, paragraph 3 to 7, inclusive, paragraphs 9, 10, 11, 12, 13, 14, 23, 24, 25, 26, 27, 28, 29, 30, 31, 32, 33, 34, 37, 38, 39, 40, and then place a support under the gearbox casing and follow paragraph 43 with the support taking the weight.

4   Carefully pull out the driveshafts from each side of the differential housing. Watch for the seals on the housing. They should pull out now that the suspension is disconnected. Tie them back and up out of the way.

5   Now obtain a further support and place it carefully under the engine, just behind the gearbox.

6   The car should now be supported itself, as should the engine and the gearbox, still. If possible slightly lower the gearbox support, so that it tips forward just a litle.

7   Remove the bolts which attach the engine block to the transmission unit.

8   If possible have an assistant to help you at this point. From the front of the vehicle get him to hold onto the transmission unit with both hands taking some of the weight of the unit from the gearbox support. This will give the required support to the unit when the nuts are removed which connect the unit to the engine block. Once these are removed it will be possible to wriggle the unit down and out, with help from the gearbox support and the assistant. Do not allow the engine to be supported on the primary shaft of the gearbox at any stage. It is a tight fit. One person can easily carry the transmission unit even if bending right down.

9   Replacement of the transmission unit to the engine and then back into the vehicle is a direct reversal of the removal sequence but an extra special watch must be kept on the primary shaft not being placed under strain. See Chapter 7, for driveshaft reconnection.

10 Refill the gearbox with the correct grade of oil before running the vehicle. It helps in all cases to place the car in reverse gear before filling so to allow a better oil flow in. It is possible, of course, to fill the gearbox when out of the vehicle.

Special note: It may seem unnecessary to remove the radiator and alternator to remove the gearbox by itself. It is done simply to aid the otherwise cramped working conditions.

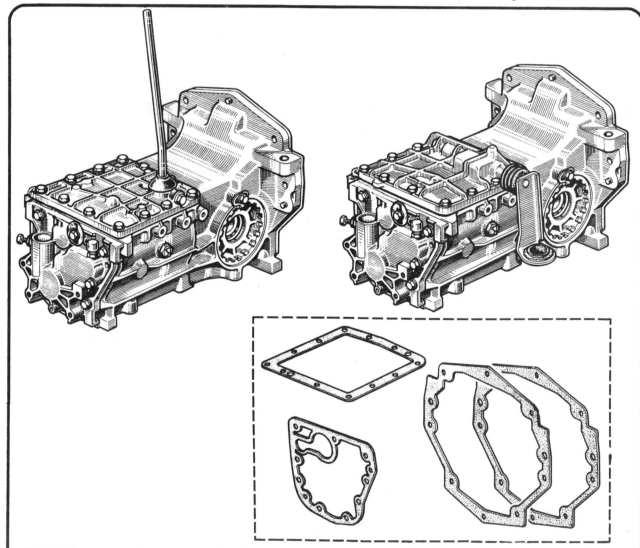

Fig. 6.1 The two types of gearbox fitted: (left) standard dash board change type; (right) floor change model. A gasket set is also shown

3 Transmission unit (R1221) - removal and replacement

1 The removal and replacement of the gearbox by itself from the R1221 is a very similar operation to that described for the 1222 model. There are several differences in actual components but all those removed to facilitate gearbox removal (as described in Section 2), are also removed. It is essential, however, to remove the radiator and its forward support brace.

2 The gearbox is, of course, attached to the sump and engine block and there will also be a bracing bar.

4 Transmission unit - dismantling

1 Before proceeding according to the directions given in this Section read the 'General description' Section first. It is assumed that the unit is out of the vehicle and on the bench. (It is not advisable to dismantle it on the floor. It will do the kitchen table no harm as it is not heavy). Do not throw away gaskets when dismantling for they will act as a guide for the fitment of the new ones supplied in the gasket set which should have already been purchased. Always renew all gaskets, locking washers and roll pins. Clean the outside casing thoroughly, all the nooks and crannies, and allow to dry. Start work with clean hands and a plentiful supply of clean rag. A set of metric Allen keys will be necessary.

2 Remember that the type 354 used in the R1221 has no bellhousing and that the crownwheel and pinion is on the 'opposite' in the casing compared with the unit used in the R1222. Once the bellhousing has been removed from the gearbox (four setscrews) on the R1222 unit, the two types of gearbox using the 'type 354' classification are the same (photos).

3 Remove the clutch thrust bearing mechanism with the cover plate of the R1221 version. See Chapter 5.

4 Mark the position of the differential adjusting ring nuts relative to the casing. Use a pin punch to dot mark them. Undo the locking tab nut and remove. Now tap gently each ring nut round using a screwdriver and hammer. Count the number of turns the ring nut has to go through to remove. This will enable

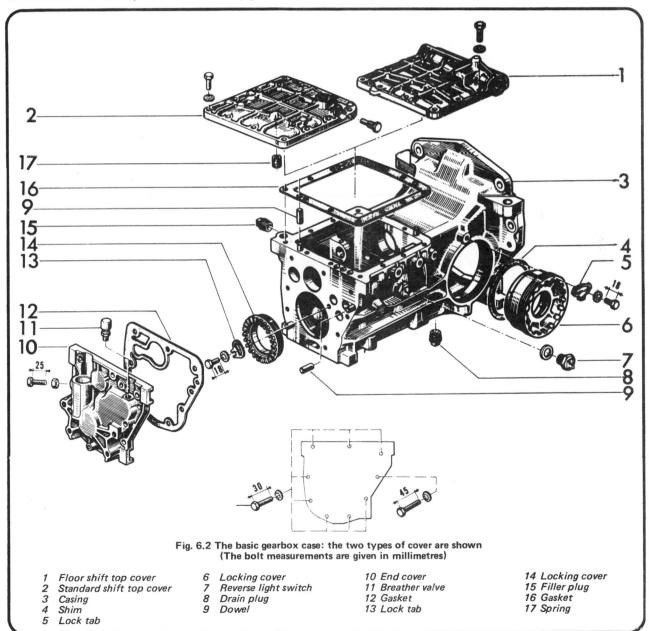

Fig. 6.2 The basic gearbox case: the two types of cover are shown
(The bolt measurements are given in millimetres)

1 Floor shift top cover	6 Locking cover	10 End cover	14 Locking cover
2 Standard shift top cover	7 Reverse light switch	11 Breather valve	15 Filler plug
3 Casing	8 Drain plug	12 Gasket	16 Gasket
4 Shim	9 Dowel	13 Lock tab	17 Spring
5 Lock tab			

exact repositioning upon reassembly (photos).

5 To free the primary/on clutch shaft and thereby the differential pull out the roll pin, with a pair of strong grips, which locks the two halves of the primary shaft together. Withdraw the shaft. This will now allow the differential to come out of the end of the casing (clutch end) (photos).

6 Now remove the top cover. Retain the washers and setscrews. Undo all screws progressively (photo).

7 When the cover is removed three springs will appear on the casing edge. Remove these. A small plunger (1st/2nd gear) will be on top of one of these. A small selector shaft locking ball will be below all of these. Turn the casing upside down allowing these to drop out. Retain them (photo).

8 Remove the end cover, its setscrews and washers. Pick out the primary shaft setting shims (photos).

9 Unlock and remove the primary shaft rear bearing retaining plate (bellhousing end). It is held by two setscrews (photo).

10 Punch out (parallel pin punch) the two roll pins holding the

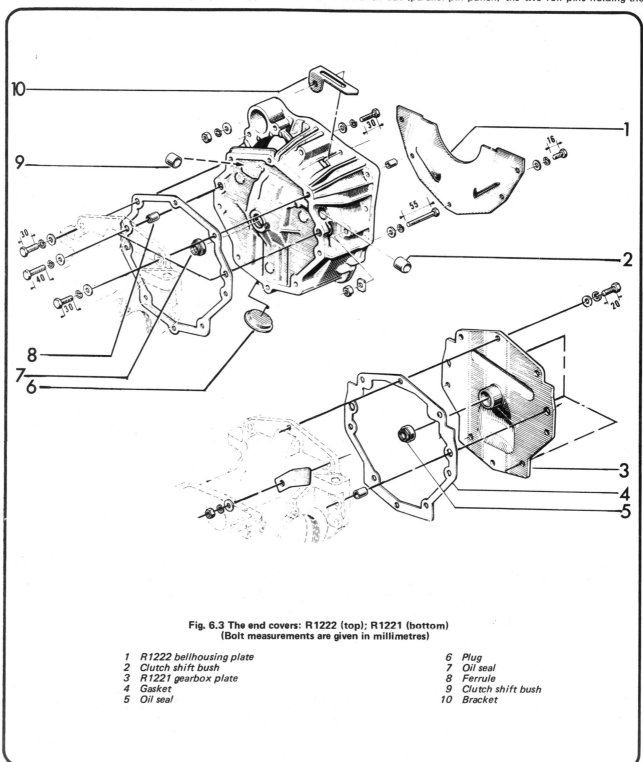

Fig. 6.3 The end covers: R1222 (top); R1221 (bottom)
(Bolt measurements are given in millimetres)

1 *R1222 bellhousing plate*
2 *Clutch shift bush*
3 *R1221 gearbox plate*
4 *Gasket*
5 *Oil seal*

6 *Plug*
7 *Oil seal*
8 *Ferrule*
9 *Clutch shift bush*
10 *Bracket*

4.2a On the R1222 it is essential to remove the bellhousing before any other work can take place

4.2b Ease the bellhousing away to save the oil seal

4.4a Note the two punch marks to the right of the spanner head; now count the number of turns

4.4b Another successful method of loosening this ring

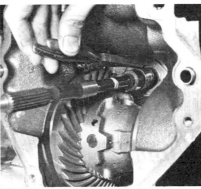

4.5a A tricky job but with patience not too difficult

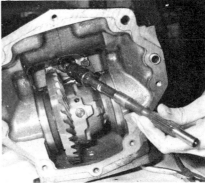

4.5b It is necessary to pull out the shaft before the differential can be removed

4.5c Note the 'way round' of the differential

4.6 Watch the detent springs when the top cover comes away

4.7 Record the location of each spring

4.8a Never lever the cover off; if stiff, a slight tap sideways should work

4.8b Record the number of shims which fall away

4.9 It is a delicate job to bend back the locking tab

reverse gear pinion shaft. Then remove the reverse gear selector shaft (photo).

11 Punch out the roll pins holding the two other gear selector shafts. Remove the 3rd/4th selector shaft and retain the locking disc which appears between the 3rd/4th and reverse gear selector shafts. Remove the 1st/2nd selector shafts. All shafts pull out through the primary end of the gear casing (photos).

12 Select two speeds by sliding two gearshafts along so that neither shaft will turn.

13 Using a very wide but thin spanner (a Calor Gas spanner will work), unlock and unscrew the speedometer drive nut from the primary end. Then release the two gears selected (photo).

14 Tap gently with a hide headed hammer the end of the final drive pinion towards the differential end. Remove the taper

roller bearing shims with the final drive pinion (photo).

15 Push the primary shaft towards the differential end so to free its rear bearing cage. Pull out its front bearing plus shims for it is a free fit (photos).

16 Pull out of the top of the casing the primary shaft. This will enable the reverse gear shaft to be pulled out of the casing, then the gear itself (photos).

17 Now lift out the 3rd/4th and 1st/2nd selector forks (photo).

18 Mark with punched dot marks the secondary shaft adjusting nut lockplate as you have the differential housing. Remove the lock tab and nut and then unscrew the adjusting nut counting the number of turns. Remove the 4th speed gear thrust washer, and the 4th gear from the end of the casing (photo).

19 Remove the rest of the gear cluster from the top of the

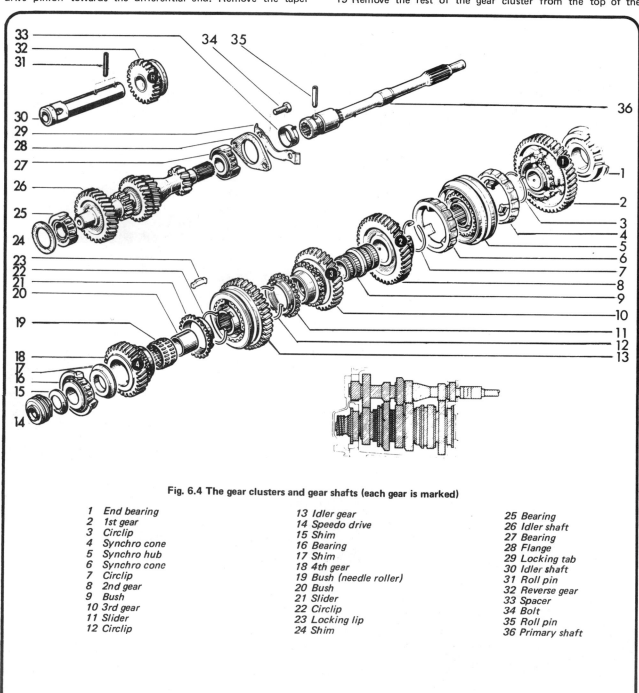

Fig. 6.4 The gear clusters and gear shafts (each gear is marked)

1 End bearing	13 Idler gear	25 Bearing
2 1st gear	14 Speedo drive	26 Idler shaft
3 Circlip	15 Shim	27 Bearing
4 Synchro cone	16 Bearing	28 Flange
5 Synchro hub	17 Shim	29 Locking tab
6 Synchro cone	18 4th gear	30 Idler shaft
7 Circlip	19 Bush (needle roller)	31 Roll pin
8 2nd gear	20 Bush	32 Reverse gear
9 Bush	21 Slider	33 Spacer
10 3rd gear	22 Circlip	34 Bolt
11 Slider	23 Locking lip	35 Roll pin
12 Circlip	24 Shim	36 Primary shaft

4.10 Gearboxes need careful handling; ease this shaft out by hand

4.11a It's best to hold the selector head when removing the shaft

4.11b Here, a nail was used to ease the locking ring out

4.11c The gearbox looks complicated but is one of the simplest made

4.13 Renault use a special tool; we used a 'Calor-Gas spanner'

4.14 The most expensive component in the gearbox; it has to be matched with the crownwheel

4.15a This bearing and shaft have to be tapped out gently

4.15b First out towards the bellhousing end and then ...

4.16a ... out through the top

4.16b Retain the reverse gearwheel when pulling out the shaft

4.17 Record how the selectors fit and remove carefully

4.18 This gear does not come out of the top of the gearbox

4.19a Remove this complete gear cluster as one unit

4.19b The final gear cluster and the gearbox should be empty

casing (photos).

20 Further dismantling is possible of both the gear clusters and the final drive as well as the gear selectors. However, it is not recommended to undertake any further dismantling to the bearings and to the final drive because of the necessity of presses to undertake the work properly. If at this stage it is found necessary to replace any bearings or the final drive you must seek the services of a Renault agent with suitable equipment. Take him the parts needing work. Read Section 5 now.

21 To replace the synchro units mark the two parts of the synchronising 1st/2nd and 3rd/4th, then separate them. This will obviously apply when replacing individual gears. Reassembly is covered in Section 8.

22 The top cover is easily dismantled if necessary. See the appropriate illustration to show the components which will enable you to disassemble them.

5 Inspection for wear of transmission components

Once decided that the transmission unit will have to be stripped down because of some minor irritant or major fault it is still not necessary to strip the unit completely. For example there is no need to remove the reverse gear cluster shaft if the synchromesh is being replaced on an otherwise properly functioning gearbox. Consequently you should go slowly once the three major components are removed from the unit because you may be doing unnecessary work. You may also have to face the fact that even when once dismantled that you will do better to reassemble the box there and then (do it properly though) and exchange it for a replacement unit from Renault. The economics of replacing large components is not always on when compared to a complete exchange unit. Remember also that exchange units are likely to be more readily available than individual component parts and that they will carry a guarantee.

Once dismantled into its three major components, the primary shaft and final drive, inspection should be detailed. Clean the inside of the unit thoroughly first with a mixture of petrol and paraffin and wipe dry.

1 Check the casting for cracks or damage, particularly near the bearing housings and on the mating surfaces.

2 Check all the gears for chips and possible cracks and replace where necessary. You should be able to tell whether this should be so from the inlet diagnosis before dismantling.

3 Check all the shafts and splines for wear and flat spots and replace if necessary. The gears through which the shafts pass should be a good slide fit and not rock about.

4 Check the synchromesh rings and assembly. All models are prone to early synchromesh failure which should really be replaced as a matter of course as it is cheap enough to do so. The springs should also be renewed.

5 Check the bearings: Primary shaft bearings are generally speaking very reliable and long lived and these are the only bearings apart from the double taper roller bearing on the pinion shaft which can be easily and economically replaced. Check them for scoring and 'wobble'. Pinion shaft bearings: The double taper roller bearing at the opposite end from the final drive is easily replaced although generally long lived. Replace it if in doubt. The pinion bearing next to the pinion wheel will have to be replaced at a cost of approximately one third of an exchange unit. If this has 'gone' and there are other necessary replacements within the transmission unit, then reassemble (properly) the gearbox and exchange the whole unit for a replacement transmission. It is not economic to do otherwise. The two outer differential bearings should be inspected in the same way. These may be replaced by the home mechanic but he may have difficulty in setting up the final drive in the casing afterwards. This was not done on the gearbox we dismantled but it is briefly explained. Again these bearings are usually reliable.

6 Any failure within the final drive unit will mean replacement of the whole unit, crownwheel assembly in total. Under certain circumstances it will mean changing the bearing and speedo drive gear. See the specifications at the start of the Chapter. We did not dismantle the crownwheel and pinion because it is not a task which can be undertaken, at least at the reassembly stage, by the home mechanic. The cost of purchasing a new crownwheel without a new pinion, madness anyway, is again approximately half that of a new exchange transmission unit. Purchasing the two together, crownwheel assembly and pinion assembly, to enable them to mesh and set-up correctly is approximately the cost of the exchange transmission and you will not get the guarantee.

7 Check that the nylon speedometer drive gearwheel is in good condition and running easily in its bush.

8 Check the selector forks for wear. Measure them with a pair of calipers and compare their ends with the thickest point; if in doubt replace. They should be only fractionally worn.

9 Check the gear shift mechanism. The tongue which also slots into the top of the selectors wears quite rapidly often resulting in non-selected gears and sloppy action.

Special Note: Such is the construction of these transmission units that they are generally speaking very reliable but often noisy. They all whine from new to some degree and this should not frighten owners. Obviously, it is not possible to detect any

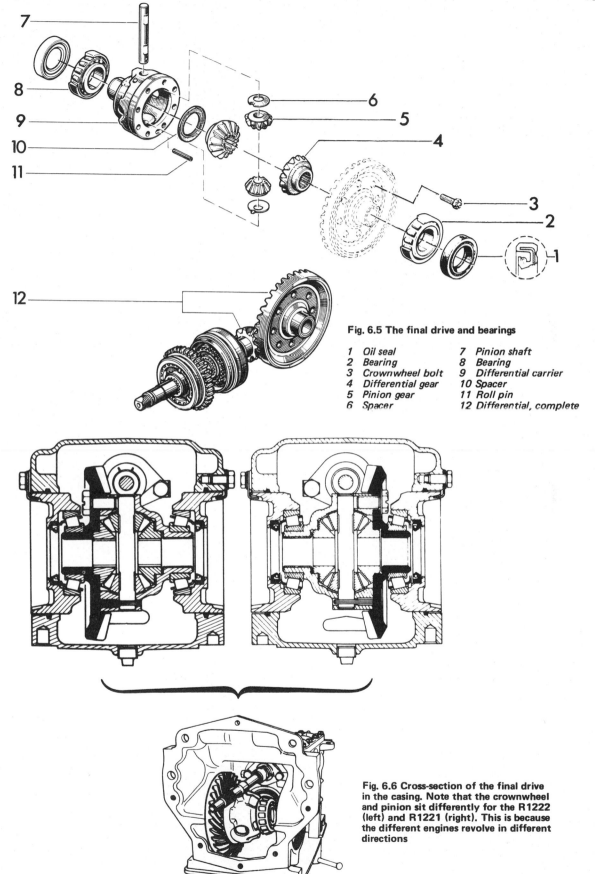

Fig. 6.5 The final drive and bearings

1 Oil seal   7 Pinion shaft
2 Bearing   8 Bearing
3 Crownwheel bolt   9 Differential carrier
4 Differential gear   10 Spacer
5 Pinion gear   11 Roll pin
6 Spacer   12 Differential, complete

Fig. 6.6 Cross-section of the final drive in the casing. Note that the crownwheel and pinion sit differently for the R1222 (left) and R1221 (right). This is because the different engines revolve in different directions

increase in whine over a period of time only to suddenly think that it is doing it more than perhaps it should. However, this is not good reason in itself to remove and disassemble the unit. The usual reason for discontent is the gradual failure of the synchromesh, particularly on first and second gears. This again is not really good reason for disassembly until it is completely non-functioning and the whine is excessive, from a mechanical point of view. Provided the unit still selects its gears, keeps them there and functions smoothly there is no mechanical reason for worry. Only at a point where it becomes unbearable for the individual owner should this action be taken. See the 'Fault diagnosis' at the end of this Chapter before jumping to conclusions.

6   Transmission unit - reassembly

1   Make sure all the components are spotlessly clean. Then look at the component drawings relevant to this gearbox. Picture the assemblies in your mind.

2   Make sure the top cover is assembled, complete. Reassemble it in a reverse sequence to its disassembly.

3   Reassemble the two synchro hubs. For the 1st/2nd unit fit the recessed inner of the hub facing towards the 2nd speed sliding gear. Fit the two springs correctly. If original parts are fitted match up the two marks. For the 3rd/4th fit the two springs, positioning each one correctly with the three keys in their recesses. See the diagram. Fit the sliding gear with the groove facing the inner part of the hub with the biggest offset.

4   Put the gear casing on its end; bellhousing end down.

5   Fit the secondary/pinion shaft gear cluster into the casing. See the photos.

6   Now fit the 4th gear and ring its split needle roller cage. Hold the cage halves in light grease. Fit the gear sleeve (photos).

7   Screw in the thrust washer and bearing adjusting ring nut.

Tighten and lock it using the same number of turns counted and having the dot marks aligned (photos).

8   Turn the gearbox onto its lower side.

9   Insert the 1st/2nd and 3rd/4th selector forks (photo).

10   Insert the reverse gear and its shaft. Punch its roll pins but not too far. See photos.

11   Put in the primary shaft, pushing the reverse gear up and down its shaft to allow it to fit. Punch the reverse gear shaft roll pins home (photos).

12   Refit the rear end plate of the primary shaft and lock it (photo).

13   Insert the pinion shaft gently through the gear cluster. Once inserted tap the taper roller bearing onto the shaft at the other end (photos).

14   Select two speeds and lock the gearbox. Refit the speedometer skew gear. Tighten fully. Select neutral. The secondary shaft must now revolve easily and without play. If not something has gone wrong. To rectify unlock the pinion shaft adjusting ring nut and loosen or tighten appropriately. Then relock. If new bearings have been fitted a preload on the secondary shaft of 1 to 3½ lbs will indicate correct fitment. Use a spring balance round the 3rd/4th groove (photo).

15   Now refit the selector shafts in the exact reverse order. 1) 1st/2nd selector shaft and roll pin. 2) 3rd/4th selector shaft and roll pin. 3) Locking disc between the selector shafts (photos).

16   Drop the three locking balls above the selector shafts through the edge of the casing. Follow here with the springs and the 1st/2nd spring plunger (photos).

17   Use a new gasket and refit the top cover. Move the end of the selector lever (longest finger) in the top cover towards its nearest corner and having used some gasket cement on both the casing and the cover, place the gasket on the casing and tighten the top cover. If it does not go on easily take it off and slide the reverse gear along so that it rests on the 4th gear on the primary shafts. Make sure the gearbox is neutral. Try again; the selector lever

6.5a The first gear cluster to go in has to go over this bridge and down into the depths ...

6.5b Note the previously installed gear cluster below; these are next

6.6a Don't be afraid of using thick grease to hold the bearing cage

6.6b This is the correct way up

6.7a Oil the thread of the locking ring and screw in by hand

6.7b Tighten and lock at the previously recorded fixing point

6.9 Both selectors in together will ensure correct location

6.10a Note the selector groove on the inside

6.10b Two roll pins located but not driven home yet

6.11a Careful, gear sliding will allow this shaft to fit

6.11b Make sure everything meshes and slides well before ...

6.11c ... driving home the roll pins in the reverse gear shaft

6.12 Now fix the flange here

6.13a Carefully push through the pinion shaft

6.13b Don't forget the shim here

6.13c Gently drive home the bearing race; we used this piece of pipe for proper location

6.14 The speedometer drive gear should be fixed in this way

6.15a First one shaft; don't forget the roll pin in the selector arm head on the far right

6.15b Roll pins hold this gearbox together; treat them carefully and try to use new ones

6.15c Don't forget the locking ring, to be fitted now

6.15d Before doing any more check that all the gears mesh and that the roll pins are home

6.16a The three detent balls should be followed ...

6.16b ... by their appropriate, previously recorded, detent spring

6.17 The top cover needs careful fitting; the shift mechanism has to mesh

6.18 We had two shims fitted upon disassembly; two must be refitted

6.19 Use a new gasket every time and gasket cement

6.20 The final stages, relocate the differential the right way round

6.21a Oil the threads and hold the differential whilst turning

6.21b The ring should be relocked in the same position as before disassembly

6.22 A new gasket for the bellhousing too

should slide into its correct notch (photo).

18 Now refit the primary shaft front bearing. Tap the outer track ring push with the casing. Refit the same number of shims which were removed (photo).

19 Refit the end cover. Use a new gasket and gasket cement (photo).

20 Replace the differential inside the housing. Make sure the crownwheel is on the correct side. See the appropriate diagram: R1222 is on the opposite side to the R1221 (photo).

21 Screw in each adjusting ring nut the same number of turns that were used in its removal. Make sure the dot punch mark aligns. If new bearings have been used your number of turns and dot alignment marks are not valid. Screw in the ring marks until the differential becomes 'slightly hard' to turn. Then check the preload. Revolve the differential to settle the bearings and then use a spring balance to test. It needs 2 to 7 lb to turn the differential easily. Adjust the ring nuts until all is well. Replace the lock tab and set screw (photos).

22 Now assemble the bellhousing of the R1222 model and the cover plate of the R1221. Bolt the relevant part to the gearbox casing in the reverse sequence of its removal (photo).

23 Replace the primary shaft using a new roll pin on the R1222. This can be 'gripped' in (photo).

24 Check that the gears can be selected easily.

6.23 The last job; always a new roll pin

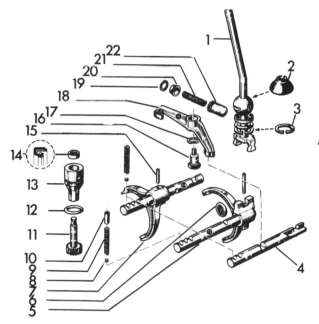

Fig. 6.8 The floor-change gearshift mechanism and selectors
(Note the gear numbers marked)

1 Shift lever	12 Seal
2 Rubber boot	13 Speedo cable housing
3 Rubber collar (inner)	14 Oil seal
4 Reverse shift shaft	15 Roll pin
5 1-2 selector shaft/fork	16 Special bushed bolt
6 Spacer	17 Spring washer
7 3-4 Selector shaft/fork	18 Reverse gear selector fork
8 Detent ball	19 Rubber seal
9 Detent spring	20 Collar
10 Plunger	21 Spring
11 Speedo drive shaft	22 Rubber collar (outer)

Fig. 6.7 The standard dashboard type gearshift and selectors.
(Note the gear numbers marked)

1 Shift lever	12 Seal
2 Rubber boot	13 Speedo cable housing
3 Circlip	14 Oil seal
4 Reverse shift shaft	15 Roll pin
5 1-2 selector shaft/fork	16 Special bushed bolt
6 Spacer	17 Spring washer
7 3-4 Selector shaft/fork	18 Reverse gear selector fork
8 Detent ball	19 Circlip
9 Detent spring	20 Collar
10 Plunger	21 Spring
11 Speedo drive shaft	22 Housing

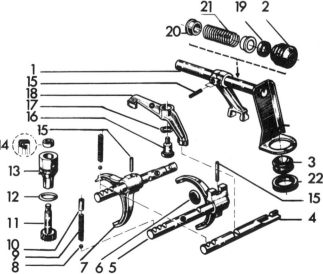

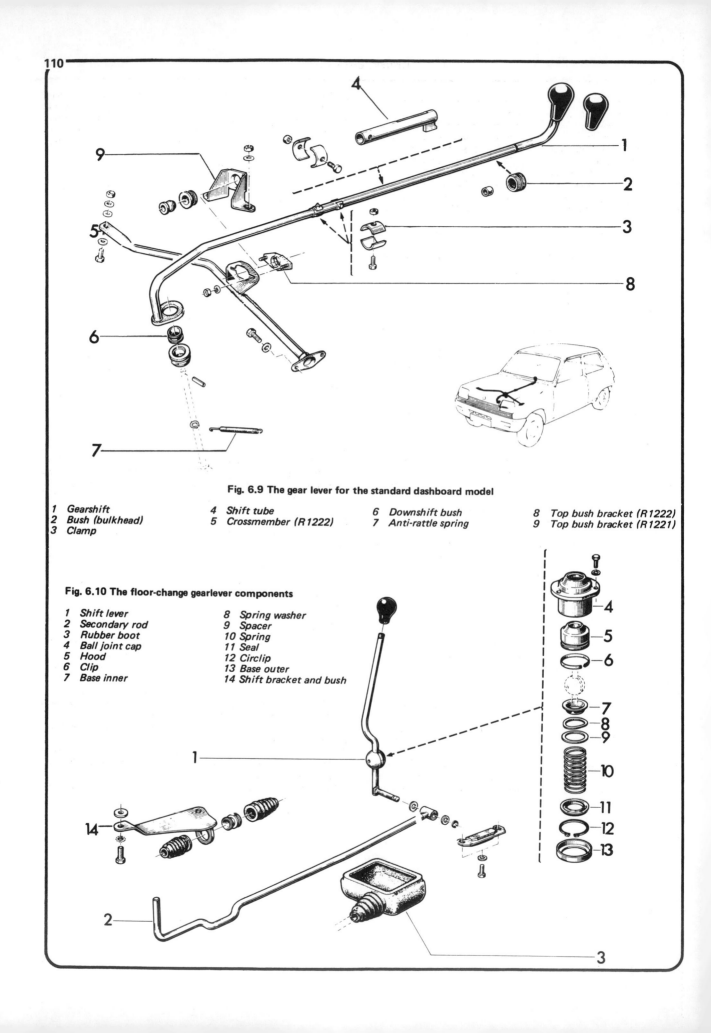

Fig. 6.9 The gear lever for the standard dashboard model

1 *Gearshift*	4 *Shift tube*	6 *Downshift bush*	8 *Top bush bracket (R1222)*
2 *Bush (bulkhead)*	5 *Crossmember (R1222)*	7 *Anti-rattle spring*	9 *Top bush bracket (R1221)*
3 *Clamp*			

Fig. 6.10 The floor-change gearlever components

1 *Shift lever*	8 *Spring washer*
2 *Secondary rod*	9 *Spacer*
3 *Rubber boot*	10 *Spring*
4 *Ball joint cap*	11 *Seal*
5 *Hood*	12 *Circlip*
6 *Clip*	13 *Base outer*
7 *Base inner*	14 *Shift bracket and bush*

7 Dashboard gearchange mechanism - general

1 The 'push-me, pull-you' gearchange is Renault's traditional type. From under the bonnet it can be seen in almost its entirety. It is as simple as it looks. This system is very efficient and easy to use. Only the bushes in which it runs wear out.

2 Sloppy gear changes and rattling gear knobs are usually due to worn bushes. The shift rod passes through two nylon bushes, both mounted in rubber, one on the radiator (R1221) or centre cross brace (R1222) and one in a shift tube in the bulkhead. The rod itself has a further bush on its end, over the lever into the gearbox.

3 To replace the cross brace bushes on the radiator, disconnect the shift rod in its middle and push out the rod. Lever out the nylon bush through the rubber one and discard both. Lubricate the new nylon and rubber bush as a pair with washing up liquid. Insert one into the other and then push into the bracket. Reassemble the shift rod.

4 The end bush on the shift rod is changed in the same way. At the same time make sure the bias spring is fitted.

5 The bulkhead bush is more difficult to replace. The shift tube must be removed from under the facia. It is fixed by four setscrews. Again the shift rod must be halved under the bonnet. Poke out the bush and push in a new one, inside its keeper. Reassembly is a simple reverse process.

6 Make sure all grommets are fitted to the bodywork where the gearshift passes through the bulkhead. A considerable draught will build up if this is not done!

8 Floor gearchange mechanism - general

1 The newer floor mounted gearchange is equally as simple as the dashboard mounted shift. There is likely to be no less wear on this system than the other, although it will manifest itself in different places.

2 Take a close look at the accompanying diagrams. Those bushes most likely to wear are indicated. The diagram illustrates the mechanism best of all. Its removal and replacement is as simple as it looks.

9 Speedometer cable - general

1 Speedometer cable removal and replacement is a simple task at the gearbox end but more difficult at the speedometer in the facia panel. A frequent occurrence is inner speedometer cable breakage. If this happens the complete inner and outer cable has to be replaced as a 'sealed' unit.

2 Release the outer cable at the gearbox by undoing the little fixing screw in the gearbox casing.

3 If it is certain the cable is broken cut the inner and outer cable at the bulkhead under the bonnet and remove and discard the rest of the cable.

4 Unscrew the knurled nut behind the facia panel using your fingers. It may be necessary to remove some of the trim first. Remove the now short piece of cable into the vehicle. Take off the two bulkhead rubber grommets.

5 Tape the knurled nut to the end of the new outer cable and thread it through the bulkhead from under the bonnet. Locate this taped end with your fingers from inside the vehicle. Before securing to the facia panel bush on the two rubber grommets.

6 Once located in the facia and screwed tight, locate the rubber grommets and feed the cable to the gearbox. Again locate properly and do up the little fixing screw.

Special Note: These cables are prone to squeaking and causing speedometer needle flutter. There is little that can be done short of replacing the whole cable!

10 Fault diagnosis - gearbox

1 Faults can be sharply divided into two main groups: Some definite failure with the transmission not working: Noises implying some component worn, damaged, or out of place.

2 The failures can usually be tracked down by commonsense and remembering the circumstances in which they appeared. Thus, if the car will not go at all a mechanical failure will occur in different circumstances to a broken linkage from the gear lever!

3 If there is a definite fault within the transmission then it has got to be removed and dismantled to repair it, so further diagnosis can wait until the parts can be examined.

4 But if the problem is a strange noise the decision must be taken whether in the first place it is abnormal, and if so whether it warrants action.

5 Noises can be traced to a certain extent by doing the test sequence as follows:

6 Find the speed and type of driving that makes the noise. If the noise occurs with engine running, car stationary, clutch disengaged, gear engaged: the noise is not in the transmission. If it goes after the clutch is engaged in neutral, halted, it is the clutch.

7 If the noise can be heard faintly in neutral, clutch engaged, it is in the gearbox. It will presumably get worse on the move, especially in some particular gear.

8 Final drive noises are only heard on the move. They will only vary with speed and load, whatever gear is engaged.

9 Noise when pulling is likely to be either the adjustment of preload of the differential bearings, or the crown wheel and pinion backlash.

10 Gear noise when free-wheeling is likely to be the relative positions of crown wheel and pinion.

11 Noise on corners implies excessive tightness or excessive play of the bevel side gears or idler pinions in the differential.

12 In general, whining is gear teeth at the incorrect distance apart. Roaring or rushing or moaning is bearings. Thumping or grating noises suggest a link out of a gear tooth.

13 If subdued whining comes on gradually, there is a good chance the transmission will last a long time to come.

14 Whining or moaning appearing suddenly, or becoming loud, should be examined quickly.

15 If thumping, or grating noises appear stop at once. If bits of metal are loose inside, the whole transmission, including the casing, could quickly be wrecked.

16 Synchromesh wear is obvious. You just 'beat' the gears and crashing occurs.

Chapter 7 Driveshafts, hubs, wheels and tyres

Contents

Specifications

Driveshafts

Type	Removable, double universal joints
Inner end	Spider GI 62 or GI 69 coupling
Outer end	Spider GI 76
Joint lubricant	Special Renault Oil

Hubs

Front hub bearings	2 ball bearing races of Renault manufacture
Rear hub bearings	2 proprietary taper roller bearing races

Wheels ... ...

Pressed steel disc (R1222 drilled. R1221 slotted), 3 stud fixing, solid centre, 13 inch diameter, 4 inch rim width (4B)

Tyres

Type ... ...

Always tubed and radial (Michelin 2X).
Normal UK fitment 145 x 13

Pressures	Front	Rear
Normal	24 psi (1.7 kg/cm^2)	27 psi (1.9 kg/cm^2)
For heavy loading or continuous high speed running	26 psi (1.8 kg/cm^2)	28 psi (2.0 kg/cm^2)

(Check manufacturers' recommendations with your fitment)

Torque wrench settings

	lb f ft	kg fm
Stub axle nut	90	12.3
Wheel nuts	40 to 45	5.5 to 6.2

1 General description

The driveshafts fitted to the Renault 5 drive the front wheels direct from the final drive in the transmission casing. They also undergo the steering movement of the car with the front wheels. Consequently they are fitted with totally universal joints at the outer (wheel) end and sliding joints at their inner (transmission) end. They are effectively single units, the joints being totally integral with the shafts. Little maintenance can be done on them and when worn out they must be replaced as a whole, although they can obviously be replaced singly.

Several types of shaft have been fitted with different styles of joint, depending on the model. It is most important that you replace the shafts with the correct type. They are not interchangeable, necessarily, from car-to-car although they are from side-to-side. Spider sliding joints have been fitted at both ends, see the Specifications at the start of this Chapter for types fitted.

The front wheel hubs themselves are special Renault manufacture caged ball bearings whilst the rear hubs are conventional taper roller bearings (two). The front hub bearings are therefore not adjustable as are the rear but must be replaced if worn or failed.

The disc road wheels are conventional, at least to Renault and French cars in general in that they have solid centres and are three stud fixings. Each model has a different style of wheel. Radial tyres are fitted as standard and must be considered as obligatory on these vehicles, and must be used with inner tubes.

2 Driveshaft - disconnection and connection

1 To be able to remove the engine and transmission unit, the driveshafts have to be disconnected at the inner end and the suspension ball joints at the outer end have to be forced from fresh mounting points.

2 Unlike other earlier small front wheel drive Renaults, the Renault 5 driveshafts are not fixed at the inner end by a roll pin and can be pulled straight out of the gearbox.

3 Disconnect the top ball joint as mentioned in the next Section, then 'wire-up' the inner Spider joint so that it does not become disconnected inside the rubber gaiter. Simply loop wire around the spline and then around the shaft 'to hold it together'.

4 Connection is the reverse process. Grease the splines first.

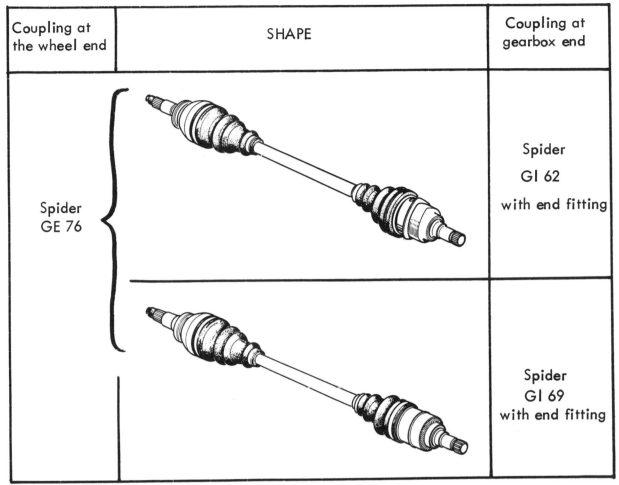

Coupling at the wheel end	SHAPE	Coupling at gearbox end
Spider GE 76		Spider GI 62 with end fitting
		Spider GI 69 with end fitting

Fig. 7.1 Visual identification of the two types of driveshaft fitted

3 Driveshaft - removal and replacement

1 Total removal of a driveshaft would only need to be done when it was deemed worn out and needing replacement when the inner joint has been disconnected or rubber bellows needed refitting. Obviously crash repairs may necessitate a shaft removal but all other suspension or brake repairs can be undertaken with the shaft remaining in the car.

2 With the purchase or borrowing of two more special tools, one of which is totally unique to this job, the do-it-yourself mechanic can easily replace a driveshaft.

3 Disconnect the inner end of the driveshafts as far as Section 2, paragraph 4. Remove the roadwheels. Then disconnect the suspension ball joints as in Chapter 1.

4 With the appropriate sized ring-spanner undo the nut on the end of the driveshaft on the outer side of the brake drum or disc. Hold the drum or disc so that you can obtain leverage, by placing a tyre lever on two wheels studs, one on either side, and press in the opposite rotational direction of the spanner. Remove the nut.

5 Borrow or hire a three-legged puller which you can bolt to the three wheel studs, to enable you to push the end of the drive-shaft back through the hub. Fit the puller and firmly screw the bolt in. It should gradually drive out the outer spline through the hub. (Fig. 7.3).

6 When released disconnect the steering arm ball joint as you have done the suspension ball joints and remove the driveshaft.

7 Replacing the driveshaft is an exact reversal of its removal except that you will require a special tool from Renault to

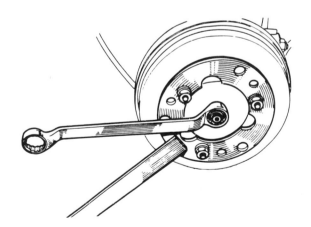

Fig. 7.2 The official tool for holding the hub to release the shaft nut. A similar home made tool can be used (Sec. 3)

enable you to pull the shaft through the hub. This is tool No. T.Av.409. Slide the driveshaft into the hub stub axle carrier assembly and screw on the fitting tool. Tighten up this tool and it will draw the shaft towards you. Once fully home remove the tool and replace the outer nut and torque to 90 lb f ft (12.3 kg f m) Figs. 7.4 and 7.5).

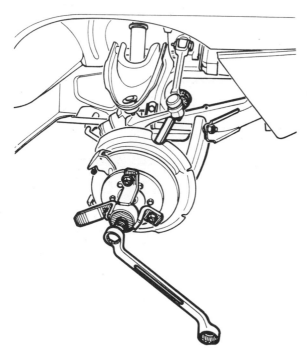

Fig. 7.3 Using a hub puller to extract the hub from the shaft
(Sec. 3)

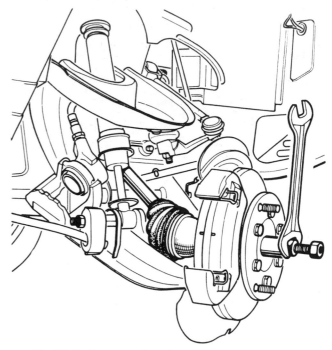

Fig. 7.5 Replacement of the front hub onto the driveshaft
using the Renault special tool (Sec. 3)

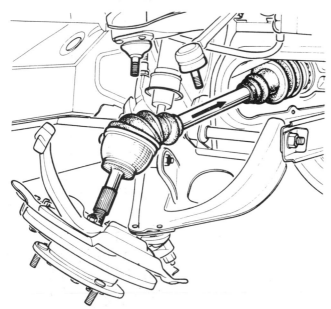

Fig. 7.4 The beginnings of shaft replacement. Note all the
disconnected joints (Sec. 3)

Note 1

It is only economic to purchase the tool T.Av.409 if more than
one shaft is going to be replaced during work on the car. It is
unlikely to be economic to purchase the three legged puller for
this purpose. New driveshafts are fitted with an inner joint
retaining clip when purchased. It is worthwhile keeping these for
they can be used instead of the wire and jubilee clip when disconnecting a driveshaft in the future.

Note 2

Earlier front wheel drive small Renaults, had problems with the
driveshafts wearing at their axle joints very quickly. The shafts
fitted to the Renault 5 are a vastly improved component and can
now be considered of good quality and reliable manufacture.

4   Driveshaft joints

As has been stated in the 'General description', there is very
little maintenance which can be carried out on the driveshaft
joints. The joints can be dismantled by the do-it-yourself
mechanic but he will find that he is unable to reassemble them.
No matter which type of shaft is fitted special tools are needed
to effect a repair. Even replacing the rubber bellows and re-
lubricating the joint is beyond the use of ordinary tools. Under
all circumstances it is more efficient to remove the driveshaft and
then take it to a Renault garage (only) to have them effect any
repair or maintenance. With the specific special tools available to
them all repairs to the joint can be carried out very quickly and
safer than attempting it yourself.

For Spider joints it is possible to have the bellows, yoke and
spider itself replaced, together or separately. Experience shows
that unless the bellows is punctured and lubricant allowed to
escape and joint to become dry, the outer universal joint wears
at a far greater rate than the inner, consequently the shaft is
nearly always replaced before the total life of the inner joint is
reached. An illustration is given of the various component parts
of a driveshaft (Fig. 7.11).

5   Front hub bearings - removal and replacement

1   Only ever replace the inner and outer front hub bearings as a
pair. It is quite uneconomic to do them singly.

2   Remove the relevant driveshaft as described in Section 2 and
3.

3   Undo the flexible brake pipe from that side as described in
Chapter 8.

4   Separate the lower suspension arm ball joint from the upright
using the same method as used in the driveshaft removal.

5   Remove the suspension upright, hub and bearings.

6   Hold the suspension upright in a vice and tap out the hub and
outer bearing and bearing spacer. Use a soft headed hammer.

7   Extracting the outer bearing can be difficult as there is
insufficient room between the bearing and hub to accommodate

115

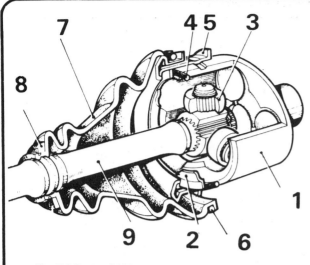

Fig. 7.6 Spider G162 coupling cross-section

1	Yoke	6	Retaining spring
2	Anti-separation plate	7	Rubber bellows
3	Spider	8	Retaining clip
4	Seal	9	Driveshaft
5	Cover		

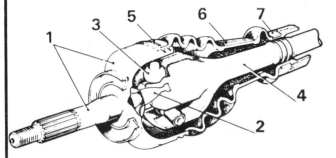

Fig. 7.7 Spider GE76 coupling cross-section

1	Bell-shaped stub axle	5	Retaining collar
2	Retaining starplate	6	Rubber bellows
3	Spider	7	Retaining clip
4	Shaft yoke		

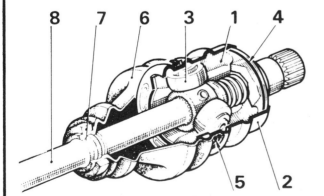

Fig. 7.8 Spider G169 coupling cross-section

1	Yoke	5	Retaining collar
2	Cover	6	Rubber bellows
3	Spider proper	7	Retaining ring
4	Grease seal	8	Driveshaft

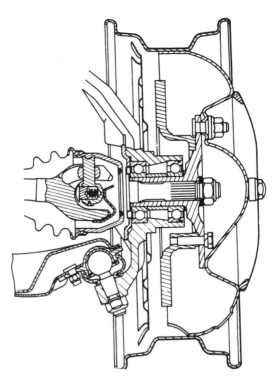

Fig. 7.9 Cross-section of the R1222 front hub

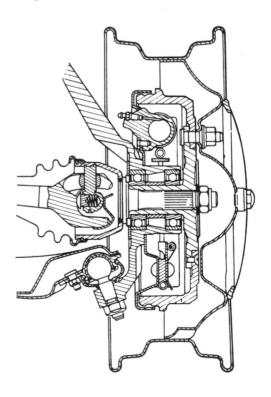

Fig. 7.10 Cross-section of the R1221 front hub

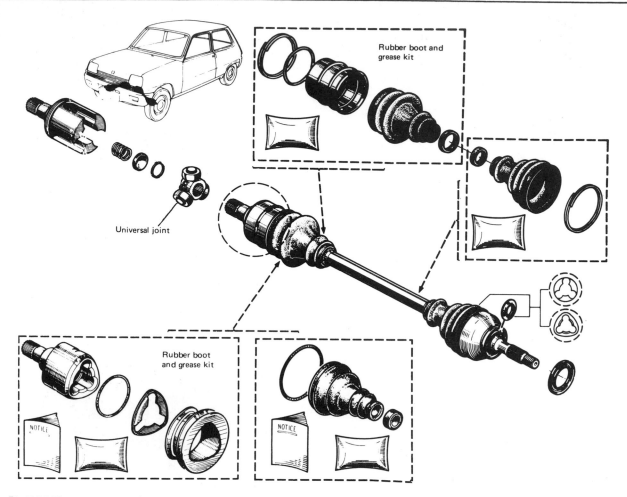

Fig. 7.11 The components of a driveshaft together with the available repair kits

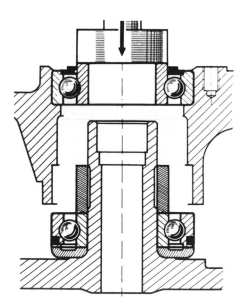

Fig. 7.12 Using a special extractor to remove the outer front bearing from the front hub (Sec. 5)

the feet of a strong conventional three-legged puller. Alternatively break-up the cage of the outer bearing so that the outer track and ball bearings drop out leaving the inner track in position on the hub. Now heat the inner track evenly with a blow lamp and grip it when hot in the jaws of the vice. Using a suitably sized drift and a heavy hammer drive the hub out from the race. Note that several applications of the blow lamp may be required to remove the race.

8 Replacement of the outer bearing to the hub utilises a suitably sized piece of tubing (32 mm) or a socket which should be used to tap in the new bearing. The sealed end of the bearing should be towards the brake drum or disc. Put aside the hub until the inner bearing has been removed from the upright.

9 To remove the inner bearing keep the upright in the vice and remove the brake backing plate or caliper dust shield by undoing the closure plate nuts and bolts. These are square headed bolts and hexagonal nuts. Remove the backing plate and the bearing closure plate.

10 Push out the inner bearing race by tapping the upright onto a piece of suitably sized tube (70 mm).

11 Push in a new bearing, sealed end facing that brake drum, using another piece of tube (58 mm). If a press is available this will ease the task. To ease both bearing races into their respective housings, wax smeared on the outer races will help.

12 Reassemble the upright, backing plate and closure plate. Use gasket cement on the closure plate. This will stop water from entering the housing - this is the most usual cause of failure.

13 Reassembly the front hub to the upright by pressing it. Do not forget the bearing spacer and place some high melting point grease between the two bearings.

14 Further reassembly is a reversal procedure of the dismantling sequence.

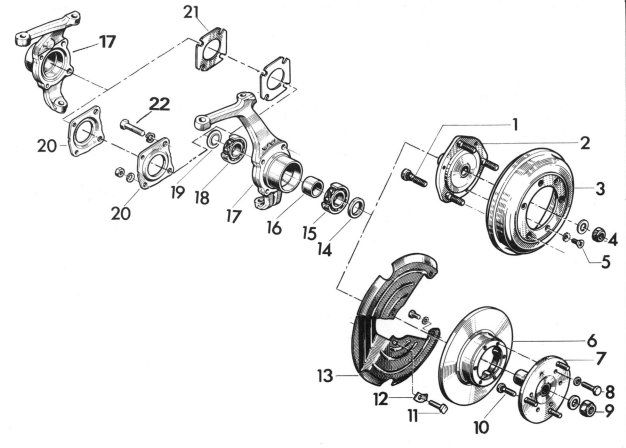

Fig. 7.13 The front hub components for both disc and drum brake hubs

1 Wheel stud (1221)	7 Front hub (R1222)	13 Dust shield (R1222)	18 Wheel bearing (inner)
2 Front hub (R1221)	8 Hub/disc bolt (R1222)	14 Shim	19 Shim
3 Drum (R1221)	9 Shaft nut (1222)	15 Wheel bearing (outer)	20 End caps
4 Shaft nut (R1221)	10 Wheel stud (R1222)	16 Bush	21 Spacer
5 Drum securing screw (R1221)	11 Dust shield screw (R1222)	17 Suspension uprights	22 Bolt
6 Brake disc (R1222)	12 Lock tab (1222)		

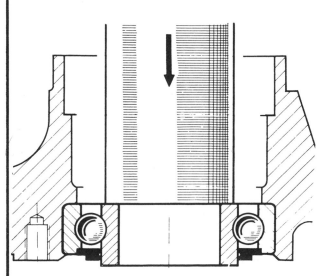

Fig. 7.14 Removal of the inner front hub bearings from the
stud axle carrier (Sec. 5)

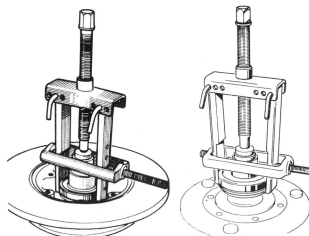

Fig. 7.15 Replacement of the front hub bearings (Sec. 5)

Top — new bearing into stub axle carrier
Bottom — new bearing on disc/hub

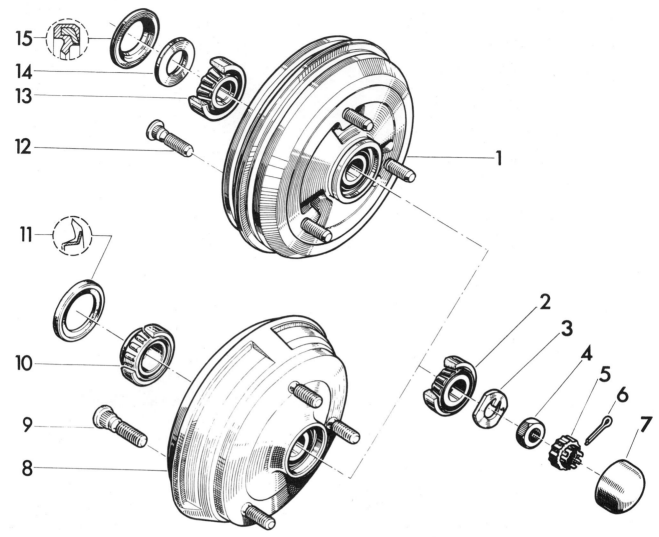

Fig. 7.16 Hub/drums for the rear axle: (top) R1222; (bottom) R1221

1 R1222 rear drum	5 Castellated nut	9 R1221 wheel stud	13 R1221 inner bearing
2 Outer wheel bearing	6 Split pin	10 R1221 inner bearing	14 R1222 spacer
3 'D' washer	7 Grease cap	11 R1221 oil seal	15 R1222 oil seal
4 Nut	8 R1221 rear drum	12 R1222 wheel stud	

6 Rear hub bearings - removal and replacement

1 Only ever replace the inner and outer rear hub bearings as a pair.

2 Remove the brake drum, as described in Chapter 8.

3 Remove the grease seal from the drum and have a new one ready for replacement. A screwdriver will easily remove this.

4 Tap the two outer bearing housings out of the drum using a large screwdriver and hammer, from the other side of the drum to the bearing. The roller bearing race of the outer bearing is already loose. Extract the inner bearing roller race using a bearing extractor. This could be a simple two legged extractor.

5 Replacement of the races and housing is an obvious reversed sequence of their removal. Tap the inner bearing race onto the stub axle using a suitably sized socket and very carefully ease in the outer housings into the drum.

6 Drum replacement is the reverse of the removal procedure, but in addition it is necessary to adjust the hub bearings. To do this, tighten the hub nut to a torque of 25 lbf ft (3.3 kgf m)

whilst rotating the drum, then back-off the nut ¼ turn. This should provide a bearing endfloat of 0.001 to 0.002 in (0.01 to 0.05 mm), but ideally it should be checked using a dial gauge.

7 Fit the castellated locking cap and a new split pin. Fill the grease cap with approximately 1/3 oz (10 gm) of a general purpose grease, then carefully tap it into position on the hub.

7 Wheels - general

1 Because the design of the suspension of the car the strength and the trueness of the roadwheels is critical, particularly at the front. A great deal of excessively fast wear on the wheel bearings and universal joints can be attributed to buckled and deformed wheels. Check every 3000 miles or when there is a sudden difference of feeling at the steering wheel that the wheels are not buckled or dented. Check also that the front wheels are balanced. (Remember that the wheels do not have holes in their centres, consequently not all electronic balancing machines can be used on these wheels). If any deformity is noticed the wheel concerned should be replaced by new. Do not attempt to 'repair'

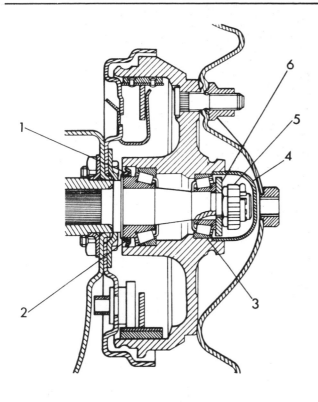

Fig. 7.17 Cross-section of the R1222 rear hub

1 Inner spacer   4 Grease cap
2 Inner roller bearing   5 Locking nut
3 Outer roller bearing   6 D washer

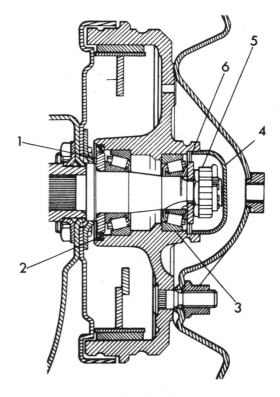

Fig. 7.18 Cross-section of the R1221 rear hub

1 Inner spacer   4 Grease cap
2 Inner roller bearing   5 Locking nut
3 Outer roller bearing   6 D washer

8. The tyres play a critical part in the suspension and steering systems; they need constant attention

wheel rims.

2 Do not overtighten the wheel nuts for this can deform the rim. Always check that the inner side of the wheel is free from mud and grit for the accummulation of these can create in-balance.

3 Grease the hub cap securing thread in the centre of the wheels. The spare wheel soon becomes rusty! Always fit the hub cap with its rubber seal surround.

8 Tyres - general

In the same way that the condition and suitability of the wheels fitted is critical so it is with the tyres. Because of the long suspension travel and fully independent suspension it is always wise to fit radial tyres on all wheels of these cars. Tyre wear is not great under any circumstances but the front tyres wear faster than the rear. Do not fit oversize tyres. The wheel rims are not readily able to take a larger section tyre. Always fit inner tubes. See Specifications for suitability of tyres. Tyre pressures are critical too (photo).

Fault diagnosis - See the fault diagnosis for Chapter 10.

Chapter 8 Braking system

Contents

Specifications

Type

R1222	Hydraulically operated front disc and rear drum brakes. Cable operated handbrake to rear wheels.	
R1221	Hydraulically operated front and rear drum brakes. Cable operated handbrake to the front wheels.	

Brake pressure limited valve fitted to the rear wheels

Front brakes

	R1222	R1221
Diameter	*Disc 228 mm (9 in)	Drum 228.5 mm (9 in)
Caliper/cylinder diameter	45 mm (1.772 in)	23.8 mm (0.937 in)
Pad/lining thicknesses including backing	14 mm (0.551 in)	6 mm (0.236 in)

*Disc thickness 10 mm (0.393 in). Minimum thickness 9 mm (0.355 in)

Rear brakes

Diameter	180.25 mm (7.096 in)	160.25 mm (6.305 in)
Brake lining width	30 mm (1.3/16 in)	25 mm (1.3/64 in)
Wheel cylinder diameter	20.6 mm (0.811 in)	

Master cylinder

R1222 Dual system, diameter	20.6 mm (0.811 in)	
R1221 Single system, diameter	19 mm (0.748 in)	

Free-play at pedal ... ...   5 mm (13/64 in)

Brake fluid ... ...   Hydraulic fluid conforming to SAE 1703C

Torque wrench settings

	lb f ft	kg f m
Brake hose to front wheel drum cylinder	15	2.07
Brake hose to disc caliper	15	2.07
Brake caliper securing bolt to stub axle carrier	50	6.91
Deflector securing bolt on caliper bracket	15	2.07
Front hub securing nuts	90	12.3
Disc to hub bolts	20	2.76
Bleed screws	7	0.96
Brake pipe unions:		
Copper	9	1.24
Steel	10	1.38

1 General description

The braking system of the Renault 5 models is conventional. The 1221 is fitted with hydraulically operated drum brakes at both the front and rear. They are operated by the front pedal whilst an independent parking (hand) brake operates the front wheels only. The R1222 however has front disc brakes and drum rear brakes and the handbrake operates the rear brakes.

Adjustment is done manually at each brake drum individually to compensate for wear on the brake shoe linings. The disc brakes of the R1222 are self-adjusting. The handbrake operation is adjusted automatically by the adjustment of the front brakes although there is a separate method of adjustment for the operating mechanism itself when this wears.

The R1221 has a single hydraulic line braking system. The R1222 will have dual line with tandem master cylinder. There is little difference in the methods of overhaul between the two types.

A separate restricting valve to the rear brakes is fitted in the hydraulic system. The brake light switch is operated at the master cylinder.

2 Routine maintenance

1 Every week remove the hydraulic fluid reservoir cap, having made sure that it is clean, and check the level of the fluid which should be just below the bottom of the filler neck. Check also that the vent hole in the cap is clear. Any need for regular topping-up, regardless of quantity, should be viewed with suspicion and the whole hydraulic system carefully checked for signs of leakage.

2 Every 3000 miles adjust the drum brakes to compensate for wear. Never ignore this task. Lubricate the adjuster **every time.**

3 Every 9000 miles remove the brake drums and examine the shoe linings. They should be renewed when the friction material has very nearly reached the level of the rivet heads or within 1/8 inch (3 mm) if bonded linings are used. If either the rivets or the shoes themselves come into contact with the brake drum they will cause scoring and greatly reduced braking efficiency. Never interchange worn shoes to even-out wear.

For the disc brakes - inspect the disc pad wear, the total pad and backing should not be less than 6 mm. If less they must be replaced in full sets.

Make sure the handbrake functions at all times. At the same time as friction material is examined the hydraulic pipes and unions should be examined for any signs of damage or corrosion. Brake lining pad wear varies according to driving style but no set of brake shoes should be expected to last more than 20,000 miles. The front pads are likely to wear at a faster rate than the rear linings.

4 Every 18 months to 2 years, depending on usage, it is good policy to renew all hydraulic cylinder seals and disc caliper piston seals as a matter of routine, together with the fluid and flexible hoses. Any repair work in the interior should also, of course, be taken into account.

5 If you have just acquired a secondhand car it is strongly recommended that all brake drums and shoes and/or disc and pads are thoroughly examined for condition and wear immediately. Even though braking efficiency may be excellent the friction materials could be nearing the end of their useful life and it is as well to know this without delay. Similarly, the hydraulic cylinders, pipes and connections should be carefully examined for leaks or chafing. Faults should be rectified immediately. It should be remembered that three year old cars will be subject to safety tests and that apart from safety, which is paramount, defects in the system even though they may not yet affect stopping power cause the vehicle to fail the test.

3 Bleeding the hydraulic system

1 The system should need bleeding only when some part of it has been dismantled which would allow air into the fluid circuit; or if the reservoir level(s) has been allowed to drop so far that air has entered the master cylinder.

2 Ensure that a supply of clean non-aerated fluid of the correct specifications is to hand in order to replenish the reservoir(s) during the bleeding process. It is advisable, if not essential, to have someone available to help, as one person has to pump the brake pedal while the other attends to each wheel. The reservoir level has also to be continuously watched and replenished. Fluid bled out should not be re-used. A clean glass jar and a 9 - 12 inch length of 1/8 inch internal diameter rubber tube which will fit tightly over the bleed nipples is also required.

3 Bleed the rear brakes first as these are furthest from the master cylinder. On dual line systems bleed 'one' system first keeping its reservoir topped up. Then bleed the by-pass circuit from the bleed nipple on the top of the unit.

4 Make sure the bleed nipple is clean and put a small quantity of fluid in the bottom of the jar. Fit the tubes onto the nipple and place the other end in the jar under the surface of the liquid. Keep it under the surface throughout the bleeding operation.

5 Unscrew the bleed screw ½ turn and get the assistant to depress and release the brake pedal in short sharp bursts when you direct him. Short sharp jabs are better than long slow ones because they will force any air bubbles along the line ahead of the fluid rather than pump the fluid past them. It is not essential to remove all the air the first time. If the whole system is being bled, attend to each wheel for three or four complete pedal strokes and then repeat the process. On the second time around operate the pedal sharply in the same way until no more bubbles are apparent. The bleed screw should be tightened and closed with the brake pedal fully depressed which ensures that no aerated fluid can get back into the system. Do not forget to keep the reservoir topped up throughout.

6 When all four wheels have been satisfactorily bled depress the

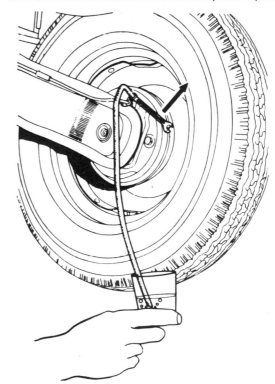

Fig. 8.1. Brake bleeding. Bleed nipple location (Sec. 3)

foot pedal which should offer a firmer resistance with no trace of 'sponginess'. The pedal should not continue to go down under sustained pressure. If it does there is a leak or the master cylinder seals are worn out.

7　Automatic brake bleed valves are available for these cars which will enable you to do this work unaided.

4　Drum brakes - adjustment

1　The procedure for adjusting the drum brakes is exactly the same for both front and rear wheels. It is necessary only to have the correct sized metric spanner to turn the square headed adjuster although the job is always better done with the correct Renault brake spanner which can cover all four sides of this adjuster. The adjusters seize easily and soon become chewed-up, if the incorrect tool is used. To this end it is wise to lubricate the adjusters with some penetrating oil in advance of the time you wish to do the task. Soak the adjuster with this fluid at the back of the backing plate. All eight adjusters are exposed to road dirt! (photos).

2　Jack-up each wheel individually having loosened the hub cap and wheel nuts. Release the handbrake when doing the fronts (R1221) or rears (R1222) and chock the other wheels.

3　Remove the wheel and turn the drum with the wheel studs. If it revolves easily the drums are in need of reasonable adjustment. (At the front the driveshaft will possibly rub on the chassis frame in this position). Place the adjusting spanner on each adjuster in turn, loosen it by turning and then revolve the drum very slowly and tighten up the adjuster until the drum is just locked by the shoe. Slacken it off fractionally so that the drum rotates, just, under slight, but not binding, friction. Proceed with the other adjuster on that backing plate. Then go on and do the other three wheels. Never adjust only one wheel, always do them all.

4　Road test the car and check that it pulls up firmly and straight, without an increase in foot pressure. The pedal should not need pumping.

5　Brake drum and shoes - removal, inspection and replacement

1　Jack-up the car and remove the roadwheel. Block the relevant wheel and release the handbrake.

2　The drums on the front wheels of the R1221 are easily removed. Slacken both adjusters right off. Remove the three holding screws interspaced between the three wheel studs. Loosen the handbrake mechanism under the bonnet. Pull off the drum over the wheel studs. If it seems stuck fast use a little

4.1a The adjusters are easily used if they are not rusty; keep both adjusters constantly lubricated

4.1b A rear drum brake with handbrake mechanism. It can be seen how the brake adjusters work

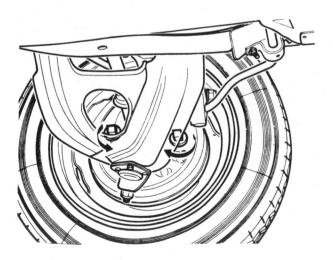

Fig. 8.2. R1221 front drum brake adjustment. Arrows show 'take up' direction (Sec. 4)

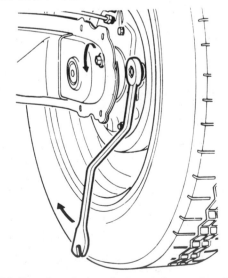

Fig. 8.3. Rear drum brake adjustment. Arrows show 'take-up' direction (Sec. 4)

penetrating oil at the roots of the wheel studs and tap it with a soft headed hammer around the edge. Do not hit the drum with a hammer as it is brittle and may well crack.

3   Removal of the rear drums is a little more complicated. Slacken off the adjusters and then remove the rear drum hub grease cap with a pair of small Stilsons. Wipe any excess grease away from the castellated nut and split pin and pull out the split pin. Undo and remove the castellated nut and 'D' washer. With luck the drum/hub will pull off the stub axle easily together with most of the bearings, inners and outers. If this is not possible a roadwheel can be replaced on the hub and this used for something to pull on. Do not waggle the wheel though. Failing both these possibilities a three-legged puller will have to be used fixed to the wheel studs and pushing on the centre of the stub axle. This puller will have to be hired or borrowed (photos).

4   With the drum removed brush out any dust and examine the rubbing surface for any signs of pitting or deep scoring. The surface should be smooth and bright but minor hairline scores are of no consequence and could have been caused by grit or brake shoes with linings just worn to the rivets. A drum that is obviously badly worn should be renewed. A perfectly satisfactory replacement can sometimes be obtained from a breaker's

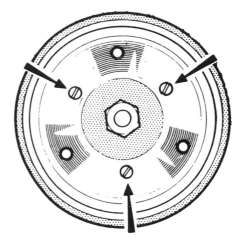

Fig. 8.4. R1221 front drum brake drum fixing screws (Sec. 5)

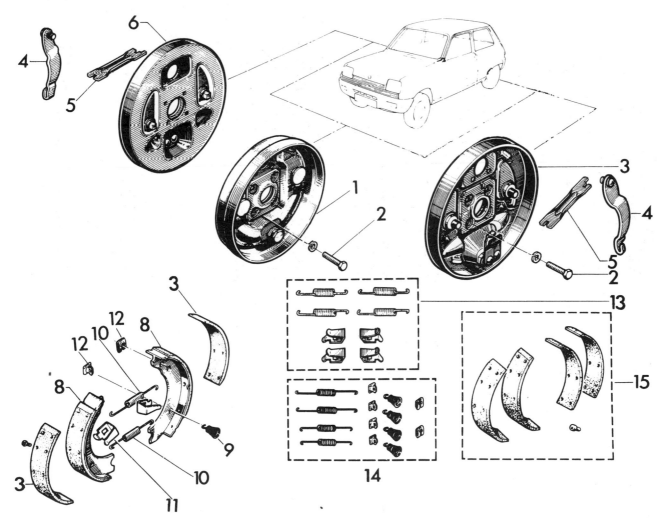

Fig. 8.5. The basic rear brake components (the boxed components show various repair kits)

1 R1221 rear brake backing plate	4 Handbrake lever (R1222)	8 Brake shoe	12 Bracket (R1222)
2 Bolt	5 Brace rod (R1222)	9 Anti-rattle spring (R1222)	13 Pressure spring and clip kit (R1221)
3 R1222 right rear brake backing plate	6 R1222 left rear brake backing plate	10 Pressure spring	14 Pressure spring and anti-rattle spring kit (R1222)
	7 Rivet	11 Clip (R1221)	15 Friction material kit

5.3a A pair of water pump grips will be needed to pull off the grease cap

5.3b A special type of locking nut; it is best to replace if you can

5.3c A 'D' washer and fairly 'thin' nut

5.3d The outer taper roller races comes away easily; now wrench off the drum

5.3e Watch the lip of the oil seal located in the drum

yard. It is no economy having drums turned up on a lathe (unless you can have it done for nothing!). Also, as the radius is altered if the rubbing surfaces are machined out, standard shoes will not match properly until a lot of bedding-in has taken place and re-radiused the linings.

5 The brake shoes should be examined next. There should be no signs of contamination by oil and the linings should be above the heads of the rivets. If the level is close (less than 1/32 inch) it is worth changing them. If there are signs of oil contamination they should be renewed also and the source of oil leakage found before it ruins the new ones as well.

6 To remove the shoes (having, of course, removed the drum) use a screwdriver to push one end of the top inner spring, which pulls the two shoes towards each other to hold-in the two pistons of the wheel cylinder, back through its locating hole in the shoe. This should loosen the spring at the top, the two shoes and the lower shorter spring. Ease each shoe in turn towards the outer rim of the backing plate and then out and away from the anti-rattle clip. The R1222 rear brakes have spring anti-rattle clips which are a push/twist fit through the shoes. Remove this clip before pushing the shoes outwards. Disconnect the lower shorter spring from the shoe. Remove the other shoe, and both springs. This procedure is the same for all the drums but on the fronts (R1221) or rears (R1222) a handbrake steady bar is fitted between the two shoes which the shorter spring rests on. This should come away too. Do not press the brake pedal and use some sort of cylinder holding device to stop the pistons easing out (if possible).

7 Before fitting new shoes check that the wheel cylinder is not distorted and is securely bolted on. Also see that the hydraulic piston moves freely and that there are no fluid leaks.

8 Replacing the brake shoes is almost an exact reversal of removal. Place both shoes under the anti-rattle clips and affix the lower retention spring in place. (On the front (R1221) or rears (R1222) place the steady bar in place underneath it). Place the

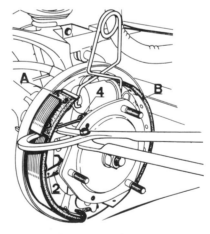

Fig. 8.6. R1221 front drum shoe removal; 'A' and 'B' indicate difference in brake shoes; '2' shows the anti-rattle spring; and '4' shows the top return spring
Note the special piston spring fitted to the cylinder (Sec. 5)

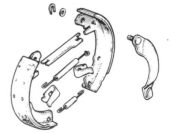

Fig. 8.7. The components of the front drum brake of the R1221 (Sec. 5)

end of the spring which you originally pushed in towards the backing plate to release the brake shoes in its position under the shoes and hooked in. Wedge it there with a crosshead screwdriver or similar tool. This just holds the little clip firm. With a pair of Stilsons grip the other end of the top spring and squeezing the two shoes together onto the piston faces with the other hand, drag the spring over the other shoe and slot in the curved end into the hole in the shoe. This is quite difficult but not dangerous. It will soon be seen exactly where to grip the spring to do this. Be patient and be sure not to damage the wheel cylinder rubber seals.

9 When replacing the drums try to make sure the drums go back on in the original positions. See Chapter 7 to check on the tightening of the rear/hub bearing.

10 When the drum has been replaced operate the brakes to check that they do not bind. It is possible for light binding to occur initially, in which case they should be checked again after a few miles motoring.

6 Drum brake wheel cylinders - inspection and repair

1 If it is suspected that one or more of the wheel cylinders is malfunctioning, jack-up the suspect wheel and remove the brake

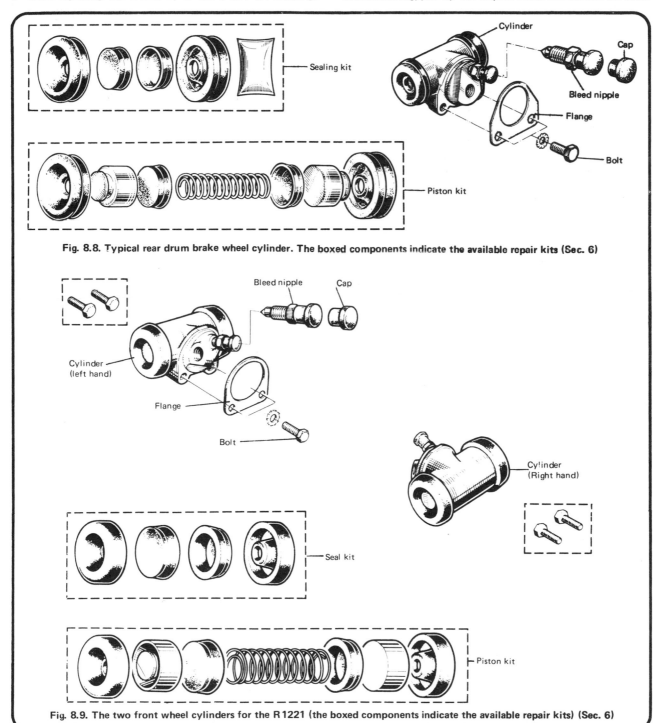

Fig. 8.8. Typical rear drum brake wheel cylinder. The boxed components indicate the available repair kits (Sec. 6)

Fig. 8.9. The two front wheel cylinders for the R 1221 (the boxed components indicate the available repair kits) (Sec. 6)

drum, as described in Section 5.

2 Inspect for signs of fluid leakage around the wheel cylinder and if there are any, proceed as described in paragraph 6.

3 Next get someone to press the brake pedal very gently and a small amount. Watch the wheel cylinder and see that the pistons move out a little. On no account let them come right out or it will need reassembly and bleeding. On releasing the pedal pressure, make sure that the retraction springs on the shoes move the pistons back into position without delay. If both pistons move all is well in the cylinder. If only one piston moves, only one shoe has been effective and repair is necessary.

4 If there is a leak, or the piston does not move (or only moves very slowly under excessive pressure) then the rubber piston seals will need renewal at least.

5 Seal the reservoir cap and remove the brake shoes as described in Section 4.

6 Disconnect the brake fluid pipes where they enter the cylinder and plug the ends of the lines to minimise loss of fluid.

7 Remove the cylinder from the backing plate by undoing the two setscrews from the rear side of the backing plate. Remove them and push the cylinder through and away. Do not attempt any cylinder repair whilst the cylinder is in place on the backing plate. It will be necessary to remove the backing plate to get at the two setscrews on some models.

8 Then pull out the piston, complete with seal and the spring. Examine the piston and cylinder for signs of wear or scoring and if there are any the whole assembly must be renewed. If they are in good condition only the seal needs renewal. Pull the old one off the piston and thoroughly clean the whole assembly using clean hydraulic fluid or methylated spirit.

9 Fit the new seal to the piston so that the lip faces away from the centre of the piston.

10 Lubricate the components in hydraulic fluid before reassembly which is carried out in the reverse order. Make sure the lip of the seal on the piston enters the cylinder first.

11 Replace the cylinder back on the backing correctly.

12 Reconnect the hydraulic pipe, replace the brake shoes and drum as described in Section 5. Bleed the hydraulic system as described in Section 3.

Special note: The wheel cylinders are never interchangeable wheel for wheel. They can only be fitted in one place, one way up. Because of the various size changes that have taken place in wheel cylinders be absolutely sure any replacement cylinders or cylinder kits are of the correct size and type.

---

7 Disc pad (R1222) - inspection and replacement

1 Before dismantling any parts of the brakes they should be thoroughly cleaned. The best cleaning agent is hot water and a mild detergent. Do not use petrol, paraffin or any other solvents which could cause deterioration to the friction pads or piston seals.

2 Jack-up the car and remove the wheel.

3 Inspection does not necessitate the removal of the disc pads themselves. The pads abut the disc surface at all times. Therefore it is possible to put the end of a steel rule (the measure must start at the end of the rule) into the recess above the caliper and the tops of the pads. It should then be evident where the outer edge of the pad comes to, on the rule, from the surface of the disc outwards. The total thickness of the pad, and its backing, must not be less than 6 mm (0.236 in.). If less than this figure the pads must be renewed.

4 To remove the pads take out the four clips which hold the caliper locking blocks in place. Hold the caliper and punch out the locking pins and then remove the second pin, and swing the caliper out to one side out of the way, and then hang with a piece of string without straining the flexible hose (photos).

5 The pads may be taken out of the caliper support bracket. If they are not being renewed note which side they come from so they may be put back in th same place. The pad friction material plus the backing should be no less than 6 mm (0.236 in.). If the pads are not worn out but have a black and shiny surface it is helpful to roughen them up a little on some emery cloth before replacing them. Disc pads last normally about 12,000 miles (photo).

6 Behind the pads on the carrier bracket are two pad anchor springs. Remove these and clean them up after ensuring that they are intact. Renew them otherwise.

7 Check the disc and caliper before replacing the original on new pads.

8 Replacement of the pads and calipers is a reversal of the removal procedure, but when fitting new pads certain additional matters must be attended to.

9 Make sure that the new pads are exactly similar to the ones taken off. Push back the piston in the caliper with a suitable blunt instrument to provide the necessary clearance for the new thicker pads.

10 Make sure the pads are the correct way up. The drilling on the back is downwards.

11 Refit the pads into the carrier, after the two pad anchor springs. The longest spring goes on the outside whilst the shortest on the inside.

12 Fit one side of the caliper between the spring and the keyway on the caliper bracket and then fit the other side of the caliper by compressing both springs.

13 Punch in the first locking pin. Using a screwdriver press in the other keyway and then in the second locking pin.

14 Refit the four spring clips with their flat portion facing the caliper bracket.

15 Refit the roadwheel, lower the car and pump the brake pedal.

Note: Disc pads must be renewed in sets. Always renew pads on both front wheels - never just one.

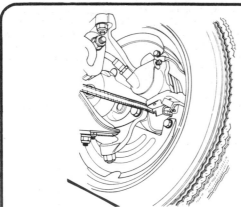

Fig. 8.10. Disc pad thickness being measured on the R1222 (Sec. 7)

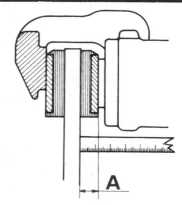

Fig. 8.11. 'A' shows how to measure the disc pad for minimum thickness (R1222) (Sec. 7)

7.4a The pads are held in simply; do not leave this clip out

7.4b You may have to tap this block out

7.4c The pads are readily removed in this situation

7.5 Try to use your fingers only

8 Caliper and disc (R1222) - removal, overhaul and replacement

1 Remove the caliper from the car, as described in Section 7 which is necessary when changing the disc pads. Then remove totally by undoing the flexible hose from the caliper end. This is simpler than removing from the bodywork. Let the hydraulic fluid drain on to a piece of rag.

2 The caliper is constructed in two parts. The piston is connected to the mounting bracket by a pin. Before working on the caliper, even to change the piston rubbers, always separate the piston from the bracket. Punch out the pin with a 3 mm (1/8 in.) pin-punch. Then remove the piston out of its bracket by holding the bracket in a vice and drilling the piston out. Be careful. With a brake caliper, if the piston is only partially seized it should be possible to force it right out under pressure from an air line on the hydraulic fluid inlet. With an air line at a petrol station this should be fairly easy but on a foot pump it will be necessary to make up a suitable air tight adaptor.

3 If the pistons are seized solid it is more than likely that you will be unable to get the piston out without damaging the cylinder or piston. However it is worthwhile having a go. Pull out

the rubber dust seal and leave the whole assembly to soak in methylated spirit for a time. If this does not soften things up then a new caliper assembly will have to be bought.

4 Assuming the pistons have been removed without difficulty, clean them thoroughly with methylated spirit and remove the seal from the annular groove in the cylinder bore. Any hard residue deposits may be removed with careful use of some 600 grade wet and dry paper. If there are any ridges or scores in the cylinder or on the piston the parts must be renewed (Fig. 8.14).

5 Fit new seals in the cylinder groove, lubricate the cylinders and pistons with hydraulic fluid and replace the pistons. Fit the dust seals, so that they fit in the cylinder groove and on the piston.

6 When the calipers have been reassembled and fitted back to the car bleed the hydraulic system as described in Section 3.

7 Discs do not last forever. Under ideal conditions and with proper and regular maintenance of caliper pistons and brake pads they will last a long time. Under other circumstances they can warp, wear irregularly, get rusted and pitted, develop score lines and as a result provide poor braking and rapid consumption of pads. Remember, disc brakes are only better than drum brakes if they are in good condition.

8 A disc in good condition should have a smooth, shiny bright

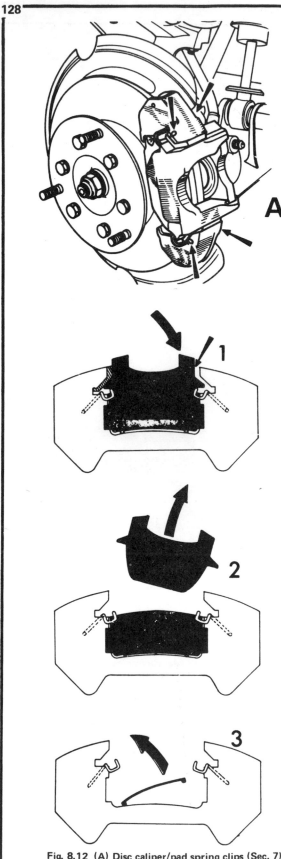

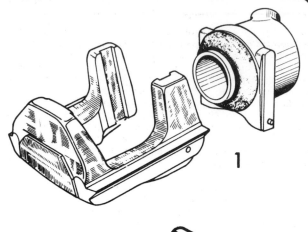

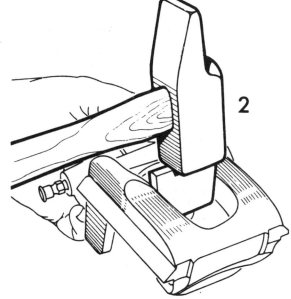

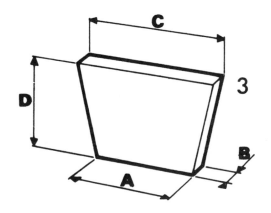

Fig. 8.12 (A) Disc caliper/pad spring clips (Sec. 7)

1   *Pad removal started*
2   *Pad away*
3   *Anti-rattle shim*

Fig. 8.13. Caliper splitting using the proper wedge (Sec. 8)

1   *Caliper parts*   A   2 1/32 in. (51.5 mm)
2   *Wedge splitting*   B   5/16 in. (8 mm)
3   *Wedge dimensions*   C   2 7/32 in. (56 mm)
                                    D   1 3/8 in. (35 mm)

surface on the pad contact area. Do not hope to improve a deteriorated disc by the burnishing effect of new pads! Another fault which a disc may have, even though the surfaces are good, is a warp (or run-out). This means it does not run true. If bad it can be seen when the wheel is spun. However, to measure the run-out accurately a clock gauge pointer should be set against one face. The deviation should not exceed 0.15 mm (0.006 in.). If you do not possess a clock gauge it is worth holding a steel pointer firmly on a nearby support with the point up to the disc face. Variations can be detected in this way also. Remember that the wheel bearings must be completely devoid of any endfloat in order to check disc run-out. Worn or maladjusted bearings can be a contributory factor in disc deterioration.

9 To renovate a disc calls for either refacing or renewal and for this they must be taken off as described next. The cost of refacing should be checked against the cost of a new disc. Remember also that the thickness of the disc should not be less than 9 mm (0.355 in.). If it is very deeply scored or pitted, or the run-out is excessive the only remedy may be a new one. If the disc is too thin it loses some of its capability to disperse heat and also its rigidity.

10 To remove a disc, a difficult task, first remove the roadwheel and the caliper. Hang the caliper up so that the flexible hose is not strained.

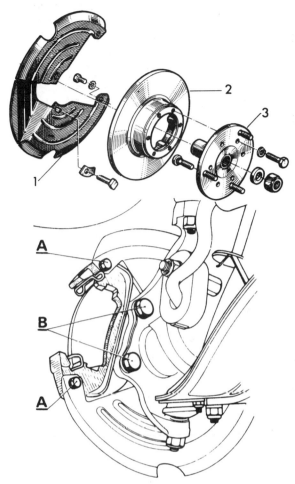

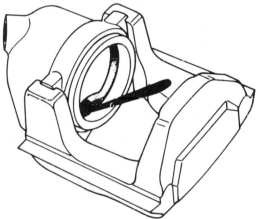

Fig. 8.14. Caliper piston seal removal (Sec. 8)

Fig. 8.15. Front disc brake components

1	Dust shield	A	Dust shield fixing bolts
2	Disc	B	Caliper fixing
3	Hub		

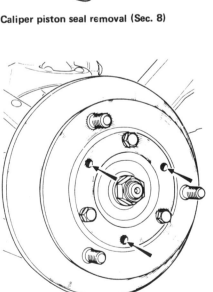

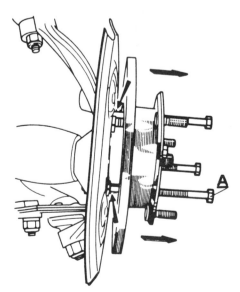

Fig. 8.16. Disc/hub extraction. The arrows on the left show the position of the 'push' screws, 'A' shows a sample 'push' screw (Sec. 0)

11 Remove the caliper bracket by removing the two deflector securing bolts and then the two bracket to stub axle carrier bolts. Free the bracket; no shimming is necessary on refitment.

12 Unscrew three of the six disc to hub securing screws. Obtain three other 8 mm setscrews about two inches long and three pieces of steel rod about 4 mm in diameter, two inches long.

13 Place one piece of rod in each of the drillings from which the bolts have just been removed. Then screw in a new setscrew pushing them through to the face of the stub axle carrier.

14 Remove the stub axle nut (90 lb f ft/12.3 kg fm is needed). Hold the hub with a tyre lever placed appropriately across the wheel studs.

15 Now progressively tighten the three setscrews and push the hub/disc off the stub axle carrier. It is not easy and quite a crude but effective method.

16 Once off the disc can be separated from the hub quite easily. Hold the disc in padded jaws of a strong vice.

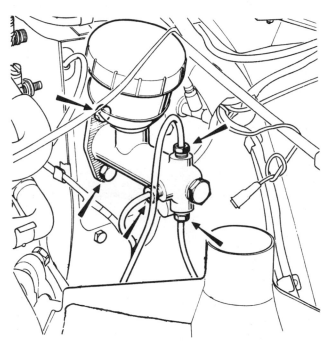

Fig. 8.17. The R1221 master cylinder in position (Sec. 9)

17 Replacement is almost a direct reverse motion of the removal except that hub/disc must be replaced using the method described in Chapter 7 for refitting a driveshaft.

Note: Only use high tension bolts for the hub to disc fitment.

9 Master cylinder - removal and replacement

1 If the wheel hydraulic cylinders and/or caliper pistons are in order and there are no leaks elsewhere, yet the brake pedal still does not hold under sustained pressure then the master cylinder seals may be presumed to be ineffective. To renew them the master cylinder must be removed.

2 Disconnect the master cylinder pushrod from the brake pedal by removing the clevis pin.

3 Unscrew the hydraulic pipe union(s) and push the pipe to one side.

4 Remove the two nuts and washers holding the master cylinder to the bulkhead, one inside the car the other under the bonnet, and lift the unit away. Empty the contents of the reservoir into a clean container.

5 Replacement is a reversal of the removal procedure, after which the braking system must be bled completely and the pedal clearance checked. See Section 17.

10 Master cylinder - inspection and repair

1 Unless there are obvious signs of leakage any defects in the master cylinder are usually the last to be detected in the hydraulic system.

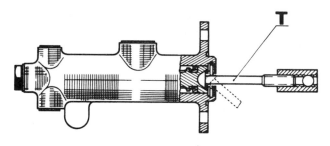

Fig. 8.18. 'T' shows the angle to which the pushrod must be moved for removal

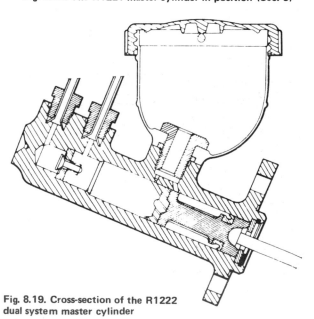

Fig. 8.19. Cross-section of the R1222 dual system master cylinder

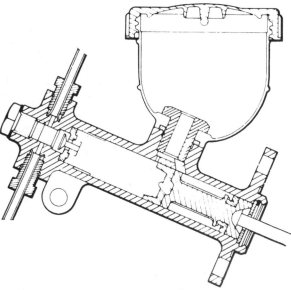

Fig. 8.20. Cross-section of the R1221 master cylinder

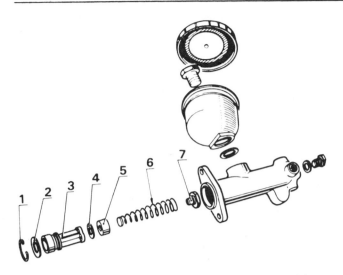

Fig. 8.21. The components of the R1221 master cylinder. '1' to '7' shows the order of the piston components - circlip, spacer, piston, spacer, rubber, spring, end cap (Sec. 10)

2 Before assuming that a fault in the system is in the master cylinder the pipes and wheel cylinders should all be checked and examined as described in Section 6.

3 Remove the master cylinder from the car as described in the previous Section.

4 Single or dual line master cylinders are similar in principle. The tandem cylinder has a by-pass unit fitted to it. Dismantle and reassemble in the same way as you would a wheel cylinder, with the same care and cleanliness. Note however the additional final circlip which holds the piston and spring and seals in the cylinder. You will need to remove the stop light switch (Section 14).

5 Adjust the brake pedal rods, as described in the next Section.

6 Completely bleed the hydraulic system.

Special note: Be absolutely sure you have repaired the master cylinder with the correct repair kit. Some kits which will physically fit some master cylinders are dangerous.

11 Hydraulic fluid pipes - inspection and replacement

1 Periodically and certainly well in advance of the DoE (MoT) test, if due, all brake pipes, connections and unions should be completely and carefully examined.

2 Examine first all the unions for signs of leaks. Then look at the flexible hoses for signs of fraying and chafing (as well as for leaks). This is only a preliminary inspection of the flexible hoses as exterior condition does not necessarily indicate interior condition which will be considered later.

3 The steel pipes must be examined equally carefully. They must be thoroughly cleaned and examined for signs of dents or other percussive damage, rust and corrosion. Rust and corrosion should be scraped off and, if the depth of pitting in the pipes is significant, they will need replacement. This is most likely in those areas underneath the chassis and along the rear suspension arms where the pipes are exposed to the full force of road and weather conditions.

4 If any section of pipe is to be removed, first of all take off the fluid reservoir cap, line it with a piece of polythene film to make it airtight and screw it back on. This will minimise the amount of fluid dripping out of the system when the pipes are removed.

5 Rigid pipe removal is usually quite straightforward. The unions at each end are undone and the pipe drawn out of the connection. The clips which may hold it to the car body are bent back and it is then removed. Underneath the car exposed unions can be particularly stubborn, defying the efforts of an open ended spanner. As few people will have the special split ring spanner required, a self-grip wrench (mole) is the only answer. If the pipe is being renewed new unions will be provided. If not then one will have to put up with the possibility of burring over the flats on the union and use a self-grip wrench for replacement also.

6 Flexible hoses are always fitted to a rigid support bracket where they join a rigid pipe, the bracket being fixed to the chassis or rear suspension arm. The rigid pipe unions must first be removed from the flexible union. Then the locknut securing the flexible pipe to the bracket must be unscrewed, releasing the end of the pipe from the bracket. As these connections are usually exposed they are more often than not rusted up and a penetrating fluid is virtually essential to aid removal (try Plus-Gas). When undoing them, both halves must be supported as the bracket is not strong enough to support the torque required to undo the nut and can easily be snapped off.

7 Once the flexible hose is removed examine the internal bore. If clear of fluid it should be possible to see through it. Any specks of rubber which come out, or signs of restriction in the bore, mean that the inner lining is breaking up and the pipe must be replaced.

8 Rigid pipes which need replacement can usually be purchased at any local garage where they have the pipe, unions and special

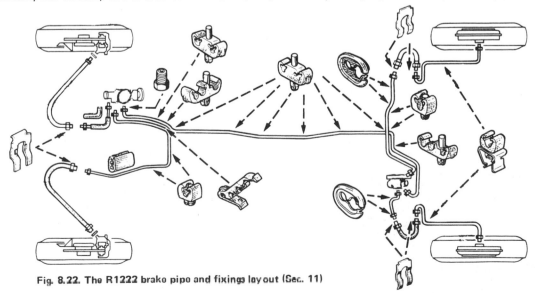

Fig. 8.22. The R1222 brake pipe and fixings layout (Sec. 11)

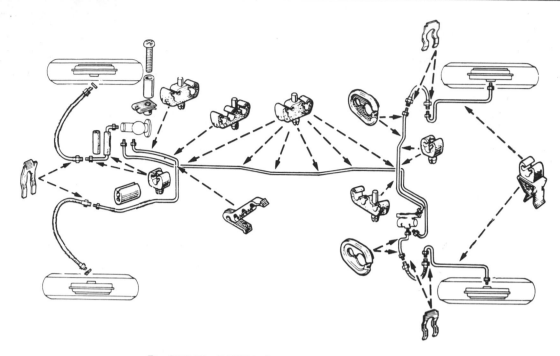

Fig. 8.23. The R1221 brake pipe and fixings layout (Sec. 11)

tools to make them up. All that they need to know is the pipe length required and the type of flare used at the ends of the pipe. These may be different at each end of the same pipe.

9   Replacement of pipes is a straightforward reversal of the removal procedure. It is best to get all the sets (bends) in the pipe made preparatory to installation. Also any acute bends should be put in by the garage on a bending machine otherwise there is the possibility of kinking them and restricting the bore area and fluid flow.

10 With the pipes replaced, remove the polythene from the reservoir cap and bleed the system as described in Section 3.

---

12 Brake pressure limiting valve and bypass unit - general

1   All models are fitted with a brake pressure limiting valve which is fitted in the hydraulic circuit to limit the maximum amount of fluid pressure going to the brakes at the rear and

thereby distribute pressure between front and rear to ensure a balanced and effective braking effort at all times. If it is suspected of malfunctioning it is important that it is replaced. It is located in the hydraulic pipe circuit on the chassis at the rear right-hand side at the end of the torsion bars. It has a special steel cover plate. It is not possible to dismantle this unit and not practical to test it (photo).

2   Always fit a new unit. Removing the old unit is a similar operation to the removal of rigid hydraulic pipes as described in Section 11. Try to bleed the unit before actually fitting to ease the system bleeding and to ensure satisfactory operation immediately. It is never wise to leave it out of the system - in fact it is positively dangerous.

3   It is not practical to adjust the adjustable limiting valves at home. Once a new unit is fitted and the hydraulic system bled, have it adjusted by a reputable Renault agency. It does not take long and is easy for them.

4   Those cars fitted with tandem master cylinders are fitted

12.1 The brake pressure limiter works best if it is clean

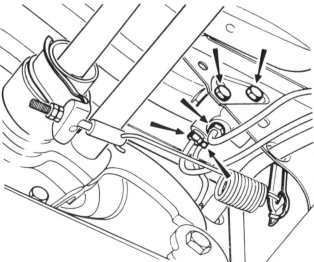

Fig. 8.24. The brake pressure (to the rear brakes) limiting valve fixings (Sec. 12)

with bypass units. It enables pressure to the rear wheels to be increased in the event of a leak in the front wheel circuit. Both this unit and the pressure limiter are fitted.

5 The bypass unit is attached to the tandem master cylinder by conventional hydraulic system fittings. It is not repairable and can oly be checked by a Renault agency. If in doubt replace the fitting.

6 Bleed the bypass system from the bleed screw on the top of the unit once the four roadwheels have been bled.

7 These are reliable instruments which should be left alone.

13 Stoplight switch - general

1 The stoplight switch is located on the outer end of the master cylinder just below the fluid reservoir. It can be removed with the master cylinder still in the car.

2 To remove, only when it is absolutely certain it in itself is malfunctioning and there is not some other electrical fault, disconnect the two cables and mark their position. Place a piece of polythene sheet over the reservoir and replace its cap - this will stop, to some extent, the loss of fluid. Place a rag

underneath the switch and with the correct sized open ended spanner unscrew the switch.

3 Replace, always using a new copper washer and tighten sufficiently. Replace the cables and bleed the brakes, having removed the polythene sheet. (Try and leave the replacement of this switch to another time when you have to bleed the brakes anyway. However, do not contravene the law).

14 Handbrake - general

1 Both the R1222 and R1221 have a centrally mounted, between the two front seats, handbrake 'handle' on lever and although the R1222 handbrake operates on the rear wheels and the R1221, the front, work in much the same way.

2 Day-to-day adjustment is taken up automatically when the rear drum brakes (R1222) and front drum brakes (R1221) are adjusted. Therefore any other adjustment necessary must be because of handbrake cable stretch which cannot be compensated for by the normal automatic adjustment. Adjusting the handbrake (only to be undertaken once the drums have been adjusted and there still remains more than 6 notches of lever

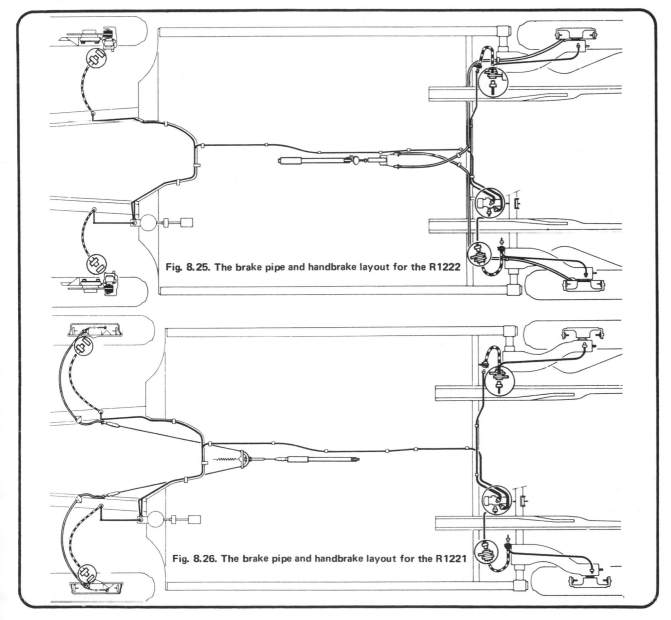

Fig. 8.25. The brake pipe and handbrake layout for the R1222

Fig. 8.26. The brake pipe and handbrake layout for the R1221

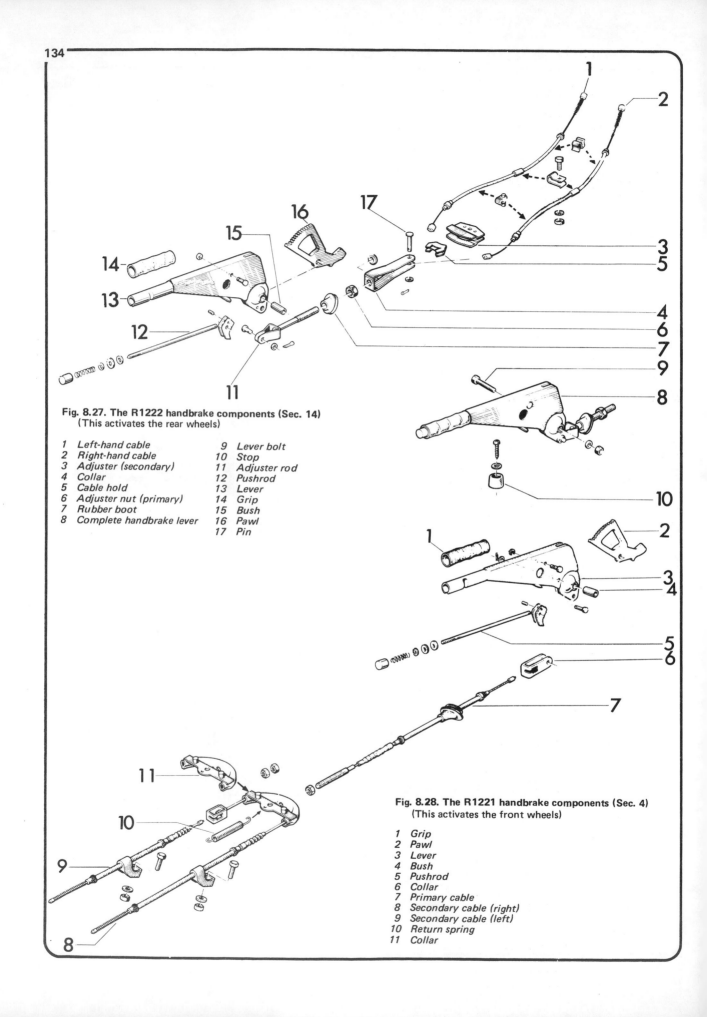

Fig. 8.27. The R1222 handbrake components (Sec. 14)
(This activates the rear wheels)

1	Left-hand cable	9	Lever bolt
2	Right-hand cable	10	Stop
3	Adjuster (secondary)	11	Adjuster rod
4	Collar	12	Pushrod
5	Cable hold	13	Lever
6	Adjuster nut (primary)	14	Grip
7	Rubber boot	15	Bush
8	Complete handbrake lever	16	Pawl
		17	Pin

Fig. 8.28. The R1221 handbrake components (Sec. 4)
(This activates the front wheels)

1 Grip
2 Pawl
3 Lever
4 Bush
5 Pushrod
6 Collar
7 Primary cable
8 Secondary cable (right)
9 Secondary cable (left)
10 Return spring
11 Collar

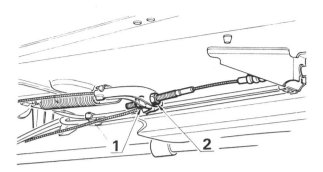

Fig. 8.29. The handbrake cable adjustment (Sec. 14)

1   Adjuster nut   2   Locknut

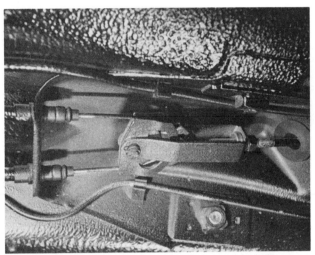

14.2 The secondary handbrake cable adjuster can be seen on the right

travel), is done from underneath the car. Chock the wheels, release the handbrake and then jack-up the rear (R1222), or front (R1221), of the car. Unlock the locknut on the handbrake rod and then tighten the adjusting nut until the rear (R1222) or front (R1221) brake linings just rub on the drums. Tighten the locknut and then try the handbrake lever. It should be fully on at **4 - 6 notches** (photo).

3   To remove the handbrake lever, tilt the front seats forward, release the handbrake, chock the wheels and raise the rear (R1222), or front (R1221), of it off the ground. Remove the primary cable from the secondary cables' junction underneath the car. The fitting will be either a split and ferrule or threaded rod. Then pull up the handbrake lever and release the primary cable from it, from inside the car - this fitting may be a bowden cable/nipple or ferrule and split pin. Then unscrew the pivot pin and nut and remove the lever. It is possible to replace the ratchet alone. Replacement is a reverse process. Adjust the handbrake.

4   Both ends of the primary cable have been disconnected in paragraph 3. This leaves only the secondary cables to be removed. The secondary cables differ between R1222 and R1221 models, although in principle work the same way. The illustration accompanying this Section best describes their removal up to the point of the brake drum. To remove the cables from the brake drums, remove the drums, remove the brake shoes and then pull out the captive end of the cable from the operating mechanism by prising open the two lips with a screwdriver. Pull the end of the cable through the backing plate. Replacement is a simple reverse process.

15 Brake, clutch and throttle pedals - general

1   The brake and clutch pedals pivot on the same shaft and one cannot be removed without the other. The throttle pedal is mounted separately.

2   To remove the pedals (necessary together) unclip the two pedal return springs from the arms, having once removed the glove tray. Punch out the roll pin, to the right of the brake pedal, on the pivot. Push out the pivot shaft to the left.

3   Let the pedals fall away. Disconnect the clutch cable from the clutch pedal by pulling out the split pin and locking pin. The pedals will now come off the pivot shaft. Note the order of washers, springs etc.

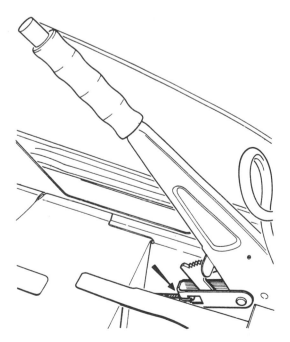

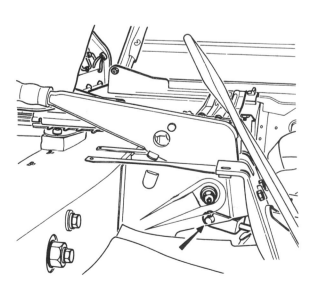

Fig. 8.30. Handbrake cable removal from the lever (left), R1221 (right) R1222 (Sec. 14)

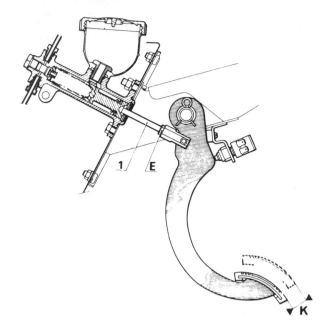

Fig. 8.31. Brake pedal clearance adjustment (Sec. 15)

K *Position of measurement*
E *Adjuster nut*
1 *Brake pedal pushrod*

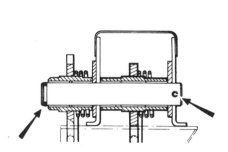

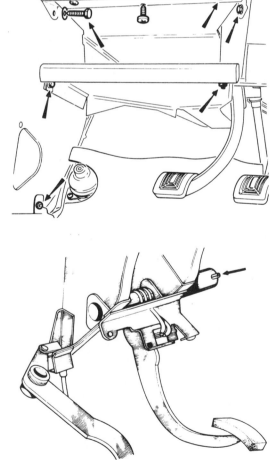

Fig. 8.32. Pedal removal. The top illustration shows the parcel shelf screws; the other two show the position of the pivot shaft and its circlip and roll-pin (Sec. 15)

4 Replacement is the reverse of removal but be sure to pregrease everything.

5 The throttle pedal is integral with its pivot bracket. The bracket is fixed to the bulkhead by three studs. The nuts of these are accessible from inside the car. Remove the throttle cable from the pedal in the same way as for the clutch.

6 The brake pedal push-rod clearance must be checked. It should have a clearance of 5 mm (13/64 in.). There is a locknut on the pushrod. This should be loosened until the clearance (between pushrod end and master cylinder) is correct at the pedal end. Tighten the locknut when all is correct.

16 Fault diagnosis - braking system

Before diagnosing faults from the following chart, check that any braking irregularities are not caused by:

1 *Uneven and incorrect tyre pressures*
2 *Incorrect 'mix' of radial and crossply tyres*
3 *Wear in the steering mechanism*
4 *Defects in the suspension*
5 *Misalignment of the 'chassis'*

Symptom	Reason/s	Remedy
Pedal travels a long way before the brakes operate	Brake shoes set too far from the drums	Adjust the brake shoes to the drums.
Stopping ability poor, even though pedal pressure is firm	Linings/pads and/or drums/disc badly worn or scored	Dismantle, inspect and renew as required.
	One or more wheel hydraulic cylinders or caliper pistons seized, resulting in some brake shoes not pressing against the drums/discs/pads	Dismantle and inspect. Renew as necessary.
	Brake linings/pads contaminated with oil	Renew linings/pads and repair source of oil contamination.
	Wrong type of linings/pads fitted (too hard)	Verify type of material which is correct for the car, and fit it.
	Brake shoes/pads wrongly assembled	Check for correct assembly.
Car veers to one side when the brakes are applied	Brake linings/pads on one side are contaminated with oil	Renew linings/pads and stop oil leak.
	Hydraulic wheel cylinder(s)/caliper on one side partially or fully seized	Inspect wheel cylinders/pistons for correct operation and renew as necessary.
	A mixture of lining materials fitted between sides	Standardise on types of linings fitted.
	Unequal wear between sides caused by partially seized wheel cylinders/pistons	Check wheel cylinders/pistons and renew linings/pads and drums/discs as required.
Pedal feels spongy when the brakes are applied	Air is present in the hydraulic system	Bleed the hydraulic system and check for any signs of leakage.
Pedal feels springy when the brakes are applied	Brake linings/pads not bedded into the drums/discs (after fitting new ones)	Allow time for new linings/pads to bed in after which it will certainly be necessary to adjust the shoes to the drums as pedal travel will have increased.
	Master cylinder or brake backplate mounting bolts loose	Retighten mounting bolts.
	Severe wear in brake drums/discs causing distortion when brakes are applied	Renew drums/disc and linings/pads.
Pedal travels right down with little or no resistance and brakes are virtually non-operative	Leak in hydraulic systems resulting in lack of pressure for operating wheel cylinders/caliper pistons	Examine the whole of the hydraulic system and locate and repair source of leaks. Test after repairing each and every leak source.
	If no signs of leakage are apparent all the master cylinder internal seals are failing to sustain pressure	Overhaul master cylinder. If indications are that seals have failed for reasons other than wear all the wheel cylinder seals/piston seals should be checked also and the system completely replenished with the correct fluid.
Binding, juddering, overheating	One or a combination of causes given in the foregoing sections	Complete and systematic inspection of the whole braking system.

Chapter 9 Electrical system

Contents

Specifications

Battery	Tudor 30 amp 6RF3 or Fulmen 30 amp 809R as original fitment

Generator

	R1222	R1221
Alternator	SEV-Motorola type 712 28412	
Dynamo		Ducellier type 7355 or 7361
Control box	SEV 033446 or Ducellier 8364	Ducellier 8311 or 8314 (sealed)
Starter motor	Paris-Rhone D8E81 or Ducellier 6187C	Paris-Rhone D8E74 or Ducellier 6185 or 6219B
Windscreen wiper motor	SEV Marchal	
Flasher unit	Klaxon 30 860 or Cartier 161	
Brake light switch	Torix or LMP mechanical switch	
Headlamps	Cibie 'special' pre-focus	
Horn	Klaxon	
Oil pressure sender switch	Jaeger Torix	
Temperature sender switch	Jaeger, operates at: R1222 111°C +/- 5°C; R1221 115°C +/- 5°C	

Cooling fan and switch (R1222)

Motor type	Ducellier type 4921 or Paris-Rhone VR12
"Mosta" temperature switch	Jaeger: points close at 92°C +/- 1.5^{O}C; points open at 82°C +/- 1.5^{O}C

1 General description

The electrical system is 12 volt DC, negative earth and apart from the ignition system which is dealt with in Chapter 4, the main items are:

1 Battery (12 volt).
2 R1221 - Dynamo (generator) driven by the fan belt, coupled with an integral voltage and current regulator; or R1222. Alternator (generator) again driven by the fan belt.
3 Electro-mechanical starter motor.
4 Windscreen wipers.
5 Lights.
6 Heater motor.
7 Heated rear window.
8 Thermostatically controlled electric cooling fan (R1222).

The battery supplies current for the ignition, lighting and other circuits and provides a reserve of power when the current consumed by the equipment exceeds the production of the generator.

The starter motor places very heavy demands on the power reserve. The generator uses engine power to produce electricity to re-charge the battery and the rate of charge is automatically controlled by a regulator. This regulator keeps the power output of the generator within its capacity (an uncontrolled generator can burn itself out) and also adjusts the voltage and current output depends on the state of the battery charge and the electrical demands being made on the system at any one time.

2 Battery - removal and replacement

1 The battery is situated at the front right-hand side of the engine compartment.
2 Disconnect the earth lead (negative) from the terminal by unscrewing the shackle or centre screw and twisting the terminal cover off. Do not use any striking force or damage could be caused to the battery. Then remove the positive lead in the same way. Always remove the earth coil first.
3 Slacken off the nuts holding the battery clamp stays until the assembly can be disengaged sufficiently to lift the battery out.
4 Lift the battery out, keeping it the right way up to prevent spillage of the electrolyte.
5 Replacement is a reversal of this procedure. Replace the positive lead first and smear the terminal posts and connections beforehand with petroleum jelly (not grease) in order to prevent corrosion.

3 Battery - maintenance and inspection

1 Any new battery, if properly looked after, will last for two years at least (provided also that the generator and regulator are in correct order).
2 The principal maintenance requirements are cleanliness and regular topping up of the electrolyte level with distilled water. Each week the battery cell cover or caps should be removed and just enough water added, if needed, to cover the tops of the separators. Do not overfill with the idea of the topping up lasting longer - it will only dilute the electrolyte and with the level high the likelihood of it 'gassing' out is increased. This is the moisture one can see on the top of the battery. 'Little and often' is the rule.
3 Wipe the top of the battery carefully at the same time removing all traces of moisture. Paper handkerchiefs are ideal for the job.
4 Every three months disconnect the battery terminals and wash both the posts and lead connectors with a washing soda solution. This will remove any corrosion deposits. Dry them off and smear liberally with petroleum jelly - not grease, before

reconnection.
5 If a significant quantity of electrolyte is lost through spillage it will not suffice to merely refill with distilled water. Empty out all the electrolyte into a glass container and measure the specific gravity. Electrolyte is a mixture of sulphuric acid and water in the ratio of 2 parts acid to 5 parts water and the ready made solution should be obtained from battery specialists or large garages. The 'normal' solution can be added if the battery is in full charged state. If the battery is in a low state of charge, use the normal solution, then charge the battery, empty out the electrolyte, swill the battery out with clean water and then refill with a new charge of normal electrolyte.

4 Battery - charging

1 In winter certain conditions may result in the battery being used in excess of the generator's ability to recharge it in the running time available. This situation does not occur however on cars fitted with alternators which have a much higher rate of output at low revolutions.
2 Where necessary therefore, an external charging source is needed to keep the battery power reserve at the proper level. If batteries are being charged from an external source a hydrometer is used to check the electrolyte specific gravity. Most battery chargers are set to charge at 3—4 amps initially and as the battery charge builds up this reduces automatically to 1—2 amps. The table following gives details of the specific gravity readings, at 21°C/70°F. Do not take readings just after topping up, just after using the starter motor, or when the electrolyte is too cold or too warm. The variation in SG readings is 0.004 for every 6°C/10°F charge - the higher readings being for the higher temperatures.

Specific gravity	Battery state of charge
1.28	100%
1.25	75%
1.22	50%
1.19	25%
1.16	Very low
1.11	Discharged completely

5 Generator (dynamo) - description, maintenance and testing

1 The DC generator or dynamo consists of an armature running in bearings. It is surrounded by field coils bolted to the outer casing or yoke. At one end of the armature is the commutator consisting of copper segments. Two carbon brushes, spring loaded and in holders run on the commutator.
2 The only maintenance required is to check that the fan belts are correctly tensioned. The armature runs in ball bearings with sealed in lubrication. Some owners may wish to check the carbon brush length and this can be done by seeing that the ends are not below the ends of the brush holders. If they are, new brushes should be fitted.
3 A generator normally works properly or not at all. There are few instances of poor performance. A quick check can be made if a voltmeter is available. Disconnect both leads from the dynamo and join the two terminals together with a piece of bare wire. From the centre of the wire run a lead via the voltmeter to earth. With the engine running at a fast tickover there should be a reading of about 15 volts. If there is no voltage then suspect the carbon brushes. If the voltage is low - 208 volts then suspect the field windings or armature. Either of the latter will require renewal or re-build by specialists.

6 Generator (dynamo) - control box

1 The regulator box regulates the voltage and current, according to the demands of the system. It also prevents feed back from the battery when the generator is producing voltage

less than battery voltage. The unit is not designed for adjustment or repair and under normal circumstances it will function perfectly and last indefinitely.

2 If the charging system is not working correctly, indicated by the warning lamp not going out when the engine speed increases the generator should first be checked as this is the most usual cause of the trouble.

3 If the generator is found to be satisfactory make a careful check of the connections on the control box to make sure they are tight and corrosion free. If the vehicle has been standing unused for a long time in a damp climate the control box will probably be defective.

4 Where a control box is defective the whole unit must be renewed.

7 Generator (dynamo and/or alternator) - removal and replacement

1 Slacken the one dynamo retaining bolt and the nuts on the sliding link, and move the dynamo in towards the engine so that the fan belt can be taken off the dynamo pulley. This is most easily done by removing the handbrake tension spring and then placing the handbrake on again. This allows the necessary room to get full leverage on the nut of the retaining bolt underneath the dynamo with an open ended spanner.

2 Push the dynamo as near to the rocker cover as possible and gently ease the fan belt off its pulley. Sometimes a screwdriver can be used effectively as a 'shoe-horn'.

3 Still holding the dynamo with the left-hand undo the two terminal leads from the dynamo. Always use the correct spanners on these two.

4 Now hold the dynamo in the same position with the right hand and carefully unclip the distributor cap but leave it attached still to the plug leads resting on its edge on the rotor arm. Also unclip the throttle cable from its retainer.

5 Swing the dynamo down now so that it rests gently on the steering column. Take off the retaining nut and slide the bolt through towards the distributor. Pull out the bolt (this is why the distributor cap is off) with the left-hand and remove the dynamo with the right.

6 Replacement is a reversal of the above procedure. Do not finally tighten the retaining bolt and the nut on the sliding link until the fan belt is at its correct tension.

7 Removal and replacement of the alternator is basically similar except that the electrical contacts are push-on. Be most careful

to reconnect properly first time and do not use any force on the casing of the alternator - **do not** use the lever.

8 Generator (dynamo) - dismantling, repair and reassembly

1 It is often likely that once the dynamo is beyond just the replacement of brushes, it is more economic to have the whole unit overhauled or replaced. Overhauling should only be undertaken by qualified auto-electricians. Its total overhaul is not really a home mechanic's task.

2 Grip the pulley of the dynamo in a vice and loosen the pulley retaining nut. Then remove the nuts from the two studs at the other end of the dynamo to release the commutator end bracket.

3 Pull off the commutator end bracket.

4 Pull out the armature, pulley and end bearing cap from the body of the dynamo but hold the brushes, still attached to the body, away from the armature to avoid their damage. (Shim steel or feeler blades do this adequately). Place the armature aside for inspection.

5 Remove the brushes from the body of the dynamo by undoing the 'DYN' and 'EXC' terminal nuts and thereby releasing the brush contact wires and the brushes from their seating bodies.

6 Never attempt to release the field coils by dismantling the field terminals of both types of dynamo because an impact screwdriver is necessary. If the dynamo is in need of new field coils it should be replaced as a total unit.

7 Do not dismantle further still at this stage. Examine the carbon brushes. The length of the brushes should be no less than 7/16 inch (11.1 mm). If required fit the correct new ones which are supplied with new leads.

8 Examine next the commutator end of the armature. This should not be burnt or scored in any way. First clean it off with a little petrol on a rag. Any traces of pitting, scoring or burring, if slight, can be cleaned off with fine glass paper. Do not use emery paper. Make sure that there are no flat spots, by tearing the glass paper into strips and use it by drawing it round the commutator evenly. Do not try and clean off too much by this method as the commutator must remain circular in section.

9 To test the armature is not difficult but a voltmeter or bulb and 12 volt battery are required. The two tests determine whether there may be a break in any circuit winding or if any wiring insulation is broken down. Fig. 9.4 shows how the battery, voltmeter and probe connectors are used to test whether (a) any wire in the windings is broken or (b) whether there is an

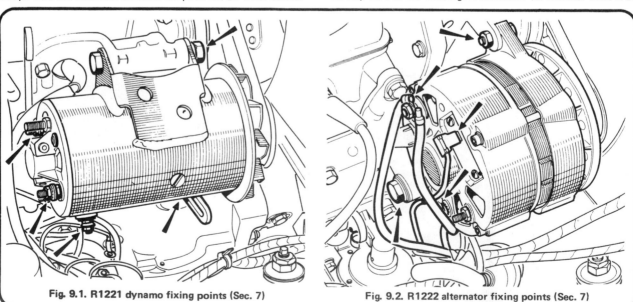

Fig. 9.1. R1221 dynamo fixing points (Sec. 7)   Fig. 9.2. R1222 alternator fixing points (Sec. 7)

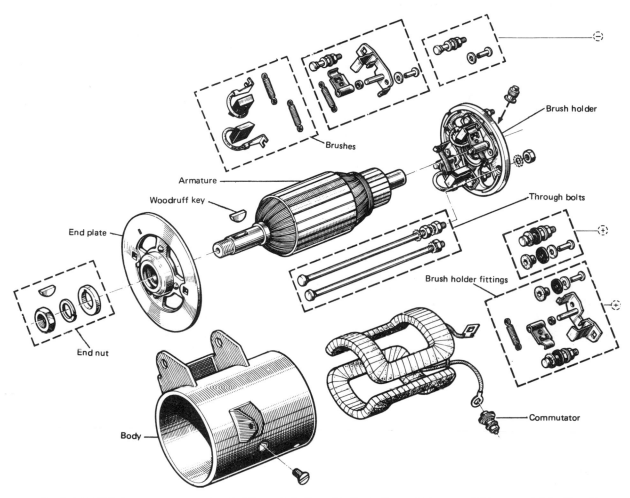

Fig. 9.3. R1221 dynamo component parts. The parts in 'boxes' indicate those which are available as repair kits (Sec. 8)

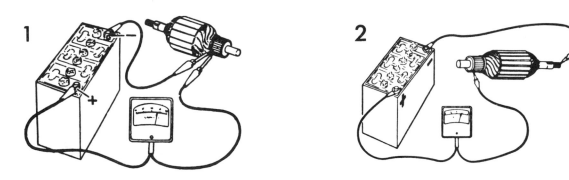

Fig. 9.4. Armature winding tests (Sec. 8)

1 Testing the armature for a broken wire   *2 Testing for insulation between windings*

insulation breakdown. In the first test the probes are placed on adjacent segments of a clean commutator. All voltmeter readings should be similar. If a bulb is used instead it will glow very dimly or not at all if there is a fault. For the second test any reading or bulb lighting indicates a fault. Test each segment in turn with one probe and keep the other on the shaft. Should either test indicate a faulty armature the wisest action in the long run is to obtain a replacement dynamo altogether. The field coils may be tested if an ohmmeter or ammeter can be obtained. With an

ohmmeter the resistance (measured between the terminal and the yoke) should be 6 ohms. With an ammeter, connect it in series with a 12 volt battery again from the field terminal to the yoke. A reading of 2 amps is normal. Zero amps or infinity ohms indicate an open circuit. More than 2 amps or less than 6 ohms indicates a breakdown of the insulation. Unless you can get the field coil readily repaired it is better to obtain a replacement unit.

10 The drive end bearing should have no play but in the event

that it also needs renewal (very rare except where the fan belt
has been persistently overtight), first remove the pulley nut and
washers and draw off the pulley. Then tap the woodruff key out
of the shaft using a screwdriver under one end. Be careful to
guard against it flying off and getting lost. If the end cover is
now supported across the jaws of a vice, with the armature
hanging down, the end of the shaft may be tapped with a soft
faced mallet to drive it out of the bearing housing with the
bearing. The bearing itself can next be taken off the shaft by the
same method. When fitting a new bearing make sure it is
thoroughly packed with grease and fit it into the end cover first,
making sure that the pressure ring and retaining plate are all
assembled correctly. Then place the retaining cup over the
armature shaft so that the open end faces the armature. Then the
end cover may be supported over the vice jaws and the armature
carefully tapped through the bearing with a mallet. Refit the
spacer, then the woodruff key, followed by the pulley, washer
and nut.

11 Reassembly is a straight reverse sequence of the disassembly
just described. **Note:** always replace the armature before refitting
the brushes.

Replace the through bolts and before tightening them right
up, check that the end plates are fully and correctly in position.
Spin the armature to ensure it is not binding or touching the
field coils and then unhook the brush springs and lower the
brushes onto the commutator with the springs on top. Finally
place a few drops of engine oil in the oil hole of the commutator
bearing bush.

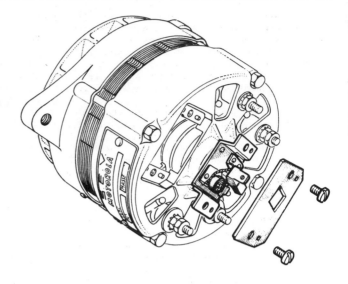

Fig. 9.5. R1222 alternator brush holder location (Sec. 9)

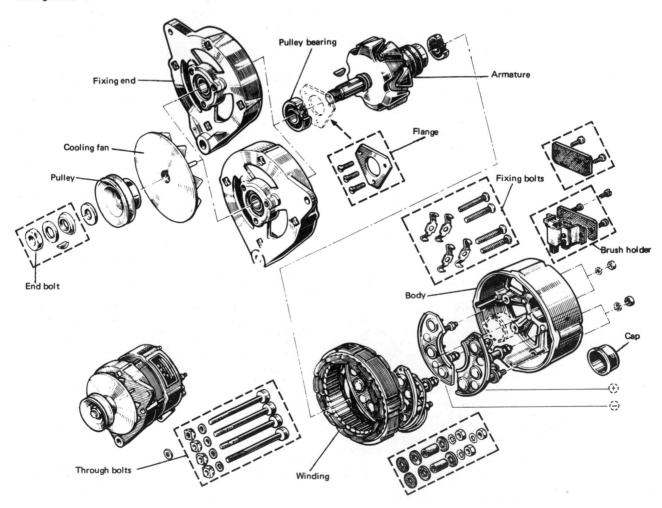

Fig. 9.6. R1222 alternator component parts. The parts in 'boxes' indicate those which are available as repair kits (Sec. 9)

9 Generator (alternator) - description and precautions

The R1222 imported into the United Kingdom is fitted with an alternator in place of the more generally well-known DC 'dynamo'. The alternator generates alternating current (AC) which is rectified by diodes into DC and is the current needed for battery storage.

The regulator is a transistorized unit which is permanently sealed and requires no attention. It will last indefinitely provided no mistakes are made in wiring connections.

Apart from the renewal of the rotor slip ring brushes and rotor shaft bearings, there are no other parts which need periodic inspection. All other items are sealed assemblies and must be replaced if indications are that they are faulty.

If there are indications that the charging system is malfunctioning in any way, care must be taken to diagnose faults properly, otherwise damage of a serious and expensive nature may occur to parts which are in fact quite serviceable.

The following basic requirements must be observed at all times, therefore, if damage is to be prevented:

1 **All** alternator systems use a **negative** earth. Even the simple mistake of connecting a battery the wrong way round could burn out the alternator diodes in a few seconds.
2 Before disconnecting any wires in the system the engine and ignition circuits should be switched off. This will minimise accidental short circuits.
3 The alternator **must never** be run with the output wire disconnected.
4 Always disconnect the battery from the car's electrical system if an outside charging source is being used.
5 Do not use test wire connections that could move accidentally and short circuit against nearby terminals. Short circuits will not blow fuses - they will blow diodes or transistors.
6 Always disconnect the battery cables and alternator output wires before any electric welding work is done on the car body.
7 Never lever on the alternator body when adjusting its fan belt drive. The casing is easily fractured. Fault diagnosis on alternator charging systems requires sophisticated test equipment and even with this action required to rectify any fault, is limited to the renewal of one or two components. Knowing what the fault is is only of academic interest in these circumstances.

10 Starter motor - general description

1 The starter motor is mounted on the engine block where the bellhousing would be on a conventional car. It is secured by two bolts on the left-hand side of the engine under the exhaust manifold. It has four field coils and four commutator brushes, two of which are earthed. The switch, in addition to making the electrical connection, also operates a lever which moves the pinion into mesh with the ring gear just before the power is switched to the motor. This results in quieter operation and reduces much of the shock loading on the starter motor. To prevent the engine driving the starter, should the pinion stick, the drive is through a one-way roller type clutch. Also, the pinion is spring loaded, so that in the event of an exact abutment of gearteeth preventing engagement the switch will still continue and make power contact and the pinion will move into engagement automatically as soon as the shaft moves. The operating lever, which connects the plunger to the pinion, pivots on an eccentric pin so that the pinion engagement may be set correctly in relation to the switch contacts. The switching method is by solenoid plunger (electrically activated).
2 Although the starter motors of the two engines are different components they can be dealt with as if they were actually the same.

11 Starter motor circuit - testing

1 If the starter motor fails to turn the engine when the switch is operated there are four possible reasons why:

a) The battery is no good.
b) The electrical connections between switch, solenoid, battery and starter motor are somewhere failing to pass the necessary current from the battery through the starter to earth.
c) The solenoid switch is no good, or the cable is not operating properly.
d) The starter motor is either jammed or electrically defective.

2 To check the battery, switch on the headlights. If they go dim after a few seconds, the battery is definitely unwell. If the lamps glow brightly, next operate the starter switch/cable and see what happens to the lights. If they go dim then you know that power is reaching the starter motor but failing to turn it. Therefore, check that it is not jammed. The starter will have to come out for examination. If the starter should turn very slowly on to the next check.
3 If when the starter switch is operated, the lights stay bright, then the power is not reaching the starter. Check all connections from battery to solenoid switch or cable to starter for perfect cleanliness and tightness. With a good battery installed this is the most usual cause of starter motor problems. Check that the earth link cable between the engine and frame is also intact and cleanly connected. This can sometimes be overlooked when the engine is taken out.
4 If no results have yet been achieved turn off the headlights, otherwise the battery will go flat. You will possibly have heard a clicking noise each time the switch was operated. This is the solenoid switch operating but it does not necessarily follow that the main contact is closing properly. (nb: if no clicking has been heard from the solenoid it is certainly defective). The solenoid contact can be checked by putting a voltmeter or bulb across the main cable connection on the starter side of the solenoid and earth. When the switch is operated, there should be a reading or lighted bulb. If not, the solenoid switch is no good. (Do not put a bulb across the two solenoid terminals. If the motor is not faulty the bulb will blow). If finally, it is established that the solenoid is not faulty and 12 volts are getting to the starter then the starter motor must be the culprit.

12 Starter motor - removal and replacement

Note: Before removing the starter motor from the car make sure it is absolutely necessary. With the engine in the car on the R1222 it is not a nice job; its really no better on the R1221.

Starter motor removal with the engine out of the car is however, simple. (The engine is easily removed with the starter left in place. Just the electrical and/or cable connections removed). Always disconnect the battery first.
1 With the engine in the car proceed as follows: Undo the electrical cables from the starter motor and tape back to the bulkhead. Undo and remove the two (R1221) or three (R1222) fixing bolts and remove the starter motor back, up (forwards) and out. Be patient with the two fixing bolts, it is quite fiddly. A tubular spanner is easiest (photo).
2 You may find it easier if you remove the carburettor air cleaner and the exhaust pipe between the manifold and silencer. It gives more working room. On the R1222 further ease of working, depending on the type of spanners availble, to remove the engine support arm on that side (photo).
3 Replacement is in each case a reversal of removal. Be sure to tighten the fixing bolts well.

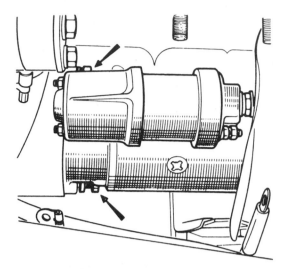

Fig. 9.7. Starter motor fixing bolts (Sec. 12)

12.1 Another shot of the starter motor electrical connection

12.2 The starter motor is heavy and may be a struggle to remove

13 Starter motor - dismantling and reassembly

1 Such is the inherent reliability and strength of the starter motors fitted that it is very unlikely that a motor will ever need dismantling until it is totally worn out and in need of replacement. It is not a task for the home mechanic because although reasonably easy to undertake the reassembly and adjustment before refitting is beyond his scope because of the need of specialist equipment. It would under all circumstances be realistic for the work to be undertaken by the specialist auto-electrician. It is possible to replace solenoids and brushes on starter motors quite easily.

2 Remove the solenoid by undoing the two holding nuts and unhooking the solenoid plunger from the lever. This may mean pushing out end locating pin in the plunger. Then lift away.

3 To remove the brushes undo the two nuts at the opposite end to the pinion and remove the end cap. Pull off the insulation and spring and ease out the commutator end bracket. On this bracket is located the brushes. Remove and inspect in the same way and replace if necessary. Do not disrupt the rest of the starter motor. Replacement is the direct reversal on all starter motors. Solenoids should always be replaced if they have ceased to function properly - there is little that can be done to them in the way of repair.

4 If the motor has been disassembled right down to its component parts the checking of the armature field coils and subsequently bearing bushes should be carried out as described in Section 7.

5 Reassembly of a totally dismantled starter motor is easy for the experienced auto-electrician but not for the home mechanic if he is to have any measure of success. Each type of starter motor has a different bearing and pinion adjustment which you will find impossible to measure without costly equipment. It is better even at this stage of disassembly to realise, that to pay for the work to be done on this unit is more economic than to do it yourself.

14 Starter motor drive pinion - inspection and repair

1 Persistent jamming or reluctance to disengage may mean that the starter pinion assembly needs attention. The starter motor should be removed first of all for inspection.

2 With the starter motor removed thoroughly remove all grime and grease with a petrol soaked rag, taking care to stop any liquid running into the motor itself. If there is a lot of dirt this could be the trouble and all will now be well. The pinion should move freely in a spiral movement along the shaft against the light spring and return easily on being released. To do this the spiral splines should be completely clean and free of oil. (Oil merely collects dust and grime and gums up the splines). The spring should be intact.

3 If the preceding cleaning and check does not actually remove the fault the starter motor will need to be stripped down to its component parts and a further check made. This, as has been explained in the preceding Section, is really beyond the scope of the home mechanic and should be left to the professional auto-electrician. Removal of the pinion itself from the armature is not difficult but requires skill and special tools to replace. If you think that the starter motor needs further inspection take it to the auto-electrician.

15 Fuses - general

The electrical system of the UK import vehicles is fused. All vehicles fitted with a six fuse system which is deemed sufficient for the whole vehicle. The fuse box is mounted under the instrument panel. The top can be lifted off and inspected easily. Always replace fuses with the correct type, see the end of this Section. They are a straight pull-out/push-in fit. Never think that you can leave them out, by-pass them or substitute a piece of tin

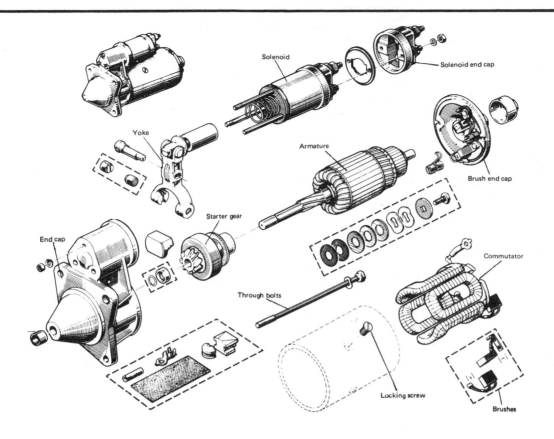

Fig. 9.8. R1222 Paris-Rhone D8E81 starter motor components. The parts in 'boxes' indicate those which are available as repair kits (Sec. 13)

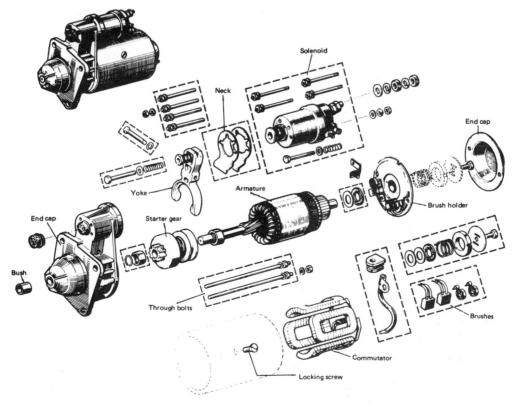

Fig. 9.9. R1222 Ducellier 6187C starter motor components. The parts in 'boxes' indicate those which are available as repair kits (Sec. 13)

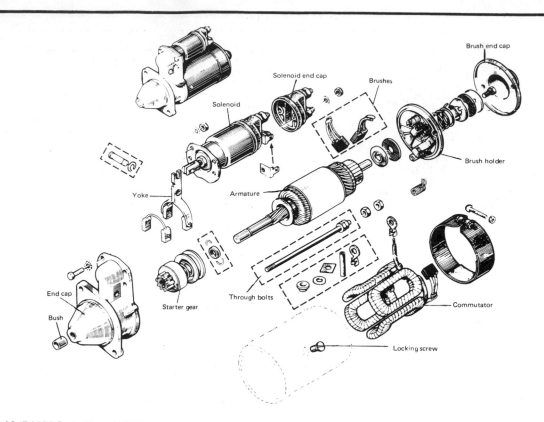

Fig. 9.10. R1221 Paris-Rhone D8E74 starter motor components. Those parts in 'boxes' indicate those which are available as repair kits (Sec. 13)

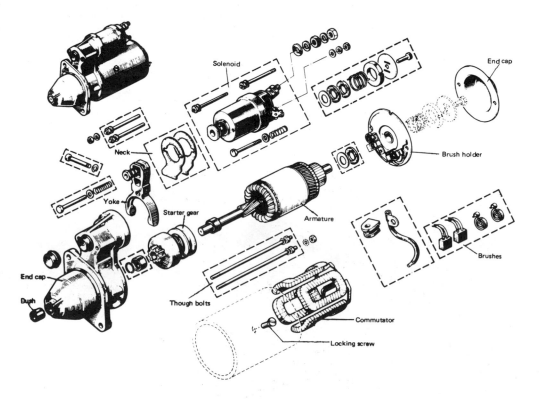

Fig. 9.11. R1221 Ducellier 6185 or 6219B starter motor components. Those parts in 'boxes' indicate those which are available as repair kits (Sec. 13)

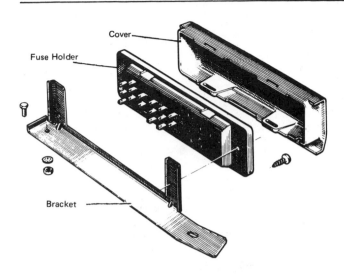

Fig. 9.12. Components of the fusebox

foil or other conductive material unless in a real emergency. Replace the make-shift fuse as soon as possible.

No 1   *Windscreen wipers*
No 2   *Headlights*
No 3   *Heater fan and sidelights*
No 4   *Flashers*
No 5/6 *Brake lights and heated rear window*

16 Direction indicator flasher circuit - fault tracing and rectification

1 The unit which causes the lights to flash intermittently is contained in a two inch long box clipped under the dashboard. It has three terminals.
2 If the flashers fail to work properly first check that all the bulbs are serviceable and of the correct wattage. Then check that the screws which hold the lamp bodies to the car are tight and free from corrosion. These are the means by which the circuit is

completed and any resistance here could affect the proper working of the coils in the flasher unit.
3 If there is still no success, bridge the 'COM' and 'REP' terminals on the flasher unit. When the switch is operated the lights should go on (on the appropriate side) and stay on. If they do the flasher unit is faulty. If they do not go on first make quite sure that with the ignition switched on current is reaching the 'COM' terminal at the flasher circuit. If it is then the indicator switch is faulty. If it is not, then the connection from the ignition switch to the flasher unit is faulty (via a fuse - 5 amp).

17 Windscreen wipers and drive motor - fault diagnosis

1 If the wipers fail to operate first check that current is reaching the motor. This can be done by switching on and using a voltmeter or 12 volt bulb and two wires between the (+) terminal on the motor and earth.
2 If no current is reaching the motor check whether there is any at the switch. If there is then a break has occurred in the wiring between switch and motor.
3 If there is no current at the switch go back to the ignition switch and so isolate the area of the fault.
4 If current is reaching the motor but the wipers do not operate, switch on and give the wiper arm a push - they or the motor could be jammed. Switch off immediately if nothing happens otherwise further damage to the motor may occur. If the wipers now run the reason for them jamming must be found. It will almost certainly be due to wear in either the linkage of the wiper mechanism or the mechanism in the motor gearbox.
5 If the wipers run too slowly it will be due to something restricting the free operation of the linkage or a fault in the motor. In such cases it is well to check the current being used by connecting an ammeter in the circuit. If it exceeds three amps something is restricting free movement. If less, then the commutator and brush gear in the motor are suspect. The shafts to which the wipers are attached run in very long brushes and often suffer from lack of lubrication. Weekly application to each shaft of a few drops of light penetrating oil, preferably, helps to prevent partial or total seizure. First pull outwards the rubber grommets, afterwards, wipe off any excess.
6 If wear is obviously causing malfunction or there is a fault in the motor it is best to remove the motor or wiper mechanism for further examination and repairs.

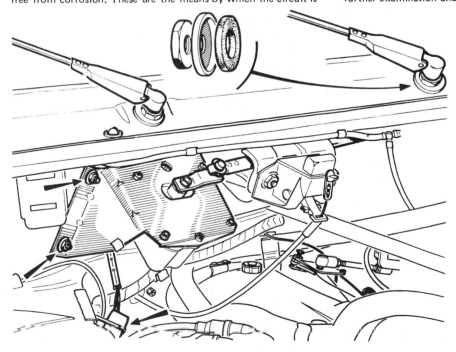

Fig. 9.13. The location under the windscreen of the wiper motor and mechanism

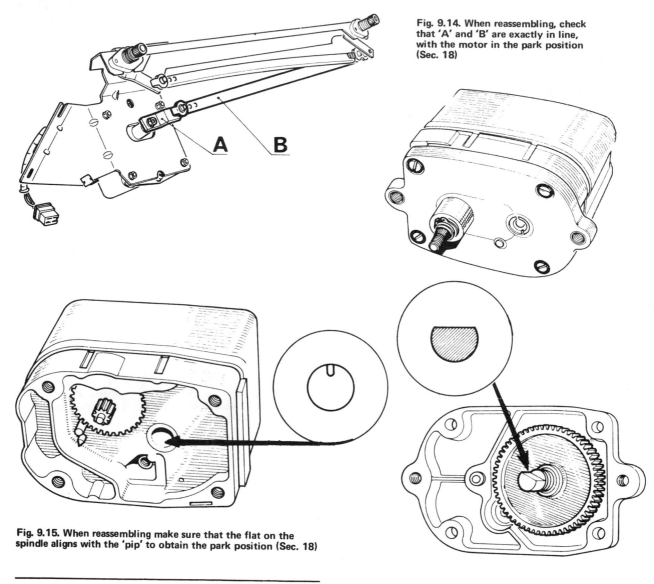

Fig. 9.14. When reassembling, check that 'A' and 'B' are exactly in line, with the motor in the park position (Sec. 18)

Fig. 9.15. When reassembling make sure that the flat on the spindle aligns with the 'pip' to obtain the park position (Sec. 18)

18 Windscreen wiper motor and mechanism - removal, replacement and overhaul

1 The windscreen wiper mechanism must be removed from the car separately from the wiper motor. Both fortunately are fairly simple, if a little fiddly.

2 To remove the mechanism first remove the wiper arms. Open the bonnet and disconnect, just below the centre of the windscreen, the motor drive arm from the driving link. Its a push fit only.

3 Unscrew the four mounting plate fixing screws. Remove the plate and linkage by turning it towards the top, having pushed the wiper arm spindles through their drillings.

4 Replacement is a straight reverse process.

5 Fortunately wiper motors are very reliable: failure is usually in the linkage. Check the fuses before attempting necessary overhaul. Disconnect the battery.

6 Open the bonnet and disconnect the linkage as in paragraph 2.

7 From inside the car get a clear view of the motor underneath the facia just above the heater 'on-off' switch. Remove any panelling surrounding to clear the working area.

8 Undo the four nuts which afix the motor to its mating plate. This will be very fiddly. Once undone wriggle the motor out

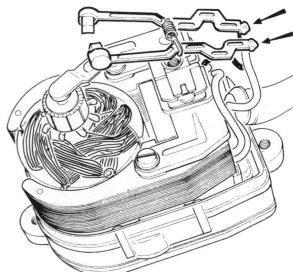

Fig. 9.16. Wiper motor brush holder location (Sec. 18)

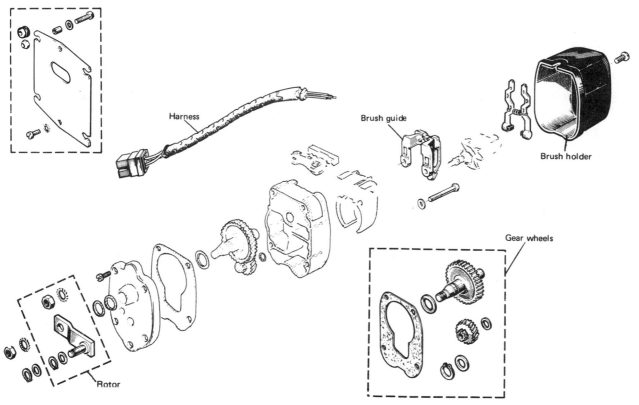

Fig. 9.17. The replaceable components of a wiper motor (Sec. 18)

having disconnected its three feed wires.

9 Replacement is a reverse sequence: patience is needed because of the restricted room.

10 The motor is secured to the plate by three screws. Check the operation of the spindles. They go rusty and therefore seize very quickly. The individual spindles are available as a spare. Retain the small fixing circlips.

11 Failure of the motor, even brush deterioration, is rare. If this **does happen, either exchange the motor or have it rebuilt by an auto-electrician** - it is an intricate mechanism with its 'Park' facility.

19 Horn - general

1 The horn fitted to the Renault 5 is a very reliable unit, although it can get wet if the car is driven in any depth of water. If it fails to operate check all the other parts in the circuit first - the push is much more likely to fail.

2 Should the horn fail to work the first thing to do is make sure that current is reaching the horn terminal. This can be done by connecting a 12 volt test lamp to the feed wire and pressing the horn button with the ignition switch on. If the bulb lights then the fault must lie in the horn or the horn mounting. The tightness and cleanliness of the horn mounting is important as the circuit is made to earth through the fixing bolt. The connections should, of course, be a clean, tight fit on the horn terminals.

3 If no current is reaching the horn check wiring connections as indicated in the wiring diagram.

4 If it is found that the fault lies in the horn unit then it will have to be replaced. Removal of all types of horn is simply the undoing of the nut which secures the horn to the mounting arm. The horn is located on the front cross panel adjacent to the gearbox. It is not important to replace the horn with exactly the same type.

5 A horn cannot be adjusted or repaired.

20 Headlamps and bulbs - adjustment, removal and replacement

1 The headlamps used are unique to the Renault 5 as is their method of fitting and adjustment. There are two types of adjustment - one to suit a laden and unladen condition and one to suit alignment and 'legal' adjustment.

2 To adjust for laden or unladen condition, open the bonnet, and find a small plastic, paddle type lever on the outer, top, rear edges of the headlamps. For an unladen condition, ie: normal usage, the levers should be up. For a laden condition, the levers should be down.

3 Once the previously mentioned levers are in the 'unladen' condition, ie: up, the headlamps can be adjusted for side

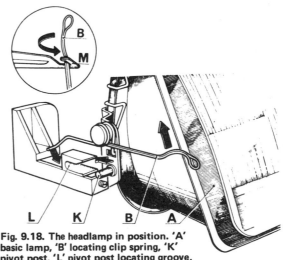

Fig. 9.18. The headlamp in position. 'A' basic lamp, 'B' locating clip spring, 'K' pivot post, 'L' pivot post locating groove, 'M' clip 'home' (Sec. 20).

alignment by a screwdriver in the adjuster screw (1 in Fig. 9.20). For 'up and down' adjustment turn the knurled screw on the top inner edge of the rear of the headlamp (2 in Fig. 9.20). Screw 3 is used to obtain a flush fitting of the headlamp in relation to the bonnet.

4   Headlamp adjustment is best done using proper optical equipment at your local Renault agency. Should you require to do it yourself, the car must be placed in an unladen condition, on level ground, at right angles to a wall some 25 feet from it. On main beam the centre of the two headlamp beams must be parallel to the centreline of car, if drawn out to the wall. On dipped beam the height of the horizontal cut-off to the left of the illuminated area must be between 4 to 6 inches less than the headlight centres.

5   To replace a headlamp bulb, the headlamp unit must be removed from the car. Lift the bonnet and prop it. Lift the wire spring clip, at the outer edge of the headlamps, from its slot, hinge the headlamp shell forward and then back slightly on its peg/slot and then lift the shell out, towards the centre of the car. Pull off the bulb connector. Replacement is a simple reverse process.

6   Bulb removal is conventional Cibie practice. Unclip the two wire clips which hold the bulb flange into the shell and pull out the bulb. Replacement is a simple reverse process.

7   Right or left-hand dipping is available from any type of bulb. Follow the instructions given on the back of the headlamp shell if any change is required.

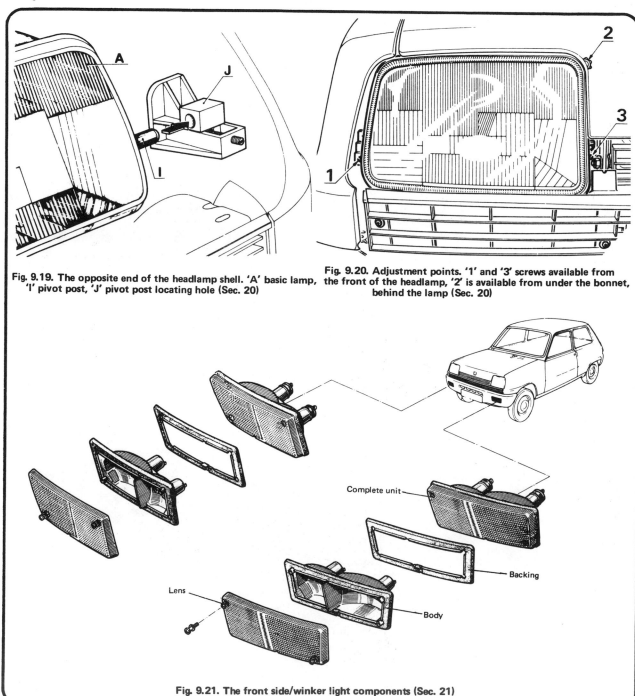

Fig. 9.19. The opposite end of the headlamp shell. 'A' basic lamp, 'I' pivot post, 'J' pivot post locating hole (Sec. 20)

Fig. 9.20. Adjustment points. '1' and '3' screws available from the front of the headlamp, '2' is available from under the bonnet, behind the lamp (Sec. 20)

Fig. 9.21. The front side/winker light components (Sec. 21)

21 Front and flasher lights - general

1 The combined front side and flasher light unit is in the front bumper. The lens is a combined orange/white lens with a divided fixing base and two bulbs (photo).
2 The lens is removed by unscrewing its two fixing screws which are captive through the lens (photo).
3 The individual bulbs are a push-screw-in fit.
4 The unit itself is removed once having removed the lens and bulb by unscrewing the two fixing self-tapping screws visible at opposite corners of the unit. Pull the unit away from the bonnet and carefully slide it from its rubber cover. The electrical connection(s) is then easily removed.
5 Replacement of the unit is exactly a reversal of the removal but make sure you do not overtighten the fixing screws and that the rubber cover is correctly positioned around the lens.

22 Rear side, stop and flasher lights - general

1 All that has been said in Section 21 for the front lights applies for those at the rear (photo).

23 Number plate lights - general

1 The number plate lights are situated in the centre of the tailgate. Lens can be removed by unscrewing the two visible Phillips screws (photo).
2 The bulbs are a push-in-and-twist fit.
3 The units as a whole can be removed completely after the lens and bulbs have been removed by releasing the electrical connection and unscrewing the two locating self-tapping screws visible.

21.1 The side flasher lights are surprisingly well protected in the bumper

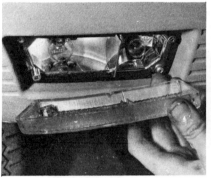

21.2 It is easy to cross the threads in the light units; be careful they are expensive!

22.1 The rear lights use three locating screws; note the drain hole

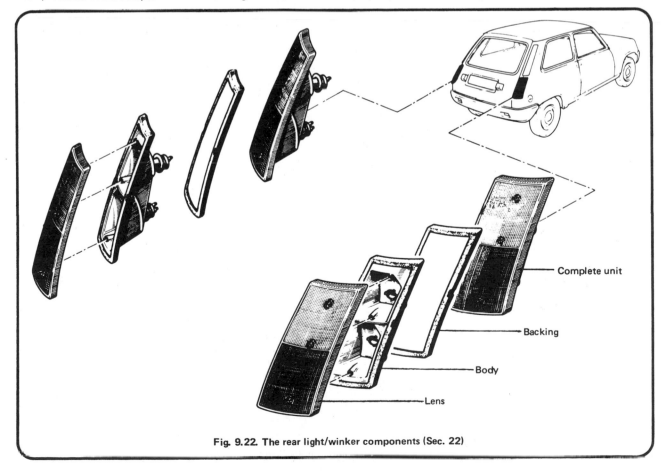

Complete unit

Backing

Body

Lens

Fig. 9.22. The rear light/winker components (Sec. 22)

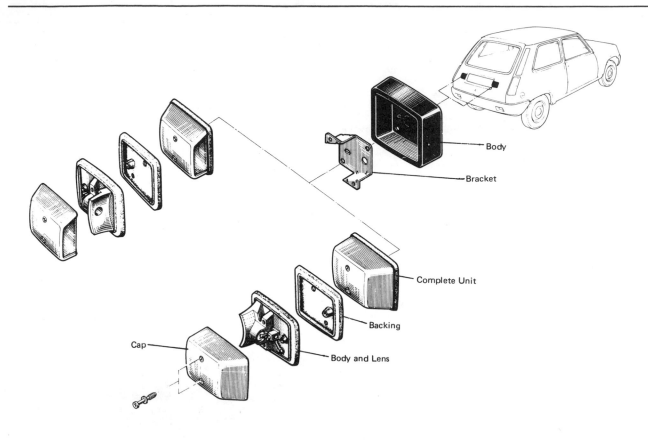

Fig. 9.23. Rear number plate light components (Sec. 23)

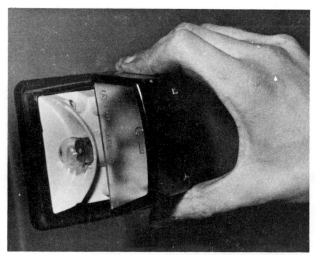

23.1 It will be necessary to clean this lens fairly regularly

4   Replacement is a reversal of removal. Check again that you have the correct replacement parts.

24 Ignition switch - general

1   See Chapter 10 on steering as this unit is an integral part of the steering column. It is a simple switch with three electrical contacts.

25 Interior light and switches - general

1   The interior light is situated over the centre of the driver's door. Its manual switch is the lens itself, working on a rocking principle. Otherwise the light comes on when the doors are opened, using a traditional on-off switch in the front door pillar.
2   Bulb replacement is simple - remove the lens which is a push-on fit. The bulb is then clipped in and out.
3   The door pillar plunger switches are fixed by one screw. Once removed, the switch pulls out with the wire connection behind.
4   No repairs are available on these switches. Replacement only is possible.

26 Lighting, dip, main beam, horn and indicator switches - general

1   The light and horn switch uses one stalk whilst the indicator uses another. However, both are part of the same switch body. If any part fails the whole switch must be replaced. No repair is possible - these switches are expensive.
2   Disconnect the battery before undertaking any work. To remove start by removing the lower protective panel under the instrument panel. Lift the top panel and remove the securing screws.
3   Leave the Lucar clips on the rear of the switch(s) attached and uncouple the junction blocks plus the two loose connections. The new switch comes with wings and junction blocks attached.
4   Replacement is a straightforward reverse sequence.

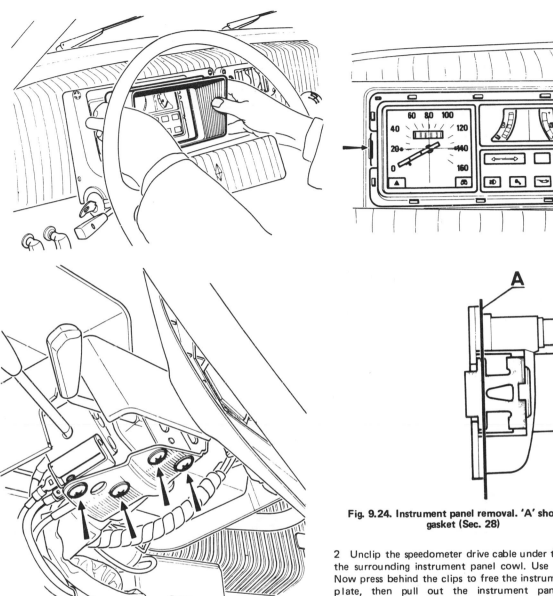

Fig. 9.25. The locating screws of the main switch cluster (Sec. 26)

Fig. 9.24. Instrument panel removal. 'A' shows a necessary gasket (Sec. 28)

27 Wiper/washer and other switches - general

1 The wiper/washer switch is removed and replaced in the same way as the lighting/horn switch as described in the previous Section.

2 The other switches are standard push-in rocker switches. With careful leverage these switches can be pulled out of the facia. Their electrical connection obviously appears from behind. No repair is possible on any of these switches - replacement only is possible.

28 Instrument panel, instruments and bulbs - general

1 The instrument panel is easily removed. Once removed access is available to the instruments and their bulbs. Disconnect the battery.

2 Unclip the speedometer drive cable under the bonnet. Unclip the surrounding instrument panel cowl. Use your fingers only. Now press behind the clips to free the instrument panel support plate, then pull out the instrument panel. Unscrew the speedometer cable, disconnect the two junction blocks and free panel.

3 The instrument panel is made up of two instruments, a printed circuit, a casing and a number of bulbs. It is possible to replace the individual parts.

4 The bulbs are readily visible push-in fits to the rear of the printed circuit.

5 The instruments are removed from the printed circuit and casing by removing the glass front (bend over the locating tabs).

6 Delicate handling is needed throughout. Parts are expensive. Replacement is a reverse process.

29 Heated rear window - general

1 The R1222 is fitted with a heated rear window. This consists of a special tailgate glass with wires threaded through its centre - as if it were an electric blanket. It is fused. You are advised not to fiddle with it. Replace the fuse - but do not attempt anything more. If it is found to be faulty take the car to a Renault agency or preferably to an auto-electrician who can test it. Let them advise to its removal and replacement - it is very costly and delicate (photo).

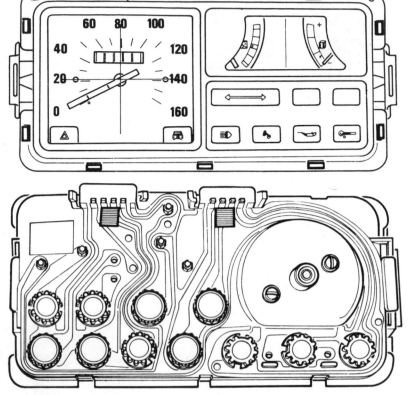

Fig. 9.26. The instrument panel with its locating clips. The back of the panel shows a standard printed circuit with bulb location (Sec. 28)

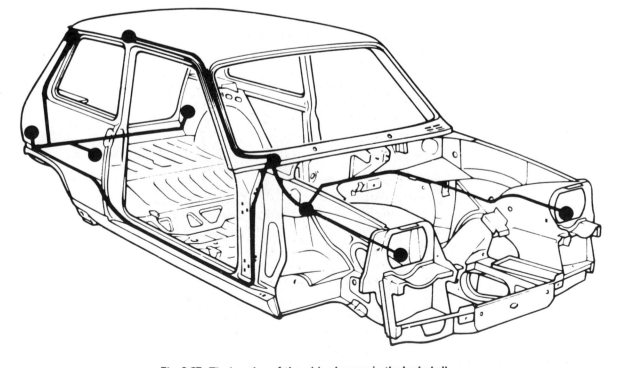

Fig. 9.27. The location of the wiring harness in the bodyshell

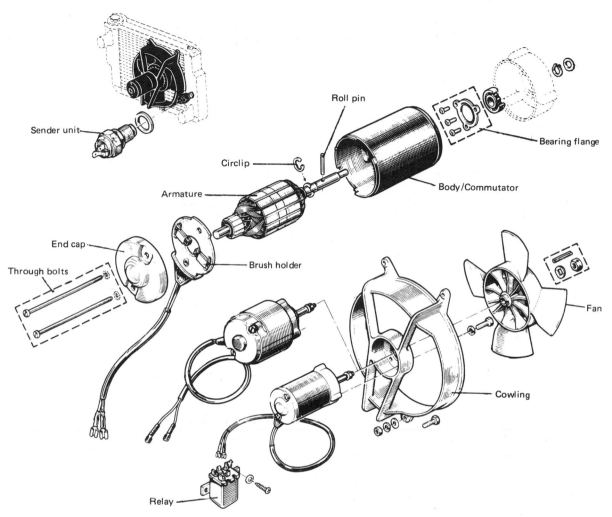

Fig. 9.28. R1222 cooling fan electric motor. Both types are illustrated here

29.1 One of the heated rear window electrical connections

---

30 Windscreen washer pump - general

1   An electric windscreen washer pump can be fitted to the

Renault 5. It is located adjacent to the windscreen washer bottle. No repair is possible - upon failure replacement is necessary.

31 Fault diagnosis - electrical system (general)

Symptom	Reason/s
Starter fails to turn engine	Battery discharged Battery defective internally Battery terminal leads loose or earth lead not securely attached to body Loose or broken connections in starter motor circuit Starter motor switch or solenoid faulty Starter motor pinion jammed in mesh with flywheel gear ring Starter brushes badly worn, sticking, or brush wires loose Commutator dirty, worn or burnt Starter motor armature faulty Field coils earthed
Starter turns engine very slowly	Battery in discharged condition Starter brushes badly worn, sticking or brush wires loose Loose wires in starter motor circuit
Starter spins but does not turn engine	Starter motor pinion sticking on the screwed sleeve Pinion or flywheel gear teeth broken or worn Battery discharged
Starter motor noisy or excessively rough engagement	Pinion or flywheel gear teeth broken or worn Starter motor retaining bolts loose
Battery will not hold charge for more than a few days	Battery defective internally Electrolyte level too low or electrolyte too weak due to leakage Plate separators no longer fully effective Battery plates severely sulphated Drive belt slipping Battery terminal connections loose or corroded Alternator not charging Short in lighting circuit causing continual battery drain Regulator unit not working correctly
Ignition light fails to go out, battery runs flat in a few days	Drive belt loose and slipping or broken. Alternator brushes worn, sticking, broken or dirty Alternator brush springs weak or broken Internal fault in alternator Regulator incorrectly set Cut-out incorrectly set Open circuit in wiring of cut-out and regulator unit

Failure of individual electrical equipment to function correctly is dealt with alphabetically, item-by-item, under the headings listed below

Horn

Horn operates all the time	Horn push either earthed or stuck down Horn cable to horn push earthed
Horn fails to operate	Cable or cable connection loose, broken or disconnected Horn has an internal fault
Horn emits intermittent or unsatisfactory noise	Cable connections loose

Lights

Lights do not come on	If engine not running, battery discharged Wire connections loose, disconnected or broken Light switch shorting or otherwise faulty
Lights come on but fade out	If engine not running battery discharged Light bulb filament burnt out or bulbs broken Wire connections loose, disconnected or broken Light switch shorting or otherwise faulty
Lights work erratically - flashing on and off, especially over bumps	Battery terminals or earth connection loose Lights not earthing properly Contacts in light switch faulty

Wipers

Wiper motor fails to work	Blown fuse
	Wire connections loose, disconnected or broken
	Brushes badly worn
	Armature worn or faulty
	Field coils faulty
Wiper motor works very slowly and takes excessive current	Commutator dirty, greasy or burnt
	Armature bearings dirty or unaligned
	Armature badly worn or faulty
Wiper motor works slowly and takes little current	Brushes badly worn
	Commutator dirty, greasy or burnt
	Armature badly worn or faulty
Wiper motor works but wiper blades remain static	Wiper motor gearbox parts badly worn

32 Fault diagnosis - radio interference

Noise	Source	Remedy
'Machine gun' rattle when engine running	Ignition system coil or HT lead	Renew HT leads
		Install 0.5 uF capacitor to + (switch) terminal of ignition coil
Undulating whine according to engine speed	Alternator	Install 0.5 uF capacitor to alternator terminal A
Crackle when accelerator pedal depressed or released	Voltage regulator	Install 0.5 uF capacitor to 'IGN' terminal of voltage regulator

R1222 and R1221 Wiring Diagram code
(See pages 157 to 161 for Wiring Diagrams)

1	LH front sidelight		45	Stoplight switch
2	LH front direction indicator		46	Instrument panel
3	LH front headlight		47	RH door pillar switch
6	RH front headlight		48	Front - rear harness junction
7	RH front direction indicator		49	Combination lighting switch - front harness junction
8	RH front sidelight		50	Direction indicator switch - front harness junction
9	'Mosta' temperature switch (R1222)		51	Flasher unit
10	Cooling fan motor (R1222)		53	Rear screen switch (R1222)
20	Horn		54	Heating - ventilating fan switch
21	Reversing lamps switch (R1222)		55	Windscreen wiper switch
22	Dynamo or alternator		60	Interior light
23	Battery		61	Combination lighting switch
24	Dynamo or alternator regulator		62	Direction indicator switch
25	Cooling fan motor relay (R1222)		63	Ignition - starter switch
26	Coolant temperature switch		65	Rear screen (R1222)
27	Starter		66	Fuel tank
28	Distributor		67	LH rear direction indicator
30	Heating - ventilating fan motor		68	LH rear and stoplights
31	Ignition coil		69	LH rear reversing lamp (R1222)
32	Oil pressure sender switch		70	Licence plate lights
33	Windscreen wiper motor		71	RH rear reversing lamp (R1222)
40	LH cowl side earth (ground)		72	RH rear and stoplights
41	LH door pillar switch		73	RH rear direction indicator
44	Fusebox			

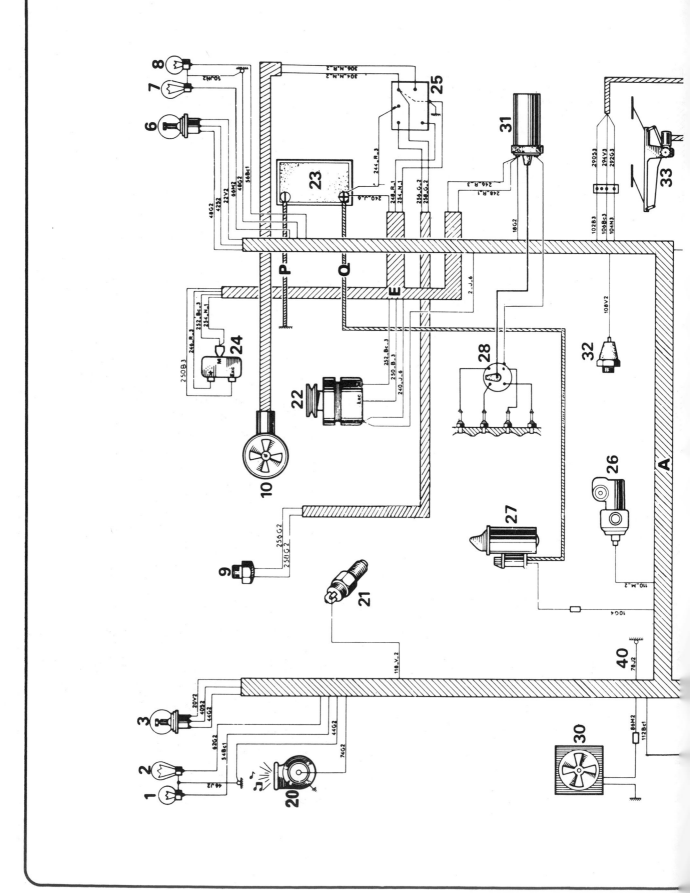

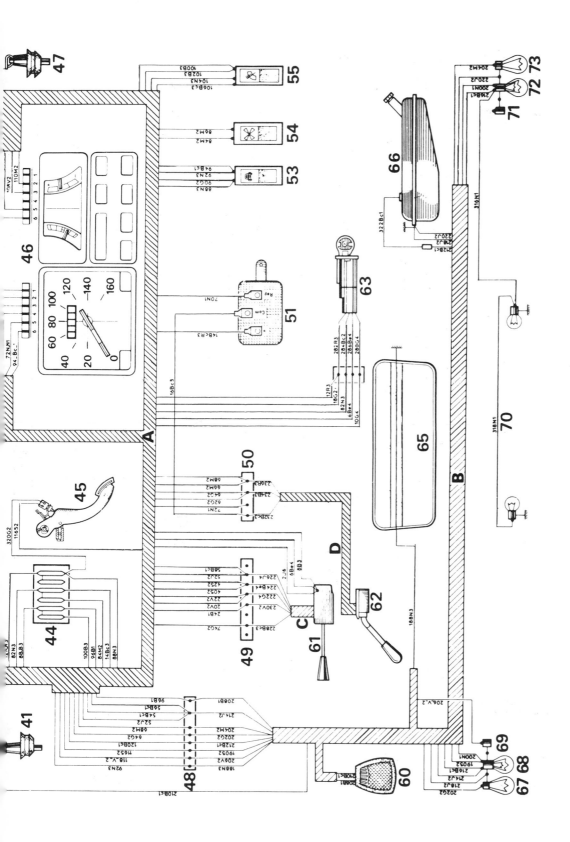

R1222 Wiring Diagram

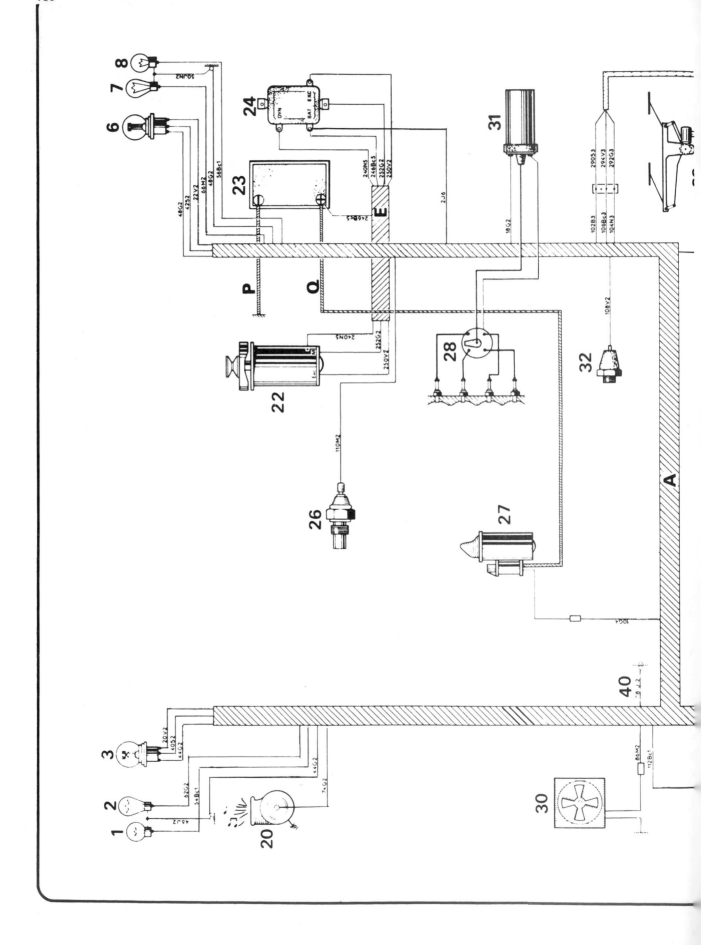

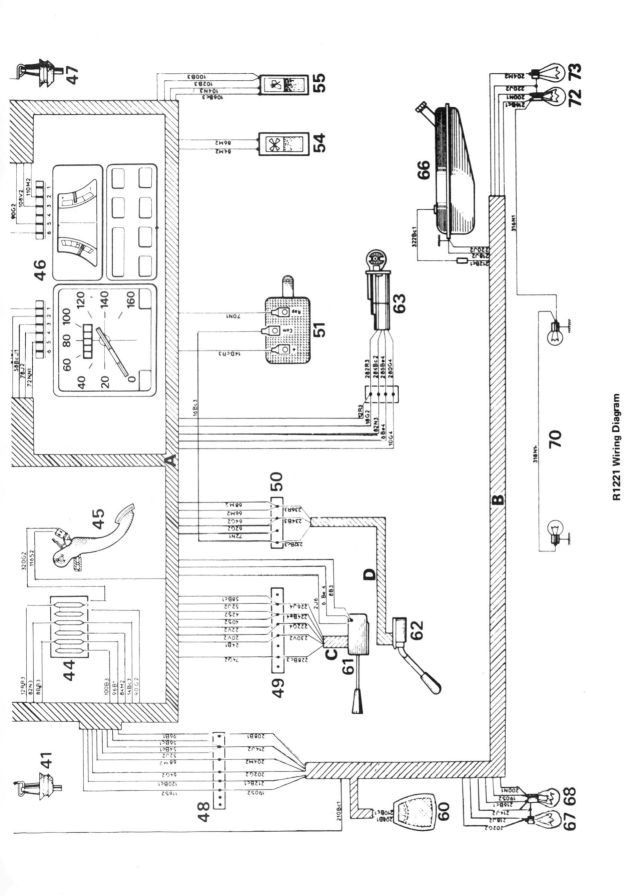

R1221 Wiring Diagram

Chapter 10 Suspension and steering

Contents

Specifications

Front suspension
Type ... ...   Independent, torsion bars with single lower arms and wishbone upper arms and anti-roll bar

Rear suspension
Type ... ...   Independent, single lever arms pivoting. Torsion bars

Shock absorbers
Type ... ...   Telescopic double acting front and rear
Front - vertical
Rear - horizontal

Steering
Type ... ...   Rack and pinion
Steering geometry and measurements:
    Castor angle (normal) ... ...   10º 31' to 11º 31'
    Camber angle ... ...   0º to 1º
    Toe-out (unladen) ... ...   0 to 5 mm (0 to 13/64 in.)
    Track on level ground:
        Front ... ...   4 ft 2 3/8 in. (R1221) 4 ft 2 13/16 in. (R1222)
        Rear ... ...   4ft 3/16 in

    Wheelbase:
        Right (offside) ... ...   7 ft 10½ in.
        Left (nearside) ... ...   8 ft 0 in.
    Turning circle (between walls) ... ...   33 ft 3 5/8 in.
    Steering wheel turns (lock-to-lock) 4.5

Torque wrench settings

	lb f ft	kg fm
Steering rack securing bolts	25	3.45
Balljoint nuts (upper) and steering	25	3.45
Balljoint nuts (lower)	35	4.83
Steering wheel nut	35	4.83
Driveshaft nut	90	12.3
Shock absorber nuts	30	4.14

1 General description

The Renault 5 is fitted with independent front and rear suspension by means of torsion bars and telescopic hydraulic shock absorbers. Double wishbone suspension, with the double acting shock absorber with built in bump stops fixed vertically, is utilised with torsion bars, one each side, running along the floor of the car. Single arms are used at the rear, with horizontal double acting shock absorbers, and torsion bars run across the car. Bump stops are built into the suspension arms. Unlike the other small Renaults, the Renault 5 has vertical rear shock absorbers. The wheelbase is greater on one side of the car than the other because of the transverse torsion bars at the rear. Anti-roll bars are always fitted to the front suspension. Underbody height is adjustable.

A rack and pinion steering unit is fitted, with self-centring action.

Much of any necessary repair and maintenance work is easily undertaken on the suspension and steering by the home mechanic although some special tools, which may possibly be home made, will be necessary. Before starting any such work be absolutely sure that you have the knowledge and facilities for finishing it and have the correct replacement parts for your model. There have been detailed changes during the production run from model to model, particularly on the steering. Asking the local Renault garage to come out and replace a torsion bar which you have removed and find you cannot replace will be very expensive!

Potential tasks are described in an order which indicates their ease and to an extent their likelihood.

2 Routine maintenance

1 The sales brochures for the Renault 5 will tell you that the suspension and steering systems are 'maintenance free'. Superficially this is true - what is necessary, however, is a good, periodic visual and manual inspection. Grease is used in the suspension joints and steering rack, rubber sleeves and gaiters are used on some components and leakage and splitting is possible. To stop eventual component failure check the suspension and steering systems.
2 Inspect the wishbone outer top and bottom ball joints for wear - there should be no looseness, and then check that there is no grease leaking from the rubber seal on each ball joint. If wear is apparent replace the ball joint - if leakage is there, it may be possible simply to regrease and replace the cover seal.
3 Inspect the torsion bar rubber sleeves. If perished or split, talk to your Renault agency for their advice.
4 Inspect the shock absorbers for looseness in their mountings - look at the top and bottom rubber bushes and check for leakage of the unit itself. If it leaks replace it and the other on the opposite too. Shock absorbers must be replaced in parts.
5 Check the tightness of the steering rack mountings. Check the steering joints as you would the ball joints on the wishbones, check the rack gaiters for splits and leakage, check the rubber/canvas steering joints and the column universal joints and replace as and when necessary.
6 Such is the design and construction of the suspension and steering, and the consequent superbness of the ride and handling, that wear tends to take place perhaps a little sooner than on conventional cars.

3 Suspension and steering - testing

1 Because of the construction of these vehicles the suspension cannot be viewed in isolation from the steering and vice versa. The safety of a car depends more on the steering and suspension than anything else and this is the reason why the compulsory tests made for vehicles over three years old pay attention to the condition of all these components.

2 Any parts which are weak or broken must be replaced immediately. Take great care to check the following. The first list is of those parts which will wear with use and the second list is of special check points:

Check for wear:
  a) *Upper and lower ball joints.*
  b) *Upper and lower wishbone and rear suspension arm inner bushes.*
  c) *Shock absorbers and/or their mounting bushes.*
  d) *Steering arm ball joints and inner bushes.*

All these points may be tested with a tyre lever or screwdriver to see whether there is any movement between them and a fixed component.

Check:
  e) *Torsion bar sleeves for perishing.*
  f) *Steering rack mounting bolts for looseness.*
  g) *Steering rack to column coupling.*
  h) *Steering wheel to column.*
  i) *Steering column bush.*
  j) *Front and rear hub bearings (see Chapter 7).*
  k) *Anti-roll bar bushes.*

There should be no play nor failure in any single part of any of the forementioned components. It is dangerous to use a vehicle in a doubtful condition of this kind.

4 Front anti-roll bar and bushes - removal and replacement

1 It is easiest if the vehicle is over a pit when removing the anti-roll bar to replace the bushes or to replace other suspension parts, although it matters little. Make sure the vehicle is properly secure on stands (if available) or on the ground with the handbrake on. It is not always necessary to remove the front wheels.
2 Remove the four bolts or nuts, and washers, which locate the anti-roll bar at its centre section under the car, and pull off the two clamps. Remove the two rubber bushes and their seats. That is all that need to be done to replace these bushes. Return new bushes, seats and refix the clamps (photo).
3 To remove the bar from the vehicle completely undo the nut which holds the two-way bush to the pin which fixes the bottom end of the shock absorber to the lower wishbone. Pull off this two-way bush from each side and remove the bar. Inspect this bush at each insert and replace if doubtful.
4 Replacement is a direct reversal of its removal. It is not possible to refit the two-way bushes incorrectly. Never drive the vehicle without the anti-roll bar fitted, located in solid, unworn bushes.

4.2 This locates the anti-roll bar bushes; check them for wear

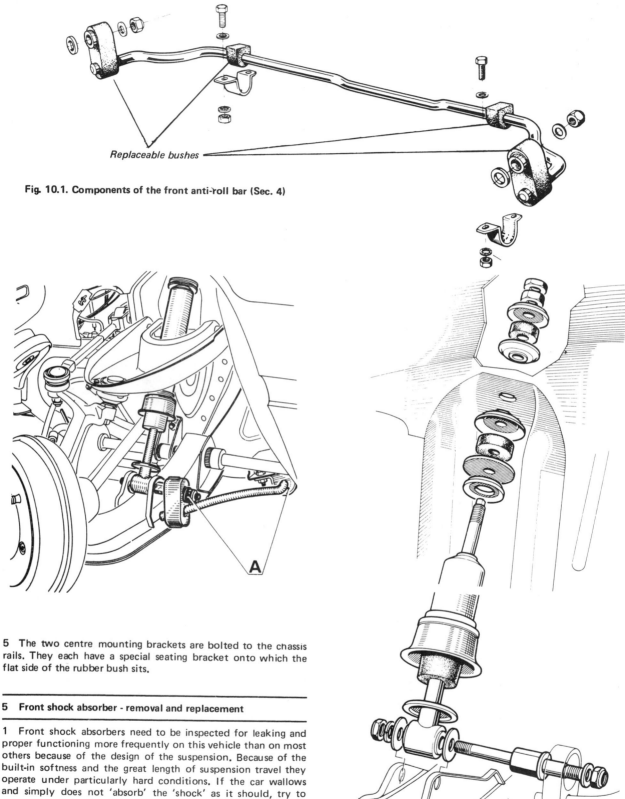

Replaceable bushes

Fig. 10.1. Components of the front anti-roll bar (Sec. 4)

A

5   The two centre mounting brackets are bolted to the chassis rails. They each have a special seating bracket onto which the flat side of the rubber bush sits.

5   Front shock absorber - removal and replacement

1   Front shock absorbers need to be inspected for leaking and proper functioning more frequently on this vehicle than on most others because of the design of the suspension. Because of the built-in softness and the great length of suspension travel they operate under particularly hard conditions. If the car wallows and simply does not 'absorb' the 'shock' as it should, try to compare a suspect vehicle with a new one, by bouncing each corner by hand. If the shock absorber leaks fluid it should be replaced immediately. Try to replace fronts in pairs, and only with the correct specified type.

2   Jack-up the front of the car, remove the front wheels, having place the car on stands, and remove the anti-roll bar as described

Fig. 10.2. Front shock absorber fixing. 'A' shows the location of the anti-roll bar at the bottom end (Sec. 5)

in Section 4.

3 Place a scissor or pump jack under the relevant lower suspension arm and jack up the arm until a firmness is felt, with the car still solid on the stands. This counterbalances the torsion bar effect and allows the shock absorber to be withdraw down through the upper wishbone.

4 Remove the shock absorber nut at the top. Do this from under the bonnet using a ring spanner and a pair of mole grips to hold the stud still.

5 Remove the bottom shock absorber mounting pin. Compress the shock absorber by hand until it is at its shortest length and remove down and outwards. Retrieve all the washers and bushes.

6 Replacement is an exact reversal of removal but check that the top rubber bushes and their cups are correctly positioned and that the bottom pin is smeared with grease. No repair to a shock absorber is possible; it, as must the old rubber bushes, should be renewed if unserviceable. Tighten all fixing nuts well, to 30 lb f ft (**4.14 kg fm**).

6 Rear shock absorber - removal and replacement

1 The principle of checking the conditon of the rear shock absorbers as frequently as the fronts is valid, although they do not generally take such abuse. They do need a little more care in removing and replacing.

2 Jack-up one side of the vehicle at a time and remove the wheel. Undo the nut on the lower attachment point and remove,

and then the two nuts at the top of the shock absorber, inside the back of the car, as for the top nuts on the front shock absorbers.

3 Using a scissor, trolley or pump jack, raise the suspension arm, free the shock absorber and remove it.

4 Replacement is an exact reversal of the removal sequence, but do not forget to smear the front attachment pin with grease before refitting and check that the bush cups are correctly fitted. Finally try to tighten the nuts to 30 lb f ft (**4.14 kg fm**).

7 Ball joints - removal and replacement

1 The four suspension ball joints, two on each side of the front suspension, at the outer end of each wishbone, are sealed for life. Their only possible maintenance is to replace the rubber cover. They therefore need replacing rather than servicing.

2 For either top or bottom ball joint replacement jack-up that side of the vehicle and place on a stand.

3 Remove the relevant front wheel.

4 With a patent ball joint remover or two wedges, having undone the nyloc nut, dislocate the ball joint from the suspension upright. Tie up the suspension upright so that it does not rest on the hydraulic brake pipe whether the top or bottom joint is being removed (Fig. 10.6).

5 The original ball joints are riveted onto the wishbone. These rivets will have to be drilled out. Clean up the rivet heads with a wire brush and file a good flat onto their heads. Use an electric

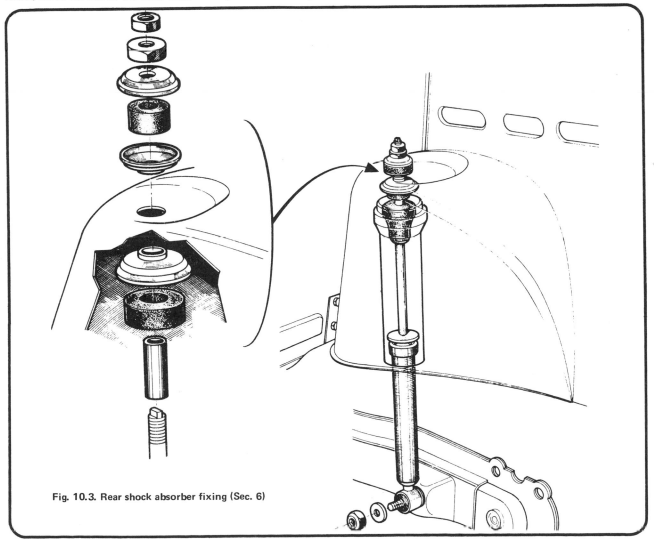

Fig. 10.3. Rear shock absorber fixing (Sec. 6)

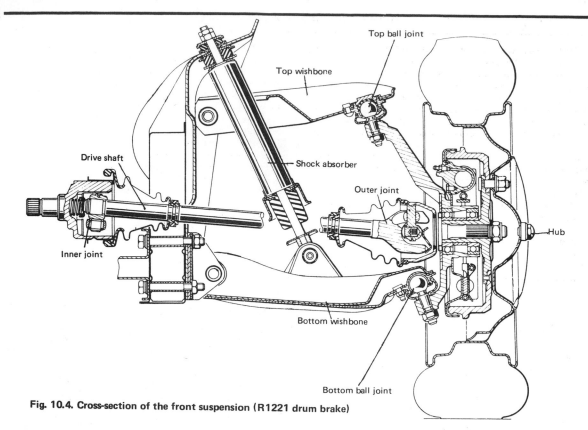

Fig. 10.4. Cross-section of the front suspension (R1221 drum brake)

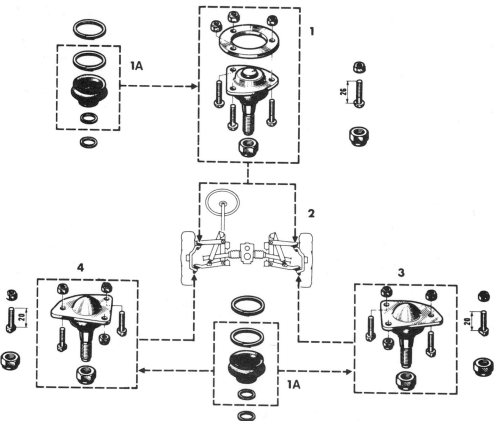

Fig. 10.5. Front suspension ball joint fitment (Sec. 7)

1   Top ball joints are interchangeable
1a Ball joint gaiter kit
2   Cross section profile of ball joint fitment

3   Nearside lower handed ball joint
4   Offside lower handed ball joint
    (Figures on setscrews indicate length in millimetres)

drill if possible. Be patient and very careful. It is not a 'rush' job. Do not attempt to drill from below and try not to drill into the wishbone itself. If done carefully it is not necessary to remove the wishbones from the vehicle (photo).

6 When purchasing new ball joints make sure that the **correct** fixing setscrews and nuts, to replace the rivets are also supplied. This is important. Also only the top ball joints are interchangeable, the bottoms can only be fixed in one way, on one side.

7 Replace the new ball joint into its correct seating and place the setscrews from below up through the ball joint and then wishbone. Tighten the nyloc nuts firmly.

8 Replace all the parts in an opposite procedure to their removal. Be sure that the ball joints are finally tight onto the upright when the car is resting on all four wheels.

9 Removal and replacement of just the ball joints' rubber bellows is only an effective repair for a new leaking joint. This will not help a worn one. It is undertaken, if new rubber bellows are in fact available for the vehicle, as in this Section (7) from

paragraphs 1 to 4 inclusive. Then remove the old bellows and clean the ball joint. Make sure the plastic sleeves are intact.

10 Pack the new bellows with specified grease, fit onto the ball joint and press up the outer plastic sleeve. The bellows retaining clip should then be fitted. It may be pinched with a piece of string to allow the clip to go on.

11 Replace the ball joint into the suspension upright, bolt up and replace, as in paragraph 8.

8 Upper wishbone and bushes - removal and replacement

1 Proceed as in Section 7, paragraphs 1 to 4 inclusive, removing the top ball joint.

2 Undo the hinge pin and remove it. It may need a gentle tapping through with a soft metal drift.

3 Remove the wishbone and retain the special pin, nut and washers.

4 Upper wishbones are not interchangeable from side to side

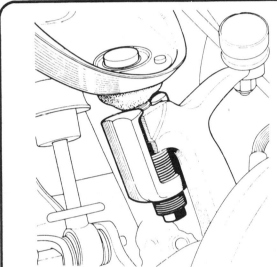

Fig. 10.6. Universal ball joint 'remover' in place on a top ball joint (Sec. 7)

7.5 On manufacture the ball joints are riveted in; they will have to be drilled through

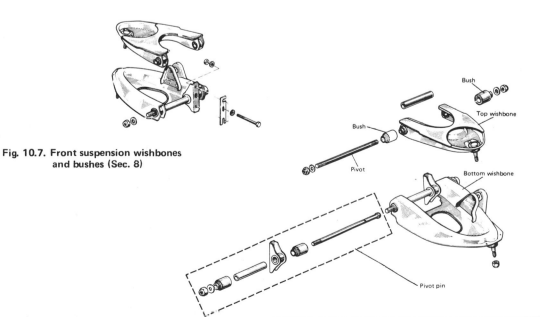

Fig. 10.7. Front suspension wishbones and bushes (Sec. 8)

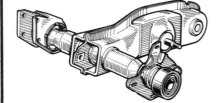

Fig. 10.8. Rear suspension arms (Sec. 10)

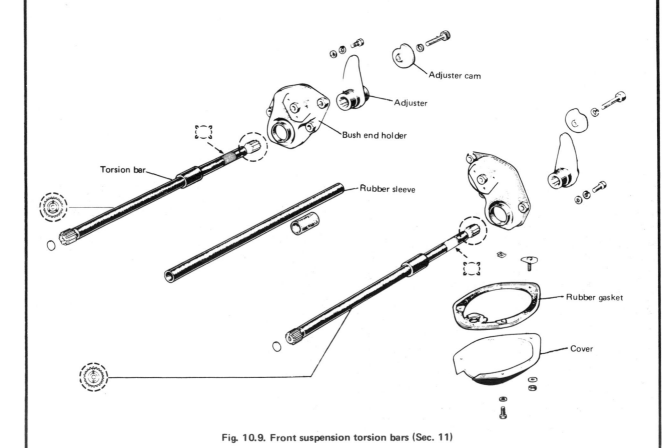

Adjuster cam

Adjuster

Bush end holder

Torsion bar

Rubber sleeve

Rubber gasket

Cover

Fig. 10.9. Front suspension torsion bars (Sec. 11)

and again it is essential that the correct type is fitted.

5   The removal of the inner brushes is not a practical do-it-yourself task. Take the wishbone to the local Renault garage and have them remove the old and press in the new. Order the new brushes beforehand. It may under some circumstances be more economic to replace the whole wishbone if the bushes and the ball joint are worn - new wishbones are supplied with both already fitted.

6   Replacement of the upper wishbone is a straight reversal of the removal procedure.

7   Have the steering/suspension alignment checked upon the replacement of new inner wishbone bushes.

9   Lower suspension arm and bushes - removal and replacement

The suspension arm or lower wishbone is attached directly to the chassis 'frame' and to the front torsion bar. Although a simple suspension system, such is the need for special tools to work on the system it is not possible for the home mechanic to work on this part. It is not possible to make suitable tools at home and their purchase price from the Renault garage does not make a once-only use viable. It is better under nearly all circumstances to gain a quotation from the Renault garage for any work needed in this area. It does not normally take a great deal of time to remove the suspension with the correct tools. It is dangerous to dismantle any part of the suspension connected to the torsion bars without the correct equipment. Read on to the next Section and Section 12 which covers the removal of the front torsion bars on the two types of vehicle, and then Section 8 for bush replacement.

10   Rear suspension arm and bushes - removal and replacement

1   Rear suspension arm removal is a very simple operation once the rear torsion bar has been removed. However as has been explained in Section 12, 'Rear Torsion Bar Removal', this is not a task able to be tackled by the do-it-yourself mechanic although it is briefly explained. For this reason little can be said here except to say once the relevant torsion bar is removed and the flexible brake pipe disconnected the rear suspension arm can be removed by undoing and withdrawing the three locating bolts. The suspension arm will then pull away from the chassis. Replacement is obviously a direct reversal procedure.

2   Once the arm is removed from the vehicle the bushes can be removed and replaced but only with the help of a press. It is not safe to use any other method.

3   Under most prevailing circumstances it is much safer and more economic to allow an official Renault garage do this work for you. It may also be cheaper if a replacement arm, complete with bushes is fitted. Fortunately these bushes often outlast the rest of the vehicle. If, however, a non-franchise garage tackles this repair make sure it fits the correct suspension arm and bushes as several non-interchangeable types have been used.

11   Front torsion bar - removal and replacement

1   Because of what has already been said about the need for special tools to undertake the proper dismantling of the front suspension in Section 9 no special details will be given in this Section except to reiterate the necessity to go to the local Renault garage with any problem relating directly to the torsion bars. However, there is included a basic procedure of dismantling and reassembly following.

2   Removal of a front torsion bar would only normally be necessary if it had broken or the suspension had been bent or in extreme cases of excess weakness, sagging. It is essential to use a pit or hydraulic lift to remove torsion bars on these vehicles.

3   Jack-up the front of the car leaving both sides of the front suspension hanging free. Remove the relevant roadwheel.

4   Remove the anchor housing protective cover and loosen bolts from inside the car (photos).

5   Inside the car push the front seats forward and tilt them. See Fig. 10.10 and loosen bolt (1) without removing it. Then turn cam (2) to zero by moving it towards the outside of the vehicle. Then insert special tool 'SUS. 545' in the adjusting lever to counter-balance the torsion effect of the bar from outside the car. Inside, unscrew the adjusting lever housing fixing bolts (3), (4) and (5). Withdraw the 'housing cover-cam assembly' from the adjusting lever, then gradually release the special tool.

6   Mark the position of the torsion bar at the adjusting lever end. See (A). Then at the suspension arm end at (B). Remove the torsion bar. Check that the mark made on the arm end aligns with the production mark on the very end of the bar. If not, note the number of splines to which it is offset.

7   Refitting is a reverse procedure - smear the splines of the bar with high quality molybdenum disulphide grease. Align all the marks, except when fitting a new bar position the adjusting lever distance (see C) about 10 to 20 mm (25/64 to 25/32 in.) from the edge. Insert special tool 'SUS. 545'. Take up torsion, then line up the cover by entering the cam in its location. Hold the assembly up against the gusset with a mole wrench and bolt it together. Remove the special tool and the mole wrench.

8   Lower the vehicle and adjust the ride height as necessary, after the vehicle has settled.

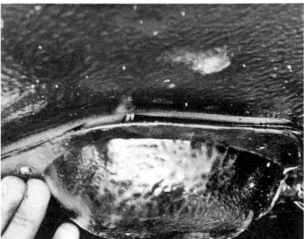

11.4a The torsion bar end cover locates on one stud and two set-screws ...

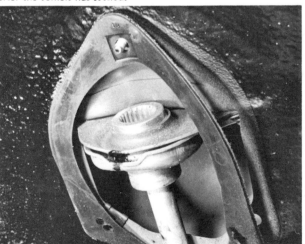

11.4b ... and should have a rubber seal

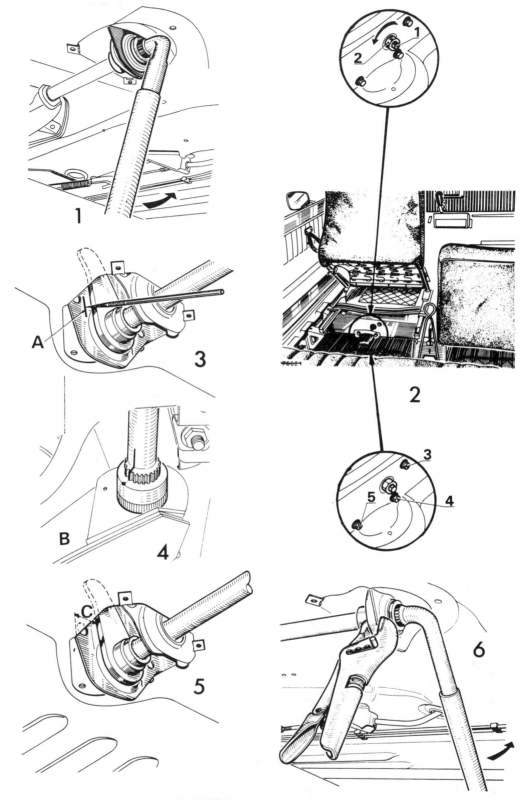

Fig. 10.10. Front torsion bar removal
(See the text to give sequence: Section 11. Further drawings help
with replacement)

1	Special tool	3	Scribed mark	5	Point at which to measure
2	Position under seat	4	'Dot' and 'line' position	6	Use wide grips

12 Rear torsion bar - removal and replacement

1 Place the rear of the vehicle on stands over a pit or on a hydraulic ramp with both roadwheels clear. Remove the relevant wheel. (On the right-hand side it is necessary to remove the brake limiter valve protective cover).

2 Set the adjusting cam to zero.

3 Remove the shock absorber as described in Section 6.

4 Replace the shock absorber with a special tool (dimensions given as Fig. 10.12) and tighten the nut until the anchor lever lifts off the cam. (See Fig. 10.12).

5 The torsion bar can now be removed from the vehicle.

6 To replace the torsion bar first tighten the special tool which has replaced the shock absorber until the length of 'X' (590mm/23¼" for the rh arm, 600mm/23.5/8" for the lh arm) is achieved. When this has been done slide the torsion bar through the bearing, having smeared the splines with molybdenum disulphide grease.

7 Position the anchor lever so that its cam is at zero adjustment.

8 When the lever is in this position slide the torsion bar into it. If this position is correctly aligned then the torsion bar should slide freely into the suspension arm and lever splines. It may however be necessary to try the torsion bar several times to achieve this, for the bar will only enter the splines in one position. Tighten the cam fixing nut. Remove the special tool and replace the shock absorber.

9 Lower the vehicle, settle the suspension and adjust the ride height as necessary.

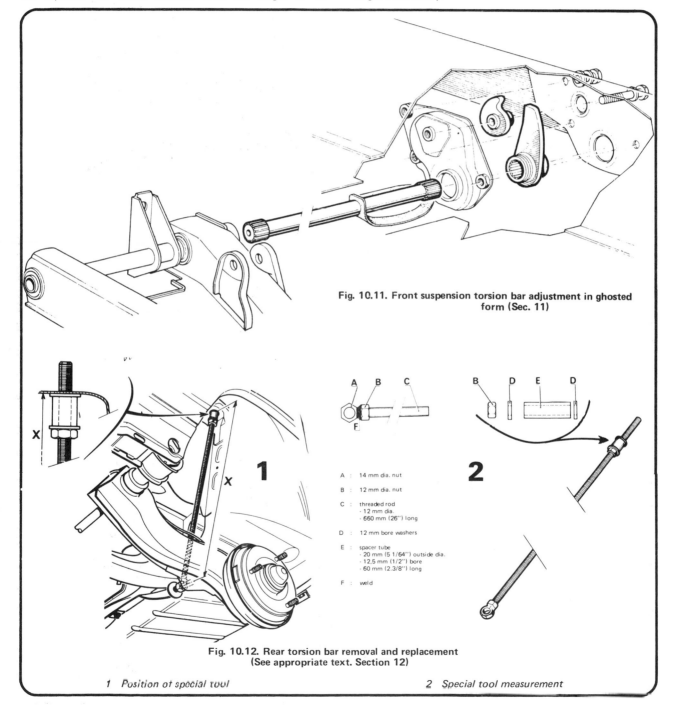

Fig. 10.11. Front suspension torsion bar adjustment in ghosted form (Sec. 11)

A : 14 mm dia. nut

B : 12 mm dia. nut

C : threaded rod
- 12 mm dia.
- 660 mm (26") long

D : 12 mm bore washers

E : spacer tube
- 20 mm (5 1/64") outside dia.
- 12,5 mm (1/2") bore
- 60 mm (2.3/8") long

F : weld

Fig. 10.12. Rear torsion bar removal and replacement
(See appropriate text. Section 12)

1 *Position of special tool*   2 *Special tool measurement*

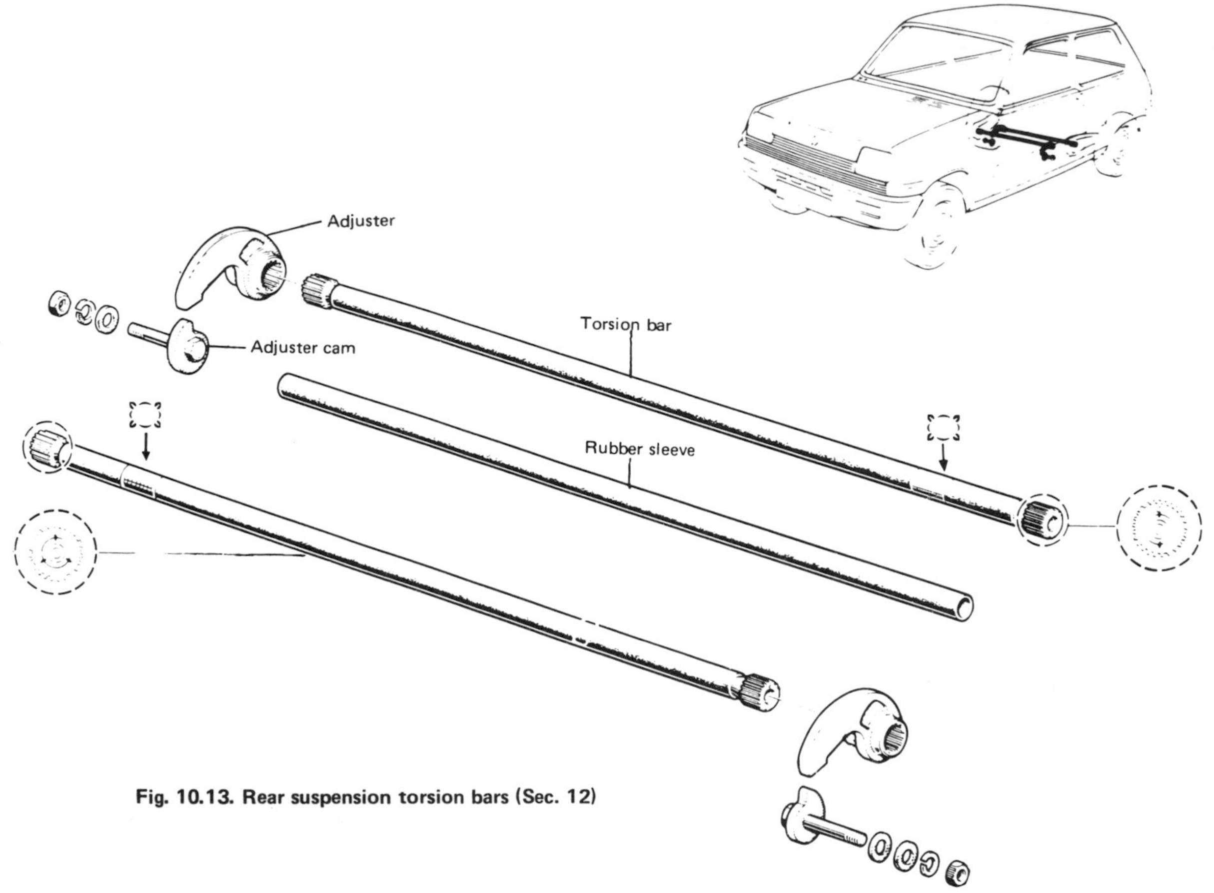

172

Adjuster

Adjuster cam

Torsion bar

Rubber sleeve

Fig. 10.13. Rear suspension torsion bars (Sec. 12)

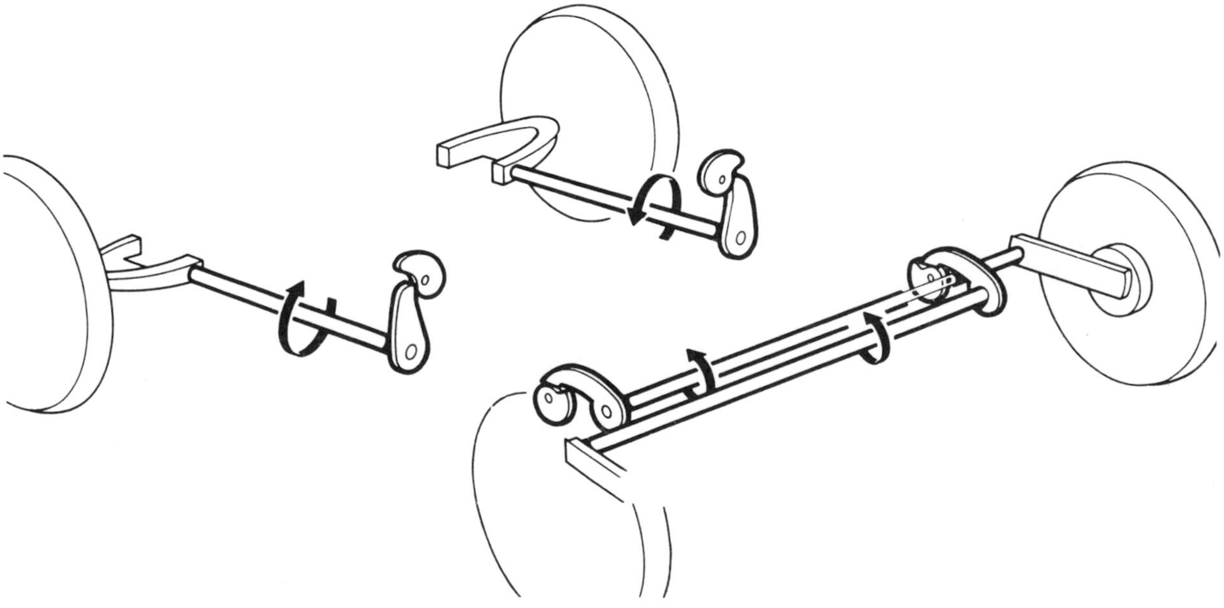

Fig. 10.14. Torsion bar adjustment. Direction of movement for height adjustment (Sec. 12)

13 Vehicle ride height - adjustment

1   Ride height adjustment is necessary whenever any part of the suspension has been removed and replaced an possibly when heavy loads are to be carried for a large mileage. Read Sections 11 or 12.
2   Ride height adjustment is altered by moving the adjusting cam in a clockwise direction. Measurement is taken at the front and rear hubs to a level ground surface.
3   See Fig. 10.14 for the direction of settings. The difference between left and right-hand side should not exceed 10 mm for setting operations.

14 Torsion bar rubber sleeve - removal and replacement

All torsion bars are fitted with a rubber sleeve which may perish with the passing of time. Also sometimes rubber bushes are fitted over these sleeves to hold off the torsion bar from the underside of the chassis and absorb vibration. It is not usually necessary to replace these sleeves unless a torsion bar breaks or the vibration is unbearable. Once the torsion bar is removed from the car rip off the old sleeve and grease the torsion bar with a non-corrosive grease. Slide on the new rubber. Compressed air greatly assists this process if it is available. Do not scratch or score the torsion bar.

15 Steering rack - removal and replacement

1   Different steering racks are fitted to the R1222 and R1221 as are different columns. However, there is little practical difference when it comes to removal and replacement.
2   To remove just the steering rack, remove the flexible coupling bolts connecting the steering column to the rack.
3   Uncouple the steering arms from the rack by undoing the two through bolts.
4   Undo the two fixing bolts which fix the steering rack and radiator (R1221) to the chassis and remove the bolts. The steering rack will now lift up and around and out. Retain and record any shims which may be fitted. See the next Section.
5   It is not possible under any circumstances to repair a steering rack. It must always be replaced. No maintenance is necessary.
6   Replacement is again a straight reversal of the removal sequence. Replace the shims, if fitted, in the correct order to avoid resetting. Should resetting be necessary you must have this done by your local Renault (only) garage. It is wise to replace the flexible coupling and the front wheel track must always be re-adjusted if the rack is ever removed or replaced. Check the tightness of the rack-to-chassis bolts, to 25 lb f ft (3.45 kg fm).

16 Steering arms - removal and replacement

1   When replacing a steering rack it is advisable to look at the condition of the bushes at the ends of the adjustable arms. If these are worn have the short removable arm replaced. At the same time check the condition of the steering arm and ball joint. No maintenance is available for this joint except the replacement of the rubber dust cover. If it is worn replace the whole steering arm. Make sure that the replacement part is for the correct side and is of the right specification, as these arms have been modified. They are not interchangeable from side-to-side.
2   To remove the steering arm remove the through bolt connecting it to the rack and then with a ball joint remover on two wedges release the ball joint from the suspension upright (photo).
3   Replacement is a reversal sequence. Have the front wheel track checked once reassembled.

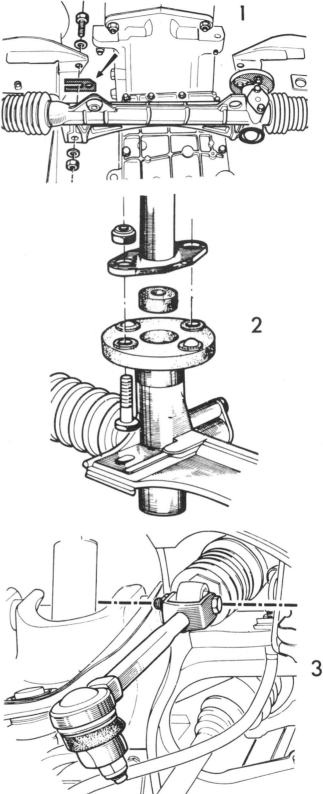

Fig. 10.15. Steering rack fixing (Sec. 15)

1   Rack fixing on chassis rails. Note the shims
2   Steering column flexible coupling
3   Steering arm bush fitting

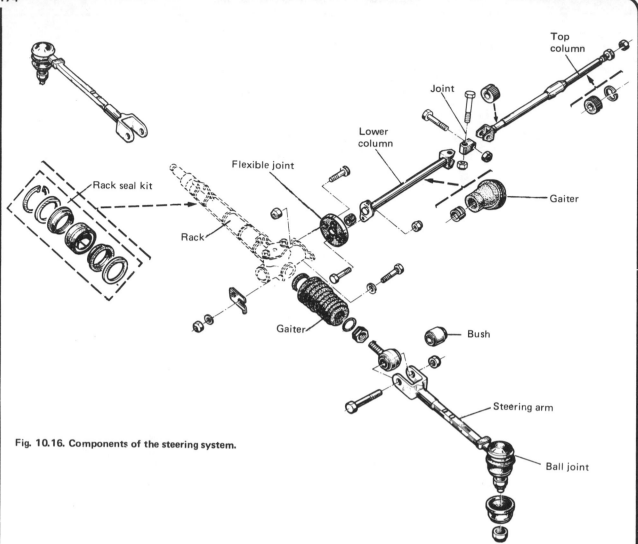

Fig. 10.16. Components of the steering system.

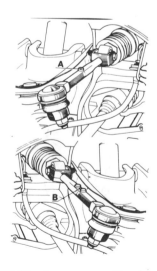

Fig. 10.17. Steering arm recognition (Sec. 16)

A   One boss in the centre - right
B   Two bosses in the centre - left

16.2 There is an easy and a difficult way of fitting these bolts; this is the easy way

lexible couplings free. All four wear
placement. It is best to replace both
her parts can be replaced seperately.
reversal of removal, but make sure
ted with a graphite based grease and
housing between the indentations.
push the bushes in.
may use rivets on its lower flexible
ng rack. Drill these out and replace

integral part of the ignition switch,
d with the other. It is possible to
se parts separately.
battery.
anel below the facia panel.
el.
block to the ignition switch. Insert

screws and then press down on the
e of the barrel and push from below
witch/lock should come away.
om the lock remove the ignition key
screws half way down the barrel.
ottom.
are in the reverse sequence.

alignment and geometry

f steering and suspension adjustment
the total correct functioning of the
adjustment of this type be made by
which will be equipped with the
ring jigs. If any major suspension or
and/or replaced it is absolutely
le checked. The following measure-
ending on what has been removed.
eir tolerances. To some extent you
Renault garage as to what they will
omponent mentioned in the Specifi-
place the vehicle in need of one or
ng. Tell the garage to make the
rt on any adjustment found to be

hich cannot, in fact, be altered).

ng.

wheels in relation to the steering

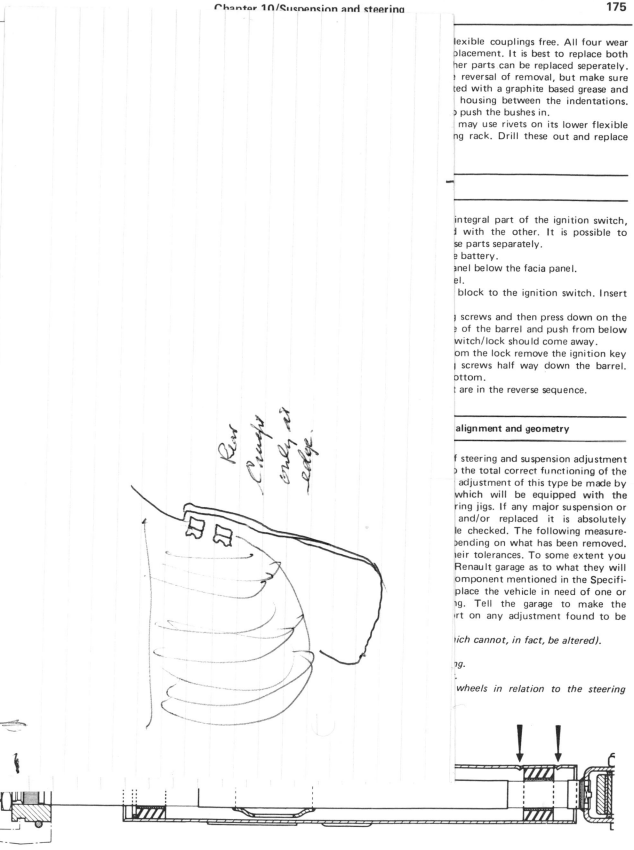

Fig. 10.19. Steering column bush location in cross-section
(Sec. 17)

20 Fault diagnosis - suspension and steering

Before diagnosing faults from the following chart, check that any irregularities are not caused by:

1 *Binding brakes*
2 *Incorrect 'mix' of tyres*
3 *Incorrect tyre pressures*
4 *Misalignment of the bodyframe or rear suspension*

Symptom	Reason/s	Remedy
Steering wheel can be moved considerably before any sign of movement of the wheels is apparent	Wear in the steering linkage, gear and column coupling	Check movement in all joints and steering gear and renew as required.
Vehicle difficult to steer in a consistent straight line - wandering	As above	As above.
	Wheel alignment incorrect (indicated by excessive or uneven tyre wear)	Check wheel alignment.
	Front wheel hub bearings loose or worn	Renew as necessary.
	Worn balljoints or suspension arms	Renew as necessary.
Steering stiff and heavy	Incorrect wheel alignment (indicated by excessive or uneven tyre wear)	Check wheel alignment.
	Excessive wear or seizure in one or more of the joints in the steering linkage or suspension arm balljoints	Renew as necessary.
	Excessive wear in the steering unit	Renew.
Wheel wobble and vibration	Road wheels out of balance	Balance wheels.
	Road wheels buckled	Check for damage.
	Wheel alignment incorrect	Check wheel alignment.
	Wear in the steering linkage, suspension arm balljoint or suspension arm inner bushes	Check and renew as necessary.
Excessive pitching and rolling on corners and during braking	Defective shock absorbers and/or broken torsion bar, anti-roll bar broken away	Check and renew as necessary.

Chapter 11 Body and fittings

Contents

1 General description

1 The Renault 5 is of monocoque construction, ie it uses a bodyshell like the Renault 16 not a seperate chassis and body as the Renault 4 and 6. Obviously this is a departure with the small front wheel drive Renaults. This makes for a very stiff, rigid construction. The engine, transmission, suspension and steering are all bolted directly into the bodyshell. The front wings, bonnet, doors and tailgate are seperate panels, and are therefore not stressed as are, for example, the roof and rear panels.

The R1222 and R1221 share the same basic bodyshell, the differences are merely cosmetic and difficult to distinguish apart! The bodyshells are available with a factory built roll-top sunroof as an option, but are always two door with a tailgate acting as a third 'door'. The interior floor is flat. All models are factory undersealed.

2 Maintenance - body exterior

1 The general condition of a car's bodywork is the one thing that significantly affects its value. Maintenance is easy but needs to be regular and particular. Neglect - particularly after minor damage - can quickly lead to further deterioration and costly repair bills. It is important also to keep watch on those parts of the bodywork not immediately visible, for example the underside, inside all the wheel arches and the lower part of the engine

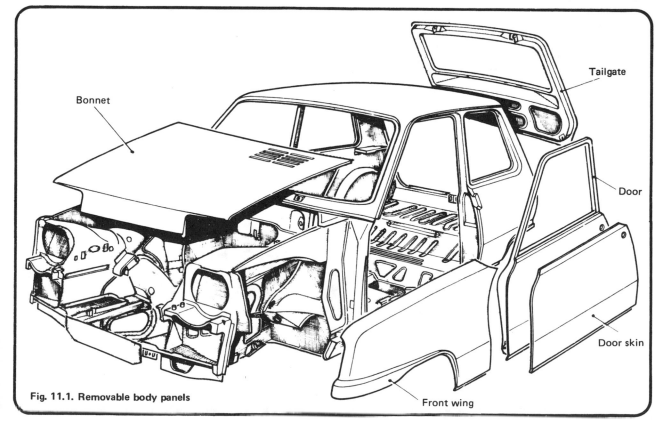

Fig. 11.1. Removable body panels

Bonnet

Tailgate

Door

Door skin

Front wing

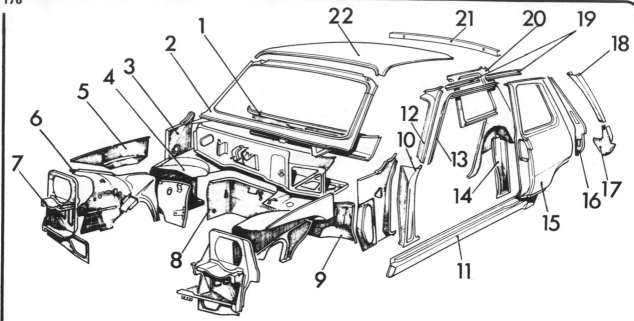

Fig. 11.2. Welded bodyshell components

1 Windscreen frame lower cross member	8 Scuttle centre section	15 Wing panel
2 Windscreen frame	9 Scuttle side section	16 Rear reinforcing flange
3 Front pillar lining	10 Front pillar	17 Rain channel lower gusset
4 Scuttle upper cross member	11 Sill panel	18 Side rain channel
5 Cowl side upper section	12 Windscreen pillar lining	19 Top stretcher lining
6 Cowl side	13 Top stretcher	20 Rear quarter panel lining
7 Headlight panel	14 Centre pillar lining	21 Extreme rear cross member
		22 Roof

Fig. 11.3. Chassis pan welded components (these are all welded to those of Fig. 11.2)

1 Closure panel
2 Front cross member
3 Front side member
4 Front face
5 Floor panel
6 Rear side member
7 Closure panel
8 Fuel tank cross member
9 Rear floor panel

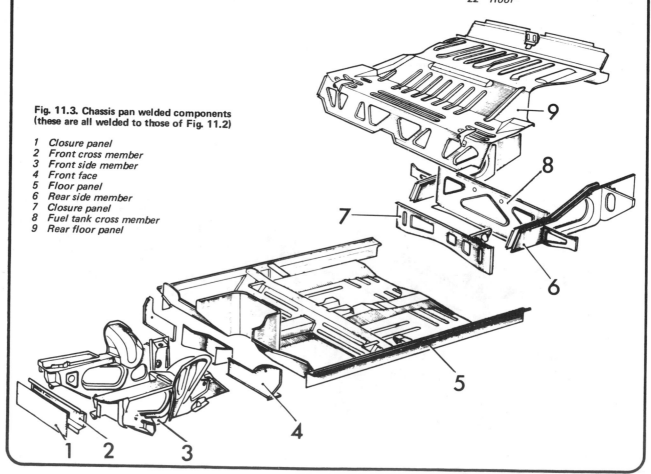

compartment.

2 The basic maintenance routine for the bodywork is washing - preferably with a lot of water from a hose. This will remove all the loose solids which may have stuck to the car. It is important to flush these off in such a way as to prevent grit from scratching the finish. The wheel arches and underbody need washing in the same way, to remove any accumulated mud which will retain moisture and tend to encourage rust. The Renault 5 collects mud in the inner side of the rear bumper and at the inner edge of the tailgate. This is thrown up by the rear wheels. Wash this out too.

Paradoxically enough, the best time to clean the underbody and wheel arches is in wet weather when the mud is thoroughly wet and soft. In very wet weather the underbody is usually cleaned of large accumulations automatically and this is a good time for inspection.

If you have the energy, jack-up the car, remove all the road wheels and clean their inner sides. The wheel offset keeps mud captive for a long time and could unbalance the wheel! **Do not** hose excessive quantities of water at the windows, heater vents etc.

3 Periodically have the whole of the underside steam cleaned, engine compartment as well so that a thorough inspection can be carried out to see what minor repairs and renovations are necessary. Steam cleaning is available at some garages and is necessary for removal of the accumulation of oily grime which sometimes collects thickly in areas near the engine and gearbox. If steam facilities are not available there are one or two grease solvents available which can be brush applied. The dirt can then be simply hosed off. Any signs of rust on the underside panels must be attended to immediately. Thorough wire brushing followed by treatment with an anti-rust compound, primer and underbody sealer will prevent continued deterioration. If not dealt witth the car could eventually become structurally unsound and therefore unsafe.

4 After washing the paintwork wipe it off with a chamois leather to give a clear unspotted finish. A coat of clear wax polish will give added protection against chemical pollutants in the air and will survive several subsequent washings. If the paintwork sheen has dulled or oxidised use a cleaner/polisher combination to restore the brilliance of the shine. This requires a little effort but is usually because regular washing has been neglected! Always check that door and drain holes and pipes are completely clear so that water can drain out. Brightwork should be treated the same way as paintwork. Windscreens and windows can be kept clear of the smeary film which often appears if a little ammonia is added to the water. If glasswork is scratched a good rub with a proprietary metal polish will often clean it. Never use any form of wax or other paint/chromium polish on glass.

3 Maintenance - interior

The flooring cover should be brushed or vacuum cleaned regularly to keep it free of grit. (This is a 'rubber' cover). If badly stained, remove it from the car for scrubbing or sponging and make quite sure that it is dry before replacement. Seat and interior trim panels can be kept clean with a wipe over with a damp cloth. If they do become stained (which can be more apparent on light coloured upholstery especially when of the nylon 'cloth' type) use a little liquid detergent and a soft nail-brush to scour the grime out of the grain of the material. Do not forget to keep the headlining clean in the same way as the upholstery. When using liquid cleaners inside the car do not over-wet the surface being cleaned. Excessive damp could get into the upholstery seams and padded interior, causing stains, offensive odours or even rot. If the inside of the car gets wet accidentally it is worthwhile taking some trouble to dry it out properly. **Do not** leave oil or electric heaters inside the car for this purpose. If, when removing mats for cleaning, there are signs of damp underneath, all the interior of the car floor should be uncovered and the point of water entry found. It may only be a missing grommet, but it could be a rusted through floor panel

and this demands immediate attention as described in the previous Section. More often than not both sides of the panel will require treatment. On cars fitted with the factory sunroof avoid touching the interior canvas. Keep it clean and rectify all tears immediately. Consult your local Renault agent as to the most suitable type of repair depending on the material used. Keep the stays and fixings very lightly but frequently oiled, particularly at the front of the roof, and periodically release and roll back the roof so that it does not become too stiff and weak.

4 Minor body damage - repair

The photograph sequence on pages 182 and 183 illustrates the operations detailed in the following sub-sections.

Repair of minor scratches in the car's bodywork

If the scratch is very superficial, and does not penetrate to the metal of the bodywork, repair is very simple. Lightly rub the area of the scratch with a paintwork renovator (eg; T-Cut), or a very fine cutting paste, to remove loose paint from the scratch and to clear the surrounding bodywork of wax polish. Rinse the area with clean water.

Apply touch-up paint to the scratch using a thin paint brush, continue to apply thin layers of paint until the surface of the paint in the scratch is level with the surrounding paintwork. Allow the new paint at least two weeks to harden; then, blend it into the surrounding paintwork by rubbing the paintwork, in the scratch area with a paintwork renovator (eg; T-Cut), or a very fine cutting paste. Finally apply wax polish.

An alternative to painting over the scratch is to use Holts "Scratch-Patch". Use the same preparation for the affected area; then simply pick a patch of a suitable size to cover the scratch completely. Hold the patch against the scratch and burnish its backing paper; the patch will adhere to the paintwork, freeing itself from the backing paper at the same time. Polish the affected area to blend the patch into the surrounding paintwork. Where the scratch has penetrated right through to the metal of the bodywork, causing the metal to rust, a different repair technique is required. Remove any loose rust from the bottom of the scratch with a penknife, then apply rust inhibiting paint (eg; Kurust) to prevent the formation of rust in the future. Using a rubber or nylon applicator fill the scratch with bodystopper paste. If required, this paste can be mixed with cellulose thinners to provide a very thin paste which is ideal for filling narrow scratches. Before the stopper-paste in the scratch hardens, wrap a piece of smooth cotton rag around the top of a finger. Dip the finger in cellulose thinners and then quickly sweep it across the surface of the stopper-paste in the scratch; this will ensure that the surface of the stopper-paste is slightly hollowed. The scratch can now be painted over as described earlier in this Section.

Repair of dents in the car's bodywork

When deep denting of the car's bodywork has taken place, the first task is to pull the dent out, until the affected bodywork almost attains its original shape. There is little point in trying to restore the original shape completely, as the metal in the damaged area will have stretched on impact and cannot be reshaped fully to its original contour. It is better to bring the level of the dent up to a point which is about 1/8 inch (3 mm) below the level of the surrounding bodywork. In cases where the dent is very shallow anyway, it is not worth trying to pull it out at all.

If the underside of the dent is accessible, it can be hammered out gently from behind, using a mallet with a wooden or plastic head. Whilst doing this, hold a suitable block of wood firmly against the impact from the hammer blows and thus prevent a large area of bodywork from being 'belled-out'.

Should the dent be in a section of the bodywork which has a double skin or some other factor making it inaccessible from behind, a different technique is called for. Drill several small holes through the metal inside the dent area - particularly in the deeper sections. Then screw long self-tapping screws into the holes just sufficiently for them to gain a good purchase in the metal. Now the dent can be pulled out by pulling on the protruding heads of the screws with a pair of pliers.

The next stage of the repair is the removal of the paint from the damaged area, and from an inch or so of the surrounding 'sound' bodywork. This is accomplished most easily by using a wire brush or abrasive pad on a power drill, although it can be done just as effectively by hand using sheets of abrasive paper. To complete the preparations for filling, score the surface of the bare metal with a screwdriver or the tang of a file, or alternatively, drill small holes in the affected area. This will provide a really good 'key' to the filler paste.

To complete the repair see the Section on filling and re-spraying.

Repair of rust holes or gashes in the car's bodywork

Remove all paint from the affected area and from an inch or so of the surrounding 'sound' bodywork, using an abrasive pad or a wire brush on a power drill. If these are not available a few sheets of abrasive paper will do the job just as effectively. With the paint removed you will be able to gauge the severity of the corrosion and therefore decide whether to replace the whole panel (if this is possible) or to repair the affected area. Replacement body panels are not as expensive as most people think and it is often quicker and more satisfactory to fit a new panel than to attempt to repair large areas of corrosion.

Remove all fittings from the affected area except those which will act as a guide to the original shape of the damaged bodywork (eg; headlamp shells etc.,). Then, using tin snips or a hacksaw blade, remove all loose metal and any other metal badly affected by corrosion. Hammer the edges of the hole inwards in order to create a slight depression for the filler paste.

Wire brush the affected area to remove the powdery rust from the surface of the remaining metal. Paint the affected area with rust inhibiting paint (eg; Kurust); if the back of the rusted area is accessible treat this also.

Before filling can take place it will be necessary to block the hole in some way. This can be achieved by the use of one of the following materials: Zinc gauze, Aluminium tape or Polyurethane foam.

Zinc gauze is probably the best material to use for a large hole. Cut a piece to the approximate size and shape of the hole to be filled, then position it in the hole so that its edges are below the level of the surrounding bodywork. It can be retained in position by several blobs of filler paste around its periphery.

Aluminium tape should be used for small or very narrow holes. Pull a piece off the roll and trim it to the approximate size and shape required, then pull off the backing paper (if used) and stick the tape over the hole; it can be overlapped if the thickness of one piece is insufficient. Burnish down the edges of the tape with the handle of a screwdriver or similar, to ensure that the tape is securely attached to the metal underneath.

Polyurethane foam is best used where the hole is situated in a section of bodywork of complex shape, backed by a small box section (eg; where the sill panel meets the rear wheel arch - most cars). The unusual mixing procedure for this foam is as follows: Put equal amounts of fluid from each of the two cans provided in the kit, into one container. Stir until the mixture begins to thicken, then quickly pour this mixture into the hole, and hold a piece of cardboard over the larger apertures. Almost immediately the polyurethane will begin to expand, gushing out of any small holes left unblocked. When the foam hardens it can be cut back to just below the level of the surrounding bodywork with a hacksaw blade.

Bodywork repairs - filling and re-spraying

Before using this Section, see the Sections on dent, deep scratch, rust hole and gash repairs.

Many types of bodyfiller are available, but generally speaking those proprietary kits which contain a tin of filler paste and a tube of resin hardener (eg; Holts Cataloy) are best for this type of repair. A wide, flexible plastic or nylon applicator will be found invaluable for imparting a smooth and well contoured finish to the surface of the filler.

Mix up a little filler on a clean piece of card or board - use the hardener sparingly (follow the maker's instructions on the packet) otherwise the filler will set very rapidly.

Using the applicator, apply the filler paste to the prepared area; draw the applicator across the surface of the filler to achieve the correct contour and to level the filler surface. As soon as a contour that approximates the correct one is achieved, stop working the paste - if you carry on too long the paste will become sticky and begin to 'pick-up' on the applicator. Continue to add thin layers of filler paste at twenty-minute intervals until the level of the filler is just 'proud' of the surrounding bodywork.

Once the filler has hardened, excess can be removed using a Surform plane or Dreadnought file. From then on, progressively finer grades of abrasive paper should be used, starting with a 40 grade production paper and finishing with 400 grade 'wet-and-dry' paper. Always wrap the abrasive paper around a flat rubber, cork, or wooden block - otherwise the surface of the filler will not be completely flat. During the smoothing of the filler surface the 'wet-and-dry' paper should be periodically rinsed in water. This will ensure that a very smooth finish is imparted to the filler at the final stage.

At this stage the dent should be surrounded by a ring of bare metal, which in turn should be encircled by the finely 'feathered' edge of the good paintwork. Rinse the repair area with clean water, until all of the dust produced by the rubbing-down operation is gone.

Spray the whole repair area with a light coat of grey primer - this will show up any imperfections in the surface of the filler. repair these imperfections with fresh filler paste or bodystopper, and once more smooth the surface and abrasive paper. If bodystopper is used, it can be mixed with cellulose thinners to form a really thin paste which is ideal for filling small holes. Repeat this spray and repair procedure until you are satisfied that the surface of the filler, and the feathered edge of the paintwork are prefect. Clean the repair area with clean water and allow to dry fully.

The repair area is now ready for spraying. Paint spraying must be carried out in a warm, dry, windless and dust free atmosphere. This condition can be created artificially if you have access to a large indoor working area, but if you are forced to work in the open, you will have to pick your day very carefully. If you are working indoors, dousing the floor in the work area with water will 'lay' the dust which would otherwise be in the atmosphere. If the repair area is confined to one body panel, mask off the surrounding panels; this will help to minimise the effects of a slight mis-match in paint colours. Bodywork fittings (eg; chrome strips, door handles etc.,) will also need to be masked off. Use genuine masking tape and several thicknesses of newspaper for the masking operation.

Before commencing to spray, agitate the aerosol can thoroughly, then spray a test area (an old tin, or similar) until the technique is mastered. Cover the repair area with a thick coat of primer; the thickness should be built up using several thin layers of paint rather than one thick one. Using 400 grade 'wet-and-dry' paper, rub down the surface of the primer until it is really smooth. While doing this, the work area should be thoroughly doused with water, and the 'wet-and-dry' paper periodically rinsed in water. Allow to dry before spraying on more paint.

Spray on the top coat, again building up the thickness by using several thin layers of paint. Start spraying in the centre of the repair area and then, using a circular motion, work outwards until the whole repair area and about 2 inches of the surrounding original paintwork is covered. Remove all masking material 10 to 15 minutes after spraying on the final coat of paint.

Allow the new paint at least 2 weeks to harden fully; then, using a paintwork renovator (eg; T-Cut) or a very fine cutting paste, blend the edges of the new paint into the existing paintwork. Finally, apply wax polish.

5 Major body damage - repair

1 Major repairs to the bodywork of any Renault 5 are only viable where they do not require the use of welding gear - straightening of the body is generally speaking outside the scope of the home mechanic. Wing, door and bonnet replacement as well as their fittings are quite possible and economic for the home mechanic provided additional structural work is not required. See the various Sections in this Chapter.

2 Because of the method of construction of this vehicle, little rusting takes place. Where it usually comes is on the removable panels - the remedy here is simple: if beyond a minor cutting - out and filling repair job, replace the total panel, it will be more economic in the long run. The second most common rusting point is on the door panels and again the same premise applies.

3 Floor pan repairs can be quite safe using fibreglass matting, resin and filler (full instructions are always given on the kit of materials), and riveting in zinc perforated sheet. However if it is suspected that the box section is affected seek the advice of a Renault garage first as they will be able to inform you of the significance and cost of a satisfactory repair.

4 If accident damage has taken place, more than just a dented wing, immediately seek the advice of a Renault garage (only a Renault garage at first) to ascertain whether the chassis has been pushed out of alignment. The car will almost certainly be unsafe after a heavy impact - it is better to be sure as to its condition at this stage. Steering and suspension only work correctly on a straight bodyshell!

6 Doors - tracing and silencing rattles

Having established that a rattle does come from the door(s) check first that it is not loose on its hinges and that the latch is holding it firmly closed. The hinges can be checked by rocking the door up and down when open to detact any play. If the hinges are worn at the pin the hinge pin and possibly the 'inner' hinge will need renewal. When the door is closed the panel should be flush. If not then the hinges or latch striker plate need adjustment. The door hinges are welded to the door and bolted to the pillars. The hinge pins can be tapped out once the circlips are removed. To adjust the setting of the door catch first slacken the screws holding the striker plate to the door pillar just enough so that it can be moved but will hold its position. Then close the door, with the latch button pressed, and then release the latch. This is so that the striker plate position is not drastically disturbed on closing the door. Then set the door position by moving it without touching the catch, so that the panel is flush with the bodywork and the other door. Then set the door position by moving it without touching the catch, so that the panel is flush with the bodywork and the other door. This will set the striker plate in the proper place. Then carefully release the catch so as not to disturb the striker plate, open the door and tighten the screws. Rattles within the door will be due to loose fixtures or something having been dropped inside them. Do make sure that all sealing rubbers are effective and that the prop stay is not itself loose.

7 Bolt-on panels - removal and replacement

1 Unlike the other small front wheel drive Renaults, the Renault 5 has only two bolt-on panels - the two front wings. They are easily and economically removed and replaced. Before replacing any panel make sure that a sealer, such as 'Glasticon Dum Dum' type putty is available.

2 To remove a front wing it helps first to remove the parcel shelf (on the relevant side) inside the car. Using a ring spanner, undo and remove all the top bolts, in fact spire screws, and washers. Do not dislodge the wing at this stage. It is not necessary to remove the bonnet or bumper.

3 Remove the securing screws at the front bottom cornor of

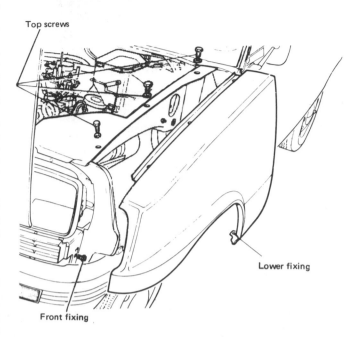

Fig. 11.4. Front wing fixing

the wing to the front crossmember, the screw at the lower wheel arch edge and through the bulkhead inside the car.

4 From the top running edge pull the wing away from the inner wing and scuttle. It may have to be tapped and levered slightly if well established.

5 To replace the wing, whether old or new, clean all the mating edges completely with a penknife and re-apply a long length of the slightly stiff sealer which has been rolled out by hand as you would a piece of plasticine. Check also that all the spire screws and their locating clips are in good usable condition. Some screws have different threads. Place the wing over the sealing strip and press down by hand so that the sealer just begins to compress and ooze out.

6 Locate all the screws and washers before tightening any fully home. Tighten them all, finally locating the nut and bolt, carefully checking periodically that the profile appears correct.

7 Painting of a new wing can be done either on or off the car. The refitting process should not damage it.

Special note: It is worth underseling new wings before they are placed on the car - it is much easier. Also while the wing is off it is profitable to clean the wheel arch and check for chipped underseal. Repair any damaged areas, as necessary.

8 Bonnet and catch - removal and replacement

1 The bonnet hinges on two swan-necked hinges at the front. Removal and replacement require the services of an assistant otherwise damage is bound to result. Remove both headlamps first - it's easier.

2 The bonnet can be removed at two points: hinge on bonnet with 4 bolts and washers or at the front top cross-brace, hinge pin to fixing, with two large bolts. If a new bonnet is to be fitted undo the 4 bolts, if not, save yourself the need to adjust its position and undo the two large hinge pin bolts.

3 Its fit position is adjusted by loosening the 4 fixing bolts.

4 Replacement is the reverse sequence to removal.

5 The bonnet catch and cable control is best described by the diagrams (Figs. 11.5 and 11.7). If left alone they seldom give trouble. Cable and catch spring replacement are obvious. Do not adjust the bonnet fitting by playing with this catch.

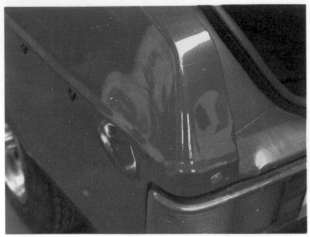

This sequence of photographs deals with the repair of the dent and scratch (above rear lamp) shown in this photo. The procedure will be similar for the repair of a hole. It should be noted that the procedures given here are simplified - more explicit instructions will be found in the text

In the case of a dent the first job - after removing surrounding trim - is to hammer out the dent where access is possible. This will minimise filling. Here, the large dent having been hammered out, the damaged area is being made slightly concave

Now all paint must be removed from the damaged area, by rubbing with coarse abrasive paper. Alternatively, a wire brush or abrasive pad can be used in a power drill. Where the repair area meets good paintwork, the edge of the paintwork should be 'feathered', using a finer grade of abrasive paper

In the case of a hole caused by rusting, all damaged sheet-metal should be cut away before proceeding to this stage. Here, the damaged area is being treated with rust remover and inhibitor before being filled

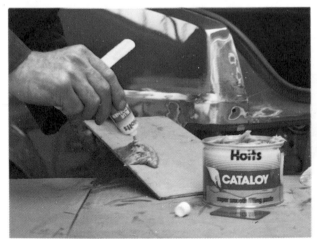

Mix the body filler according to its manufacturer's instructions. In the case of corrosion damage, it will be necessary to block off any large holes before filling - this can be done with zinc gauze or aluminium tape. Make sure the area is absolutely clean before ...

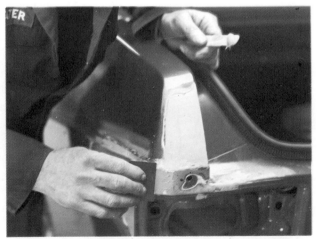

... applying the filler. Filler should be applied with a flexible applicator, as shown, for best results: the wooden spatula being used for confined areas. Apply thin layers of filler at 20-minute intervals, until the surface of the filler is slightly proud of the surrounding bodywork

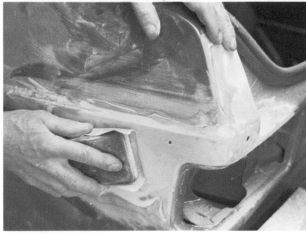

Initial shaping can be done with a Surform plane or Dreadnought file. Then, using progressively finer grades of wet-and-dry paper, wrapped around a sanding block, and copious amounts of clean water, rub-down the filler until really smooth and flat. Again, feather the edges of adjoining paintwork

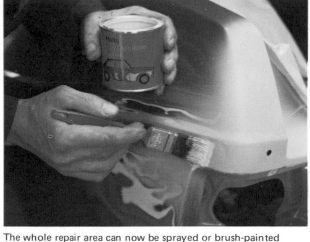

The whole repair area can now be sprayed or brush-painted with primer. If spraying, ensure adjoining areas are protected from over-spray. Note that at least one-inch of the surrounding sound paintwork should be coated with primer. Primer has a 'thick' consistency, so will fill small imperfections

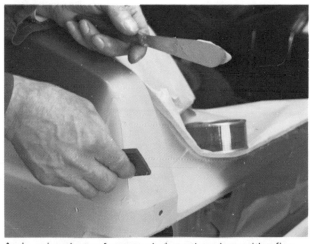

Again, using plenty of water, rub down the primer with a fine grade of wet-and-dry paper (400 grade is probably best) until it is really smooth and well blended into the surrounding paintwork. Any remaining imperfections can now be filled by carefully applied knifing stopper paste

When the stopper has hardened, rub-down the repair area again before applying the final coat of primer. Before rubbing-down this last coat of primer, ensure the repair area is blemish-free - use more stopper if necessary. To ensure that the surface of the primer is really smooth use some finishing compound

The top coat can now be applied. When working out of doors, pick a dry, warm and wind-free day. Ensure surrounding areas are protected from over-spray. Agitate the aerosol thoroughly, then spray the centre of the repair area, working outwards with a circular motion. Apply the paint as several thin coats.

After a period of about two-weeks, which the paint needs to harden fully, the surface of the repaired area can be 'cut' with a mild cutting compound prior to wax polishing. When carrying out bodywork repairs, remember that the quality of the finished job is proportional to the time and effort expended

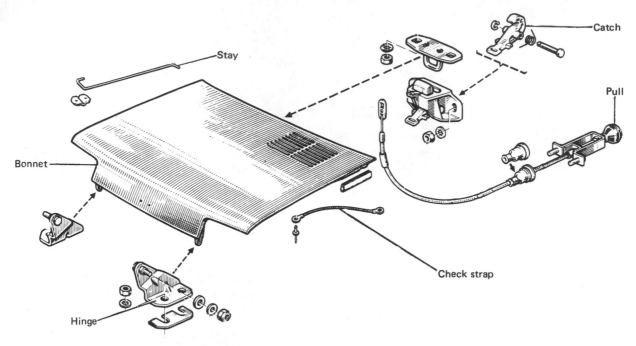

Fig. 11.5. Components of the bonnet fixing and catch mechanism (Sec. 8)

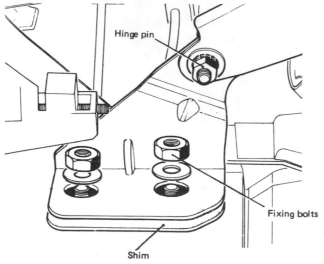

Fig. 11.6. Bonnet hinge fixing (Sec. 8)

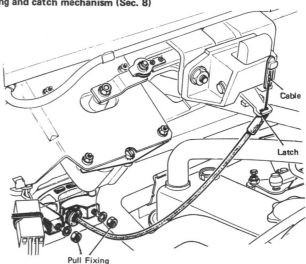

Fig. 11.7. Bonnet catch mechanism (Sec. 8)

9   Door and window winder - removal and replacement

1   Door removal on this model is relatively easy. Punch out the top hinge pin with a tapered pin. A special tool is available (Car. 543) but a suitable pin-punch should work. 'Plus-Gas' or 'WD40' will help to ease the top hinge pin. The bottom hinge is best removed on the door itself. Pull open a small black plastic panel inside the car at the bottom of the door pillar and unbolt the hinge bolts. The door will now be free (Fig. 11.8).

2   The door is heavy, have someone support it. Replacement is a direct reverse process.

3   On these models the window winders and door mechanisms are not connected. One can be removed without the other.

4   Remove the door trim slowly and carefully. It is expensive to replace if ruined. Pull back the plastic covering on the window winder handle, push back the locking tab of the fixing nut and remove the nut and then the handle. Remove the door pull (2 crosshead screws) and remote control catch for the door (two

screws) (Fig. 11.9).

5   Insert a piece of wood (make sure the window is fully closed) approximately 3 feet long and 1 inch by 1½ inches between the doorframe and the trim and twist it to spring out the trim panel clips. Do not use a screwdriver around the edges. Unseal the doorframe and see the window winder mechanism.

6   Remove the three fixing screws and then wind down the window so that it is only open 1.3/8''. Disconnect the winder mechanism from the lower glass frame (three screws) and pull out the mechanism in a downward direction towards the trailing edge of the door.

7   To remove the window glass, first remove the door catch mechanism. See Section 12. Remove the inside between it and the doorframe using a screwdriver and then lift out the glass through its frame (inner side) by pivoting it at the bottom. Then remove the outer seal held by six clips (Fig. 11.10).

8   All replacement sequences are the exact reversal of the removal sequences.

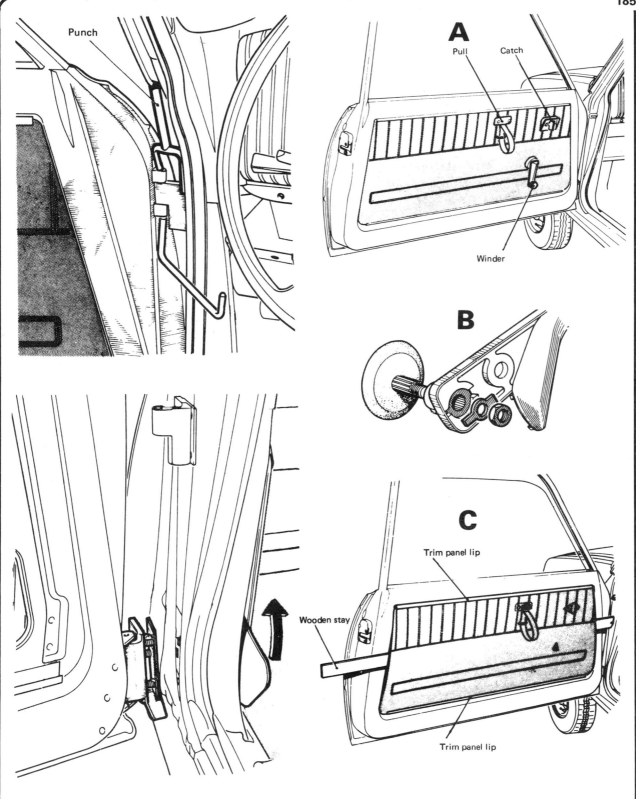

Fig. 11.8. Door hinge removal. 'Top' shows the special tool for punching out the hinge pin, 'bottom' shows the trim flap to then release the hinge on the bodyshell (Sec. 9)

Fig. 11.9. Door trim panel removal (Sec. 9)

10 Tailgate and catch - removal and replacement

1   To remove the tailgate an assistant is essential otherwise the panel could fall on your head! Remove the rear light lens and

bodies on the offside, and the extacter grille above it.

2   Disconnect the feed wire from the rear number plate lights inside the extractor and feed the wire out to free the tailgate. Disconnect the feed to the heated rear window (R1222) and the tailgate earth connection.

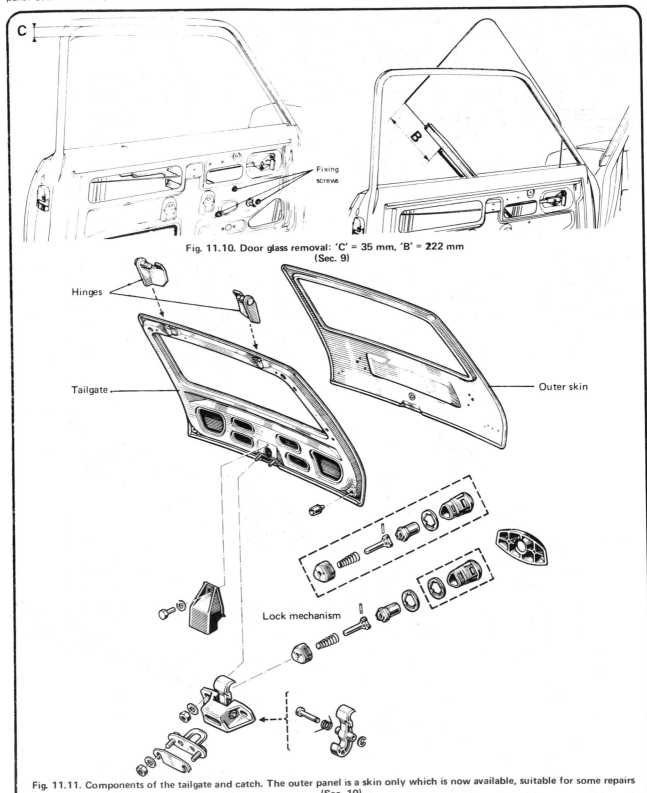

Fig. 11.10. Door glass removal: 'C' = 35 mm, 'B' = 222 mm
(Sec. 9)

Fig. 11.11. Components of the tailgate and catch. The outer panel is a skin only which is now available, suitable for some repairs
(Sec. 10)

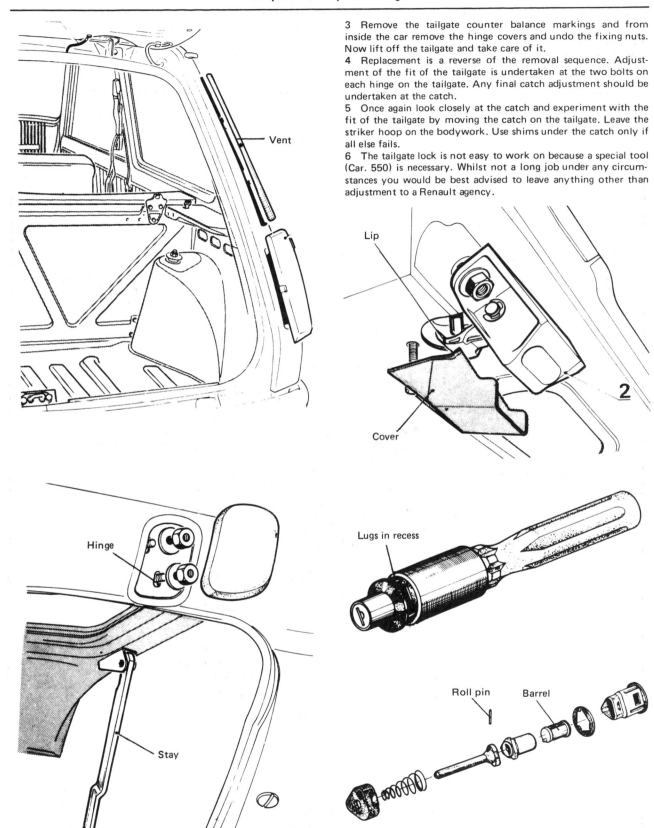

3   Remove the tailgate counter balance markings and from inside the car remove the hinge covers and undo the fixing nuts. Now lift off the tailgate and take care of it.

4   Replacement is a reverse of the removal sequence. Adjustment of the fit of the tailgate is undertaken at the two bolts on each hinge on the tailgate. Any final catch adjustment should be undertaken at the catch.

5   Once again look closely at the catch and experiment with the fit of the tailgate by moving the catch on the tailgate. Leave the striker hoop on the bodywork. Use shims under the catch only if all else fails.

6   The tailgate lock is not easy to work on because a special tool (Car. 550) is necessary. Whilst not a long job under any circumstances you would be best advised to leave anything other than adjustment to a Renault agency.

Fig. 11.12. Rear tailgate removal. 'Top' shows necessary side vent and tail light removal to release wiring. 'Bottom' shows hinge location (Sec. 10)

Fig. 11.13. The components of the tailgate catch. 'Top' shows the catch and its cover, 'middle' shows the lugs which need pressing into the recess to release the push button 'bottom' the components of the lock (Sec. 10)

11 Windscreen and glass - preparation and replacement

1 The windscreen and rear screen are curved and all the other glass fitted to the Renault 5 is flat. Various types of fitting, rubber surround and trim have been fitted through its production life and it is essential that an exactly similar fitting is used.

2 To replace a front or rear screen or any non-opening window glass clean out the window surround and remove the rubber seal. Check that it is in good condition - not stretched, perished or cracked. However, do make sure that your fitting the glass is necessary - many windscreen replacement companies fit free. On windscreen fitting, if the previous glass has been broken plug the gap between the facia panel and window as well as closing the ventilator flap, to avoid splinters entering.

Special Note: Refitment of the heated rear window (R1222) takes special care. If you are in any doubt, don't! Leave it to one with this experience.

3 Fit the rubber seal around the glass and lay on a good flat working surface. Insert a piece of string 3 to 4 mm (0.11 to 0.15 in) in diameter into the slot of the seal. Pass it totally around the seal and exit it with about 5 inches overlap and 8 inches hanging near a bottom corner.

4 Position the glass and seal into the window from outside with the string inside hanging, with the help of an assistant.

5 Square the glass up, hold, press where the string overlaps. Inside, pull each string in turn and gradually feed glass into the seal. Withdraw string pressing from outside, and check for good seal.

12 Door catch - removal and replacement

1 Have confidence when dealing with door catches on this car - they are relatively simple. To remove, remove the trim panel, the waterproof sheet and then wind the window right up.

2 Remove the catch plate fixed with one screw to the inner catch panel and to the catch (door edge) with three screws. You now have the inner catch plate and the catch removed.

3 Remove the remote control housing markings fixed by two screws and nuts and the rod bearing clip. Pull out the remote control housing and separate the rod from the lock and then pull out the control rod assembly.

4 Replacement is an easy reverse process.

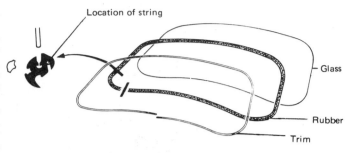

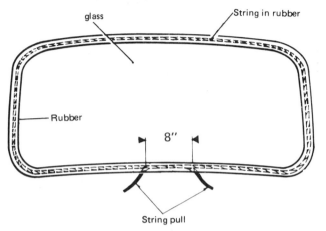

Fig. 11.14. Screen fitment (1) (Sec. 11)

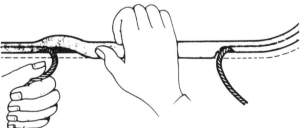

Fig. 11.15. Screen fitment (2) (Sec. 11)

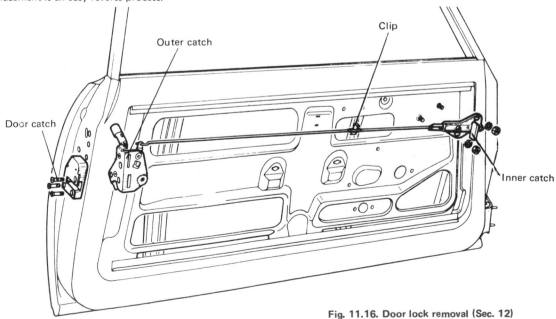

Fig. 11.16. Door lock removal (Sec. 12)

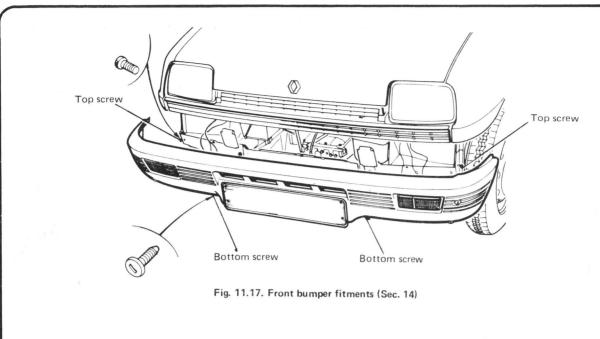

Top screw

Top screw

Bottom screw

Bottom screw

Fig. 11.17. Front bumper fitments (Sec. 14)

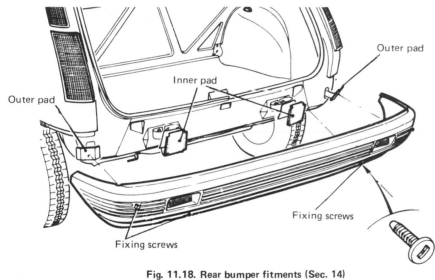

Outer pad

Inner pad

Outer pad

Fixing screws

Fixing screws

Fig. 11.18. Rear bumper fitments (Sec. 14)

14.2 The plastic bumpers are fixed by these special screws; use a well fitting screwdriver to release

14.5 The bumpers are mounted to the body by these special brackets

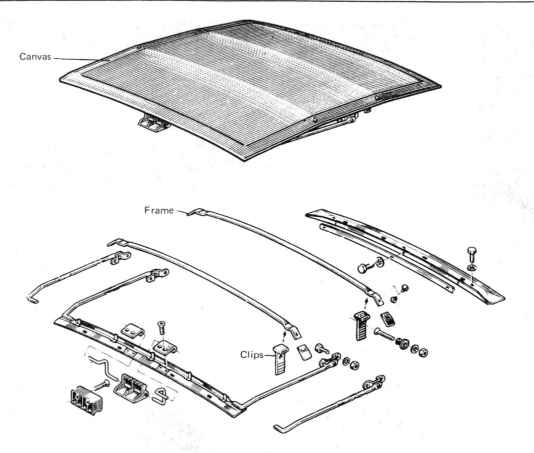

Fig. 11.19. Sunroof fitting components

5   Adjustment can be made at the catch and at the striker plate on the opposite pillar.

6   Door catches can be repaired only by replacing the return spring and the push-button lock, both of which have obvious removal and replacement methods, once the catch is removed.

13 Trim - removal and replacement

1   The trim fitted both internally and externally is of very simple and utilitarian construction. Its removal is obvious in each case. If a screw is not visible then it is either a push-on fit or is slid on. Check each part - but never force anything. Door trim is covered in Section 9 dealing with the window winder.

2   The front grille, apart from the model identification markings, is the only major piece of external trim. The headlamp surrounds are dealt with in Chapter 9.

3   The grille is removed by unscrewing the three top self-tapping screws and the four lower retaining bar self-tapping screws. Be gentle, it is constructed of moulded plastic and aluminium and is relatively expensive to replace. The grille is removed by pulling out and down.

14 Bumpers - removal and replacement

1   The front and rear plastic bumpers are unique to the Renault 5. Not only are they designed to take a 5 mph impact safely but are part of the integral bodyshell design, not simply tacked onto the car. Their replacement is simple although they are expensive.

2   At the front there are four special bolts, two to the side of the sidelights and two on the lower edges of the front number plate. Undo all four and pull the bumper away gently. Disconnect the sidelight wiring from behind. Retain the shock absorbing pads, which are clipped onto bolted-on brackets.

3   The rear bumper is similarly fixed (photo).

4   Replacement is a direct reverse process.

5   The shock absorbing pads must be in good condition, not deteriorated nor squashed. Replace if either (photo).

15 Facia panel and parcel trays - removal and replacement

1   The facia panel, underneath the fluted plastic covering, is a welded sheet steel pressing. Look at Fig. 11.2; item 1 is the windscreen frame lower crossmember - that is the facia panel: it cannot be removed. By undoing two crosshead screws fixing the two end panels, it is possible to remove these covers and then to peel away the stuck-on plastic covering completely once the instrument panel and heater bracket are removed. The central ventilator will have to be removed too.

2   Unless something has fallen inside the facia panel box section, there should be no reason to want to gain access behind it. Anything that should find its way there can be recovered by simply removing the instrument panel. See Chapter 9, Section 28. The plastic covering should be restuck (see your Renault agent for advice on adhesives).

3   The parcel shelves are held by a series of crosshead screws along the edges. Depending on which one will determine exactly how they can be juggled free. For example, the passenger side parcel shelf should be tackled by removing the screws at the back of the shelf, on the underside, then the side fixings.

4   Replacement is an obvious reverse sequence.

The Renault 5 GT L (R1225) UK Version

Chapter 12 Supplement

A Introduction

The purpose of this supplement to the Renault 5 Owner's Workshop manual is to bring the information up-to-date, to fill a few gaps in information found in the first editions and finally to include the 5GTL/5TL (USA) models and the 5GTL/TS (UK) models.

The USA 5GTL/5TL models are termed as the R1228, the UK 5GTL is the R1225 and the 5TS is the R1224.

Basically, the R1224, R1225, and R1228 models are re-designed version of the R1222 with a 1289 cc (78.6 cu in) engine fitted.

The R1225 (5GTL) introduced onto the UK market in April 1976 was designed with economy in mind and was not fitted with the twin-choke Weber carburettor as are the R1224 and R1228 models.

The R1224 (5TS) introduced in May 1975 is the sports model in the UK range of Renault 5s and is also more refined than the basic R1225.

The R1228 (USA) models have round headlights and larger bumpers fitted which give the car a different appearance when compared with the UK versions. The R1228 GTL is better equipped than the more 'basic' R1228 TL model although externally they appear identical. Further differences between R1224, R1225 and R1228 models when compared with the R1222 models are noted in Chapter 12 and the Specification Section, but, before undertaking a repair, removal or adjustment of any item read the relevant section of Chapter 12 and in most cases refer to the previous Chapters for instructions. Remember also that the Specifications Section will also give further information which is essential when making checks or adjustments etc.

B Routine Maintenance

In addition to the tasks listed on pages 10, 11 and 12 of the manual, the following should be added, where applicable.

Every 12,000 miles (20,000 km) or 12 months, whichever comes first

Arrange for your Renault dealer to check the operation of the emission control system(s) (as applicable).

Every 6,000 miles (10,000 km) or every 6 months, whichever comes first

Dismantle, clean and check the condition of the positive crankcase ventilation system and hoses. Renew parts as necessary.

Fig. 12.1. The Renault 5TS (R1224) UK version

C General Specifications

Engine

Engine - general (R1224)
Specifications are the same as the R1222 model except for the following:

Renault type number	810-25
Cubic capacity	1289 cc (78.66 cu in)
Bore	2.874 in (73 mm)
Stroke	3.032 in (77 mm)
Compression ratio	9.5 : 1
BHP (maximum) SAE	64 at 6,000 rpm
Torque (maximum) SAE	67 lb/ft at 3,500 rpm
Normal operating temperature	86°C (187°F)

Connecting rods and big-end bearings (R1224)

Regrind size of big-end bearings	0.009 in (0.23 mm)
Grinding tolerances	0 - 0.001 in (0.- 0.02 mm)

Crankshaft and main bearings (R1224)

Nominal diameter	2.158 in (54.80 mm)
Regrind size of big-end bearings	0.010 in (0.25 mm)
Grinding tolerances	± 0.0004 in (0.01 mm)

Pistons and cylinders (R1224)

Liner bottom locating diameter	3.091 in (78.5 mm)
Liner protrusion	0.0015 to 0.005 in (0.04 to 0.12 mm)
Gudgeon pin length	2.8125 in (62 mm)
Gudgeon pin diameter	0.787 in (20 mm)
Thickness of liner base seal	
Blue spot	0.003 in (0.08 mm)
Red spot	0.004 in (0.10 mm)
Green spot	0.005 in (0.12 mm)

Pushrods (R1224)

Length	6.8125 in (173 mm)
Diameter	0.217 in (5.5 mm)

Spark plug electrode gap ... ...
0.025 to 0.029 in (0.65 to 0.75 mm)

Engine oil - sump capacity (inc. filter) ... ...
6 Imp pts (6.7 US pts, 3.25 litres)

Engine - general (R1225)
Specifications are the same as the R1224 model except for the following:

Renault type number	810 - 26
BHP (maximum) SAE	44 at 5.000 rpm
Torque (maximum) SAE	62.2 lb/ft at 2.000 rpm

Engine - general (R1228)
Specifications are the same as the R1224 model except for the following:

Renault type number	810 - 28
Compression ratio	8.5 : 1
BHP (maximum) SAE	58 at 6.000 rpm
Torque (maximum) SAE	69.6 lb/ft at 3.500 rpm

Pushrods (R1228)

Length	6.93 in (176 mm)

Carburation and Fuel Systems

Fuel pump

Type	Mechanical plunger
Application	*R1222, R1224, R1225 and R1228

    *late (689-10) engine fitted with oil - bath type cylinder block

Carburettor type

Carburettor type	Application
Solex 32 SE1A (507 or 586)	R1221
Solex 32 SE1A (561, 586 or 639)	R1222
Solex 32 SE1A (702)	R1225

Weber 32 DIR (11 or 62) R1224
Weber 32 DIR (46) R1228

Carburettor settings

	Solex 32 SE 1A		
Mark (last 3 serial numbers)	507	561-586-639	702
Choke tube	23 mm	23 mm	23 mm
Main jet	125	122.5	117.5
Air compensator jet	150	170	140
Slow running jet	40	40	44
Needle valve	1.5	1.5	1.5
Accelerator pump jet	40	40	40
Choke	Manual by cable		

Carburettor settings

	Weber 32 DIR 11		Weber 32 DIR 62		Weber 32 DIR 46	
	1st barrel	2nd barrel	1st barrel	2nd barrel	1st barrel	2nd barrel
Choke tube	23	24	23	24	24	24
Main jet	125	145	125	145	122	130
Air compensator jet	180	150	185	185	175	180
Idle speed jet	52	60	50	60	45	60
Emulsion tube	F53	F6	F53	F6	F57	F6
Accelerator pump jet	50		50		50	
Needle valve	1.75		1.75		1.75	
Float	11 grams		11 grams		11 grams	
Float level (with gasket)	9/32 in (7 mm)		9/32 in (7 mm)		9/32 in (7 mm)	
Initial throttle opening	0.039 in (1 mm)		0.039 in (1 mm)		0.047 in (1.2 mm)	
Choke initial opening mechanical	11/64 to 14/64 in (4.5 to 5.5 mm)				13/64 in (5 mm)	
Choke initial opening (vacuum)	19/64 to 21/64 in (7.5 to 8 mm)		1/4 in (6 mm)		1.4 in (6 mm)	
Idle speed	675 to 725 rpm		675 to 725 rpm		800 ± 50 rpm	
CO analysis percentage					2.3 to 3.0%	
Fast idle speed					1500 rpm	

Ignition system

R1224 and R1225 same as R1222 unless indicated otherwise

Spark plug

	R1224	R1225 and R1228
Type	AC 42 FS, Champion L87Y	AC 43 FS, Champion L92Y
Electrode gap	0.024 to 0.028 in (0.6 to 0.7 mm)	

Distributor

Type
R1221 Ducellier 4493 or SEV 4000 3102
R1224 Ducellier 4442
R1225 Ducellier 4360
R1228 Ducellier Number not known

Ignition timing

R1221 $6° ± 1°$ BTDC or $28/64 ± 5/64$ in $(11 ± 1.9$ mm$)$
R1222 and R1225 $5° ± 1°$ BTDC or $25/64 ± 5/64$ in $(10 ± 1.9$ mm$)$
R1224, R1225 and R1228 $0° ± 1°$ BTDC or $0 ± 5/64$ in $(0 ± 1.9$ mm$)$

Clutch

	R1224	R1225 and R1228
Type	170 DB310	180 DBR335
Plate diameter	6.69 in (170 mm)	7.08 in (180 mm)
Disc thickness	0.291 in (7.4 mm)	0.303 in (7.7 mm)
Adjustment	End of release fork 1/8 to 5/32 in (3 to 4 mm)	

Gearbox

	R1224	R1225	R1228
Renault type number	354-11,17,26,27	354	354-35
Gearchange type	Floor mounted		
Number of gears	4 forward 1 reverse		
Synchromesh	All forward gears		
Forward gears	Helical cut		
Reverse gear	Straight cut		

Oil capacity   ...   .   3 Imp pts (2 Us qts, 1.8 litres)
Oil grade EP80W

Ratios

	R1221/ R1222	R1224	R1224	R1225	R1228
1st	3.83	3.67	3.83	3.83	3.67
2nd	2.24	2.37	2.37	2.24	2.24
3rd	1.46	1.52	1.52	1.46	1.46
4th	1.03	1.03	1.03	1.03	1.03
Reverse	3.23	3.23	3.23	3.25	3.54
Final drive	4.125	3.625	3.625	3.100	3.625

Braking system
R1224, R1225 and R1228 same as R1222 unless indicated otherwise

Brake disc (Front)
Thickness (new) ...   .   0.393 in (10 mm)
Minimum permissible thickness   ...   .   0.355 in (9 mm)

Rear brakes (R1222, R1224, R1225 and R1228)
Wheel cylinder diameter   ...   .   0.867 in (22 mm)

Master cylinder (R1224)
Type   ...   .   Dual circuit
Diameter ...   .   0.748 in (19 mm)

Brake vacuum servo (R1224)
Diameter ...   .   6 in (152 mm)

Electrical system

Alternator
R1221   ...   .   SEV-motorola 71220802
R1222   ...   .   Ducellier 7577
R1224, R1228   ...   .   Paris-Rhone A13R154
R1225   ...   .   Not known

Control box
R1221   ...   .   Not known
R1222 and R1224   ...   .   Ducellier 8364 or 8371
R1228   ...   .   Paris-Rhone AYB218

Starter motor
R1222   ...   .   Paris-Rhone D8E 121 or Ducellier 6187 - 6231
R1224   ...   .   Ducellier 6231
R1225   ...   .   Not known
R1228   ...   .   Paris-Rhone D8E121

Headlights
R1224 (1976 onwards) H4

Rear screen wiper motor
R1224 and R1228   ...   .   Ducellier 2738

Torque wrench settings (R1224 and R1228)

	lb f ft	kg f m
Crankshaft main bearing bolts	50	6.5
Big-end bolts	35	4.5
Flywheel bolts	40	5.0
Water pump pulley nut (later type without key)	35	4.5

D Engine

1 Engine - modifications and descriptions

The Renault 5 GTL and TL are referred to as model R1228

in the USA. In the UK the 5GTL is referred to as the R1225 and the 5TS as the R1224.

These models are fitted with a five-bearing 1300 cc (78.7 cu in) engine designated as 810 - 28 in the USA and 810 - 25 in the UK. This 1300 cc (78.7 cu in) engine is a development of the engine used in the 12TS/15TL models. This engine is also very similar in layout and installation to the 956 cc (58.3 cu in) engine fitted to the Renault 5TL model (R1222).

As the 1300 cc (78.7 cu in) engine is almost identical to the 956 cc (58.3 cu in) engine the same instructions given in Chapter 1 can be likewise applied. However, having said this, it is essential that both the engine sections and specification lists of Chapter 12 and Chapter 1 are referred to before commencing any work. There is a significant change in the design of the cylinder block casting of later R1222 models which have the 689-01 engine fitted. This later type block incorporates an oil bath under the camshaft and can be identified by the points shown in Fig. 12.2. .

When fitting this later type block in place of the early type two modifications will be necessary. A plunger type fuel lift pump must be fitted to this new block and Fig. 12.18 shows the pump components. It will also be necessary to modify the right-hand engine mounting on the cowl side by making a recess in the top front part of the mounting. The purpose of this modification is to allow the pump to move when the engine is oscillating on its mountings. Failure to make this modification will cause damage to the fuel lift pump. If during making this recess spot welds are removed then they must be remade before refitting the mountings.

2 Engine - removal (R1224 and R1225)

1 The engine removal sequence for the R1224 is basically identical to the operation described in Chapter 1, Section 5. Note that a different type of carburettor is fitted to this model and obviously the connections will be slightly different.
2 To gain better access to the engine/transaxle it will be found necessary to remove the front grille panel as described in Chapter 11, Section 13.
3 Disconnect the vacuum servo hose from the inlet manifold connection.
4 The engine removal sequence for the R1225 is practically identical to the R1222 model.

3 Engine - removal (R1228)

1 The engine removal sequence is very similar to that employed for the R1222 in Chapter 1, Section 5. However, due to the fact that USA models are fitted with emission control systems and have a slightly different layout the following steps should be taken during the removal operation.

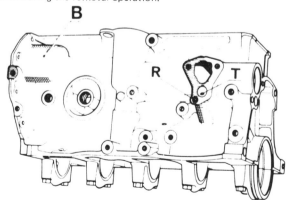

Fig. 12.2. The 689-01 oil bath type cylinder block fitted to later R1222 models

Identification marks: B = Boss at timing gear end
T = Oil return hole
R = Bottom fixing hole for the fuel pump packing

2 Remove the air pump filter, the air pump, and the air pump bracket. Section 6 of this Chapter gives instructions for the removal of these items.
3 Remove the bolts retaining the shift rod support bracket to the transaxle casing.
4 Disconnect the clutch cable from the clutch fork by using a screwdriver to push back the sleeve retainer from the support bracket.
5 To gain better access to the engine/transaxle unit during the removal operation it will be found necessary to remove the front grille panel as described in Chapter 11, Section 13.

4 Engine dismantling - ancillaries (R1228)

1 During the dismantling operations it will be found necessary to remove items not listed in Chapter 1. It will be necessary therefore to refer to various Sections in Chapter 12 for details of their removal particularly in the case of emission control equipment which is not fitted to UK models.

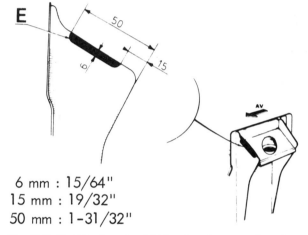

6 mm : 15/64"
15 mm : 19/32"
50 mm : 1-31/32"

Fig. 12.3. Modifications to right-hand engine mounting when fitting later type oil bath cylinder block to R1222 models
E = recess in the top part of the mounting bracket

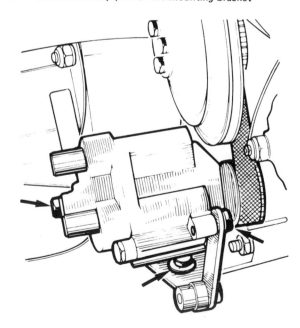

Fig. 12.4. The air pump mountings and drive belt (R1228)

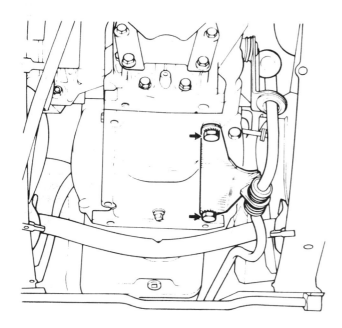

Fig. 12.5. The gearchange bracket bolted to the transaxle casing (R1228)

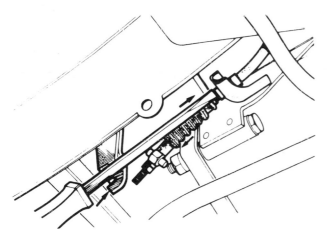

Fig. 12.6. Releasing the clutch cable from the clutch fork (R1228)

5 Cylinder head - removal and refitting (R1228)

1   Removal of the cylinder head is virtually identical to the instructions given in Chapter 1, Section 11. However, it will be necessary to disconnect the vacuum servo hose from the inlet manifold connection and to remove the air pump drive belt.
2   Refitting the cylinder head is the reversal of the dismantling procedure.

6 Camshaft - removal and refitting (R1228)

The camshaft and its associate components are similar to those used and fitted to the R1222 engine described in Chapter 1. Note that the R1228 model is fitted with a double row timing chain and drives a toothed pulley wheel at its forward end. A camshaft oil seal is fitted to the forward end of the cylinder block. Care must be taken when removing and renewing the seal to ensure that the camshaft and new oil seal are not damaged.

E Cooling system

1 Cooling system - layout (R1224 and R1228)

The cooling system layout of these models is very similar to that of the R1222 model (see Fig. 2.1, Chapter 2 and compare it with Fig. 12.8).

2 Fan belt - adjustment (current R1221 model)

1   Current R1221 models are fitted with a different 'fan' belt water pump drive adjuster (see Fig. 12.9).
2   Adjustment of the inner belt is achieved by slackening the slider bar and adjusting screw (v) locknuts and turning the adjusting screw in a clockwise direction, to achieve the desired belt tension. Tighten the locknuts after adjustment.
3   The end of the adjusting screw butts against the water pump body and as the adjusting screw is turned in a clockwise direction the jockey pulley is forced outwards thus tensioning the belt.
4   To slacken the belt reverse the above instructions.
5   Removal of the belt is identical to the instructions given in Chapter 2 apart from the above instructions.

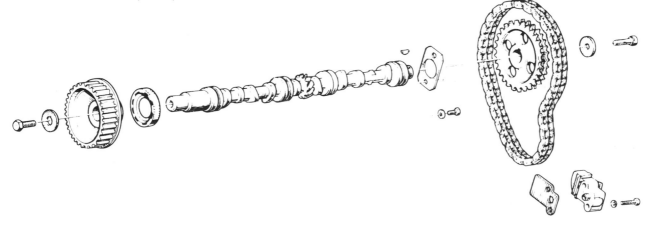

Fig. 12.7. The camshaft, timing chain and tensioner components (R1228)

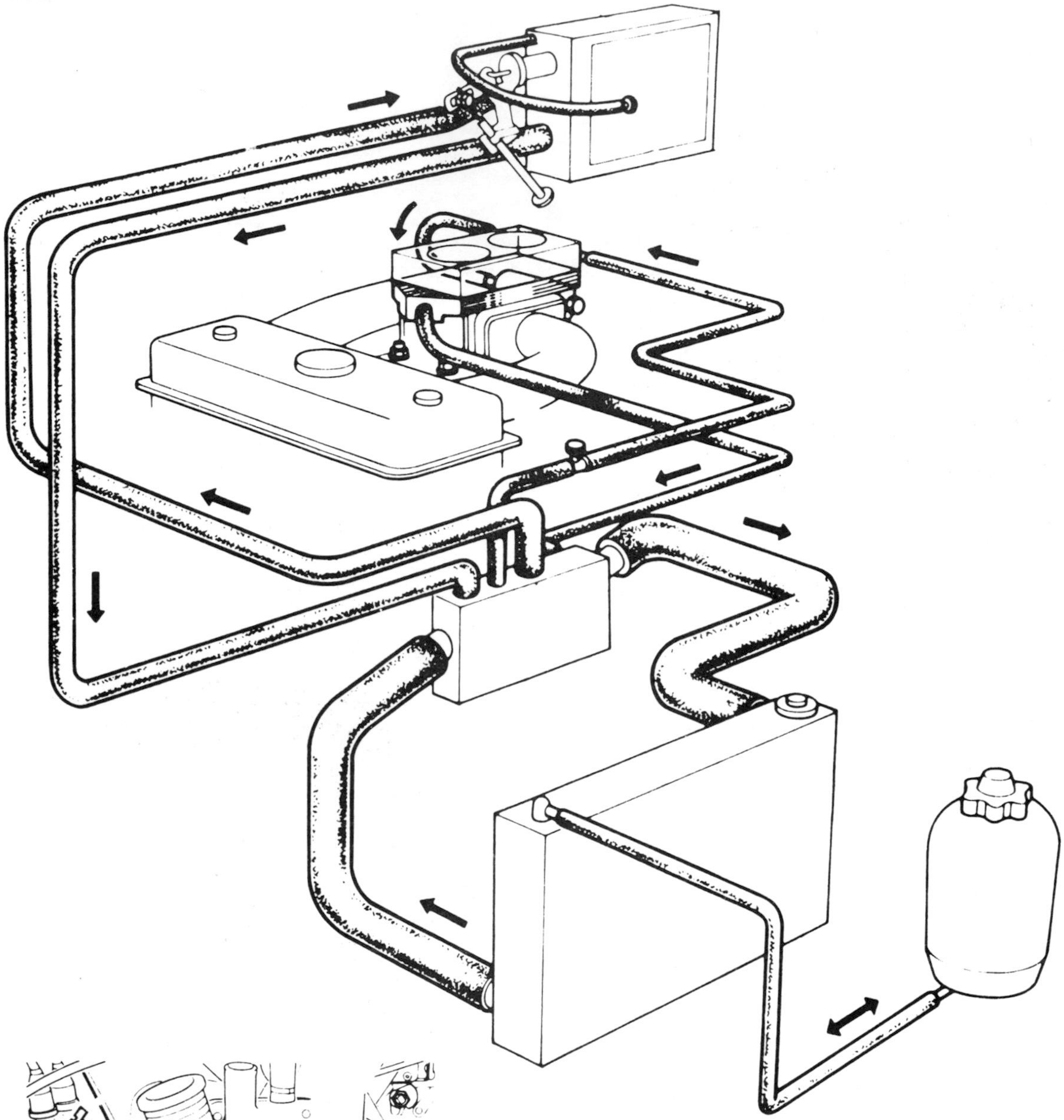

Fig. 12.8. Typical cooling system layout
for R1224 and R1228 models

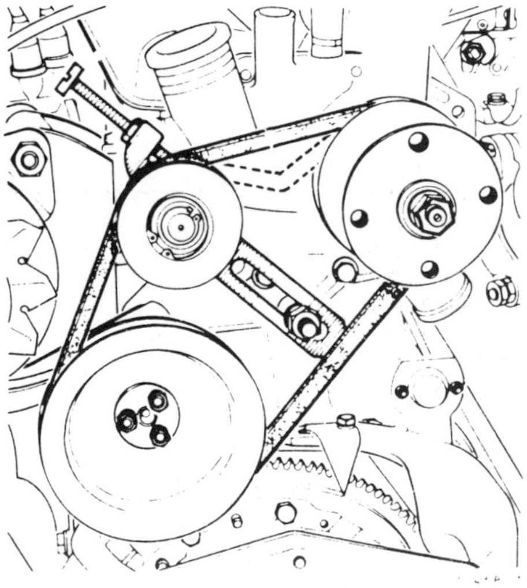

Fig. 12.9. The fan belt and jockey pulley adjuster mechanism
(R1221)

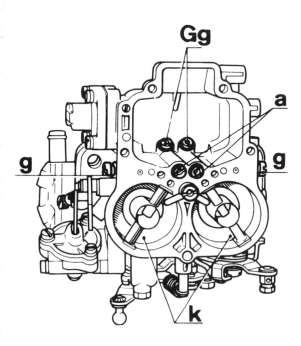

Fig. 12.10. The Weber carburettor with the top removed

a   Air compensator jet
g   Idling jet
Gg   Main jet
k   Choke tube

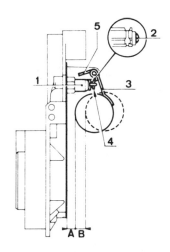

Fig. 12.11. Checking the float level and drop (Weber carburettor)

1   Check valve   5   Tongue
2   Check valve ball   A = 9/32 in (7 mm)
3   Float arm   B = 5/16 in (8 mm)
4   Tongue

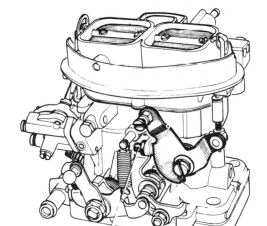

Fig. 12.12. Checking the initial throttle opening (Weber carburettor)

1   Adjusting screw and locknut

F Carburation; fuel and emission control systems

1   Weber carburettor (R1224 and R1228)

1   The Weber 32 DIR carburettor is a twin progressive choke downdraught carburettor which has the same operating principle as the Solex variety described in Chapter 3. The Weber carburettor is basically two single choke carburettors in one body. The primary (1st barrel) throttle flap valve is joined to the secondary (2nd barrel) flap valve by a special linkage. The linkage is designed so that the secondary throttle flap valve begins to open as the primary throttle flap valve approaches its fully open position hence the term 'progressive'. This facility allows for comparative economy at low speeds (operating on one choke) and extra performance when needed (both chokes operating). The carburettor is fitted with a cold start strangler (choke) device which is manually operated through a cable control on the dashboard.

2   This carburettor is an expensive component, relative to the Solex and comprises many finely engineered parts. Consequently it is advised that under no circumstances should the carburettor be dismantled further than the removal of the float chamber/choke flaps cover, and this only to clean the float chamber and to check the level of the float. If you are certain that the carburettor is at fault, and is not simply an adjustment or ignition fault then the carburettor must be removed and taken to a Renault or Weber agency for rectification. Do **NOT** attempt any home renovation - it can often only make matters worse.
3   Removal of this carburettor is almost identical to that described in Chapter 3 for the Solex type. The carburettor is located by four nuts instead of two.
4   The top cover or 'lid' of the carburettor is retained by screws which are made of a relatively soft metal. It is therefore essential when attempting to remove these screws to use the correct size of screwdriver and furthermore to ensure that a new paper gasket is available.
5   The float level and jet removal (only if absolutely necessary)

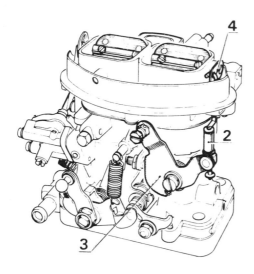

Fig. 12.13. Checking the setting of the mechanically operated choke flap (Weber carburettor)

2   Tube   3   Cam lever
                            4   Control rod link

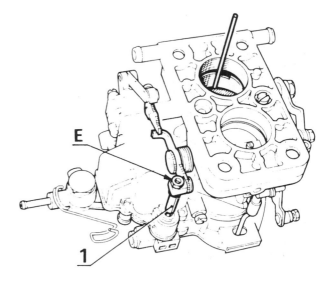

Fig. 12.14. Checking the adjustment of the de-fuming valve (Weber carburettor R1224 only)

1   Defuming valve stem   E   Adjusting nut

should be undertaken in the same way as for the Solex. Make sure you understand what you are doing first. Read the correct Section and the specification details thoroughly.

2   Weber carburettor (R1224 and R1228) - adjustments

1   Adjustments to the Weber carburettors fitted to these models is very similar to those described in Chapter 3 for the Solex type. However, in the case of the R1228 (USA) model it should be noted that incorrect adjustment of the carburettor will infringe current Federal Laws with regard to emission control. For this reason it is advisable to entrust the task to a carburation specialist or your nearest Renault dealer.
The following instructions are given for owners who feel confident enough to make the adjustments. The instructions given cover both the R1224 and R1228 models but note that the carburettor fitted to the R1228 (USA) model is slightly different in some respects which are noted in the text below.
2   Initial throttle opening (carburettor removed).
    a) Close the choke flap fully.
    b) Now measure the throttle flap valve opening with a suitable diameter gauge rod (see the Specifications for the dimension).
    c) Adjustment is made by unscrewing the locknut and turning the adjusting screw in the correct direction as shown in Fig. 12.12.
3   Mechanically activated choke flap - initial opening adjustment (carburettor removed).
    a) Close the choke flap fully.
    b) Bring the sleeve into contact with the cam by exerting pressure on the choke flap.
    c) Now, using a suitable diameter gauge rod or alternatively a twist drill of a comparable size measure the choke flap initial opening at the bottom of the flap (see the Specifications for the dimension).
    d) Adjustment of the opening clearance is made by carefully bending the link (see Fig. 12.13).

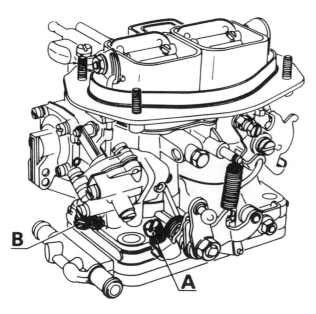

Fig. 12.15. The idling speed and mixture adjusting screws (Weber carburettor)

A   Idling speed screw   B   Idling mixture screw

4   Vacuum-activated choke flap mechanism (carburettor removed).

  a) *Push the link in as far as possible which is located in the centre of the vacuum unit.*
  b) *With the link in this position close the choke flaps until the spring between the cam and the sleeve is slightly compressed.*
  c) *With both units in this position measure the choke flap initial opening. (Refer to Fig. 12.14 and the Specifications Section for details).*
  d) *To adjust the choke flap initial opening it is necessary to remove the blanking screw from beneath the vacuum unit. Using a small screwdriver turn the adjusting screw located in the passage directly beneath the blanking screw.*

5   Defuming valve (R1224 only (carburettor removed)).

  a) *This carburettor is fitted with a defuming valve which opens the float chamber to the atmosphere on idling.*
  b) *Fully open the choke flap and press down the stem of the defuming valve.*
  c) *Measure the throttle flap valve opening which should be 0.014 to 0.025 in (0.35 to 0.65 mm).*
  d) *Adjust the clearance by turning the nut on the end of the defuming valve stem in the appropriate direction.*

6   Idling and mixture adjustments with CO analyser (R1228 model).

  a) *Run the engine until it has reached its normal operating temperature. Note, before attempting to make any adjustments to the carburettor it is necessary to ensure that the air filter element is sound and the ignition timing and contact breaker points gap are set correctly.*
  b) *Clamp the hose connecting the diverter/relief valve and the check valve.*
  c) *Now turn the throttle idling speed screw until the engine idling speed is 775 rpm, and adjust the idling mixture screw until the CO analyser reads between 2.3 and 3%.*
  d) *Repeat the adjustments detailed in paragraph c) until the engine is idling at 775 rpm with the correct CO percentage.*
  e) *Remove the clamp from the hose and check that the engine is idling at 800 $\pm$ 50 rpm.*
  f) *If the engine idling speed is incorrect adjust the idling speed screw to achieve the desired setting.*
  g) *Reclamp the hose and check the CO reading only.*
  h) *After removing the clamp recheck the engine idling speed.*

7   Idling and mixture adjustments without CO analyser (R1224 and R1228 models).

  a) *Run the engine until it has reached its normal operating temperature.* **Note:** *Before making any adjustments to the carburettor it is necessary to ensure that the air filter element is sound and the ignition timing and contact breaker points gap are set correctly.*
  b) *On R1228 (USA) model clamp the hose connecting the diverter/relief valve to the check valve.*
  c) *On both models turn the idling speed adjusting screw until the engine is idling at 725 rpm for the R1224 model and 775 rpm for the R1228.*
  d) *Adjust the idling mixture screw until the engine runs at as high a speed as possible.*
  e) *Readjust the idling speed adjusting screw as instructed in paragraph c).*
  f) *Repeat steps c) and d) if adjustment of the mixture screw causes the engine speed to peak at any other rpm than that given.*
  g) *On R1228 models turn the mixture screw clockwise to weaken the mixture. An idling speed drop of 20 - 25 rpm should be obtained without affecting the smoothness of the engine at idling speed.*
  h) *Remove the clamp from the hose and check the engine idling speed (R1228). It should now be 800 $\pm$ 50 rpm. Adjust the idling speed screw, if necessary to achieve this speed.*

---

3   Throttle cable - removal and refitting (all models)

Removal

1   Remove the clevis pin from the pedal assembly.
2   Free the other end of the cable from the swivel but take care to prevent bending or distorting the cable if it is to be reused.
3   When releasing the cable hold the locking sleeve with an open ended spanner of the correct size. Undo the locknut of the locking screw and then release the screw.
4   Now remove the compensator circlip and draw out the cable.

Refitting and adjusting

5   Position the cable and refit the compensator and its securing circlip.
6   Refit the clevis pin at the pedal and fit a new split pin.
7   Fit the copper end fitting in the swivel sleeve. Take care

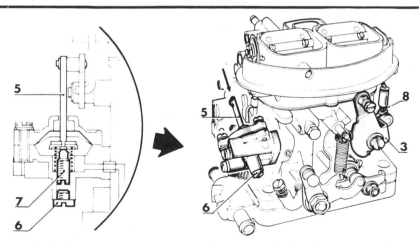

Fig. 12.16. Checking the setting of the vacuum activated choke flap (Weber carburettor)

3 Cam lever	6 Blanking screw	7 Adjusting screw	8 Spring
5 Link rod			

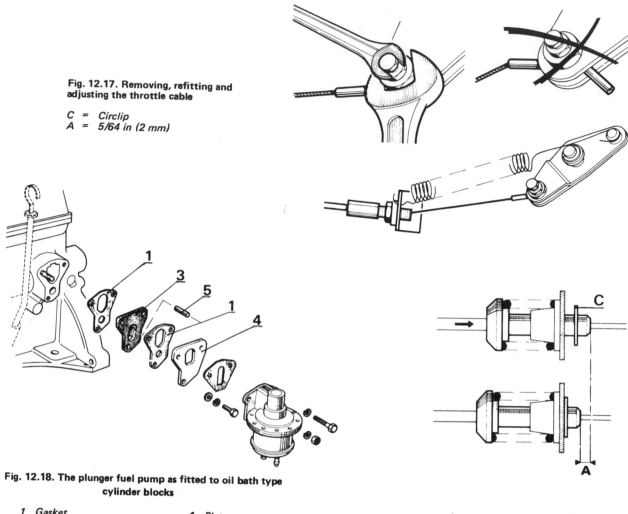

Fig. 12.17. Removing, refitting and adjusting the throttle cable

C = Circlip
A = 5/64 in (2 mm)

Fig. 12.18. The plunger fuel pump as fitted to oil bath type cylinder blocks

1   Gasket   4   Plate
3   Plunger guide and packing   5   Pump plunger

when tightening the locking bolt and nut. Ensure that the cable is central where it leaves its sleeve.

8   Press the accelerator pedal fully down to the floor, the throttle should be hard against its stop at the carburettor.

9   Now tighten the cable in the spool so that the compensator spring is compressed to a length of 5/64 in (2 mm).

10 Now recheck that the accelerator pedal is fully down to the floor, the throttle is against its stop at the carburettor and the compensator spring can still be compressed.

4   Fuel pump - changes and applications

A plunger type fuel pump is now fitted to R1222 models which have an oil-bath cylinder block. Refer to Fig. 12.2 to identify this type of block. R1224, R1225 and R1228 models have fitted both the oil-bath cylinder block and the plunger type fuel pump.

At the time of publication there was no information on the dismantling and reassembly procedure for this type of pump. Fig. 12.18 shows the order of packing and gaskets applicable to this pump. It should be noted that the plunger type fuel pump can only be fitted to the oil-bath type cylinder block.

5   Emission control systems - general description

1   The emission control system enables cars manufactured for the North American market to conform to Federal Regulations governing the emission of hydrocarbons, carbon monoxide, nitric oxide and fuel vapours from the crankcase, exhaust and fuel systems.

2   All Renault 5 models are fitted with a positive crankcase ventilation (PCV) system. In addition North American models are equipped with a thermostatic air cleaner, a throttle positioner system, and an ignition timing advance control system to control exhaust emissions. Models destined for California will have a catalytic converter and an exhaust gas recirculation (EGR) system in addition to the systems noted above.

Positive Crankcase Ventilation (PCV) System (All models)

3   All Renault 5 models are fitted with a PCV system to achieve crankcase breathing and the removal of 'blow-by' vapours by making use of the inherent partial vacuum in the carburettor and inlet manifold.

4   The system consists of various hoses and one restricting jet. The restricting jet is located in the pipe connecting the rocker cover to the inlet manifold.. USA models have a flame trap incorporated in the pipe line (see Fig. 12.22).

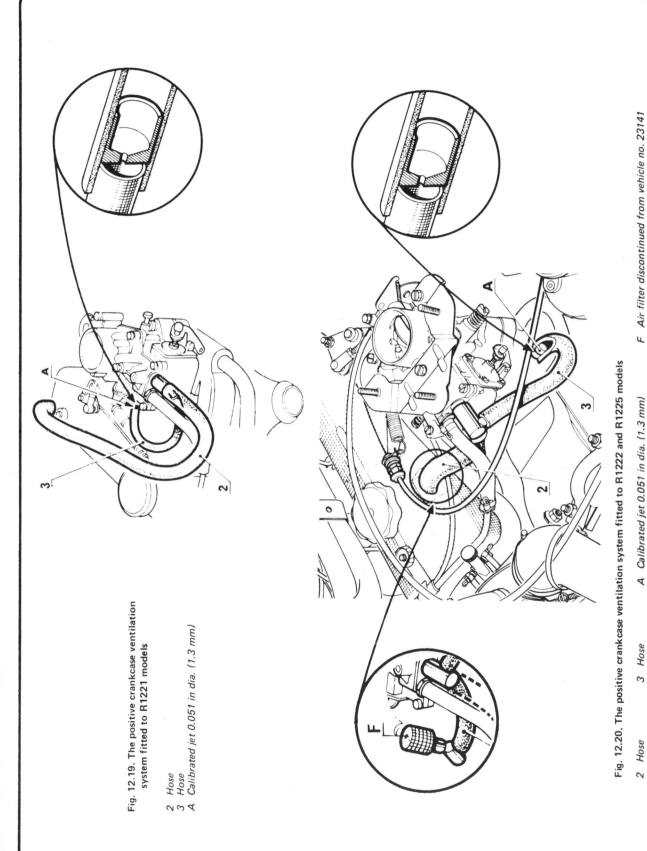

Fig. 12.19. The positive crankcase ventilation
system fitted to R1221 models

2   Hose
3   Hose
A   Calibrated jet 0.051 in dia. (1.3 mm)

Fig. 12.20. The positive crankcase ventilation system fitted to R1222 and R1225 models

2   Hose   3   Hose   A   Calibrated jet 0.051 in dia. (1.3 mm)   F   Air filter discontinued from vehicle no. 23141

Air Injection System (R1228 only)

5   This system is used to reduce the emission of hydrocarbons, carbon monoxide and nitric oxide in the exhaust gases and comprises air pump, diverter/relief valve, air shut-off/check valve and air injection manifold.

6   The rotary vane type pump is belt driven from the engine and delivers compressed air at a maximum pressure of 4.3 psi to each of the four exhaust ports.

7   The diverter/relief valve controls the air pressure delivered to the injection manifold and releases excessive pressure to the atmosphere. During deceleration the diverter/relief valve shuts off the compressed air supply to the injection manifold and the compressed air is released to the atmosphere.

8   The air shut-off valve is controlled by the choke cable and forms an integral part with the check valve. When the choke is operated the valve shuts off the air flow from the air pump to the injection manifold.

9   The check valve is a diaphragm-spring operated non-return valve. Its purpose is to protect the air pump from exhaust gas pressures both under normal operation and in the event of the drivebelt failing.

Thermostatic air cleaner

10 This device consists of an air cleaner with a double inlet. A flap fitted to the assembly meters and mixes the warm and ambient air entering the air cleaner. The flap is controlled by a wax thermostat element. The device effectively provides air at a more constant temperature to the carburettor and allows a finer control on mixture to be achieved and thus assists in reducing the exhaust emissions.

Evaporative Control System (1228 models only)

11 This system uses an activated charcoal absorption canister through which the fuel tank is vented, and incorporates the following features:

   a) *The carburettor constant depression is used to induce a purge condition through the absorption canister.*

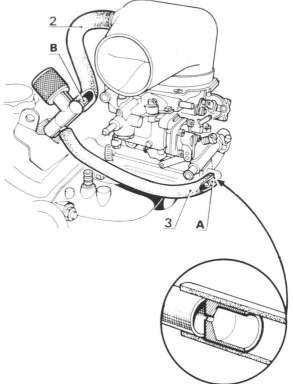

Fig. 12.21. The positive crankcase ventilation system fitted to R1224 models

2 Hose	A Calibrated jet 0.051 in dia. (1.3 mm)
3 Hose	B Calibrated jet 0.256 in dia. (6.5 mm)

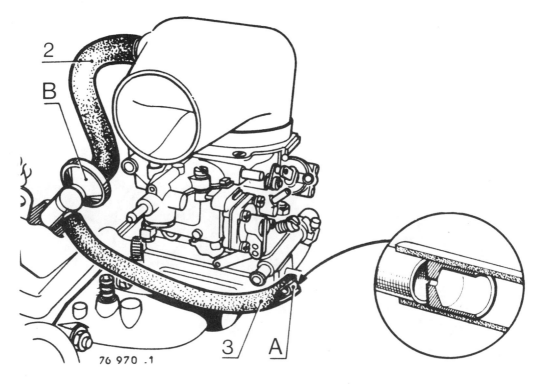

76 970 .1

Fig. 12.22. The positive crankcase ventilation system fitted to R1228 models

2 Hose   3 Hose   A Calibrated jet 0.059 in dia. (1.5 mm)   B Flame arrestor

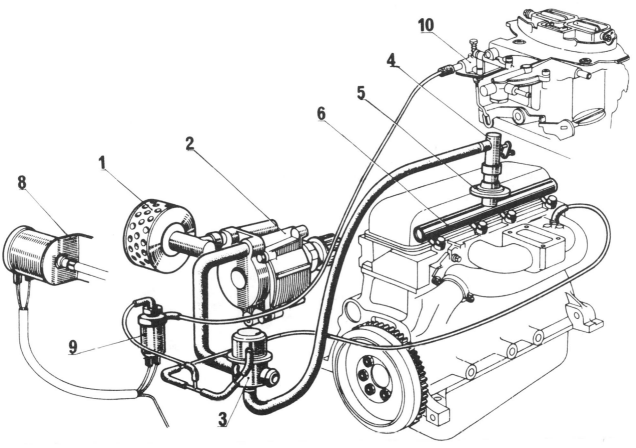

Fig. 12.23. The air injection system (R1228 models)

1 Air pump air filter
2 Air pump (rotary type belt driven)
3 Relief/diverter valve

4 Air shut off valve
5 Check valve
6 Air injection manifold

8 Centrifugal governor
9 Throttle positioner solenoid valve

10 Throttle valve positioner diaphragm unit

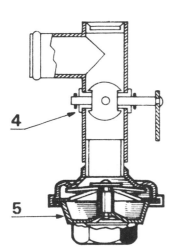

Fig. 12.24. The combined air shut off and check valve assembly

4 Air shut off valve
5 Check valve

b) A vapour-liquid separator and combined two-way check valve is provided between the fuel tank and charcoal absorption canister. When the fuel expands and the pressure in the fuel tank reaches 5 psi, the valve in the two-way check valve opens and allows the fuel vapour to travel to the charcoal canister, where the fuel vapours are absorbed and the tank is thus vented to the atmosphere. As the fuel level in the tank drops the other valve opens and air is drawn into the tank.

c) A check valve is fitted in the fuel return pipe line between the fuel pump and tank. This valve allows the fuel to flow in one direction only between the pump and tank.

d) A sealed filler cap is used to prevent loss by evaporation.

e) The fuel filler tube extends into the fuel tank to prevent complete filling; this permits the fuel to expand in hot weather.

Exhaust Gas Recirculation (EGR) System (Californian R1228 model only)

12 To minimise nitric oxide exhaust emissions, the peak combustion temperatures are lowered by recirculating a metered quantity of exhaust gas through the inlet manifold.

13 A control signal is taken from a tapping in the carburettor body. At idle, full load or when the coolant temperature is below $45^\circ C$ ($113^\circ F$) the EGR system does not function. Under part load conditions a controlled amount of recirculation is provided.

Catalytic Converter (Californian 1228 model only)

14 To further reduce the emission of carbon monoxide and hydrocarbons, a catalytic converter is fitted in the exhaust system of Californian models.

15 As the exhaust gases pass through the converter a chemical reaction occurs which reduces the exhaust emissions.

16 A protection system is provided to prevent the converter from overheating. When the temperature of the converter reaches $427^\circ \pm 32^\circ C$ ($800^\circ \pm 90^\circ F$) a temperature sensor activates a relay which energises a solenoid valve. The solenoid valve shuts off the vacuum supply to the air injection control valve which in turn stops air injection into the exhaust system.

Vacuum Advance Control System (1228 models only)

17 With the engine coolant temperature below $45^\circ C$ ($113^\circ F$) a thermal sensing switch cuts off the current feed to a relay. The relay in turn controls the flow of current to the solenoid valve.

18 When the solenoid valve is de-energised it allows the inlet manifold vacuum to act upon the vacuum advance unit of the distributor. At temperatures above $45^\circ C$ ($113^\circ F$) the solenoid valve is energised and shuts off the supply of vacuum to the distributor vacuum advance unit.

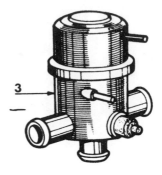

Fig. 12.25. Diverter/relief valve (R1228)

Ignition Timing Advance Control System (1228 models only)

19 A switch linked to the choke cable closes when the choke is operated. The switch when closed supplies current to the vacuum solenoid valve which then opens and allows carburettor vacuum to act upon the distributor vacuum advance unit. This arrangement allows the ignition timing to be advanced during cold engine operation. When the choke is released the switch contacts open and the system is de-energised.

Throttle Positioner System (Fast Idle) (R1228 only)

20 The system consists of a speed sensor, solenoid valve, and throttle positioner diaphragm unit.

21 When the vehicle speed exceeds 21 mph the contacts of the speed sensor switch close and energise the throttle positioner

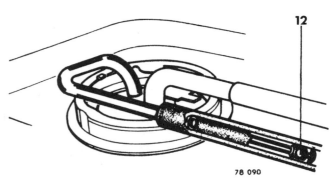

Fig. 12.26. Check ball valve, allowing fuel flow from pump to tank only

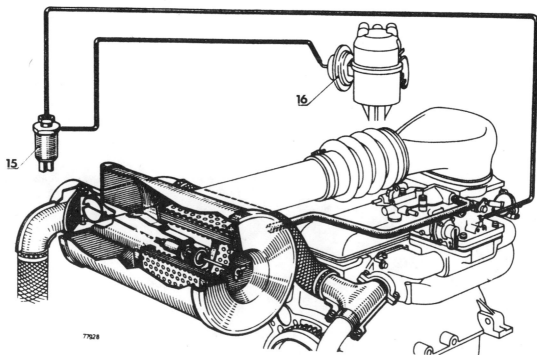

Fig. 12.27. The thermostat air cleaner assembly (R1228)

15 Solenoid valve   16 Distributor vacuum unit

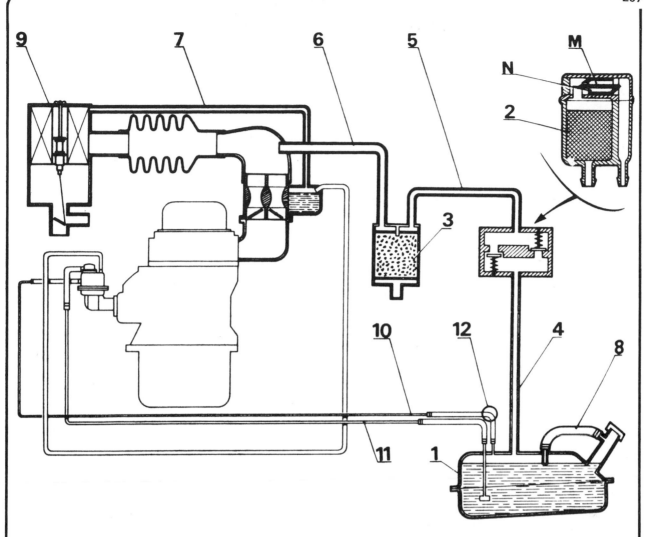

Fig. 12.28. The fuel vapour evaporative emission control system (R 1228)

1 Fuel tank
2 Fuel vapour tank with incorporated filter
3 Charcoal canister
4 Line, fuel tank to expansion tank
5 Line, fuel vapour tank to charcoal canister
6 Line, canister to carburettor air intake
7 Line, carburettor float chamber to air cleaner
8 Line, filler neck to fuel tank
9 Carburettor air intake elbow
10 Fuel return hose · pump to fuel tank
11 Fuel supply line, tank to fuel pump

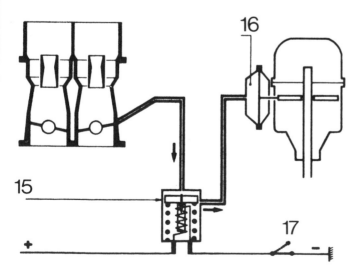

Fig. 12.29. The ignition timing advance control system

15 Solenoid control valve
16 Distributor vacuum unit
17 Switch contacts

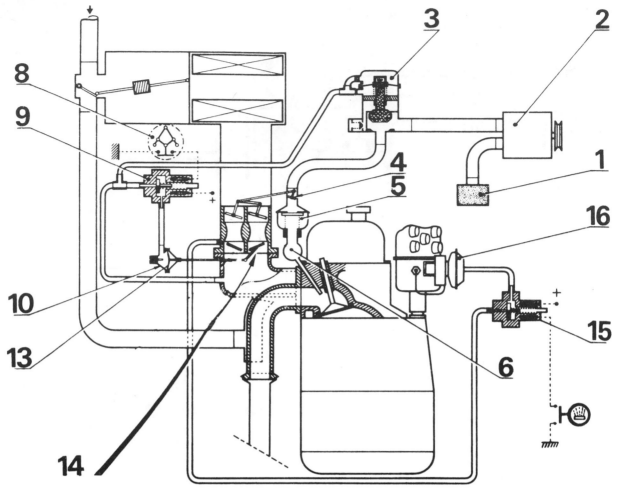

Fig. 12.30. Layout of the fast idling system (throttle positioner system) (R1228)

1 Air pump filter	5 Check valve	9 Throttle positioner solenoid	14 Throttle flap valve
2 Air pump	6 Air injection manifold	valve	15 Vacuum advance solenoid
3 Diverter/relief valve	8 Centrifugal governor	10 Throttle valve positioner	valve
4 Air shut-off valve		13 Diaphragm unit	16 Vacuum advance unit

solenoid valve. The solenoid valve opens and allows vacuum from the inlet manifold to act upon the throttle positioner diaphragm. If the vehicle is accelerating the vacuum signal is too weak to operate the diaphragm unit.

22 During deceleration of the vehicle the vacuum signal is strong enough to operate the diaphragm unit which will prevent the throttle flap valve from closing completely, thus reducing the concentration of unburned hydrocarbons in the exhaust system, by admitting a mixture sufficient to maintain complete combustion within the engine cylinders.

23 When the speed of the vehicle drops to 17 mph the contacts of the speed sensor switch separate and the throttle positioner solenoid valve is de-energised which in turn shuts off the vacuum supply to the throttle opener diaphragm. The throttle flap valve can now close completely and resume its normal idling position.

---

6 Emission control systems - inspection, repair and maintenance

Positive Crankcase Ventilation (PCV) System (All models)

1 To ensure that the PCV system functions correctly inspect

and clean the system at 6,000 mile (10,000 km) intervals.

2 Renew the hoses if they are cracked or perished remembering to fit the calibrated restricting jet in the appropriate pipe line.

Air Pump - removal and refitting

3 Remove the air cleaner and air pump filter.

4 Disconnect the hoses from the air pump.

5 Remove the bolts securing the pump in position and lift it off.

6 Refitting is the reverse of the dismantling procedure. Note that the air pump belt is not adjustable, therefore it is essential to check the belt deflection as described in the following paragraphs.

Air Pump drivebelt - removal and refitting

7 Loosen the nuts and bolts holding the alternator in position and remove the alternator drivebelt.

8 Remove the air cleaner and air pump filter.

9 Slacken the air pump mountings to allow the toothed belt to be removed.

10 Refitting the belt is the reverse of the removal procedure.

11 The toothed belt is not adjustable but it is essential after refitting it to check the deflection of the belt at a point midway between the two pulleys. The belt deflection should be 6/64 in

to 9/64 in (2.5 to 3.5 mm) if the belt is in good condition. If the deflection is greater than this dimension then a new belt must be fitted.

Air distribution manifold - removal and refitting
12 Disconnect the air hose at the air shut off valve.
13 Disconnect the shut off valve linkage from the carburettor.
14 Unscrew the four unions and withdraw the complete manifold (and check valve) from the exhaust ports.
15 If necessary, hold the manifold in a vice, and unscrew the check valve.
16 Refitting is the reverse of the dismantling procedure.

Thermostatic air cleaner - testing
17 Remove the air cleaner assembly from the engine and remove the filter element.
18 Dip the air cleaner in water so that the thermostat unit is immersed.
19 Heat the water to a temperature of 18°C (64°F). The valve should shut off the ambient air inlet after 5 minutes.
20 Raise the water temperature to 36°C (97°F). The valve should close off the hot air inlet after 5 minutes.

Fast idle speed - adjustment
21 Check and adjust if necessary the normal idling speed as described in the earlier part of this Section.
22 Now disconnect the solenoid (+) feed wire and insulate it.
23 Using a jumper lead connect a 12 volt feed wire to the solenoid terminal.
24 Start the engine and adjust the fast idling screw to obtain an engine speed of 1500 rpm.
25 Remove the jumper lead and reconnect the solenoid feed wire.

Centrifugal speed sensor device - testing
26 To test the speed sensor device which operates the fast idle device through the solenoid valve necessitates raising the front wheels off the ground.
27 Chock the rear wheels and ensure the front end is adequately supported.
28 Connect a test light between the solenoid terminal (+) and a satisfactory earthing point.
29 Start the engine and engage 2nd gear. On accelerating the bulb should go out at a speed of 21 mph. On decelerating the bulb should come on at a speed of 17 mph.

Exhaust Gas Recirculation (EGR) system - maintenance
30 At 25,000 mile intervals the EGR system should be dismantled, cleaned and checked. To remind the driver that 25,000 mile period has elapsed an EGR maintenance warning light will illuminate.
31 The task of carrying out this maintenance and check is best entrusted to your nearest Renault dealer who will have the necessary equipment to service the system and to reset the warning light.

Catalytic converter - removal and refitting
32 At the time of publication no details of the removal and refitting of this unit was available.

7 Fault diagnosis - emission control systems

Symptom	Reason/s
Oil fume seepage from engine	Split or collapsed hoses.
Erratic idling	Fault check valve Carbon canister purge line disconnected. Faulty EGR valve
Power reduced	Faulty EGR valve

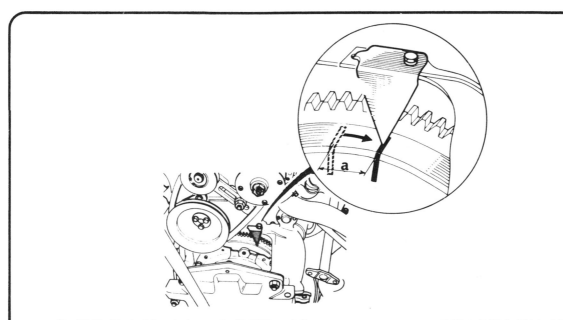

Fig. 12.31. The ignition timing marks (R1221 model) $a = 7/16 \pm 5/64$ in $(11 \pm 1.8$ mm)

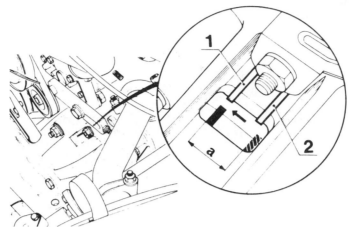

Fig. 12.32. The ignition timing marks (R1222, R1224, R1225 and R1228 models)

1   0° (TDC)   2   4° (BTDC)   a   Measurement in in. (mm) corresponding to degrees of advance

G Ignition system

1   Ignition system - modifications

1   A few changes have been made to the ignition system and reference to the Specifications Section of this Chapter will give details of the changes and the models affected.

2   The R1224 and R1228 models both use the Ducellier distributor but at the time of publication the model number fitted to the R1228 was not known, however, in all other respects it appears to be identical to the R1224 distributor.

H Clutch

1   Clutch (R1224, R1225 and R1228)

1   The clutch assemblies fitted to these models are identical to the assembly fitted to the R1222 except for the differences noted in the Specifications Section of this Chapter.

J Gearbox

1   Gearbox - general description (R1224, R1225 and R1228)

1   These models are fitted with the 354 type gearbox which is very similar to that which is fitted to the R1222 model.

2   The gearbox and final drive ratios are somewhat different between the various models, particularly in the case of the R1225 model which has a 3.1 to 1 final drive ratio purposely fitted with economy cruising in mind. Refer to the Specifications Section of this Chapter for further details of the gearbox fitted to these models.

3   The removal, dismantling and refitting of these gearboxes is identical to the R1222 model as described in Chapter 6.

2   Floor mounted gear lever - checking adjustment of stop plate

1   R1224, R1225, R1228 and some R1222 models are fitted with a floor mounted gear shift lever.

2   Select reverse gear and check the measurement from the centre of the stop button on the end of the gear shift lever to the top of the stop plate (see Fig. 12.33, dimension A).

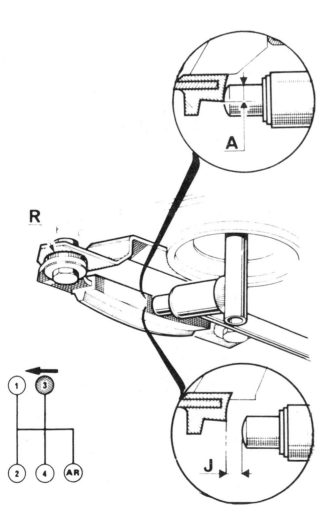

Fig. 12.33. Checking the adjustment of the stop plate (floor mounted gearchange models)

A   3/16 to 9/32 in (5 to 7 mm)
R   Spacing washer
J   1/8 in (3 mm)

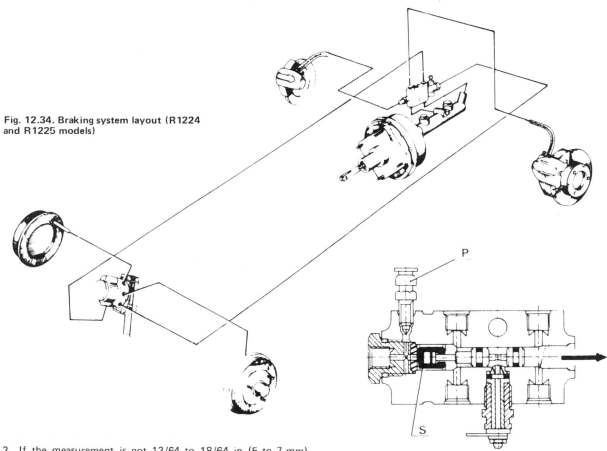

Fig. 12.34. Braking system layout (R1224 and R1225 models)

3 If the measurement is not 13/64 to 18/64 in (5 to 7 mm) adjust the stop plate height using washers placed between the stop plate and the body (Fig. 12.33 point R).

4 Now select 3rd gear position and press the lever over toward the 1st-2nd gear position.

5 With the gear lever in this position measure the distance (J Fig. 12.33) between the stop plate and the end of the stop button which should be 1/8 in (3 mm).

6 If necessary use the slotted holes in the stop plate to achieve this clearance dimension.

K Braking system

1 Braking system - modifications and general description

1 Several modifications have been made to the braking systems of current R1221 and R1222 models. A dual circuit master cylinder is now fitted to some R1221 models. Certain R1221 and R1222 models have automatic rear brake adjusters fitted.

2 Dimensional changes are given in the Specifications Section at the commencement of this Chapter.

3 The introduction of the combined bypass/pressure drop indicator on models which have a dual circuit master cylinder is a special safety feature. The operation of this unit is described later in this Section.

4 The R1224 model is fitted with a vacuum servo brake booster unit as standard and is also fitted with either manual or automatic rear brake adjusters.

5 The R1228 model is fitted with manual rear brake adjusters which can be turned by application of a screwdriver through an adjuster hole in the backplate.

6 All models are now fitted with an adjustable stop light switch which is fitted to the foot brake pedal assembly.

Fig. 12.35A. Section through the bypass/pressure drop indicator

P Bleed nipple
S Bypass valve
➡ Direction of piston travel if there is a fault in the front braking system

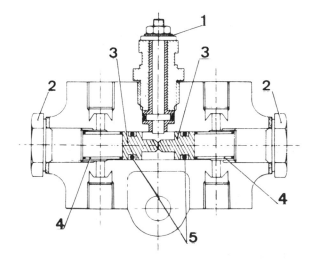

Fig. 12.35B. The simple pressure drop indicator (sectioned view)

1 Switch terminal   4 Springs
2 Closure plugs   5 Seals
3 Piston

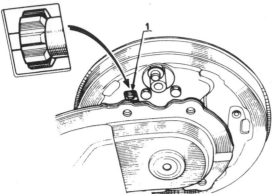

Fig. 12.36. The rear brake adjuster wheel (R1228)

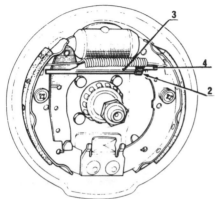

Fig. 12.37. The rear brake components shown with the brake drum removed (R1228)

2   *Adjuster wheel*   4   *Male rod*
3   *Female rod*

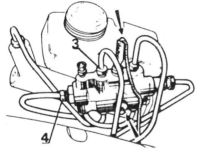

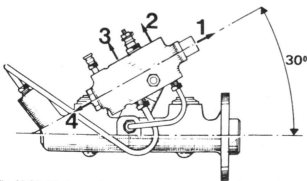

Fig. 12.38. The bypass/pressure drop indicator mounted to the master cylinder

1   *Outlet to LH front wheel*   3   *Outlet to rear wheels*
2   *Outlet to RH front wheel*   4   *Outlet to rear wheels*
                                       (additional circuit)

2   Bypass/pressure drop indicator - description and operation

1   This unit, fitted to some models equipped with dual circuit brakes, has two principal functions.

2   In the first instance the unit activates a warning light circuit if there is an out of balance state occurring between the front and rear braking circuits.

3   An out of balance state will occur if the system requires bleeding, or if there is an external brake fluid leakage and finally if there is a fault in the master cylinder.

4   The PDI unit consists of a piston head assembly which is subjected to hydraulic pressure from the front and rear brake circuits acting respectively on each side of the piston.

5   When the braking system is functioning correctly equal pressures are acting on the piston head assembly and the piston will remain in a central balanced position.

6   An out of balance condition, for one of the reasons given in paragraph 3, will cause the piston to move from the central position to make contact with an electrical sender switch unit screwed into the PDI unit.

7   When the piston makes contact with the sender unit an electrical circuit is completed and a warning light on the instrument panel is illuminated and this warns the driver of a brake system fault.

8   The second function of the bypass/pressure drop indicator is to direct brake pressure to the rear brakes in the event of a fluid leakage on the front brake circuit.

9   When there is a drop in line pressure in the front brake circuit the piston within the PDI unit will move laterally due to the unbalance.

10 Attached to the piston assembly is a valve which when opened connects the master cylinder direct to the rear brake circuit. Thus all the braking pressure is applied and transferred to the rear brakes.

11 On some models where the bypass system is not included, the PDI unit takes a simpler form and merely operates as described in paragraphs 1-7.

3   Bypass/pressure drop indicator - removal and refitting   (all models except R1222)

1   Remove the cap from the brake fluid reservoir and stretch a thin sheet of polythene over the reservoir top. Refit the cap. This will prevent excessive loss of fluid when the bypass/pressure drop indicator unit is disconnected.

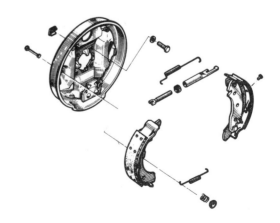

Fig. 12.39. Exploded view of the rear brake components (R1228)

2 Disconnect the PDI warning light wire at the switch unit.
3 Disconnect the various pipe line connections joined to the bypass/pressure drop indicator. Note the positions of the pipes so that they can be reconnected correctly.
4 Unscrew the indicator fixing nut and lift the unit away.
5 The unit cannot be repaired and if it is faulty fit a new unit in its place.
6 Refitting the unit is the reverse of the dismantling procedure except for the following points.
7 The pressure drop indicator should be inclined at an angle of 30° from the vertical centre line of the master cylinder.
8 When the unit has been connected bleed the system as described in the next Section of this Chapter and Section 3 of Chapter 8.

4 Bleeding the system (applicable to all models fitted with a bypass pressure drop indicator)

1 Bleed the system as described in Chapter 8, Section 3 but after bleeding the four wheels bleed the pressure drop indicator.
2 The pressure drop indicator should always be bled last.

5 Rear brake - adjustment (R1228 model)

1 Chock the front wheels and release the handbrake.
2 Raise the rear wheels clear of the ground.
3 Remove the plastic cap from the backplate to gain access to the toothed adjuster wheel.
4 Using a screwdriver turn the adjuster wheel whilst slowly turning the roadwheel.
5 Continue turning the adjuster wheel until the brake shoes have been adjusted sufficiently to prevent the roadwheel from being turned.
6 Now turn the adjuster wheel in the opposite direction until the roadwheel can be rotated without undue binding or resistance.
7 Apply the footbrake pedal and recheck the adjustment.
8 Repeat the operation for the other rear brake.
   Note that Fig. 12.37 shows the direction in which the adjuster wheel must be turned to adjust the rear brakes. This is not necessarily correct as some of the early R1228 models must be turned in the opposite direction.

6 Rear brake drum and shoes - removal, inspection and refitting (R1228)

1 Chock the front wheels and jack up the rear of the car. Remember to support the car with either axle stands or strong wooden packing blocks. Never rely on the jack as the sole method of support.
2 Remove the roadwheel and release the handbrake.
3 Remove the adjuster wheel blanking cap from the backplate and turn the adjuster wheel in the correct direction to back the brake shoes off. (Refer to the previous sub-section for details).
4 Now remove the brake drum/hub assembly as described in Chapter 8.
5 When the drum/hub assembly has been removed carry out an inspection of the lining and drum condition also described in Chapter 8.
6 If the brake shoes are to be removed proceed by removing the upper shoe return spring which links the front (leading) and rear (trailing) brake shoes together. Renault use a special spring removal tool for this operation, however, a screwdriver and a pair of pliers are just as effective.
7 Carefully release the handbrake cable from the operating link.
8 Release the shoe steady spring and cup. Use pliers or a suitable socket and extension bar to compress the shoe steady spring. With the spring in the compressed state from behind the backplate rotate the steady pin through 90° to release it from the steady spring cup.
9 Repeat this operation for the other shoe steady spring.
10 Remove the lower shoe return spring and remove the brake shoes.
11 Renault use a special tool to restrain the wheel cylinder pistons which tend to move outwards under the influence of a spring fitted between them. A strong rubber band will serve the same purpose. Remember that the brake pedal must not be pressed down with the shoes and drum removed unless the pistons are restrained.
12 Before refitting the brake shoes dismantle the adjuster mechanism and examine it for wear and operation. The threaded link can be cleaned with a wire brush and lightly lubricated. Remember to screw the adjuster wheel back to the position which would fully release the adjustment of the brake shoes.
13 Refitting the brake shoes is the reverse of the dismantling procedure but ensure that the brake shoes are refitted the

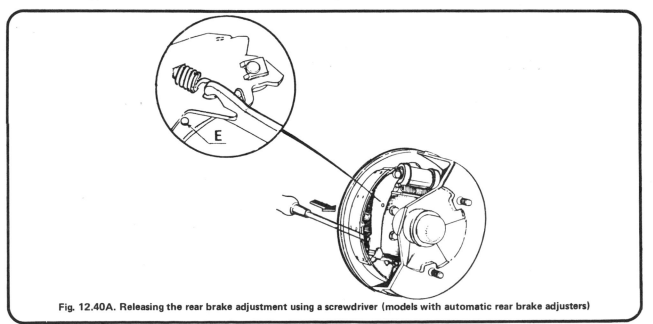

Fig. 12.40A. Releasing the rear brake adjustment using a screwdriver (models with automatic rear brake adjusters)

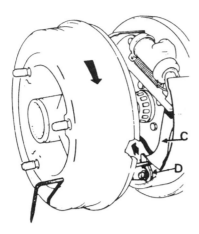

Fig. 12.40B. Releasing the rear brake adjustment using a length of 3/16 in (5 mm) diameter rod (RH side shown)

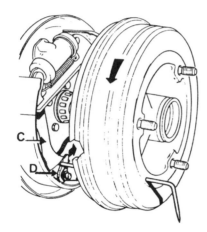

Fig. 12.40C. As 12.40B but LH side shown

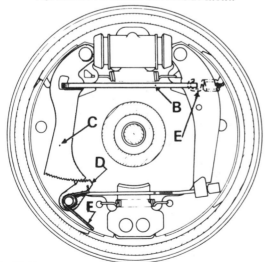

Fig. 12.41. The rear brakes with drum removed (models with automatic adjusters)

B Link
C Lever
D Toothed quadrant

E Tension spring
F Quadrant spring

correct way round, ie. with the longer lining towards the front and the shorter lining towards the rear as in Fig. 12.39.

14 Refit the drum/hub assembly as described in Chapter 8 making reference to Chapter 7 for adjustment.

15 Adjust the brake shoes as described in Section 5.

16 Remember to refit the blanking caps to the adjuster holes in the backplate.

7 Rear brake drum and shoes - removal and refitting (models with automatic rear brake adjusters)

1 Chock the front wheels and jack up the rear of the car. Support the car with either axle stands or strong wooden packing blocks.

2 Remove the roadwheel and release the handbrake.

3 The automatic brake adjuster mechanism can be backed off using a screwdriver inserted through a hole in the backplate or brake drum. Each method is described below.

4 Remove the sealing plug from the backplate and insert a screwdriver. Press the handbrake operating lever with the screwdriver to free its pip from the brake shoe. The brake shoe is drilled to allow access to the lever. (Refer to Fig. 12.40A).

5 Once the pip is free back the lever off by pushing it to the rear.

6 Alternatively, a length of 3/16 in (5 mm) diameter rod, cranked at one end, can be inserted through the hole in the brake drum which is covered by a blanking plug.

7 Insert the rod so that its end rests against the forward side of the sector.

8 Hold the rod in this position and turn the drum slowly in a forward direction. The toothed sector will be forced back out of mesh by the rod and the adjustment will be released. (Figs. 12.40B and 12.40C).

9 Remove the rear brake drum/hub assembly as described in Chapter 8.

10 Carry out an inspection of the drum and lining condition also described in Chapter 8.

11 If the brake shoes are to be removed proceed by removing the upper shoe return spring. Renault recommend that service tool FRE.572 is used to remove this spring. However, a pair of pliers and a screwdriver can be substituted in its place.

12 Disconnect the handbrake cable from the link arm.

13 Unhook the two shoe steady springs using a length of rod to press the spring downwards and at the same time tipping it slightly to release the spring.

14 Swing the forward link arm back against the stub axle and ease the brake shoes away from the backplate. Have ready a strong rubber band to wrap around the wheel cylinder to restrain the pistons from travelling outwards under the influence of the spring which lies between them. Renault use service tool FRE.05 to restrain the wheel cylinder pistons and it is shown in Fig. 12.42A

15 With the brake shoes now tipped outwards pull the link bar outwards to release it from the leading shoe.

16 Reset the toothed quadrant in its initial setting position against the forward link arm.

17 Now tilt the leading (forward) brake shoe through 90° and remove the lower shoe return spring with a screwdriver.

18 The brake shoes can now be lifted from the backplate.

19 If new brake shoes are to be fitted then it will be necessary to transfer the link arms and adjuster assembly components to the new brake shoes. In any case the component parts of this assembly should be inspected for wear and damage and renewed as necessary.

20 Refitting the shoes is the reverse of the dismantling procedure.

21 To fit the shoe steady spring clips in their backplate holes press them inwards and turn them through 90°.

22 Finally, before fitting the brake drum/hub assembly it is essential to check the initial setting of the self-adjusting system.

23 Adjustment depends on the tension of the spring which is hooked between the link and the trailing (rear) brake shoe.

Fig. 12.42A. Removing the upper shoe return spring (service tools FRE 05 and 572 shown)

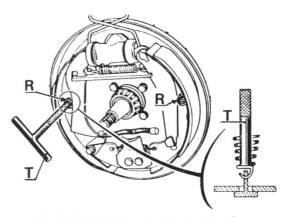

Fig. 12.42B. Releasing the shoe steady springs

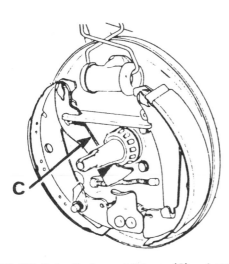

Fig. 12.42C. Swing the forward link arm (C) against the stub axle and ease the brake shoes away from the backplate

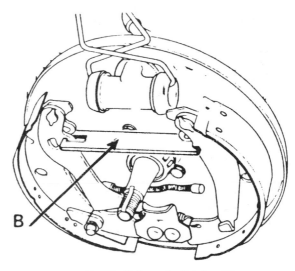

Fig. 12.42D. Release the link bar (B)

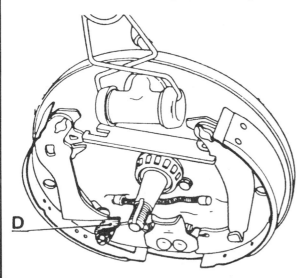

Fig. 12.42E. Reset the toothed quadrant (D)

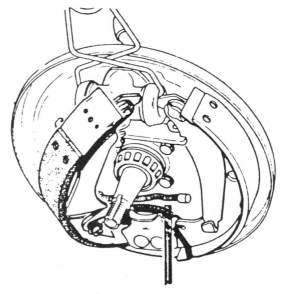

Fig. 12.42F. Tilt the leading shoe and remove the lower shoe return spring

24 This tension is measured by checking that a clearance of approximately 3/64 in (1 mm) is present between the forward edge of the link and the forward edge of the slotted hole in which it is fitted.

25 If this approximate dimension is not achieved then it will be necessary to renew the tension spring and the two shoe return springs.

26 Refit the brake drum/hub assembly as described in Chapter 8 making reference to Chapter 7 for hub adjustment.

27 Now press the brake pedal several times to centralise the brake shoes and to operate the automatic adjuster mechanism.

28 Remember to refit the blanking plug in either the backplate or brake drum depending on which method was used to release the brake adjustment.

8 Brake Servo unit - description (R1224 only)

The vacuum servo unit is fitted into the brake system in series with the master cylinder and brake pedal to provide power assistance to the driver when the brake pedal is depressed.

The unit operates by vacuum obtained from the induction manifold, and comprises basically a booster diaphragm and a non return valve.

The servo unit and hydraulic master cylinder are connected together so that the servo unit push rod acts as the master cylinder push rod. The driver's braking effort is transmitted through another push rod to the servo unit piston and its built in control system (photo).

The servo unit piston does not fit tightly into the cylinder but has a strong diaphragm to keep its periphery in contact with the cylinder wall so assuring an air tight seal between the two parts. The forward chamber is held under vacuum conditions created in the inlet manifold of the engine and during periods when the engine is not in use the controls open a passage to the

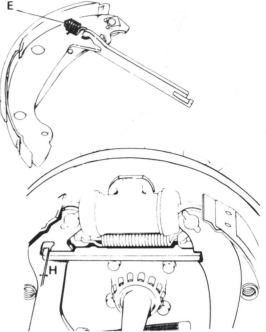

Fig. 12.43. Checking the initial setting of the automatic adjuster

E Tension spring
H Clearance gap between link bar and brake shoe hole = 3/64 in (1 mm)

rear chamber so placing it under vacuum. When the brake pedal is depressed, the vacuum passage to the rear chamber is cut off and the chamber is opened to atmospheric pressure. The consequent rush of air into the rear chamber pushes the servo piston forward into the vacuum chamber and operates the push rod to the master cylinder. The controls are designed so that assistance is given under all conditions. When the brakes are not required, vacuum is re-established in the rear chamber when the brake pedal is released.

Air from the atmosphere passes through a small filter before entering the control valves and rear chamber and it is only this filter that will require periodic attention.

9 Brake servo unit - removal and refitting (R1224 only)

1 Disconnect the battery negative (−) lead.

2 Remove the master cylinder as described in Chapter 8.

3 Disconnect the vacuum hose union on the brake servo.

4 Remove the clevis pin connecting the brake pedal to the pushrod (from within the drivers compartment).

5 Unscrew the brake servo fixing nuts and lift the unit free.

6 Refitting the servo is the reverse of the removal operation but if the unit has been dismantled or a new unit is being fitted, two dimensions must be checked to ensure correct operation of the unit.

7 Check that the protrusion of the pushrod end is 23/64 in (9 mm) from the face of the servo unit which mates with the master cylinder. If necessary adjust the pushrod nut to achieve this dimension.

8 Now check the distance between the face of the servo unit and the centre of the hole through the yoke at the pedal end of the servo. If the measurement is not 4 23/64 in (120 mm) adjust the yoke position to achieve this dimension.

9 With the servo now refitted connect the master cylinder and bleed the brakes as described in Chapter 8, Section 3, making reference to the part of this Section which deals with bleeding the bypass/pressure drop indicator.

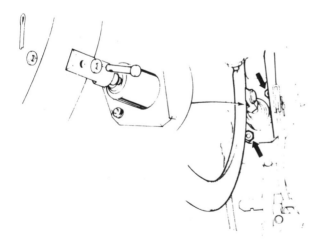

Fig. 12.44. Disconnecting the brake servo push rod clevis from the brake pedal (R1224)

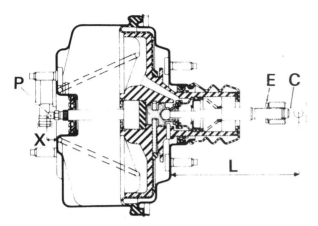

Fig. 12.45. Adjusting the brake servo clearances (R1224)

E Locknut   X 23/64 in (9 mm)
C Clevis   P Pushrod nut
L 4 23/32 in (120 mm)

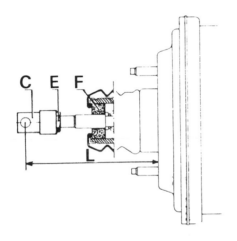

Fig. 12.46. The brake servo air filter (R1224)

C Clevis yoke   F Air filter
E Locknut   L 4 23/32 in (120 mm)

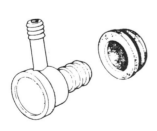

Fig. 12.47. The brake servo one-way valve and rubber grommet (R1224)

10 Brake servo unit - air filter renewal (R1224 only)

1 Under normal operating conditions the servo unit is very reliable and does not require overhaul except at very high mileages. In this case it is better to obtain a service exchange unit, rather than repair the original.
2 However, the air filter may need renewal and fitting details are given below.
3 Remove the brake servo as described in the previous Section.
4 Unscrew the pedal yoke after backing off the locknut first.
5 Remove the retaining spring from the air filter, if applicable and extract the filter with a sharp pointed object.
6 Fit the new filter and locate the retaining spring where applicable.
7 Refit the pedal yoke but check that the distance between the face of the servo unit and the centre of the hole through the yoke is as detailed in the previous Section of this Chapter.

11 Brake servo unit - one-way valve removal, checking and refitting (R1224 only)

1 Disconnect the vacuum inlet hose at the brake servo.
2 Twist and pull out the one-way valve to release it from the retaining grommet.
3 Check the condition of the one-way valve both visually and by blowing through it by mouth in both directions. If the valve is functioning correctly it should be possible to blow through in one direction only.
4 If the valve is faulty renew it.
5 Before refitting the valve check the condition of its retaining grommet. If the grommet is split or perished renew it.
6 Press the one-way valve into the servo unit and reconnect the vacuum inlet hose.

12 Dual circuit master cylinder - removal and refitting

1 Remove the cap from the brake fluid reservoir and stretch a thin sheet of polythene over the reservoir top and refit the cap. This measure will prevent excessive fluid loss from the unit when the pipe lines are disconnected. Alternatively the brake fluid reservoir can be drained with a syringe.
2 Disconnect the metal pipe lines.
3 Remove the bypass/pressure drop indicator as described in Section 3. Note that the R1222 model is different and a three way connector is fitted at the end of the master cylinder.

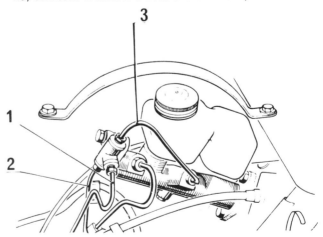

Fig. 12.48. The dual circuit master cylinder and pipes (R1222)

1 RH front wheel   3 Brake limiter
2 LH front wheel

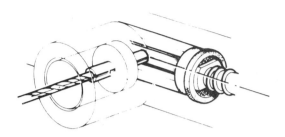

Fig. 12.49. Removing the roll pin using a 3.5 mm twist drill (R1224)

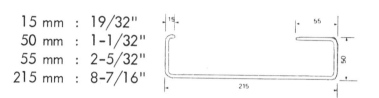

15 mm	:	19/32"
50 mm	:	1-1/32"
55 mm	:	2-5/32"
215 mm	:	8-7/16"

Fig. 12.50. The dual circuit master cylinder and fluid reservoir (R1224) along with a tool made up to the dimensions given for compressing the master cylinder pistons

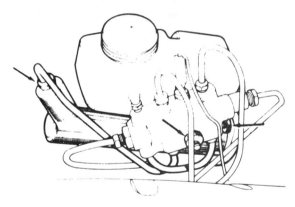

Fig. 12.51. The dual circuit master cylinder, bypass P.D.I. unit (typical for R1221, R1224, R1225, R1228 and some R1222 models)

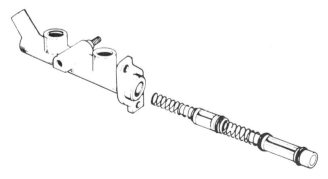

Fig. 12.52. The dual circuit master cylinder along with the primary and secondary piston assemblies (R1224)

4   Undo the two fixing nuts which secure the master cylinder to the servo unit (R1224 model) or the pedal assembly (all other models).
5   In the latter instance when withdrawing the master cylinder it will be necessary to disconnect the master cylinder pushrod.
6   Refitting the master cylinder is the reverse of the removal operation.
7   Finally bleed the system referring to Chapter 8, Section 3 and Section 4 which describes the bleeding operation when a bypass/pressure drop indicator is fitted.

13 Dual circuit master cylinder - dismantling, inspection and overhaul (R1224)

1   Remove the master cylinder as described in Section 12.
2   Drain the fluid from the cylinder reservoir and pull the reservoir off.
3   The reservoir is a push fit into two rubber sleeves which can now be removed.
4   Now make up a tool from a length of ¼ in (6 mm) steel rod to the dimensions shown in Fig. 12.50 and compress the primary and secondary piston assemblies with it.
5   With the pistons now compressed with this tool insert a 3.5 mm twist drill into the secondary piston roll pin. Rotate the master cylinder around the drill and then grip the drill shank in a vice and pull the master cylinder away from the drill.
6   The drill, if screwed far enough into the roll pin, will extract the roll pin when the master cylinder is drawn away.
7   Repeat this operation for the primary piston roll pin.
8   Remove the piston compressing tool and extract the primary and secondary piston assemblies.
9   Clean all the parts in methylated spirits and systematically inspect them for wear and damage.
10 If the bore of the master cylinder is pitted or scored then a new master cylinder assembly should be obtained.
11 If the master cylinder bore is in sound condition and a repair seal kit is available the cylinder can be rebuilt. Take care when

renewing the piston seals to fit them in the correct positions. The master cylinder bore and piston assemblies should be lubricated with brake fluid before the parts are assembled together.

12 Refit the piston assemblies so that the slots for the roll pins are vertical.

13 Fit the piston compressing tool and insert the roll pins taking care to align them with their slotted faces towards the pushrod end (see Fig. 12.54).

14 Refit the two rubber sleeves and press the fluid reservoir into position.

15 Finally fit the master cylinder and bleed the system as described in Chapter 8 with reference to Section 4 which deals with bleeding the bypass/pressure drop indicator.

14 Dual circuit master cylinder - dismantling, inspection and overhaul (R1221, R1222, R1225 and R1228 models)

1 Remove the master cylinder as described in Section 12.

2 Drain the fluid reservoir and mount the cylinder in a vice

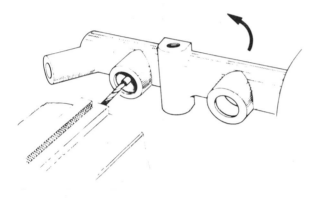

Fig. 12.53. Grip the twist drill in a vice to withdraw the roll pin (R1224)

fitted with soft faced jaws.

3 Remove the fluid reservoir by pulling it upwards and tilting it alternatively to the left and right.

4 Now remove the two rubber sleeves which locate the fluid reservoir to the master cylinder.

5 Remove the brake pipe between the three way union and the master cylinder followed by the three way union (R1221, R1222 and R1225).

6 Using a piece of wooden dowel rod or any suitable soft instrument press the piston assembly inwards by 3/16 in (5 mm) and remove the stop screw from underneath the master cylinder.

7 Using a pair of circlip pliers, with the piston still compressed, remove the circlip followed by the stop washer.

8 Slowly release the pressure on the pistons and withdraw the primary piston followed by the secondary.

9 Now clean the master cylinder bore and the piston assemblies in methylated spirits.

10 Inspect the master cylinder bore for pitting or score marks. If the cylinder bore is faulty then a new master cylinder assembly should be fitted.

11 If the master cylinder bore is in good condition and a repair seal kit is available the cylinder can be rebuilt. Take care when fitting new piston seals as they can easily be fitted the wrong way round. The master cylinder bore and piston assemblies should be lubricated with fresh clean brake fluid before the parts are assembled together.

12 Carefully insert the secondary piston followed by the primary piston.

13 Now refit the stop washer and circlip whilst carefully compressing the piston assembly with a wooden dowel rod or an alternative soft instrument.

14 Now press the piston inwards about 3/16 in (5 mm) and refit the stop screw to the base of the cylinder.

15 The three way union and brake pipe can now be refitted on R1221, R1222 and R1225 models.

16 Refit the rubber sleeves and press the fluid reservoir into position.

17 The master cylinder can now be refitted as described in Section 12.

18 Finally, bleed the system as described in Chapter 8, Section 3 with reference to Section 4 which deals with bleeding the bypass/pressure drop indicator.

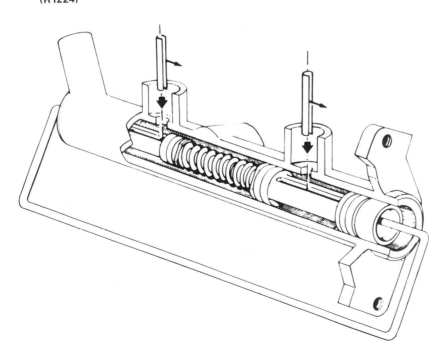

Fig. 12.54. Refitting the roll pins locating them into the piston grooves

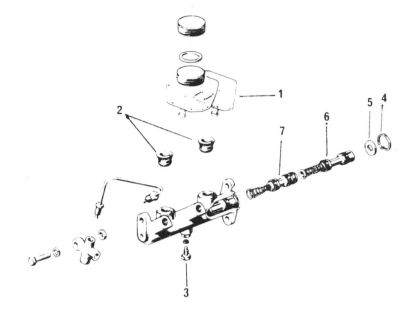

Fig. 12.55. The component parts of the
dual circuit master cylinder fitted to
R1221, R1222 and R1225 models
(similar to the R1228 master cylinder)

1   Fluid reservoir
2   Rubber sleeves
3   Piston stop screw
4   Circlip
5   Stop washer
6   Primary piston
7   Secondary piston

15 Fault diagnosis - braking system

Symptom	Reason/s
Pedal travels a long way before the brakes operate	Faulty automatic rear brake adjusters.
Brake warning light illuminates	Air in brake system Fluid leakage in system. Fault in master cylinder.
Stopping ability poor, even though pedal pressure is firm (R1224)	Fault in vacuum servo unit. Faulty vacuum servo unit one-way valve. Servo air filter blocked.

L Electrical system

1   Electrical system - modifications and description

The electrical systems of R1221 and R1222 models have
undergone slight modifications largely in connection with the
starter motor and charging system components. The detailed
changes in model type numbers and applications can be found in
the Specifications Section of this Chapter.

The R1224, R1225 and R1228 models have various electrical
fittings which are not mentioned in Chapter 9 but are individually dealt with in this Chapter, eg, rear screen wiper/washer
system.

The main external difference between the R1224, R1225
models when compared with the R1228 is the headlights. The
R1224, R1225 models use rectangular headlight units while the
R1228 is fitted with round units. Post August 1976 R1224
models are fitted with additional H4 quartz iodine headlight
bulbs which work in conjunction with the main beam application.

R1225 models have a different size alternator pulley which
drives the alternator at a faster speed. The pulley drive ratio on
this model is 2.15 : 1 whereas on other models it is 1.75 : 1. The

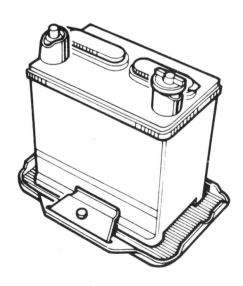

Fig. 12.56. The battery retainer fitted to cars manufactured
from 1974 onwards

reason for this change is due to the higher rear axle ratio fitted to this model which results in a reduced engine cruising speed.

The R1228 model is fitted with a seat belt warning system which comprises a dashboard warning light and a buzzer unit.

2 Battery - removal and refitting (all Renault 5 models from 1974)

1 The removal and refitting of the battery is identical to the procedure described in Chapter 9 except for one small detail.
2 The method of retaining the battery has now been redesigned and consists of a clamping plate and bolt. The battery has a moulded ledge near its base and the angled clamping plate rests on this ledge (see Fig. 12.56).
3 When refitting the battery lubricate the threaded bolt and ensure that the clamping plate is not overtightened or the moulded ledge may snap off.

3 Wiper arms - removal and refitting (R1222, R1224, R1225 and R1228)

1 The procedure described below is applicable to the wiper arm/s fitted to both the windscreen and rear window.
2 Lift the plastic cover at the base of the arm.
3 Now remove the spindle locknut and release the wiper arm. If the arm will not release from the spindle ease it carefully off with a screwdriver.
4 Before refitting ensure that the wiper spindle is in the 'parked' position.
5 Push the wiper arm back onto the spindle ensuring that the wiper blade is in the correct position.
6 Refit the spindle locknut. Do not overtighten the locknut or it may be difficult to remove the wiper arm in future.

4 Rear window wiper motor - removal and refitting

1 Disconnect the battery negative (−) lead.
2 Disconnect the rear wiper motor wires, this includes the earth wire which is screwed to the door framework.
3 Remove the wiper arm, complete with the wiper blade, as described in the previous Section.
4 The motor assembly is located on the outside by a locknut screwed onto the spindle boss and from within by two bolts.
5 With the two bolts and single locknut removed the wiper motor can be lifted away from the door.
6 The motor cannot be repaired and if it is proven to be defective then a new motor must be purchased and fitted.
7 Refitting the wiper assembly is the reverse of the removal operation.

5 Headlight unit - removal and refitting (R1228 models)

1 Remove the radiator grille panel.
2 Loosen the three screws which secure the headlight retainer ring.
3 Twist the light unit counter-clockwise until the three screw heads are aligned with the larger cutouts of the retainer ring.
4 Lift the retainer ring and headlight unit away from the headlight backing shell and detach the wiring block connector from the rear of the headlight unit.
5 Fitting the headlight unit is the reverse of the removal operation. Lugs cast into the rear of the headlight unit ensure that it will only fit in the correct position.

6 Headlight - adjustment (R1228 model)

1 It is recommended that the headlight aiming is adjusted with

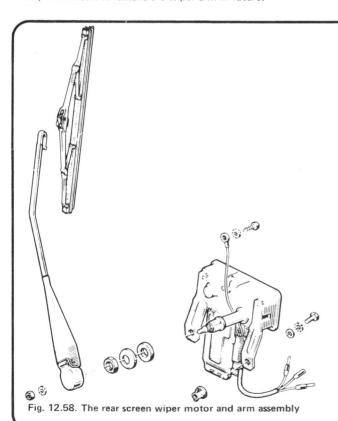

Fig. 12.58. The rear screen wiper motor and arm assembly

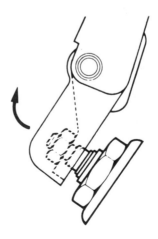

Fig. 12.57. The wiper arm fixing (all models)

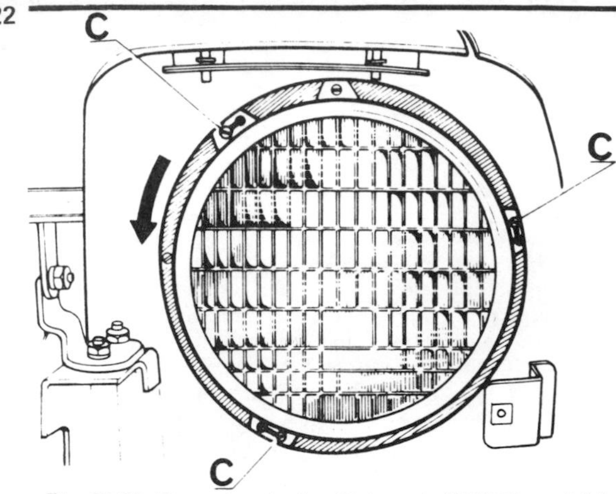

Fig. 12.59. Removing the headlight unit (R1228 models)

C Locating screws

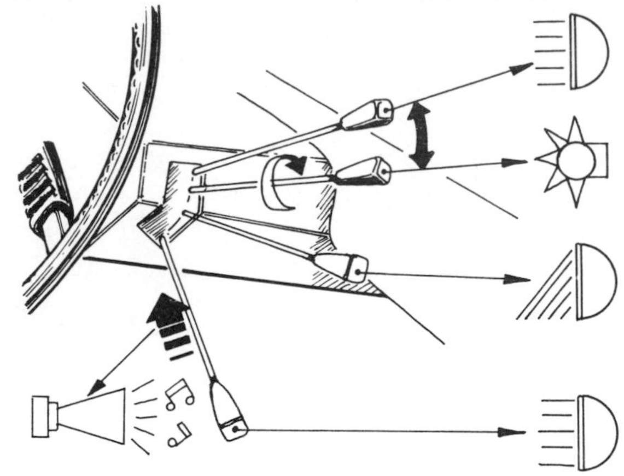

Fig. 12.60. The light switch control for R1224 models which have quartz iodine headlight bulbs fitted

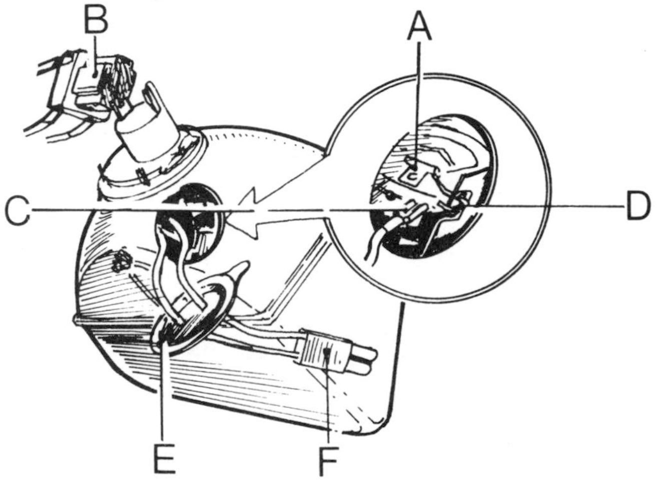

Fig. 12.61. Replacing the quartz iodine headlight bulb (Some R1224 models)

A Spade terminal
B Wiring connector block
C Spade terminal connector
D Retainer spring clip
E Rubber cover flap
F Connecting block

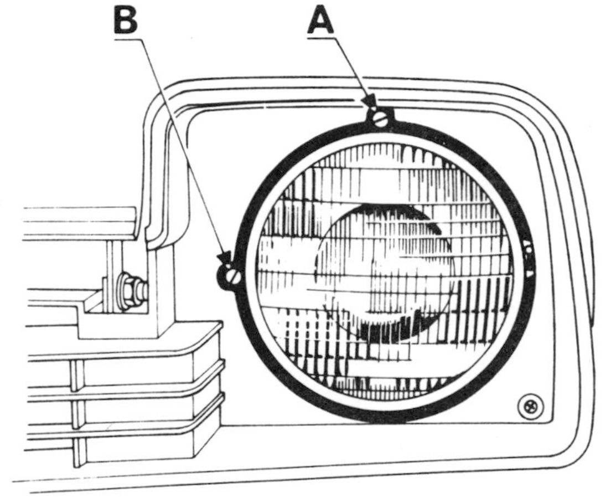

Fig. 12.62. Adjust the headlight beam setting (R1228 models)

A Vertical aiming screw   B Horizontal aiming screw

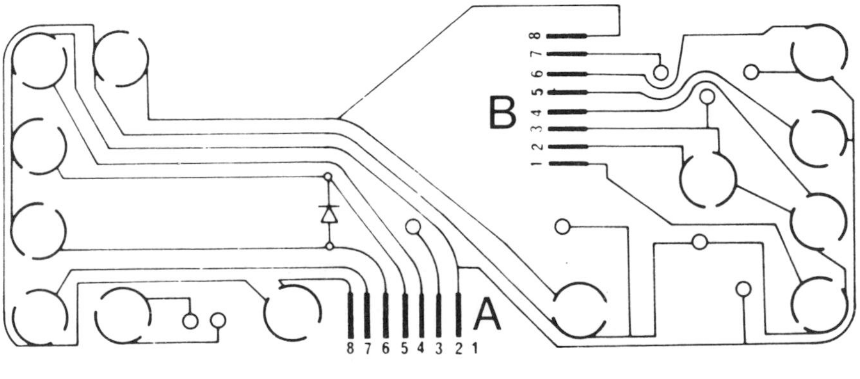

Fig. 12.63. The printed circuit as fitted to the R1224 models

A1	Not in use	B1	'Hazard' warning lights
A2	+ feed	B2	Direction indicator
A3	+ contact breaker (rev counter)	B3	Earth
A4	Choke	B4	Quartz Iodine driving lights
A5	Oil	B5	Not in use
A6	Water	B6	Brake pressure drop indicator
A7	Rear screen	B7	Fuel gauge
A8	Headlights	B8	Instrument panel lighting

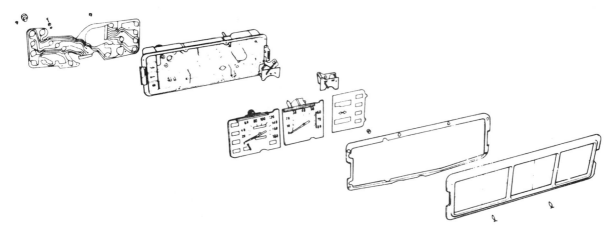

Fig. 12.64. The JAEGER instrument panel assembly as fitted to R1224 models

Fig. 12.65. Circuit diagram for R1224 models

1   LH front sidelight
2   LH front direction indicator
3   LH front headlight
6   RH front headlight
7   RH front direction indicator
8   RH front sidelight
9   Temperature switch on radiator
10   Cooling fan motor
19   RH horn*
20   LH horn
21   Reversing lights switch*
22   Alternator
23   Battery
24   Regulator
25   Cooling fan motor relay*
26   Water temperature switch
27   Starter
28   Distributor
29   QI driving lights relay*
30   Heating-ventilating fan motor
31   Ignition coil
32   Oil pressure switch
33   Windscreen wiper motor*
34   Brake pressure drop indicator*
40   LH cowl side earth (ground)
41   LH door pillar switch*
42   Wire junction
43   Wire junction
44   Fusebox
45   Stoplights switch
46   Instrument panel
47   RH door pillar switch
48   Junction - front and rear harnesses
49   Junction - front harness and combination lighting switch harness

50   Junction - front harness and - Hazard - warning lights system wiring
51   Flasher unit
52   QI driving lights switch*
53   Rear screen demister and rear screen wiper switch
54   Heating-ventilating fan switch
55   Windscreen wiper switch
56   Heating-ventilating fan resistance
57   Junction block - front and rear harnesses
58   Junction block - direction indicator and - Hazard - warning lights system harnesses
59   - Hazard - warning lights system switch*
60   Interior light
61   Combination lighting switch
62   Direction indicators switch
63   Ignition-starter switch
64   Cigar lighter*
65   Rear screen demister*
66   Fuel tank unit
67   LH rear direction indicator
68   LH rear light and stoplight
69   Reversing lights wire*
70   Licence plate lights
72   RH rear light and stoplight
73   RH rear direction indicator
74   Brake pressure drop indicator warning light switch*
75   Rear screen wiper motor*
76   Rear screen washer pump*
77   Push-in plug and socket for LH side front direction indicator repeater
78   Push-in plug and socket for brake pressure drop warning light
79   Push-in plug and socket for RH side front direction indicator repeater

Optional

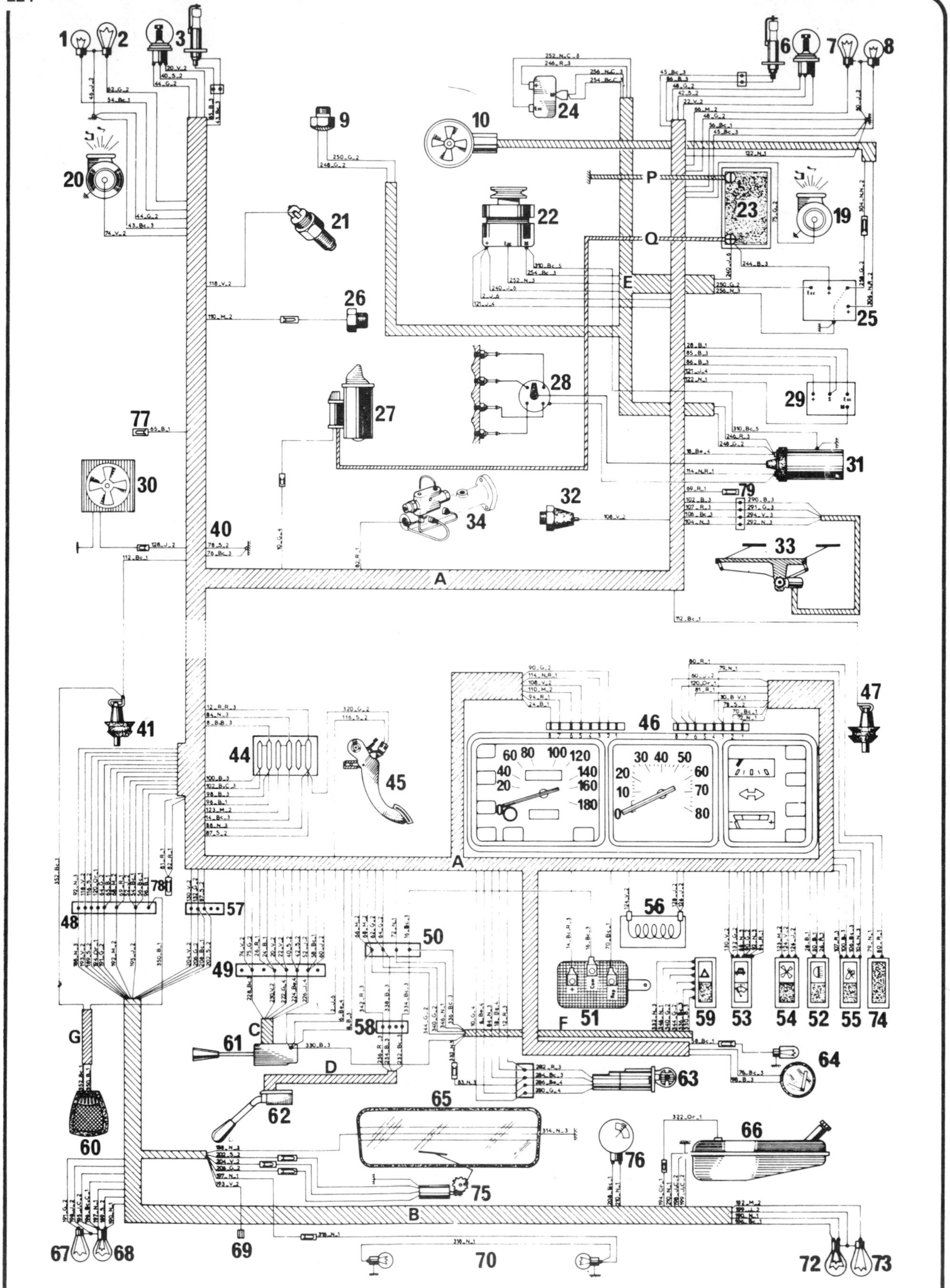

Fig. 12.65. Circuit diagram for R1224 models

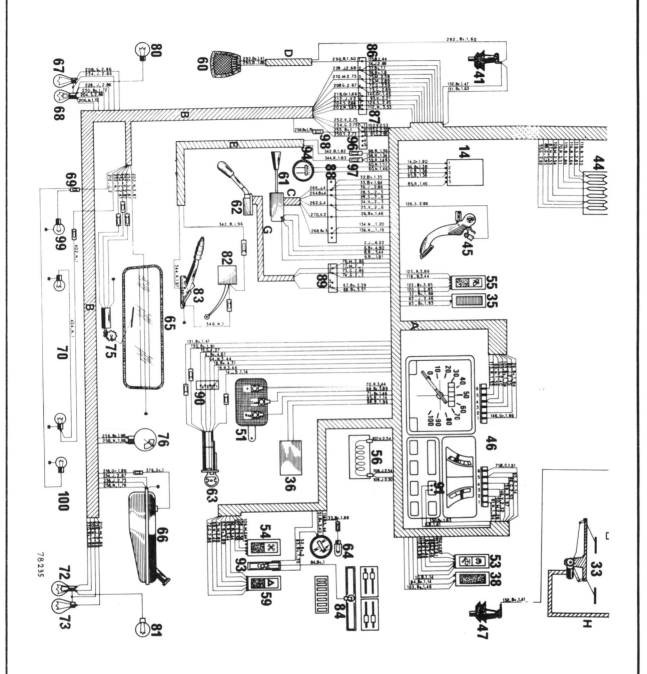

Fig. 12.66. Circuit diagram for R1228 models

78.235

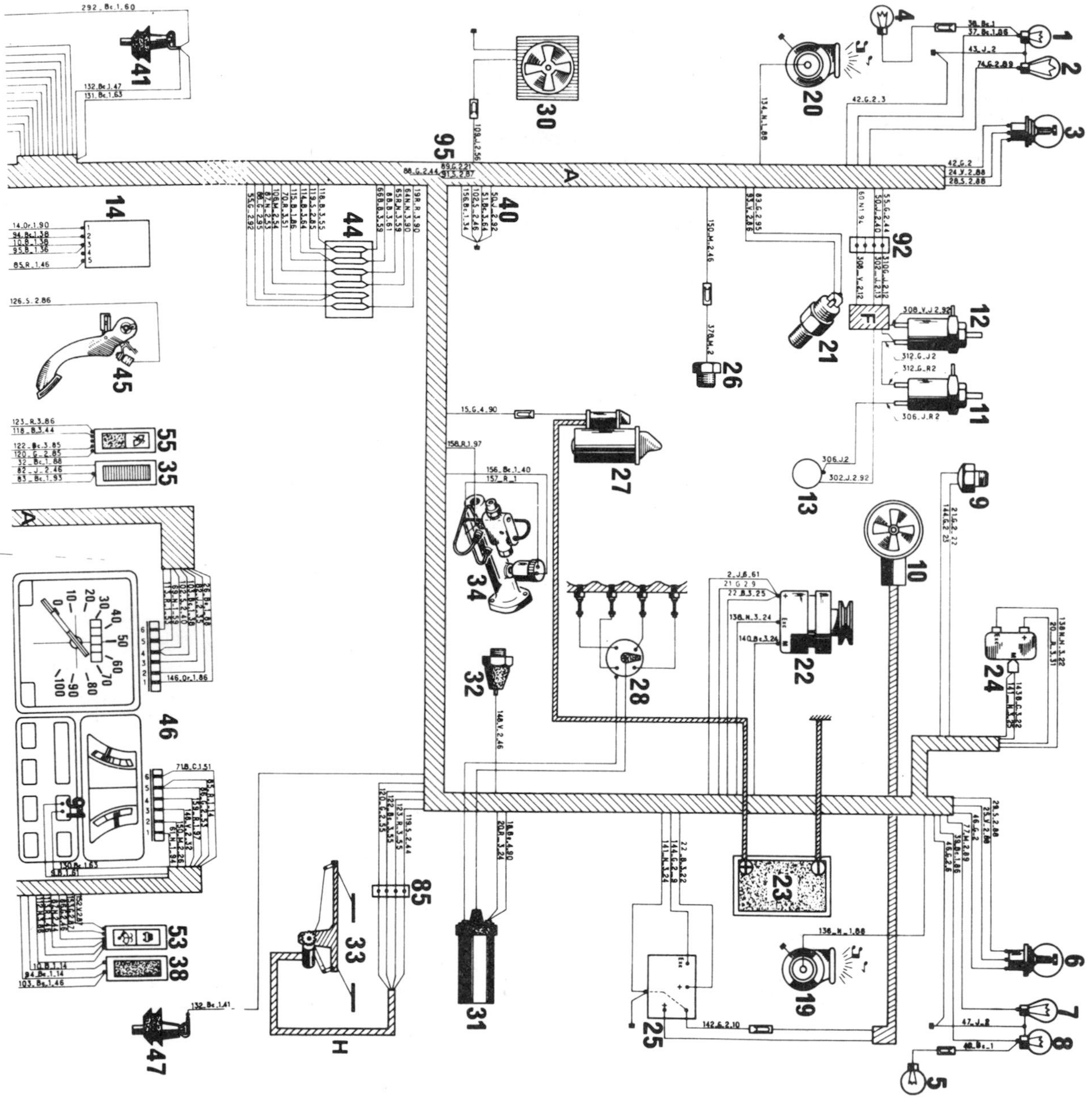

Fig. 12.66 Circuit diagram for R1228 models (Cont/d).

1	LH front parking light
2	LH front direction indicator
3	LH front reflector/side marker
4	RH front reflector/side marker
5	RH front illuminating reflector
6	RH front headlight
7	RH front direction indicator
8	RH front parking light
9	Temperature switch on radiator
10	Cooling fan motor
11	Solenoid valve
12	Solenoid valve (Ign. dist. vacuum advance
13	Centrifugal switch
14	Timer relay
19	RH horn
20	LH horn
21	Back-up light switch
22	Alternator
23	Battery
24	Regulator
25	Cooling fan motor relay
26	Coolant temperature switch
27	Starter
28	Distributor
30	Heating - ventilating fan motor
31	Ignition coil
32	Oil pressure sender switch
33	Windscreen wiper motor
34	Brake pressure indicator
35	Lighting rheostat

36	Buzzer
37	Diodes
38	Seat belt light
40	Instrument panel earth
41	LH door switch
44	Fuse box
45	Stoplight switch
46	Instrument panel
47	RH door switch
51	Flasher unit
53	Rear window demister and wiper switch
54	Heat-ventilating fan switch
55	Windscreen wiper switch
56	Heating-ventilating fan motor resistance
59	Warning light system switch
60	Overhead interior light
61	Combination lighting switch
62	Direction indicator switch
63	Ignition - starter switch
64	Cigarette lighter
65	Heater rear window
66	Fuel tank
67	LH rear direction indicator
68	LH rear tail and stoplight
69	Back-up light wire
70	License plate light
72	RH rear tail and stoplight
73	RH rear direction indicator
75	Rear window wiper motor

76	Rear window washer pump
80	LH rear reflector/side marker
81	RH rear reflector/side marker
82	Seat belt contact
83	Handbrake light switch
84	Heating controls illumination
85	Front harness - windscreen wiper harness connection
86	Front harness - rear harness connection
87	Front harness - rear harness connection
88	Front harness - combination lighting switch harness connection
89	Front harness
90	Front harness
91	Key reminder light
92	Front harness connection - solenoid valves connection
93	Switch identification illumination
94	Choke control
95	Harness splice (+)
96	Push in plug socket for seat belt and switch
97	Push in plug and socket for brake pressure drop indicator
98	Push in plug and socket for rear window wiper/pump
99	LH back-up light
100	RH back-up light

Fig. 12.66 Circuit diagram for R1228 models

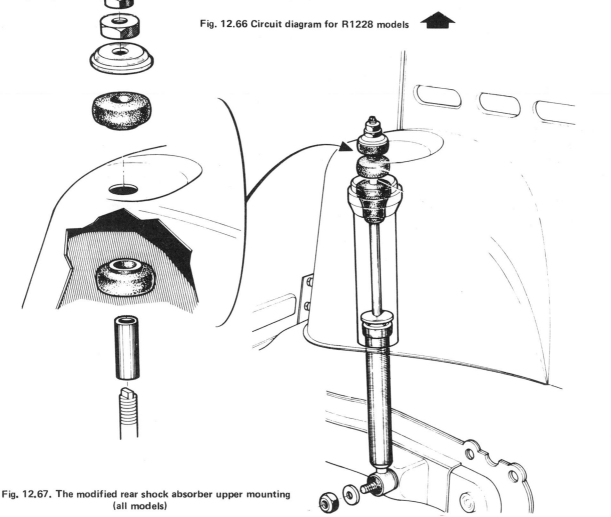

Fig. 12.67. The modified rear shock absorber upper mounting (all models)

the recommended optical equipment by your local Renault agency. However, a rough setting can be achieved using a wall or garage door as a screen on which the headlights can be set. With the car close to a wall or door mark the position of each headlight with a piece of chalk.

2   If you are adjusting the headlights in this manner the car must be positioned on a level surface, in an unladen state, at right angles, 25 feet from the projecting screen, ie. wall or garage door.

3   On main beam the centre of the two headlight beams must be parallel to the centre line of the car. On the dipped beam the height of the horizontal cut-off to the right of the illuminated area must be between 4 to 6 inches less than the headlight centres.

4   Two adjustment screws are provided. One adjusts the beam height while the other adjusts the sideways movement of the beam (see Fig. 12.60).

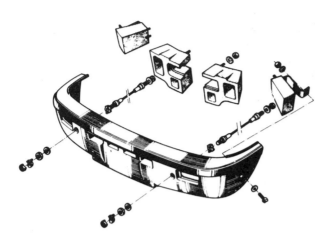

Fig. 12.68. The front bumper assembly (R1228 models)

7   Quartz Iodine headlight bulbs - removal and refitting (R1224)

1   The R1224 is fitted with headlights which have a long range beam in addition to the conventional beam. The quartz iodine lights can only be operated in conjunction with the main beam operation.

2   To remove the quartz iodine bulb it is necessary to remove the light unit as described in Chapter 9.

3   Disconnect the two wiring block connectors and lift the rubber flap cover.

4   Now, through the hole which the rubber flap covers, disconnect the spade connector.

5   The quartz iodine bulb is held in place by a spring clip which can be released by pressing it firmly on the curved end.

6   With the clip now released carefully remove the bulb. Note when handling either a new bulb or one which is still functioning correctly **DO NOT TOUCH THE GLASS PART OF THE BULB.** It is advisable to hold the bulb by its connecting spade terminal.

7   Refit the bulb holding it by the connecting spade terminal. The shape of the bulb and its socket prevents any fitting error.

8   Fit the bulb retainer spring clip in its slot.

9   Reconnect the spade terminal wire and refit the rubber flap cover.

10 Refitting the light unit is the reverse of the removal operation.

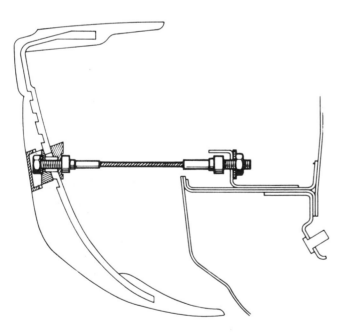

Fig. 12.69. Sectional side view of the front bumper showing the central support and cable fixing (R1228 models)

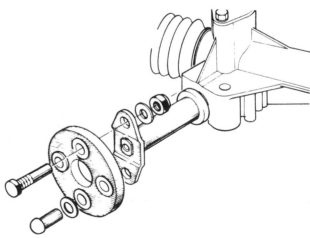

Fig. 12.70. Renewing the steering column flexible coupling (all models)

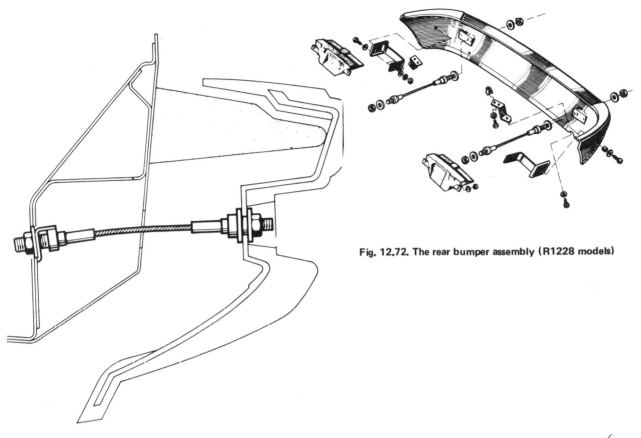

Fig. 12.72. The rear bumper assembly (R1228 models)

Fig. 12.71. Sectional side view of the rear bumper showing the
central support and cable fixing (R1228 models)

8 Instrument panel - removal, dismantling and refitting (R1224)

1 Despite the fact that the R1224 model has a tachometer (rev counter) fitted along with other warning instruments it can still be removed, dismantled and refitted in the same manner as the R1222. See Chapter 9 for details.

M Suspension and Steering

1 Rear shockabsorber mounting (all models)

The rear shockabsorber mounting has now been modified by removal of the two metal cupwashers and the fitting of rubber bushes which have a locating flange (see Fig. 12.67).

2 Steering column flexible coupling - renewal

1 Remove the steering rack as detailed in Chapter 10.
2 Drill out the flexible coupling rivets.
3 Fit the new coupling in position on the rack flange and bolt the coupling in position with 7 mm diameter bolts which are 1 3/16 in (30 mm) long. The heads of the bolts should be facing the steering wheel (see Fig. 12.68).
4 Refit the steering rack as described in Chapter 10.

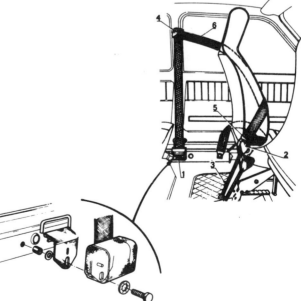

Fig. 12.73. The '2nd generation' retractor seat belts fitted to
later Renault 5 models

1 Retractor   4 Counter post
2 Buckle   5 Clasp
3 Centre stop   6 Webbing

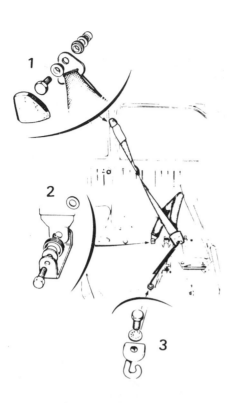

Fig. 12.74. The 'association' type of seat belt fitted to early Renault 5 models

1 *Centre pillar mounting point*
2 *Side member mounting point*
3 *Floor frame centre section mounting point*

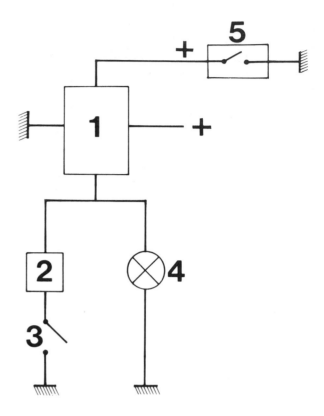

Fig. 12.75. The seat belt warning system fitted to R1228 models

1 *Timer*	4 *Fasten-seat belt warning*
2 *Buzzer*	*light*
3 *Belt switch*	5 *Starter switch*

N Bodywork and fittings

1 Front bumper - removal and refitting (R1228)

1 Remove the plastic radiator grille panel.
2 Undo the side mounting screws with a screwdriver for TORX type screws.
3 From within the engine compartment undo the two bumper support nuts.
4 Disconnect the side light feed wires and lift the bumper off.
5 Before refitting the bumper check the condition of the shock absorbing pads and renew them if necessary.
6 Refitting the bumper is the reverse of the removal operation.

2 Rear bumper - removal and refitting (R1228)

1 Remove the two reflectors which cover the two centre mounting nuts.
2 Undo the two centre mounting nuts.
3 Undo the side mounting screws with a screwdriver for TORX type screws.
4 Now remove the lower mounting bolts stamped 'tacle'.
5 The bumper can now be lifted away from the car.
6 Before refitting the bumper check and renew if necessary the shock absorbing pads.
7 Refitting the bumper is the reverse of the removal operation.

3 Seat belts - general note

1 The latest Renault 5 models are fitted with '2nd generation' retractor-type seat belts. Earlier R1221 and R1222 models were fitted with the 'association' non-retracting type of seat belt.
2 The stowage hooks provided should always be used to prevent damage to the belts whilst they are not in use.
3 In the event of an accident where the seat belt has been subjected to extreme strain, it should be renewed. This applies also if the seat belt webbing has become worn and frayed thus reducing the effective strength of the belt.
4 For cleaning the seat belt webbing, all that it requires is soap and warm water. Excess water should be wiped off and the belts then allowed to air-dry. Detergents and cleaning fluids can cause irreparable damage to the belt material and should never be used.
5 R1228 models are fitted with a seat belt warning system which functions as follows:

a) *A warning light on the dashboard lights up as the starter motor is operated.*
b) *A buzzer unit sounds for 8 to 10 seconds if the seat belts are not buckled.*

Metric conversion tables

Inches	Decimals	Millimetres	Millimetres to Inches		Inches to Millimetres	
			mm	Inches	Inches	mm
1/64	0.015625	0.3969	0.01	0.00039	0.001	0.0254
1/32	0.03125	0.7937	0.02	0.00079	0.002	0.0508
3/64	0.046875	1.1906	0.03	0.00118	0.003	0.0762
1/16	0.0625	1.5875	0.04	0.00157	0.004	0.1016
5/64	0.078125	1.9844	0.05	0.00197	0.005	0.1270
3/32	0.09375	2.3812	0.06	0.00236	0.006	0.1524
7/64	0.109375	2.7781	0.07	0.00276	0.007	0.1778
1/8	0.125	3.1750	0.08	0.00315	0.008	0.2032
9/64	0.140625	3.5719	0.09	0.00354	0.009	0.2286
5/32	0.15625	3.9687	0.1	0.00394	0.01	0.254
11/64	0.171875	4.3656	0.2	0.00787	0.02	0.508
3/16	0.1875	4.7625	0.3	0.01181	0.03	0.762
13/64	0.203125	5.1594	0.4	0.01575	0.04	1.016
7/32	0.21875	5.5562	0.5	0.01969	0.05	1.270
15/64	0.234375	5.9531	0.6	0.02362	0.06	1.524
1/4	0.25	6.3500	0.7	0.02756	0.07	1.778
17/64	0.265625	6.7469	0.8	0.03150	0.08	2.032
9/32	0.28125	7.1437	0.9	0.03543	0.09	2.286
19/64	0.296875	7.5406	1	0.03947	0.1	2.54
5/16	0.3125	7.9375	2	0.07874	0.2	5.08
21/64	0.328125	8.3344	3	0.11811	0.3	7.62
11/32	0.34375	8.7312	4	0.15748	0.4	10.16
23/64	0.359375	9.1281	5	0.19685	0.5	12.70
3/8	0.375	9.5250	6	0.23622	0.6	15.24
25/64	0.390625	9.9219	7	0.27559	0.7	17.78
13/32	0.40625	10.3187	8	0.31496	0.8	20.32
27/64	0.421875	10.7156	9	0.35433	0.9	22.86
7/16	0.4375	11.1125	10	0.39370	1	25.4
29/64	0.453125	11.5094	11	0.43307	2	50.8
15/32	0.46875	11.9062	12	0.47244	3	76.2
31/64	0.484375	12.3031	13	0.51181	4	101.6
1/2	0.5	12.7000	14	0.55118	5	127.0
33/64	0.515625	13.0969	15	0.59055	6	152.4
17/32	0.53125	13.4937	16	0.62992	7	177.8
35/64	0.546875	13.8906	17	0.66929	8	203.2
9/16	0.5625	14.2875	18	0.70866	9	228.6
37/64	0.578125	14.6844	19	0.74803	10	254.0
19/32	0.59375	15.0812	20	0.78740	11	279.4
39/64	0.609375	15.4781	21	0.82677	12	304.8
5/8	0.625	15.8750	22	0.86614	13	330.2
41/64	0.640625	16.2719	23	0.90551	14	355.6
21/32	0.65625	16.6687	24	0.94488	15	381.0
43/64	0.671875	17.0656	25	0.98425	16	406.4
11/16	0.6875	17.4625	26	1.02362	17	431.8
45/64	0.703125	17.8594	27	1.06299	18	457.2
23/32	0.71875	18.2562	28	1.10236	19	482.6
47/64	0.734375	18.6531	29	1.14173	20	508.0
3/4	0.75	19.0500	30	1.18110	21	533.4
49/64	0.765625	19.4469	31	1.22047	22	558.8
25/32	0.78125	19.8437	32	1.25984	23	584.2
51/64	0.796875	20.2406	33	1.29921	24	609.6
13/16	0.8125	20.6375	34	1.33858	25	635.0
53/64	0.828125	21.0344	35	1.37795	26	660.4
27/32	0.84375	21.4312	36	1.41732	27	685.8
55/64	0.859375	21.8281	37	1.4567	28	711.2
7/8	0.875	22.2250	38	1.4961	29	736.6
57/64	0.890625	22.6219	39	1.5354	30	762.0
29/32	0.90625	23.0187	40	1.5748	31	787.4
59/64	0.921875	23.4156	41	1.6142	32	812.8
15/16	0.9375	23.8125	42	1.6535	33	838.2
61/64	0.953125	24.2094	43	1.6929	34	863.6
31/32	0.96875	24.6062	44	1.7323	35	889.0
63/64	0.984375	25.0031	45	1.7717	36	914.4

1   Imperial gallon = 8 Imp pints = 1.16 US gallons = 277.42 cu in = 4.5459 litres

1   US gallon = 4 US quarts = 0.862 Imp gallon = 231 cu in = 3.785 litres

1   Litre = 0.2199 Imp gallon = 0.2642 US gallon = 61.0253 cu in = 1000 cc

Miles to Kilometres		Kilometres to Miles	
1	1.61	1	0.62
2	3.22	2	1.24
3	4.83	3	1.86
4	6.44	4	2.49
5	8.05	5	3.11
6	9.66	6	3.73
7	11.27	7	4.35
8	12.88	8	4.97
9	14.48	9	5.59
10	16.09	10	6.21
20	32.19	20	12.43
30	48.28	30	18.64
40	64.37	40	24.85
50	80.47	50	31.07
60	96.56	60	37.28
70	112.65	70	43.50
80	128.75	80	49.71
90	144.84	90	55.92
100	160.93	100	62.14

lb f ft to Kg f m		Kg f m to lb f ft		lb f/in^2: Kg f/cm^2		Kg f/cm^2: lb f/in^2	
1	0.138	1	7.233	1	0.07	1	14.22
2	0.276	2	14.466	2	0.14	2	28.50
3	0.414	3	21.699	3	0.21	3	42.67
4	0.553	4	28.932	4	0.28	4	56.89
5	0.691	5	36.165	5	0.35	5	71.12
6	0.829	6	43.398	6	0.42	6	85.34
7	0.967	7	50.631	7	0.49	7	99.56
8	1.106	8	57.864	8	0.56	8	113.79
9	1.244	9	65.097	9	0.63	9	128.00
10	1.382	10	72.330	10	0.70	10	142.23
20	2.765	20	144.660	20	1.41	20	284.47
30	4.147	30	216.990	30	2.11	30	426.70

Index

Printed by
Haynes Publishing Group
Sparkford Yeovil Somerset
England